TRAUMA IN FIRST PERSON

TRAUMA IN FIRST PERSON

Diary Writing During the Holocaust

AMOS GOLDBERG

Translated from Hebrew by

SHMUEL SERMONETA-GERTEL and **AVNER GREENBERG**

INDIANA UNIVERSITY PRESS

This book is a publication of

Indiana University Press
Office of Scholarly Publishing
Herman B Wells Library 350
1320 East 10th Street
Bloomington, Indiana 47405 USA

iupress.indiana.edu

The paper used in this publication meets the minimum requirements of the American National Standard for Information Sciences—Permanence of Paper for Printed Library Materials, ANSI Z39.48-1992.

Manufactured in the United States of America

Library of Congress Cataloging-in-Publication Data

Names: Goldberg, Amos, author.
Title: Trauma in first person : diary writing during the Holocaust / Amos Goldberg ; translated from Hebrew by Shmuel Sermoneta-Gertel and Avner Greenberg.
Other titles: Traumah be-guf rishon. English
Description: Bloomington, Indiana : Indiana University Press, [2017] | Includes bibliographical references and index.
Identifiers: LCCN 2017024825 (print) | LCCN 2017025462 (ebook) | ISBN 9780253030214 (e-book) | ISBN 9780253029744 (cloth : alk. paper)
Subjects: LCSH: Holocaust, Jewish (1939–1945)—Historiography. | Holocaust, Jewish (1939–1945)—Personal narratives—History and criticism. | World War, 1939–1945—Personal narratives—History and criticism. | Jews—Diaries—History and criticism.
Classification: LCC D804.348 (ebook) | LCC D804.348 .G6513 2017 (print) | DDC 940.53/18072—dc23
LC record available at https://lccn.loc.gov/2017024825

1 2 3 4 5 22 21 20 19 18 17

CONTENTS

PREFACE

Josef Zelkowicz, born in 1897, was an intellectual, affiliated with the Poalei Zion Left party (the Marxist Zionist Jewish workers' party), and a resident of Lodz. In May 1940, Zelkowicz was confined to the ghetto along with the other Jews of the city, where he remained until his deportation to Auschwitz and subsequent murder. He documented reality in the ghetto and in particular the lives of the people imprisoned there, their moods, and their collapsing consciousness.

Zelkowicz understood that conditions of severe deprivation—terrible hunger, mortality, disease, the extreme violence of the Nazis, the reign of terror imposed by Judenrat chairman Mordechai Chaim Rumkowski, and devastating poverty—create a particular social structure and generate a new kind of consciousness. Just like Primo Levi, he understood that harsh conditions do not lead to solidarity and spiritual improvement but, on the contrary, cause society to disintegrate and shatter the individual's very self and identity. They do not uplift people but, in most cases, debase them. With this understanding in mind, Zelkowicz wrote the following while inside the ghetto:

> It is not only the external form of life that has changed in the ghetto. . . . It is not only the clothing that has come to look tattered and the faces to wear masks of death, *but the entire Jewish trend of thought has been totally transformed under the pressure of the ghetto*. . . . The ghetto, the great negator of the civilization and progress that people nurtured for centuries, has swiftly obliterated the boundaries between sanctity and indignity, just as it obliterated the boundaries between mine and yours, permitted and forbidden, fair and unfair.[1]

And elsewhere, in a similar vein:

> Grave crimes were committed in the ghetto. The gravest of them was *the transformation of people who had worked for decades to maintain their culture and ways, the fruits of millennia of effort, into predatory beasts after half a year of life under inhuman conditions. Overnight they were stripped of every sense of morality and shame.* Ghetto inhabitants pilfered and stole at every opportunity, whether they needed the booty or not. Some rummaged in the trash like pigs for leftovers, which they ate then and there. Some starved to death, but others, exploiting the opportunities available to them, stole, pilfered, gorged themselves, and drank themselves silly.[2]

However, not only social solidarity, moral consciousness, cultural values, and Jewish ideals were utterly transformed under the conditions that prevailed in the Lodz ghetto, according to Zelkowicz. The personal history and identity of each and every individual were also completely undermined, sometimes to the point of collapse. The story of the pious Yaakov Eli—a deeply religious man, who made every effort to preserve his human dignity and pure faith, even in the ghetto—concludes with the following observation by Zelkowicz: "What's the purpose . . . of all the effort that Yaakov Eli invested in himself for so many years, if *a year and a half of life in the ghetto has transformed his inner essence so drastically that he repudiates his entire life*?"[3] In the harsh conditions of the Lodz ghetto, the need to survive was many times linked to the repudiation of one's former life, until one's inner self had been transformed beyond recognition. The brutal reality imposed by the Nazis on their victims rendered the latter virtually helpless—not only in terms of external circumstances, controlled almost entirely by the Nazis, but also in terms of their inner natures, their moral values, their individual traits, and their very identities. The state of radical helplessness experienced by Jews during the Holocaust also devastated their inner worlds. The most destructive consequence of this situation—beyond the blurring of the other distinctions mentioned by Zelkowicz—was the fundamental blurring of the necessary separation between "inside" (that is, the individual's inner world) and "outside" (the events and power relations occurring in reality).

Faced with this extreme historical reality, the discipline of history itself would appear to stand helpless. Although the historiography of the Holocaust, written over the past seventy years, has been remarkably successful in reconstructing Jewish life during that period, historians have found it difficult to contend with the full extent of the helplessness that the Jews experienced. History is charged with describing what *is*—events, responses, survival, and struggle, communal, personal, and family activity—not what is not, such as help*less*ness. History deals with existence, not absence; with the formation and preservation of identity, not its extreme negation; with the construction and creation of frameworks and institutions, not their disintegration; with the development of ideas and processes of producing meaning, not their erasure. How, then, should history deal with a period characterized first and foremost by what it lacked, by its helplessness, without betraying its most essential aspect? How can we write history about what is not, about what is negated, about what has disintegrated or been distorted?

The question becomes even more pressing in the context of historical consciousness and the collective memory of the Holocaust among Jews (including Israeli Jews) and significant numbers of non-Jews for whom the Holocaust acts as a central identity-founding event. How can identity be founded upon an event at the heart of which stands the disintegration of identity, negation, helplessness, and defeat?

Public consciousness in many places around the world appears at a loss when it comes to this issue as, to a great degree, does the historiography on the Jews during the Holocaust. Both tend to ignore the fundamental undermining of identity and deny the deep cracks in the image of the victim—although these are amply and vociferously reflected in writings from that period, such as those of Zelkowicz, cited above. The image of the Jews during the Holocaust in popular and historical representations generally follows the optimistic paradigm, presuming the successful preservation—with few exceptions (which naturally serve to reinforce the rule)—of social values and human and Jewish identity, at least as long as circumstances permitted.

History books thus dedicate numerous pages to Jewish institutions and organizations during the Holocaust and to the various forms of endurance and resistance. Museums shape the image of the victim as one who preserved human and social values, held on to personal beliefs, and conducted a vibrant religious, family, and cultural life under all conditions—even in the Auschwitz death camp. The social disintegration, the shattering of identity, and the internal rifts are hardly mentioned—as if the horrors of the "outside" (persecution, hardship, murder, etc.) failed to penetrate the Jewish "inside" (values, identity, social, and psychological structures) during the Holocaust. Paradoxically, the narrative of the Holocaust, from the perspective of its victims, is recounted as one of victory (of the spirit, vital force, Jewish and human identity, etc.) and not as a narrative of bitter defeat, although the writings of the period treated in this book in fact attest to the very opposite.[4] Indeed, as the scholar of Hasidism Mendel Piekarz demonstrated as early as the 1980s, such processes of "beautification" began immediately after the war and may already be observed in the writings of some of the survivors.[5] These processes are so sweeping that many later representations of the Holocaust, in historiography and museums, in textbooks and in popular culture, sometimes seem to relate to a very different event from the one described in the writings of the period itself. The internal transformation of social consciousness and the human psyche that occurred during the catastrophe—so dominant in the writings of the period—is not given sufficient attention in its later representations.

The present book seeks to address this central dimension of radical and undermining helplessness experienced by Jews during the Holocaust and to describe its effects on the individual. Based on the diaries of Jews written during the Holocaust, I have sought to examine the fundamental unsettlement and internal disintegration that shook the identity of the victims to the point of threatening to nullify their very human existence, beyond the question of their biological survival. In many ways, this is an attempt to continue the inquiry that Primo Levi began with the notes he wrote at the Auschwitz camp and that, in 1947, he encapsulated in his immense question: "If this is a Man." Levi believed that it is precisely the study of the victim—no less and perhaps more than the "murderer" or any other historical actor of that period—that fully raises the question of what remained of what is "human" in that fateful period and, moreover, how should what is "human" be understood in the first place. In the present work, I have studied the "humanity" of the victims of the Holocaust not primarily in terms of their social or moral consciousness (as Zelkowicz, for example, emphasizes in the passages quoted above), although these aspects will also be discussed, but from the perspective of the diaries written during the course of the events themselves, as "life story" texts, which—under ordinary circumstances—are considered identity-founding.

The writing of diaries by Jews is a central cultural phenomenon of the Holocaust period—one that has already been the subject of a number of comprehensive scholarly monographs.[6] In this book, I have chosen to focus on the aspect of these diaries as "life story" enactments. The premise here is that human beings find their human, cultural, and moral identity, first and foremost, by means of their life stories. The "life story" is what enables them to create themselves as unique individuals, as whole and more or less continuous subjects, and as social beings who interact with the world around them.

It is also what allows them to afford meaning to the events in which they are cast, to weave them into acceptable personal and collective history. The power of the "life story" to preserve an individual's unique, human identity was destroyed, however, by the extreme traumatic events into which Jews were cast during this period, to the point that the story appears to collapse, and with it the teller. Sometimes it seems that the Holocaust diaries are not life stories but stories of extreme trauma that, in fact, negate and dismantle those same life stories. To paraphrase Zelkowicz, they tell how the traumatic events transformed people's inner essence so drastically that they repudiated their entire lives, and seem to testify—in real time—to the reduction and at times even the disappearance of human beings, even before they were actually murdered. The tension between the concept of "life story" as identity-forming and the concept of "trauma" as undermining the foundations of identity lies at the heart of this book.

Since the 1970s, various attempts have been made to integrate psychology and history. Some scholars have written psychohistory and others have tried to apply psychoanalytic concepts to history.[7] Most of these attempts—a few of which are bold and fascinating—have been rejected by historians. Some have attributed this rejection to the weakness of the findings and methodologies proposed, while others have blamed the conservatism of the historical discipline. Nevertheless, the present work is another attempt in this direction. By combining psychoanalytic concepts, primarily that of trauma, with a literary reading of the texts examined, the book explores the depth structures of the human consciousness of those who wrote diaries as the events of the Holocaust unfolded. This inquiry, in and of itself, challenges the image of the victim created by historiography—an image that, as intimated above, is also part of the collective consciousness that preserves the memory of the Holocaust in Israel and around the world. In writing this book, I have sought to present a historical study of helpless consciousness during the Holocaust. I hope I have succeeded, if only in part.

Trauma is a central concept in this book, employed here as an interpretive key to autobiographical texts from the Holocaust period since at the heart of this concept stands the sophisticated attempt to conceptualize the experience of radical helplessness. In critical theory in general and anthropology in particular, sharp criticism has been leveled at "trauma discourse" and its conceptualizations. I am aware of this criticism and even accept many of its arguments.[8] My use of the concept of trauma here, however, is neither orthodox nor therapeutic.[9] For me, this is first and foremost a conceptual field that enables the revelation of certain aspects generally ignored by historiography and writing on the Holocaust—primarily the centrality of helplessness during this period and its dismantling and undermining effects.

This book is the product of a long and complex intellectual process, encouraged and supported by people and institutions to whom I owe a deep debt of gratitude.

First, I would like to thank my two teachers, Sidra Ezrahi and Shlomith Rimmon-Kenan. I cannot overstate the debt I owe them for all they have taught me and for the support they have given me over the years. Shlomith is a model of intellectual rigor, thoroughness, and comprehensive knowledge, and Sidra a paradigm of groundbreaking scholarly courage and ethical commitment in research.

Another teacher whose influence is evident in nearly every page of this book, and to whom I would like to offer my deepest thanks for his generosity, is Dominick LaCapra, with whom I had the great privilege of studying. I would also like to thank my colleagues and teachers at the Institute of Contemporary Jewry and Yad Vashem—in particular, the late David Bankier, who compelled me, time after time, to express my thoughts in a clear and straightforward manner; and Danny Blatman, whose support and friendship are, for me, invaluable gifts.

I would also like to thank Ruth Ginsburg, who introduced me to psychoanalytic thought and trauma studies, and Hannan Hever, who was among the first to read an embryonic version of the present work, and whose advice and comments, as well as his encouragement, have been a source of inspiration and support. Another dear friend and colleague from whom I have learned a great deal is Alon Confino, a pioneer in the field of cultural history of the Holocaust. I would also like to thank the two anonymus readers for their invaluable remarks.

A number of institutions and foundations have supported this project from its inception, including the high costs involved in its publication. I would like to express my deepest gratitude to them all, for their essential material support and, no less, for the confidence they have shown in my work, which they deemed worthy of financial backing: The Institute of Contemporary Jewry at the Hebrew University, The Hebrew University Faculty of the Humanities, The Egit Foundation for Holocaust Literature—through the Israeli General Federation of Labor (Histadrut), The Ignatz Bubis Foundation, The Memorial Foundation for Jewish Culture, Yad Vashem—which awarded me the Danek Gertner Prize, and the Van Leer Institute, which has been a second home to me. To all of them I owe a deep debt of gratitude. Without their support, this research project and its publication as a book would not have been possible.

Beyond all the material and professional support I have received, this book would never have come to be without the support of my dear family, whose encouragement has accompanied me throughout the long and arduous process of its writing, especially my wife Michal and my beloved children Sharon, Shai, Rut, and Hallel-Bracha, to whom this book is dedicated.

Notes

1. Josef Zelkowicz, *In Those Terrible Days: Notes from the Lodz Ghetto*, ed. Michal Unger, trans. Naftali Greenwood (Jerusalem: Yad Vashem, 2002), 139–141; emphasis added.

2. Ibid., 131; emphasis added.

3. Ibid., 149; emphasis added.

4. One of the few outside of Europe who recounted the narrative as one of defeat without redemption was Nathan Alterman although, immediately after the Holocaust, he returned to the national redemptive approach. See Hannan Hever, "Avru Toldot He'amim Keshod Batzaharayim: Natan Alterman Bitkufat Hashoah" [The history of the nations passed like a robbery at noon: Nathan Alterman during the Holocaust], in *Sho'ah Mimerhak Tavo* [When disaster comes from afar], ed. Dina Porat (Jerusalem: Ben-Zvi Institute, 2009), 48–84.

5. Mendel Piekarz, *Sifrut Ha'edut al Hasho'ah Kemakor Histori: Veshalosh Teguvot Hasidiyot Be'artzot Hasho'ah* [The literature of testimony as a historical source of the Holocaust and three Hasidic reflections on the Holocaust] (Jerusalem: Bialik Institute: 2003).

6. See Jacek Leociak, *Text in the Face of Destruction: Accounts from the Warsaw Ghetto Reconsidered*, trans. Emma Harris (Warsaw: Żydowski Instytut Historyczny, 2004); Alexandra Garbarini, *Numbered Days: Diaries and the Holocaust* (New Haven, CT: Yale University Press, 2006); Rachel Feldhay Brenner, *Writing as Resistance: Four Women Confronting the Holocaust: Edith Stein, Simone Weil, Anne Frank, Etty Hillesum* (University Park: Pennsylvania State University Press, 1994); David Patterson, *Along the Edge of Annihilation: The Collapse and Recovery of Life in the Holocaust Diary* (Seattle: University of Washington Press, 1999); Fiona Kaufman, "By Chance I Found a Pencil: The Holocaust Diary Narratives of Testimony, Defiance, Solace and Struggle" (PhD diss., University of Melbourne, 2010). See also a summary of these studies in Amos Goldberg, "Jews' Diaries and Chronicles," in *The Oxford Handbook of Holocaust Studies*, ed. Peter Hayes and John K. Roth (Oxford: Oxford University Press, 2011), 397–414.

7. See, for example, Saul Friedländer, *History and Psychoanalysis: An Inquiry into the Possibilities and Limits of Psychohistory* (New York: Holmes and Meier, 1978); Robert Jay Lifton and Eric Olson, *Explorations in Psychohistory* (New York: Simon and Schuster, 1975). For a recent overview of the subject, see Sally Alexander and Barbara Taylor, eds., *History and Psyche: Culture, Psychoanalysis, and the Past* (Basingstoke: Palgrave Macmillan, 2013).

8. See, for example, my article "The Victim's Voice in History and Melodramatic Esthetics," *History and Theory* 48, no. 3 (2009): 220–237.

9. I have largely followed in the footsteps of Dominick LaCapra, who wrote: "I don't try to be orthodox as a psychoanalyst, but really aim to develop the concepts in a manner that engages significant historical problems—and for me, the Holocaust is one of the most important of these problems." See Dominick LaCapra, *Writing History, Writing Trauma* (Baltimore: Johns Hopkins University Press, 2014), 141.

TRAUMA IN FIRST PERSON

INTRODUCTION

"If This Is a Man"

"There Is No One"

In his homily for *Shabbat Shuvah* 5702 (27 September 1941), delivered in the Warsaw ghetto (and transcribed after the conclusion of that same Sabbath), Rabbi Kalonymus Kalman Shapira, the Rebbe of Piaseczno, wrote the following:

> We said the following on the holy Sabbath: [Before the holiday] I thought that with troubles such as these, when Rosh Hashanah [the Jewish new year] would come, the sound of our prayers would be tumultuous and that our hearts would pour out to God like a stream of water. . . . Nevertheless our eyes are witness to the fact that before the war, during previous High Holidays, our prayers had greater fervor and enthusiasm, with a greater outpouring of the heart, than this year.[1]

In his homily, Rabbi Shapira refers to the Jewish High Holiday prayers in the ghetto that were not recited, as might have been expected, with heightened devotion but rather with surprising emotional indifference, to his great consternation.[2] At first he suggests that the reason for this may lie in "physical weakness; we have no strength," but he is not satisfied with this explanation and goes on to cite two more possible reasons for the phenomenon he described. The first concerns the psychology of one's relationship with God: "When a Jew prays and his prayers are answered, he then finds strength and enthusiasm for his subsequent prayers. But when people pray and they see that not only are they not answered, but the troubles increase even more, God forbid, then our hearts fall, and we cannot rouse ourselves in prayer."[3] In prayer, claims Rabbi Shapira, there is a psychology of reciprocity at work.

When a person prays and not only is not answered but "the troubles increase even more," the worshiper despairs, and that is the state of the worshipers in the Warsaw ghetto. This explanation, we should note, is still within the realm of psychology and traditional Jewish theodicy, retaining all the elements of the religious covenant between human beings and God: God, humans, and even faith and hope are dialectically embedded within the despair: should God answer their prayers, the worshipers' faith will be restored and they will return to praying with enthusiasm. Even this, however, fails to satisfy Rabbi Shapira, who offers a further possible explanation: "The second reason is . . . that the attainment of any spiritual state, including faith and joy, requires the existence of a person—someone to do the believing and rejoicing. But when every individual is crushed and trampled, there is no one to rejoice."[4] This final explanation is far more radical. Here the individual ceases to exist while still alive. In contrast to the psychological description of despair in the previous explanation, which assumes the existence of a human being who despairs, here there is only absence, with virtually no acting subject. "There is no one to rejoice"—the subject of the prayer no longer exists. Rabbi Shapira goes on to describe this situation as "depth within depth"—not the depth of despair, but the depth of absence. The "I" is virtually destroyed even before the person is murdered.[5]

It is important to stress that Rabbi Shapira's words do not refer to the glassy-eyed masses, mostly refugees, wasted with hunger, starving in the streets of the ghetto, or to those who lay helpless in their beds, but to those who actually came to pray in the synagogue on Rosh Hashanah and *Shabbat Shuvah*—those who sought to fulfill their religious obligations in order to preserve the continuity of their religious, Jewish, and human identity. Rabbi Shapira speaks of human nullification specifically with regard to these people![6]

In other words, Rabbi Shapira's testimony points to the fact that it is specifically by entering the realm of symbolic practices—that is, the social and cultural activities (prayer, in this case) that regulate the language of reality and its rules—that the loss of the human as such is reflected and perhaps even occurs. Rabbi Shapira's testimony raises the terrible possibility that in the extreme situation of the Warsaw ghetto in the fall of 1941—a possibility we can extend to many other traumatic situations during the course of the Holocaust—the human may disappear precisely when one is living and acting in the context of social and cultural activity.[7]

This conclusion, as it arises from the testimony of one of the most courageous and incisive witnesses of the period, highlights the fact that both individual human beings and the very concept of "the human" underwent extreme change during the Holocaust. In those circumstances in which victims of a vast trauma such as the Holocaust (but of course not essentially only the Holocaust) found themselves, "man" underwent such radical transformation that the human condition—at least in some of the historical and existential situations, not only in the camps but also in the ghettos and elsewhere—seems to have departed from the conventional conceptual realm of the way in which we usually perceive human character and nature. This autobiographical testimony regarding the nullification of human beings even during their lifetimes requires further clarification. We should thus ask, using the words of Saul Friedländer, "What is the nature of human nature?" as revealed in the writings of the Holocaust period.[8]

Rabbi Shapira's fear that the human may be "murdered" while still alive is echoed in the writings of a number of the leading theoreticians and thinkers of the 1950s and 1960s, such as Hannah Arendt and Theodor Adorno. Arendt, for example, in her monumental work *The Origins of Totalitarianism* (1951), claimed that the Nazi totalitarian project, as embodied in the concentration camps, sought to create a new kind of human—devoid of the element of spontaneity that Arendt considered essential to the definition of "humanity." The essence of the Nazi project lay in "transforming the human personality into a mere thing, into something that even animals are not."[9] As in Rabbi Shapira's testimony from the Warsaw ghetto, Arendt asserted, with regard to the camps, that they demonstrated the possibility of destroying the "psyche" without destroying the physical person. Arendt thus concludes that "indeed psyche, character, and individuality, seem under certain circumstances to express themselves only through the rapidity or slowness with which they disintegrate."[10]

Similarly, Adorno, in a 1965 lecture titled "The Liquidation of the Self," on the collapse of metaphysics in the traditional sense, argued that in light of Auschwitz and the institutionalization of torture under the Nazi regime, existence may no longer be assumed to have meaning.[11] The locus in which this crisis of metaphysics is most keenly apparent, according to Adorno, is "the self." As a political and philosophical concept, "the self" underwent a process of destruction under the regime of which Auschwitz and torture were the most emblematic institutions.

The Italian writer Primo Levi offered the most concise and trenchant formulation of this question in 1947, in his book *If This Is a Man.*[12] Levi examines human nature in one of the most extreme loci of Nazi persecution—the Auschwitz camp—specifically through observation of the prisoner's experience, based on Levi's own ordeal in the camp. Levi described and identified behavioral and cognitive patterns he found it difficult to ascribe to normal, reasonable people in twentieth-century Europe. The extreme reality of Auschwitz created a new kind of human behavior and consciousness, placing a fundamental question mark, as intimated in the book's title, next to the concept of "man," as shaped in the great western enlightenment traditions in which Levi was raised. In his famous introductory poem to *If This Is a Man,* Levi writes:

> You who live safe
> In your warm houses,
> You who find, returning in the evening,
> Hot food and friendly faces:
> Consider if this is a man
> Who works in mud
> Who does not know peace
> Who fights for a scrap of bread
> Who dies because of a yes or no.
> Consider if this is a woman,
> Without hair and without name
> With no more strength to remember,
> Her eyes empty and her womb cold
> Like a frog in winter.
> Meditate that this came about.[13]

Toward the end of the book, Levi revisits the issue, directly:

> It is man who kills, man who creates or suffers injustice; it is no longer man who, having lost all restraint, shares his bed with a corpse. Whoever waits for his neighbour to die in order to take his piece of bread is, albeit guiltless, the furthest from the model of thinking man than the most primitive pigmy or the most vicious sadist. Part of our existence lies in the feelings of those near to us. That is why the experience of someone who has lived for days during which man was merely a thing in the eyes of man is non-human.[14]

Contrary to the idea of human autonomy conceived by the enlightenment, Levi argues that our humanity is largely determined by how we are perceived by others. We are entirely dependent on their gaze, and helpless before it, when it turns us into an object to be destroyed. Levi relates primarily to Auschwitz, but his deliberation—"if this is a man"—would appear equally applicable to some of the other "zones" of the Holocaust as well as other events of extreme mass violence.

The question of the collapse of "the human" during the Holocaust was also a key element in the early historiography regarding Jews in the Holocaust. In 1964, the historian Leni Yahil—one of the pioneers of Israeli Holocaust historiography—delivered a methodological lecture titled "Holocaust: Original Sources and the Problems of Their Investigation." At that time, the field of Holocaust history was just beginning to establish itself as an independent historical field and, in her lecture, Yahil sought to outline the field's goals and primary difficulties.[15] At the very beginning of her lecture, Yahil noted that the duty of writing the history of the Holocaust stems from the fact that "our era, with all of its revolutionary changes, terrible wars, and destructive manifestations, has shaken our accepted notions of the figure of man."[16] Yahil went on to say, "the main thing that prompts us to study history—even of the distant past, but certainly in the case of the Holocaust—is the problem of the figure of man. . . . It is, therefore, inconceivable that research of the Holocaust period would not focus primarily on man, evaluating human actions and behavior."[17]

The Holocaust, as Yahil suggested, fundamentally undermined our conceptions of "man," as shaped and developed in the historical, religious, and philosophical traditions in which she was raised. Therefore she called for historical-humanistic research, with "man" (not peoples, societies, or cultures) as the central object of this study. In her essay, Yahil called for seeking a balance between what she called "man as an individual" and "man in society," and between psychological analysis and the analysis of actions. Nevertheless, in the very tracing of paradigmatic lines for the field, which were, from her perspective, also its raison d'être, Yahil established the figure of "man" as the central and terrible riddle to be addressed—and this, as noted, in the embryonic stage of historiography of the Jews during the Holocaust. In this context, she stated explicitly that the study of "man" must include both victim and murderer. In both cases, "man" during the Holocaust was not necessarily the same as "man" that had existed before.[18]

The question of "man"—the terrifying challenge that arises from the observation of the *victims* of Nazism—has thus tormented victims, survivors, philosophers, and historians, and it demands thorough scholarly investigation. It would seem, however, that after forty years of intensive development and significant achievements in the field Holocaust research this challenge has yet to be met with sufficient scope and depth.

To address the challenge posed by Primo Levi and the others I have just mentioned, I turned to the methodology and theory of "life stories" and autobiography studies. Using these disciplines, this book will examine autobiographical texts written by Jews during the Holocaust—from the 1930s in Germany and primarily during the war in Europe, in the ghettos, and even in the concentration and death camps. These are mainly diaries (that is, daily journals in which the writer describes, at more or less fixed intervals, his or her activities and most recent experiences, close to the time of their occurrence), but also memoirs (that is, long essays written retrospectively) that were written during the war (and not thereafter).[19]

The fundamental principle in life-story and autobiography studies is that only through language can people give meaning to the events of their lives and constitute their identities, that is, by weaving those events into a narrative. In other words, there is a close affinity between the autobiographical text—as language, narrative, and narration—and the constitution and existence of a subject with a distinct identity. Whether people experience their lives as narrative or merely afford their lives meaning through narrative, they can only experience them through the act of narration, which entails the varying levels of cohesion and coherence that the story imposes on the plot, as well as the processes of thematization present in various aspects of the story, without which human experience cannot, in fact, be discussed. *The "man" that will be examined in this book is, thus, autobiographical "man," that is, "man" written or constituted within the text and by the text that he or she composed in the first person.*

In light of this, over the course of the book I will relate to the diaries from the Holocaust period as autobiographical texts, through which the authors of the diaries sought to narrate, in the first person, an extended and significant part of their lives. The diaries treated here, however, were written in traumatic situations, characterized, first and foremost, by extreme *helplessness* in the face of terror, and the destructive and murderous forces acting from without. This helplessness (ostensibly) disintegrates the narrating subject, his or her narrative ability, and the story itself. Bearing this in mind, I will seek to address the following question: *In a situation of such extreme helplessness, is there any narrative at all—and consequently an "I" who tells it in the first person—and, if so, in what sense? (Or, phrased differently: Is there, in the texts before us, an "I" telling the story in the first person—and, if so, in what sense?)*

Autobiographical writing in such a traumatic period would appear to be a patently paradoxical phenomenon. On the one hand, it represents the traumatic events and in so doing seeks to cope with them. On the other hand, however, the very same autobiographical writing also presents, as I will argue, grave symptoms of the trauma itself and, sometimes, even actively embodies them.[20]

We have already seen how, in Rabbi Shapira's homily, personal disintegration may manifest itself in all its force, specifically within the context of cultural activity. This homily, as noted above, reports the terrible impact of traumatic situations—the disappearance (or radical reduction) of human beings while still alive. Moreover, the circumstances described by Rabbi Shapira are those of the Warsaw ghetto, before ever having encountered the reality of the concentration or death camps. Rabbi Shapira tells us that this disappearance became apparent or actually occurred during the course of the most important religious ritual in Hasidic life: prayer. In the present context, we must ask whether a parallel might not be drawn from one cultural practice to another—from religious ritual to autobiographical writing itself—to determine whether the same disappearance described by Rabbi Shapira with regard to prayer (the disappearance of the praying subject) might not occur in the act of narration as well. In other words, could the autobiographical text itself attest to or embody the disappearance or at least the radical diminution of the narrating subject?

If this is the case, what would be the status of autobiographical writing that *explicitly* indicates these phenomena of disappearance, diminution, and disintegration, or even manifests them in the text itself? When the text recounts these phenomena can it redeem or mitigate them? And, if so, to what extent and in what way? Or perhaps even the writer herself is swallowed up in the very process she is describing?

These questions, which pertain to the paradox of the act of autobiographical writing during the Holocaust (and other hugely traumatic events) will be dealt with at length in the book, as a key to understanding "man" during this period.

The Phenomenon and the Impulse

According to testimonies—contemporary and later—and judging by the large number of diaries in the archives, many of which have been published, autobiographical writing (understood here as writing in the first-person singular) was the central genre of writing among Jews during this period.[21]

Throughout Europe, in the cities and small towns, ghettos, forests, hiding places, concentration, labor, and even death camps, Jews wrote of their experiences under Nazi rule, in many different languages.[22] The most extreme case, perhaps, is that of three Sonderkommandos at Auschwitz, who kept a kind of diary until their murder and, in their writings, attested to the fact that many others had done the same.

Many of the diaries were, of course, written by educated people, but a considerable number were also written by ordinary people, children, and adolescents. Jews from all walks of life engaged in writing, including ultra-Orthodox Jews, in whose culture autobiographical writing was not normally practiced. There are two notable exceptions to this rule: diaries kept by women with children are rare and, to the best of my knowledge, no diaries were kept during the death marches. Writing would seem to require, above all, a constant location—even the most terrible of locations.[23]

Although no comprehensive survey of the diaries written during the Holocaust has been conducted to date, which makes it difficult to evaluate the extent of the phenomenon with any precision, it appears to be extremely impressive.[24] We must also presume that only some—perhaps a minority—of the manuscripts have survived. In all likelihood, many were destroyed or lost during the course of events. The fortuitous discoveries of the diaries we do possess may offer some indication of the probability that many others have completely disappeared. The touching diary of the child Dawid Rubinowicz, for example, was found by chance in a pile of refuse in the town of Bodzentyn, in Kielce County, Poland.[25] In many cases, diaries and other documents that have survived include explicit references to other diaries that have never been located.[26]

In any event, it is clear that the phenomenon was very widespread, and was typical of the period. This is also reflected in the fact that most of those who wrote diaries only began to do so under Nazi rule.[27]

The large number of diaries should not, however, be taken for granted. Many factors made such writing extremely difficult. First, paper and writing implements were not always readily available. Yitzhak Aron, from the town of Miory, writing after the destruction of his community, notes at the beginning of his diary that his account will be very concise, due to a shortage of paper.[28] Some of the materials on which the texts were written also attest to this difficulty—diaries written, for example, on notes or occasional scraps of paper, such as the anonymous diary of a boy from Lodz, written in the margins of a French book; the diary of Menachem Oppenheim from Lodz, written in the margins of a prayer book; the diary of Avraham Keiser from Warsaw, written on paper from cement bags; and many others.[29] Beyond the technical difficulties, however, the writing itself was almost always accompanied by a sense of danger—often mortal danger—to the writer and to people mentioned in the diary.[30]

Many of the writers addressed the danger incurred by their writing. Rabbi Yehoshua Moshe Aronson, for example, wrote in the concise and lean (linguistically and figuratively) diary he kept in the Konin camp: "May the reader forgive me for the imprecise grammar at times and lack of statistical order, for I write in the middle of the night, secretly, under threat of death. If anyone were to suspect . . ."[31] What is particularly interesting about this statement by Rabbi Aronson is that, although he was an Orthodox rabbi, bound by the religious prohibition against endangering one's own life (except to avoid committing one of the three cardinal sins: sexual immorality, idolatry, or murder), he was prepared to risk his life to write a diary. This is indicative of the powerful impulse to write and to document, which acts as a kind of compulsion that imposes itself on the writers, beyond all considerations of ethics, religious law, or effectiveness. This impulse is described explicitly by Emanuel Ringelblum in his own diary in February 1941: "The drive [*drang* in the original Yiddish] to write down one's memoirs is powerful: even young people in labor camps do it.[32] The manuscripts are discovered, torn up, and their authors beaten."[33]

In many ways, it is not surprising that Jews turned to diary writing during this period. Diary writing is a practice that has been identified with intimacy on the one hand and chaos on the other—particularly when the "outside" is repressive and menacing.[34] At times it was also identified with cultural and political subversion. Diary writing in eighteenth-century Britain, for example, was typical of a nonconformist bourgeoisie forced to adhere to social norms in public while conducting a parallel private existence.[35] So, too, some scholars explain that diary writing came to be viewed as a feminine genre in the late nineteenth and early twentieth centuries, because it was a period in which subjective self-consciousness had already begun to develop among women but had not yet been afforded social recognition and legitimacy. The contradiction between self-consciousness and social norms heightened their awareness of oppression, which was often channeled into diary writing.[36] In a similar vein, Dostoevsky described diary poetics as "poetics of the underground."[37] Furthermore, the diary genre, like all autobiographical writing, dominates in times of crisis.[38] The genre becomes particularly popular in periods or situations of tremendous change and momentous historical events, alongside massive personal repression and individuals' growing need to reorganize what remains of their own identity and document the extreme changes occurring in and around them. Indeed, the Nazi period, especially the war, is considered a "prolific" time of diary and memoir writing, also among the Germans.[39]

The recourse to diary writing must be understood in light of all these factors. When Jews sought to write their experiences in the extreme situations in which they found themselves, when the sense of peril became increasingly palpable, when the order of the world was completely overturned, when the sense of continuity was disrupted and personal identity radically unraveled, and when death became an increasingly certain presence and inevitable fate—they turned to the diary.[40] However, this tendency bears a paradoxical meaning.

On the one hand, the impulse to first-person writing is the individual expression of a writer who must repeatedly say (or write) "I," even under the most difficult of circumstances. And if the history of autobiographical writing in its various forms is also a statistical history, then the autobiographical impulse to write, given such increased quantitative expression in this period, must be seen as a significant moment—the historical moment of the individual.[41]

On the other hand, however, autobiographical writing of the Holocaust period presents certain characteristics that would appear to demand significant qualification of this conclusion, since these texts are characterized by the fundamental fragmentation enabled by the diary genre. The "poetic" (if it may be called that) of the diary is one of fragmentation. It is a text written without the perspective that would enable the organization of events into a single narrative. It is a genre (if it may be called that) that allows contradiction and even antithesis on all levels to exist within a single textual sequence.[42] In effect, as the diary scholar Peter Börner asserts, diary writing has neither thematic nor structural rules.[43] The range of diary styles and degrees of completeness and cohesion are vast.[44]

Therefore, when Dostoevsky sought a genre of writing capable of articulating the chaos and fragmentation he considered typical of his time, he turned to the journalistic diary, in which he saw an expressive genre much more suited to the spirit of the age than the coherent novel. His goal in writing the diary was, as Gary Morson put it, "to define and express the laws of decomposition."[45] Horst Rüdiger summed it up as follows: "The diary may serve as a replacement for the novel because it has wholly renounced the beautiful error of causal affinity between the events and the continuous linear story. The diary replaces the strong cohesion of the narrative form with outbursts of randomness, meaninglessness and absence of theme. This is the most appropriate form for alienating and borderline situations; for the permanent state of insecurity in which we find ourselves today."[46] There is no doubt, therefore, that among the genres that potentially enable the writing of such extreme events as those of the Holocaust—events that radically disintegrate the sense of continuity and coherence of reality—the diary is the most suitable. As such, however, this genre teaches us far more about disintegration than about cohesion.

But there is more to it. It seems that even the actual saying of "I" in the Holocaust diaries essentially undermines the very uniqueness of the individual. In many Holocaust diaries the "I," as a unique and unrepeatable experience with its special life story, is apparently almost entirely swallowed up by the universal experience, as Chaim Kaplan from Warsaw described so well in his diary, on 24 November 1939—some two months after the beginning of the Nazi occupation:

> Amidst the general horror, the tragedy of the individual is neutralized and ignored. There is no one whose existence has not been devastated. There is no one who has not had a member of his family killed. And those who remain alive are without work. The busiest and most necessary economic arteries have been paralyzed. In the face of the general disruption and destruction of the foundations of life, the tragedy of the individual is not distinct. Before a companion opens his mouth to tell of his troubles, I can anticipate all the details in advance. His words almost remain suspended in air, and his frightful story makes no impression upon me.[47]

One can clearly sense here the dissipating uniqueness of every individual life story and of the increasingly reduced autonomy of the individual and the ability to shape one's life, understand it, and give it meaning. The writers recount, in the first person, all of the tremendous forces they face and in which they are swept up. The significance of these forces in terms of determining their fate, in life and in death, is immeasurably greater than their self-understanding, decisions, passions, introspection, emotional sensitivity, personality development, and intellectual capacity. The individual stands helpless in the face of such forces. The following passage from the diary of Zvi Radlitzky, from Lvov, illustrates the extent to which the testimony overshadows the witness: "Like between the millstones, when the kernels of grain spin around with the stones until they are ground—a few kernels escape into the cracks in the stones, until the dizzying dance uproots them again from their place in order to grind them. So too are we, the few who—sometimes for a short while—escape the wild dance of death and remain as observers of the death and destruction of others."[48] In this sense, writing in the first person is paradoxical. It accentuates the "I" while, at the same time, attesting to its radical limitation.[49] Autobiographical writing during the Holocaust thus touches the very heart of the question of existence and the nature of the human individual in this period.

Between the Personal and the Documentary

In general, Holocaust diaries vary hugely in form and content—some are more personal, at times even intimate, while others tend to be more documentary or ethnographical. Some are highly descriptive in style while others contemplate the events' historical or even philosophical meaning. Some are prosaic while others are more poetic in their style. Something, however, virtually all the diaries—even the most intimate—share is the documentary impulse.[50]

Indeed many of those who had kept diaries before the war, changed the nature of their diary entries during the war, shifting from a journal focusing on the author's personal life—without openly presuming the presence of an external reader—to one seeking to document historical events and their influence on the writer, and generally intended for readers other than the author.[51] This virtue is shared by both diaries and memoirs written by Jews during the war and is of great importance.

Traditionally, the diary and the memoir represent two distinct forms of first-person writing. Diary writing, as Lejeune put it, is a form of "self-hospitality"—personal and intimate—while memoir writing tends toward historical documentation.[52] The personal diary, as it developed in the modern era, tends to focus on the experience of the moment, the writer and the writer's inner life. In the memoir, on the other hand, the writer's life is generally described within the context of the events to which the author was a witness and a party.[53] While the focal point of diary writing is the writer and the writer's inner world, in the memoir the writer serves as a kind of anchor for the events and spirit of the age. In this sense, the memoir is closer to (premodern) diaries of historical documentation, as opposed to (modern) intimate, personal diaries. The distinction between these two types of diary is nearly as old as the field of diary studies itself. Thus, for example, Richard Meyer, in his essay "On the Historical Development of the Diary" [Zur Entwicklungsgeschichte des Tagebuchs], published in 1898, distinguished between earlier diaries—"factual chronicles" or "objective diaries," as he called them—and the modern diary, which he saw as a "self-portrait of a spirit/mind in the course of its development."[54]

This trajectory, which allows us to make a sharp distinction between the memoir and the diary, is far less clear during the Holocaust. Holocaust diaries are often characterized by a historical-documentary instinct. In these diaries, the events are the real "protagonist" and even when the object of the account is the narrator's life, the writing is often not perceived as "personal" but as documenting the protagonist within the given historical context. The focus frequently shifts from the writer as the object of writing to the writer as representative of the period. For example, Calek Perechodnik writes at the beginning of his diary: "My life may be considered fairly typical. I cannot claim to have an outstanding intellect or some accidental good fortune to make me stand out among others. Oh no! All the silly mistakes, all the errors committed by the Jews, I committed as well. All the misfortunes, all the tragedies that affected them, touched me in the same measure."[55] Thus even the most individualist and intimate diaries written during the Holocaust take into account the historical-documentary impulse—contrary to the nature of diaries in "normal" times, in which the individual functions as the diary's sole center of gravity.

In effect, most of the autobiographical texts written during the Holocaust, whether in diary form or as a memoir, combine both perspectives—the historical-documentary perspective typical of the memoir and the intimate-autobiographical perspective typical of the diary—which also sustain one another.[56] Thus, for example, Batya Temkin-Berman begins her diary anew on 5 May 1944: "I will go back to writing again, like then, only for myself, although I am well aware that should these pages be preserved until the end of the war, they will no longer be my personal property—for none of us, the survivors, is a private person any longer . . . I will strive to write down all of the events that occur and to intersperse them with my memories."[57] Consequently, in most of the extensive body of first-person writing, the center of gravity shifts from the inner world of the individual's choices, feelings, achievements, expectations, hopes, deeds, and passions (personal, intimate diary) to the whirlwind of external events and their overwhelming influence on the writer and on society in general (historical-documentary diary).[58] The modern diary is driven by the impulse toward introspection and self-understanding, while the Holocaust diary arises primarily from the urge to document the incidents and historical events witnessed by the writer. This is not writing that responds directly to the question "Who am I?" but, rather, to the questions "What have I seen?" (testimony) and "What are the external forces that decide my fate and the fate of those around me?" (documentation). This runs counter to the process of historical development that the genre has undergone over the course of the modern era—from a chronicling genre that documents general and external events to one in which authors contemplate and write from the depths of their own psyches and describe their personal lives.[59] In the diaries addressed here, the process is the exact opposite.

The Double Nature of Documentation during the Holocaust

In fact, a further twist to the relationship between the "personal" and the "documentary" in these texts makes them far more complex. This is reflected, for example, in the diary of Fela Szeps, from the Grünberg camp in Silesia, which presents an interesting combination of intimate writing and historical documentation. A number of passages from the diary are worth quoting at length in this context.

The diary's first entry is dated 5 April 1942:

> There is a lot of talk here about writing a diary. Everyone thinks that there are a great deal of things that should be documented, things that don't ordinarily happen in normal life, things that we ourselves would not have believed exist in the world. Such things belonged to past ages, or were the product of the fertile imagination of story-writers. I think any of us who have read such stories have thought that were she herself to experience what the unfortunate heroines of these novels had gone through, the world would have turned upside-down, the sun and the moon would not have shone as usual, and she herself would certainly not have survived. But here, everything goes on as usual, despite the somewhat strange things that happen here, and these strange happenings are accepted with resignation, as if they were natural phenomena. Slowly, one becomes accustomed to phenomena that are out of this world, and there is nothing to write in the diary, everything seems natural.[60]

I will return to this extraordinary passage later in the book, but it is immediately apparent that in Szeps's writing the documentary and intimate registers are inextricably bound together. On the one hand, the events themselves would have been unimaginable in a normal world, which "would have turned upside-down, the sun and the moon would not have shone as usual." However, for all their horror, they are—from the camp inmate's perspective—a normal, even banal part of everyday life: "slowly, one becomes accustomed to phenomena that are out of this world." Therefore, Szeps notes, there is no point in documenting them—"there is nothing to write in the diary." Everything seems natural! Even ever-present death is taken for granted, eliciting no particular human emotions. Death in the Grünberg camp went from a shocking human event to a purely biological phenomenon.[61] Szeps's entire conceptual framework regarding what is "human" has collapsed or, as she puts it at the beginning of her entry on 23 August 1942, "All facts become nothing."[62]

If "facts become nothing," what is the purpose of writing a diary? Does it not lose its value as an instrument of documentation—communicating the experiences of the camp to those outside? How can one describe something that is, at one and the same time, normal and beyond the realm of human imagination? The documentation project thus comes to a dead end before it has even begun. The writer has no stable standpoint from which it is possible to document the events that are simultaneously banal and catastrophic. This failure creates a terrible sense of distress that cannot be fully expressed in words but then, in itself, becomes an object of writing: "Nevertheless, the desire often arises to pick up a pencil and do something with it, to write down some of what lies deep in the heart, delving restlessly in the depths and below the threshold of consciousness. For often, only the heart, in its depths, conceals some feeling of bitterness toward that . . . and seeks some handhold to express indefinable pain, and perhaps the pencil will afford it such a handhold."[63] The gap between the events requiring documentation and the inability to document them thus channels into a painful and powerful delving, not entirely accessible to the conscious mind. Such anguished subversion in the depths of the heart, accessible only indirectly, cannot be fully described or defined by means of writing. The pencil, as an object, merely affords a handhold.

According to this passage, not only the mimetic or representative aspect of documentary writing is significant—because the "event" can never truly be represented. It is always hidden within the tremendous and unbridgeable gap between the knowledge (that they are living in a catastrophic world, in which ordinary rules no longer apply) and the experience (that everything in the camp is, in fact, normal). Nonetheless, documentary writing may provide the hidden "event" with contours or an anchor around which it may be organized. In moments of severe trauma, documentary writing provides the unconscious pain with a handhold: *The documentary impulse thus becomes the autobiographical impulse of writing the trauma.*[64]

The documentation that Szeps seeks is thus a different kind of documentation—not merely an account of the events that have taken place but also, and perhaps most important, of the prisoners' inner world. It is a kind of documentation that cannot adhere to the principles of historical documentation, based first and foremost on chronological sequence. Thus, despite the regret Szeps expresses at the nearly two-month-long break in her writing, she clearly rejects the possibility of retroactive chronological writing because in such a fashion "perhaps everything would be transcribed in precise chronological order, but the heart's cry of despair would not be heard and would be absent there."[65] Szeps thus documents the events not only as facts but also as an experience of personal trauma—the heart's cry.

Already in the first paragraph of Fela Szeps's diary we see that the historical documentation of the particular events to which the women prisoners at the camp were both witnesses and victims in fact revolves around the author's need to write "what lies deep in the heart." The historical documentation in Szeps's diary is, ultimately, also a documentation of the human psyche. It is an intimate account of the "self" in the course of a traumatic experience. The diary is thus a documentary text, written with the historical awareness of the importance of documentation while, at the same time, seeking to document the prisoners' feelings and paradoxical inner consciousness. Even when it deals with external events it is, in effect, recounting the writer's inner world. In the process of focusing on the subjective and unconscious pain of the writer, historical documentation and autobiographical writing of the state of trauma converge and coalesce.[66]

In this book I apply this definition of Szeps's documentation as a kind of guide for reading texts from the period, including those—such as the diaries of Ringelblum, Kaplan, Klemperer, and others—whose authors strive to present them as documentary, mimetic texts.[67] Hence, the reading of these texts cannot be limited merely to their representational dimension but must also address the gaps and disintegrative undercurrents that flow beneath the surface and become accessible only indirectly. An analysis of this type of documentation must focus, through the text, specifically on the gaps and spaces in which the conscious but at times also unconscious pain occurs—the terrible but elusive pain that Szeps calls "indefinable"—rather than on the illusion of mimetic fullness created by the text.[68]

This position stands in a dialectical relationship to the scholarly view regarding "life stories" and autobiographies. Life-story studies implicitly assume that subjects constitute themselves or their identities by means of the stories they tell about their lives. As we have seen in the passage from Fela Szeps's diary quoted above, writing holds great value for the writer, but this value does not stem from the structure of the narrative and its organizational or representative ability but, in fact, from the gaps within it, the impossible paradoxes it subsumes, the act of writing itself, and the status of the object of writing—the pencil as focusing unconscious feelings that fundamentally undermine the subject.[69]

Structure of the Book

The central body of this book (excluding the introduction and conclusion) is divided into three parts. The first part presents the basic theoretical premises at the foundation of this work, as well as the main methodological considerations that guided me during the course of my research, some of which I have already touched on in the present introduction. The structure of this first part is dynamic. Its point of departure, as will be presented in chapter 1, is the theory of life stories and autobiographical writing. This theory posits a strong association between the establishment of the subject and the subject's ability to recount (in writing or orally) his or her life story. The autobiographical texts addressed in the book, however, were written in traumatic situations that, by their very nature, contradict (at least ostensibly) the character of narrative writing—as narrative is a mode of organization, which expresses performative power, whereas trauma is a fundamental disintegration and radical embodiment of helplessness. Chapter 1, therefore, examines the conflict between the concept of "life story" and that of "trauma," as expressed in the Holocaust diaries.[70] As I already stated in the preface, I am well aware of the criticism that has arisen in the fields of anthropology and culture studies concerning "trauma discourse" and its conceptualizations—criticism I share, to some extent.[71] My use of the concept of trauma here, however, is neither orthodox nor therapeutic.[72] For me, this is first and foremost a conceptual field that allows me to reveal certain aspects that historiography and writing on the Holocaust have largely tended to ignore—primarily the centrality of helplessness during this period. Chapter 2 is dedicated to this debate with the historiography of Jews during the Holocaust, as written primarily (but certainly not solely) in Israel, which has overlooked or even completely ignored the full significance of this aspect of the history of the period.[73]

In chapter 3, which concludes the theoretical part of the book, I will present a model—based on semiotic and psychoanalytic premises—which describes the dynamics at work within the autobiographical texts from the Holocaust period. This model reveals the (limited) therapeutic potential of writing and, conversely, its destructive and violent aspects. This chapter is, in a sense, the theoretical core of the book.

The remaining two parts of the book focus on the parallel reading of two extensive diaries written by Jews during the Nazi period: the diaries of Victor Klemperer from Dresden and Chaim Kaplan from Warsaw. This reading is based on the theoretical chapters but also deepens and broadens the discussion of questions raised in those chapters. The selection of these two diaries was not arbitrary. In some ways, they represent two extremes of the spectrum of Jewish identity at that time, as well as the historical range of Jews during the Holocaust. Klemperer, an assimilated Jew who converted to Christianity, married a Christian German woman before the war; Kaplan was a Jew with a strong and ardent sense of national consciousness. Klemperer writes in German—a language for which he has great admiration; Kaplan writes in Hebrew, of which he is an impassioned advocate. The former is a Central European intellectual; the latter is in many ways a typical member of the Eastern European Jewish intelligentsia.

The historical fate of these two men also differed. Klemperer retained a limited amount of liberty and freedom of movement; Kaplan was imprisoned in the Warsaw ghetto, along with the remainder of the city's Jews, in the fall of 1940. The conditions in which they lived were also very different in terms of their severity. While some 20 percent of the inhabitants of the Warsaw ghetto died of hunger and illness, conditions for the small, remaining Jewish population of Dresden (until the "Final Solution," of course) were less extreme. The two men were exposed to different levels of violence: while the Nazis treated the Jews in Germany with some degree of restraint, in Poland and the Eastern Territories they did not hold back at all, subjecting the Jews to murderous violence. Another difference between the two lies in the respective rates of deterioration. In Germany the persecution of the Jews was more gradual, as it was "spread" over the course of the six and a half years prior to the war. In Poland change came much faster, with far greater intensity. Klemperer's situation was thus, objectively, "better" than Kaplan's, although his experiences were also extreme. Klemperer remained in

Germany and survived due to his marriage to a non-Jewish woman; Kaplan was sent to Treblinka during the Great Deportation in the summer of 1942.[74]

Conceptually, I relate to both diaries using the same theoretical framework. Nevertheless, each diary is discussed within the cultural context of the writer and the historical circumstances of the writing—circumstances that underwent changes over the course of the writing period.

Admittedly, these two writers cannot be considered representative of the extremely diverse life stories of European Jews before the war, disrupted and destroyed during the Holocaust. In terms of gender, age, education, political consciousness, scholarly orientation, and many other elements, these biographies reflect little more than these two, very specific life stories. Nonetheless, they do share a number of characteristics that make them worthy of close reading. Both authors were assiduous and excellent diary writers. Their writing is elegant, intelligent, and incisive; both wrote almost daily and sometimes more than once a day; both kept diaries before the war, and the nature of their writing changes from the moment that they come under Nazi rule—from the personal-intimate to the historical-documentary, in which they see their mission; yet both maintain a personal, subjective perspective. Another characteristic common to both writers is their exceptional consciousness of the act of writing itself. Furthermore, neither is satisfied merely to chronicle events but rather both strive (almost obsessively) to conceptualize and understand the reality in which they found themselves in light of their old frames of reference.

Consequently, both diaries constitute rich, trenchant, and reflective autobiographical documents in which the writers not only describe the reality they experience but also struggle against it through writing. In this sense, which is at the core of this study, the analysis of these two extensive diaries can teach us a great deal about the basic forces, principles, and structures that constitute autobiographical writing in times of severe trauma and powerlessness. Although such an analysis obviously cannot exhaust all forms of Jewish autobiographical writing during the Holocaust, its findings can surely offer considerable insight into relations between self, text, and ongoing trauma. Hence, these diaries stand at the heart of two discussions regarding autobiographical writing during the Holocaust. The discussion of Klemperer's diary focuses on the writer's temporal experience, while the discussion of Kaplan's diary concentrates on the writer's stance in the face of the murderer's annihilating force, laws, language, and increasing infiltration into the writer's own voice.

The primary method applied in the discussions of the diaries of Klemperer and Kaplan is that of close reading, involving as many passages as possible from the two texts, while extending the discussion to other diaries or to additional theoretical or historical connotations, mainly through the endnotes. The principal structural reason for employing the technique of close reading is that this book presumes that language, in all its strata, cannot be ignored if we wish to understand "man." This is all the more true of diaries that are "life stories," in which the writer establishes his or her identity by means of narrative and language—two phenomena that occur, in this context, on the linguistic plane. The text of the diary is not—to paraphrase Paul Valéry—a transparent window through which man or historical reality may be observed, while ignoring the window itself.[75] In this sense, close reading is faithful, first and foremost, to language, sensitive to its subtlest variations. It examines the most basic building blocks and mechanisms of writers' discourse and narrative—thereby gaining insight into the writers themselves and their existential state at the time of writing. In many ways, the close reading of a text allows attention to be focused on what the text *does* and not just on what it *says*.

This approach stands in contrast to the prevailing approach of Holocaust historians, who have also made extensive use of diaries but have always related to them as documentary texts (i.e., as historical sources and not as events or phenomena in their own right). The conventional approach sees the diaries as transparent windows through which we can observe social processes, worldviews, concrete events, and so forth, but the text itself (the diaries, in this case) is always viewed as a means to a more or less faithful and valid reconstruction of historical or mental reality. As such, the text is never the object of focused attention. Conversely, I have sought to approach the text of the diaries and the event of their writing as the subjects and objects of my research. Close reading focuses on the subtle variations within the text that establish or, unfortunately, disintegrate both the text and its speaking subject.[76] The following is thus a literary-psychoanalytic investigation that seeks to understand the "man" in the text—contrary to previous studies, which have taken a historical approach and have focused on reconstructing the *event* from the text.

Notes

1. Kalonymus Kalman Shapira, *Esh Kodesh* [Sacred fire] (1960; reprint, Jerusalem: Yad Vashem, 1979), 56–57. Unless otherwise noted, all quotations from this text are from Nehemia Polen's English translation, in Nehemia Polen, *The Holy Fire: The Teachings of Rabbi Kalonymus Kalman Shapira, the Rebbe of the Warsaw Ghetto* (Northvale, NJ: Jason Aronson, 1994). *Shabbat Shuvah*, "The Sabbath of Return," is the Sabbath between Rosh Hashanah and Yom Kippur (the Day of Atonement), one of the most solemn days in the Jewish calendar.

2. The emotional indifference that characterized prayer in the ghetto was not unique to the Warsaw ghetto. Regarding the Lodz ghetto, see Oskar Singer, "Hamatzod Hagadol Begeto Lodz" [The great manhunt in the Lodz ghetto], *Yediot Beit Lohamei Haghetaot* 21 (1959): 80; Menachem Oppenheim, "Yomano shel Menahem Oppenheim Migeto Lodz" [The diary of Menachem Oppenheim of the Lodz ghetto], *Sinai* 28 (1951): 241–278. For a contemporary account of religious life in the Lodz ghetto, see Jerakhmil Bryman, "The Nature of Ghetto Prayer Services," in *Lodz Ghetto: Inside a Community under Siege*, ed. Alan Adelson and Robert Lapides (New York: Viking, 1989), 399–405. Rabbi Shapira was careful to corroborate his testimony: "Now as I write these words I can add that other people have told me that they share the same impression" (*Esh Kodesh*, 56). Such rhetoric is typical of historical testimony, which seeks to provide individual experience with universal validity.

3. Shapira, *Esh Kodesh*, 56.

4. Ibid., 57.

5. I say "virtually" because, later in the homily, Rabbi Shapira interprets the significance of the plural form of the word "depths" in the biblical verse "From the depths I have called You, O Lord," as an affirmation of the human ability to call out to God not only from the first depth, but even from the second depth, the depth of absence. He does not, however, explain how this is possible. For another interpretation of this passage, within a detailed analysis of Rabbi Shapira's thought, see Avichai Zur, "'The Lord Hides in Inner Chambers': The Doctrine of Suffering in the Theosophy of Rabbi Kalonymus Kalman Shapira of Piaseczno," *Dapim: Studies on the Shoah* 25 (2011): 183–237. This is undoubtedly the most comprehensive and comprehensive analysis of Rabbi Shapira's doctrine of suffering published to date. See also references, there, to other studies on Rabbi Shapira's philosophy.

6. "Sanctification of life" is a concept that is attributed to Rabbi Isaac Nissenbaum of the Warsaw ghetto but was, in fact, developed before the war. While the traditional religious demand to "sanctify God's name" requires Jews to lay down their lives, under certain conditions of persecution, the demand to "sanctify life" as part of the struggle against an enemy requires the exact opposite: to cling to life. The "sanctification of life" became a code that imbued the daily struggle for survival under Nazi oppression with religious and almost transcendental value.

7. By "during the course of the Holocaust" I mean the period, as defined by Israeli historiography, between the Nazi rise to power in 1933 and the fall of the Third Reich in 1945. Most of the texts discussed here, however, were written during World War II.

8. From a presentation given at Notre Dame University on 26 April 1998. Quoted in Sidra DeKoven Ezrahi, "Racism and Ethics: Constructing Alternative History," in *Humanity at the Limit: The Impact of the Holocaust on Jews and Christians*, ed. Michael A. Singer (Bloomington: Indiana University Press, 2000), 27.

9. Hannah Arendt, *The Origins of Totalitarianism* (Cleveland: World, 1958), 438. For a critique of Arendt on this issue, see Michal Aharony, *Hannah Arendt and the Limits of Total Domination: The Holocaust, Plurality, and Resistance* (New York: Routledge, 2015).

10. Arendt, *The Origins of Totalitarianism*, 441. See also chapter 5 in Zygmunt Bauman, *Modernity and the Holocaust* (Cambridge: Polity, 1989).

11. Theodor W. Adorno, "The Liquidation of the Self," in *Can One Live after Auschwitz? A Philosophical Reader*, ed. Rolf Tiedemann (Stanford, CA: Stanford University Press, 2003), 427–436. Adorno cites Jean Améry's essay on torture. See Jean Améry, *At the Mind's Limits: Contemplations by a Survivor on Auschwitz and Its Realities*, trans. Sidney Rosenfeld and Stella P. Rosenfeld (Bloomington: Indiana University Press, 1980).

12. See Manuela Consonni, *Rezistentzyah o Sho'ah: Zikaron, Gerush Vehashmadah Be'italyah 1945–1985* [Resistance or holocaust: The memory of the deportation and the extermination in Italy, 1945–1985] (Jerusalem: Magnes, 2009); Primo Levi, *If This Is a Man/The Truce*, trans. Stuart Woolf (London: Abacus, 2004).

13. Levi, *If This Is a Man*, 17.

14. Ibid., 177–178.

15. The lecture was later published as an article. See Leni Yahil, "Mekorot Hasho'ah Uve'ayot Mehkaran" [Holocaust: Original sources and the problems of their investigation], *Yalkut Moreshet* 2, no. 3 (December 1964): 155–161.

16. Ibid., 155.

17. Ibid., 158–159. Another pioneer of Holocaust studies in Israel, Mark Dworzecki, wrote in a similar vein. See Mark Dworzecki, "Ha'adam Vehahevrah Nokhah Hasho'ah" [Man and society in view of the Holocaust], *Yedi'ot Yad Vashem* 2 (June 1954): 10, 12.

18. Fela Szeps, who, in her diary, documented the "humanity" of women prisoners at the Grünberg camp, defined such people as "those who had not yet been discovered or interrogated." Fela Szeps, *Balev Ba'arah Hashalhevet: Yomanah shel Fela Szeps* [A blaze from within: The diary of Fela Szeps] (Jerusalem: Yad Vashem, 2002), 34. See also Geoffrey Hartman, *The Longest Shadow: In the Aftermath of the Holocaust* (Bloomington: Indiana University Press, 1996), 145.

19. These memoirs were typically written during the second half of the war, from 1943 on—mostly in hiding.

20. See Shlomith Rimmon-Kenan, "Narration as Repetition: The Case of Günther Grass's *Cat and Mouse*," in *Discourse in Psychoanalysis and Literature*, ed. Shlomith Rimmon-Kenan (New York: Methuen, 1987), 176–187; Dominick LaCapra, *Representing the Holocaust: History, Theory, Trauma* (Ithaca, NY: Cornell University Press, 1994); LaCapra, *History and Memory after Auschwitz* (Ithaca, NY: Cornell University Press, 1998).

21. It is very difficult to define the characteristics of the genre of autobiography. See Laura Marcus, *Auto/biographical Discourses: Theory, Criticism, Practice* (Manchester: Manchester University Press, 1994). I have therefore included various kinds of first-person writing in this discussion. For an article on the subject of autobiographies that draws its conclusions from the diversity of the genre, see Aviad Kleinberg, "Shalosh Otobiografiyot Miyemei Habeinayim" [Three autobiographies from the Middle Ages], *Alpayim* 13 (1996): 44–64. The "diaries" treated in this book in fact belong to two genres prevalent during the Holocaust. The first is the daily journal in which the writer describes, at more or less fixed intervals, his or her activities and most recent experiences, close to the time of their occurrence. The second genre formally resembles a memoir and was typically written during the second half of the war, from 1943 onward. Most writers of this second genre were in hiding, suffering deprivation and living in fear for their lives, when they decided to recount, retrospectively, all their experiences up to that point. The distinction between these two forms is not unequivocal. The writer of an ordinary diary may sometimes include lengthy accounts of the past and vice versa. Autobiographical

writing was indeed the central genre of writing at the time, with the exception of letter writing, which may also be included in the category of first-person writing.

22. Some diarists chose to combine several languages in their writing. For a fascinating analysis of such a case, see Batsheva Ben-Amos, "A Multilingual Diary from the Lodz Ghetto," *Gal-Ed* 19 (2004): 51–74.

23. This may explain why relatively few diaries were kept by Armenians murdered during the course of their deportation to the desert—the main extermination technique employed by the Turks. A notable exception is Vahram Dadrian, *To the Desert: Pages from My Diary* (Princeton, NJ: Gomidas Institute, 2003).

24. Jews engaged in autobiographical writing, including diaries and memoirs, before the Holocaust as well, but not to the same extent. On the development of Jewish autobiographical writing, see Marcus Moseley, *Being for Myself Alone: Origins of Jewish Autobiography* (Stanford, CA: Stanford University Press, 2006); Jeffrey Shandler, ed., *Awaking Lives: Autobiographies of Jewish Youth in Poland before the Holocaust* (New Haven, CT: Yale University Press, 2002).

25. Dawid Rubinowicz, *The Diary of Dawid Rubinowicz*, trans. Derek Bowman (Edmonds, WA: Creative Options, 1982).

26. Emanuel Ringelblum mentions a number of diaries that had been lost, drawing the following conclusion: "It is known that many in Warsaw have kept diaries. It appears that only a fraction of these will reach the general public. The deluge of deportation inundates and sweeps over everything. It leaves no trace. In vain people were sent to the flats of the deportees to search for writings they had left behind. They found nothing, because everything had been thrown in the garbage, destroyed or burned" (Emanuel Ringelblum, *Ktavim Ahronim: Yahasei Yehudim-Polanim* [Last writings: Jewish–Polish relations], vol. 2 [Jerusalem: Yad Vashem, 1994], 33–34). Some of the authors of the diaries refer to other diaries that have never been found. See, for example, Batya Temkin-Berman, *Yoman Bamahteret: Parshiyot Udmuyot Mivarshah Hakvushah* [Underground diary: Episodes from occupied Warsaw] (Tel Aviv: Hakibbutz Hameuchad and the Ghetto Fighters' House, 1956), 7, 83, 135. See also Avraham Tory on the lost diary of Israel Kaplan: Avraham Tory, *Surviving the Holocaust: The Kovno Ghetto Diary*, ed. Martin Gilbert, trans. Jerzy Michalowicz (Cambridge, MA: Harvard University Press, 1990), 278–280.

27. For the sake of comparison, the diary scholar William Matthews lists 2,500 diaries written in Britain between 1442 and 1943 (cited in Felicity A. Nussbaum, *The Autobiographical Subject: Gender and Ideology in Eighteenth-Century England* [Baltimore: Johns Hopkins University Press, 1989], 24). Dina Porat also notes the frequency of the phenomenon during the Holocaust. See Dina Porat, "The Vilna Ghetto Diaries," in *Holocaust Chronicles: Individualizing the Holocaust through Diaries and Other Contemporaneous Personal Accounts*, ed. Robert Moses Shapiro (Hoboken, NJ: Yeshiva University Press and KTAV, 1999), 157. The opposite phenomenon is also interesting: Fela Szeps linked the completion of her diary to the end of the horrors: "I very much wanted to finish writing this diary already, but world events refuse to support my wishes" (Szeps, *Balev Ba'arah Hashalhevet*, 98).

28. Yitzhak Aron, *Mayn Klayne Tsavoe* [My little Will], Yad Vashem Archives (uncataloged, in the author's possession).

29. Quoted in Jacek Leociak, *Text in the Face of Destruction: Accounts from the Warsaw Ghetto Reconsidered*, trans. Emma Harris (Warsaw: Żydowski Instytut Historyczny, 2004), 68. See also on the materiality of the diary: *Yomano shel Na'ar Almoni MiLodz* [Diary of an anonymous boy from Lodz] (Yad Vashem Archives O-33/1032); Oppenheim, "Yomano shel Menahem Oppenheim."

30. The same conclusion was reached by Renata Laqueur Weiss, who examined diaries written in the concentration camps, not necessarily those written by Jews (Renata Laqueur Weiss, "Writing in Defiance: Concentration Camp Diaries in Dutch, French and German, 1940–1945" [PhD diss., New York University, 1971], 33). See also Bruno Bettelheim, *The Informed Heart* (New York: Thames and Hudson, 1961), 135. See, for example, Zelig Kalmanovitch, "A Diary of the Nazi Ghetto in Vilna," in *YIVO Annual of Jewish Social Science*, vol. 7 (New York: YIVO, 1953), 10–12. Yitzhak Zuckerman explains Yitzhak Katzenelson's use of biblical themes in his poetry in a similar vein—as coded references, for the eyes of his Jewish readers only (cited in Yechiel Szeintuch, *Yitzhak Katzenelson: Ktavim Shenitzlu Migeto Varshah Umimahaneh Vittel* [Yitzhak Katzenelson's rescued manuscripts from the Warsaw ghetto and the Vittel concentration camp] [Jerusalem: Magnes and the Ghetto Fighters' House, 1990], 33). See also Josef Kermisz, in his introduction to Czerniakow's diary: "Czerniakow wrote . . . in a style that is simple, unadorned, and to the point. Concealment was another reason for his brevity" (Josef Kermisz, introduction to *The Warsaw Diary of Adam Czerniakow: Prelude to Doom*, ed. Raul Hilberg, Stanislaw Staron, and Josef Kermisz [New York: Stein and Day, 1979], 3). Sometimes, writers feared the Jewish leadership within the ghetto. For example, the "Lodz Ghetto Chronicle" was subject to strict supervision and censorship, overseen by Rumkowski, who was very sensitive to the ways in which he was portrayed, orally and in writing. It is important to note, however, that this was a public rather than a private chronicle. I will discuss these issues later in the book, with regard to Klemperer.

31. Yehoshua Moshe Aronson, *Alei Merorot* [Leaves of bitterness] (Bnei Brak: private publication, 1996), 122. For an interesting comparison between the diary and Aronson's memoirs, see Esther Farbstein, "Diaries and Memoirs as a Historical Source: The Diary and Memoir of a Rabbi at the 'Konin House of Bondage,'" *Yad Vashem Studies* 26 (1998): 87–128.

32. "Der drang tsu shreiben memoirn iz azoy shtark" (Emanuel Ringelblum, *Ksovim fun Geto: Togbuch fun Varshover Geto 1939–1942* [Writings from the ghetto: A diary from the Warsaw ghetto 1939–1942] [Warsaw: Yiddish Bukh, 1961], 224. The Yiddish word *drang* (like the German *Drang*) denotes a strong impulsive outburst from a very primal source.

33. Emanuel Ringelblum, *Notes from the Warsaw Ghetto: The Journal of Emanuel Ringelblum*, trans. Jacob Sloan (New York: Schocken, 1974), 133.

34. See Lorna Martens, *The Diary Novel* (Cambridge: Cambridge University Press, 2009), 55–56; Gary Saul Morson, *The Boundaries of Genre* (Austin: University of Texas Press, 1981), 8–9. For the most comprehensive study of diaries, see Gustav Rene Hocke, *Europäische Tagebücher aus vier Jahrhunderten* (Frankfurt am Main: Fischer Taschenbuch, 1991).

35. Fothergill calls this a "dissenting tradition." See Robert Fothergill, *Private Chronicles: A Study of English Diaries* (London: Oxford University Press, 1974), 27–28.

36. Some claim that autobiography also has the potential to give voice to the oppressed classes. See Julia Swindells, *The Uses of Autobiography* (London: Taylor and Francis, 1995), 7; Margo Culley, introduction to *A Day at a Time: The Diary Literature of American Women from 1764 to the Present*, ed. Margo Culley (New York: Feminist Press at the City University of New York, 1985), 3–4; Martens, *The Diary Novel*, 173. An extensive body of scholarship has developed around the subject of women's diaries since these afford access to women's voices, which lacked prominence in the male-dominated public sphere. See, for example, Suzanne I. Bunkers and Cynthia A. Huff, *Inscribing the Daily: Critical Essays on Women's Diaries* (Amherst: University of Massachusetts Press, 1996). For a historical study exploring women's voices during the American migration to the west, see Lillian Schlissel, *Women's Diaries of the Westward Journey* (New York: Schocken, 1982).

37. Quoted in Morson, *The Boundaries of Genre*, 8–9.

38. The impulse for autobiographical writing often stems from personal crisis. A clear example of this from the tradition of Jewish autobiographical writing is the unique memoir of Glückel of Hameln, which she began to write following her husband's death. Glückel of Hameln, *Memoirs of Glückel of Hameln*, trans. Marvin Lowenthal (New York: Schocken, 1977).

39. I refer to diaries written at the writer's personal initiative, as the Nazi regime encouraged Germans to write a "family-clan diary" (*Tagebuch der Sippe*), "from which their descendants will draw strength and wisdom and gain knowledge . . . of the network of ties and destiny associated with the alliance of blood" (Peter Börner, *Tagebuch* [Stuttgart: J. B. Metzlerische, 1969], 54). See also Suzanne zur Nieden, "Aus dem vergessenen Alltag der Tyrannei," in *Im Herzen der Finsternis: Victor Klemperer als Chronist der NS-Zeit*, ed. Hannes Heer (Berlin: Aufbau, 1997), 110; Peter Fritzsche, *Life and Death in the Third Reich* (Cambridge MA: Harvard University Press, 2008), 9. See also Janosch Steuwer, *"Ein Drittes Reich wie ich es auffasse": Politik, Gesellschaft und Privates Leben in Tagebüchern 1933–1939* (Göttingen: Wallstein, 2017).

40. On the variety of reasons that Jews kept diaries during this period, see Alexandra Garbarini, *Numbered Days: Diaries and the Holocaust* (New Haven, CT: Yale University Press, 2006), 129–167; and Leociak, *Text in the Face of Destruction*, 77–103.

41. See Karl Joachim Weintraub, *The Value of the Individual: Self and Circumstance in Autobiography* (Chicago: University of Chicago Press, 1978), which is based on a study of periods in which autobiographical writing flourished; and the pioneering work of Georg Misch, *A History of Autobiography in Antiquity* (London: Routledge and Kegan Paul, 1950). See also Aviad Kleinberg's critique in Kleinberg, "Shalosh Otobiografiyot."

42. Take, for example, the words of Max Frisch: "In it [the diary] one does not hide away but writes up. In it one discovers one's thoughts. The diary is, at best, indicative of the time and place to which it attests. We do not take into account the hope that the day after tomorrow, when we will think otherwise, we will be wiser. The pen is held like a seismographic needle and, in effect, we do not write but are written about" (quoted in Börner, *Tagebuch*, 60).

43. Börner, *Tagebuch*, 60. See also Garbarini, *Numbered Days*, 16–21. Garbarini discovered family diaries written by Jewish parents to children with whom contact had been lost. The parents sought to maintain family ties in an imaginary form through these diaries of virtual letters (since they were never sent or meant to be sent) to their children (95–128).

44. Philippe Lejeune, *On Diary*, ed. Jeremy D. Popkin and Julie Rak, trans. Katherine Durnin (Manoa: University of Hawai'i Press, 2009), 3.

45. Morson, *The Boundaries of Genre*, 9. Gombrowicz, too, intentionally chose the diary as the medium most suited to representing the paradoxes of modern life (quoted in Börner, *Tagebuch*, 60).

46. Quoted in Börner, *Tagebuch*, 67.

47. Chaim Aron Kaplan, *Scroll of Agony: The Warsaw Diary of Chaim A. Kaplan*, trans. and ed. Abraham I. Katsh (Bloomington: Indiana University Press, 1999), 75.

48. Zvi Radlitzky, "Reshimot Miyemei Hakibush Hagermani BeLvov (Lemberg) 1941–1943" [Notes from the days of the German occupation in Lvov (Lemberg) 1941–1943], *Yalkut Moreshet* 21 (1976): 7.

49. This is an extreme example, open to De Man's subversive claim regarding all biographies—that they merely pretend that the "I" exists, but in fact disguise its disappearance. See Paul De Man, "Autobiography as De-facement," *MLN* 94 (1979): 919–930.

50. I will cite a number of representative examples. The diary of Calek Perechodnik—given the title *Hatafkid He'atzuv shel Hati'ud* [The sad role of documentation] for its publication in Hebrew (Jerusalem: Keter, 1993), based on a passage in the diary itself—indeed has a clear documentary nature. Aryeh Klonicki's diary—titled *The Diary of Adam's Father* in English (trans. Avner Tomaschoff [Jerusalem: The Ghetto Fighters' House and Hakibbutz Hameuchad, 1973]), as in Hebrew (*Yoman Avi Adam* [Jerusalem: The Ghetto Fighters' House and Hakibbutz Hameuchad, 1969])—begins as follows: "In deciding to write this diary I was motivated by the desire to leave some remembrance at least to those of my brothers fortunate enough to be living in lands untouched by the hand of Hitler" (21, 5 July 1943). Even Anne Frank, who kept a personal diary, toys with the idea of publishing her diary after the war (*The Diary of a Young Girl: Definitive Edition*, ed. Otto H. Frank and Mirjam Pressler, trans. Susan Massotty [London: Puffin, 2007], 317, 5 April 1944); and Etty Hillesum, whose diary is an example of the most intimate kind of diary, seeks, through it, to become a "chronicler" of her time, but "not a chronicler of horrors. Or of sensations," as she notes on 3 October 1943 (Etty Hillesum, *An Interrupted Life: The Diaries of Etty Hillesum, 1941–1943*, trans. Arnold Pomerans [New York: Henry Holt, 1996], 234). Perhaps the most shocking example of the documentary intention of the diary can be found in the diaries written by the Sonderkommandos at Auschwitz. On the first page of his diary, Zalman Gradowski writes, in Polish, Russian, French, and German: "Take interest in this document which contains very important material for the historian" (Zalman Gradowski, "Writings," in *The Scrolls of Auschwitz*, ed. Ber Mark, trans. Sharon Neemani [Tel Aviv: Am Oved, 1985], 173). Similarly, Rabbi Yehoshua Moshe Aronson wrote, in an appendix to his diary, dated winter 1943: "I am writing the scroll of the Konin house of bondage, a chronicle, as scientific material for the researchers of our generation. It is written very concisely, without embellishment, only things as they are, of what my eyes have seen" (Aronson, *Alei Merorot*, 122). See also Yani Shulman, "Der Elteste der Yuden" [The eldest of the Jews], *Yediot Beit Lohamei Haghetaot* 29 (1960): 60.

51. See, for example, Josef Kermisz, introduction to Adam Czerniaków, *Yoman Geto Varshah* [Diary of the Warsaw ghetto] (Jerusalem: Yad Vashem, 1970), 8 [Hebrew]. See also chapters 4 and 7 below on the change in the focus of writing in the diaries of Victor Klemperer and Chaim Kaplan. One should nonetheless restrict this assertion, at least with regard to the external reader. The very appeal to an external reader, which seems at odds with the intimate nature of the diary, stems, at least partially, from accepted social practices. The commercial publication of diaries began in the 1880s. Diaries had been published as early as the beginning of the nineteenth century, and historical societies gradually uncovered a growing number of diaries from various periods. Nevertheless, the end of the nineteenth century saw a wave of published personal diaries sweep through Europe, especially France. One of the most prominent of these was the journal of the Swiss writer Henri-Frédéric Amiel, published in the years 1882–1884. It is worth noting that the journal was not published in an academic context, as a historical or biographical source. It simply satisfied readers' growing need for a glimpse into the private worlds of more or less known figures. The intimate diary became established public fact. See Martens, *The Diary Novel*, 115–118.

52. Lejeune, *On Diary*, 329–336.

53. Paul John Eakin, *How Our Lives Become Stories: Making Selves* (Princeton, NJ: Princeton University Press, 1999), 55–61. See also Misch, *A History of Autobiography*, 6–7; and Leona Toker, "Towards a Poetic of Documentary Prose: From the Perspective of Gulag Testimonies," *Poetics Today* 18, no. 2 (Summer 1997): 193.

54. Meyer based his research on the journals of Herder, Hebbel, and Amiel. Quoted in Börner, *Tagebuch*, 2.

55. Calek Perechodnik, *Am I A Murderer? Testament of a Jewish Ghetto Policeman*, trans. Frank Fox (Boulder, CO: Westview, 1996), xi.

56. Even a laconic, documentary diary—practically a chronicle—like that of Czerniakow, includes many references to the personal dimension of the writer's life. See, for example, Adam Czerniakow, *The Warsaw Diary of Adam Czerniakow: Prelude to Doom*, ed. Raul Hilberg, Stanislaw Staron, and Josef Kermisz (New York: Stein and Day, 1979), 105, 126, 172 (entries for 5 January 1940, 10 March 1940, and 8 July 1940).

57. Temkin-Berman, *Yoman Bamahteret*, 7.

58. The situation in children's diaries would appear to be different. In this case the declared intention in writing the diary usually has less to do with documentation and more to do with the writer's internal, emotional life and need to elaborate the experience through dialogue and reflection. Thus, for example, Moshe Flinker writes, on 24 November 1942: "I have started this diary so that I can write in it every day what I do and think; in this manner I shall be able to account for all I have done each day" (Moshe Flinker, *Young Moshe's Diary: The Spiritual Torment of a Jewish Boy in Nazi Europe*, trans. Geoffrey Wigoder [Jerusalem: Yad Vashem, 1965], 23); and Anne Frank writes on 20 June 1942: "I feel like writing, and I have an even greater need to get all kinds of things off my chest. . . . Now I'm back to the point that prompted me to keep a diary in the first place: I don't have a friend" (*The Diary of a Young Girl*, 12–13).

59. See, for example, Börner, *Tagebuch*, 1–8, and Hocke, *Europäische Tagebücher*, especially the first chapter.

60. Szeps, *Balev Ba'arah Hashalhevet*, 23. Hannah Arendt describes the unique experience of the Nazi concentration camps in almost exactly the same fashion: Hannah Arendt, "The Concentration Camps," in *A Holocaust Reader: Responses to the Nazi Extermination*, ed. Michael L. Morgan (New York: Oxford University Press, [1948] 2001), 47–63.

61. See, for example, the case of Srebnik, one of the two survivors from Chelmno interviewed in Lanzmann's film *Shoah*, whose testimony was analyzed by Shoshana Felman. He too recalls corpses as *Figuren*, rather than as murdered human beings. Only in retrospect does the witness manage to situate his testimony within a human frame of reference capable of affording significance to what he has seen. Felman thus argues that the event itself is, by definition, without witnesses. The witnesses are not conscious of what their eyes are seeing, that is to say they are incapable of situating the sight in relation to the life of the living. Shoshana Felman and Lori Daub, *Testimony: Crises of Witnessing in Literature, Psychoanalysis, and History* (New York: Routledge, 1992), 258.

62. Szeps, *Balev Ba'arah Hashalhevet*, 33.

63. Ibid., 23.

64. On the identification of testimony with autobiography in trauma literature, see Suzette A. Henke, *Shattered Subjects: Trauma and Testimony in Women's Life-Writing* (New York: St. Martin's, 1998), xvi. For a similar approach, see Margaret Ravenel Richardson, "Trauma and Representation in Women's Diaries of the Second World War" (PhD diss., University of St Andrews, 2012).

65. Szeps, *Balev Ba'arah Hashalhevet*, 33.

66. For an extensive discussion of this subject, see Amos Goldberg, "Haktivah Bitkufat Hasho'ah: Ti'ud Hahistoriyah o 'Ti'ud' Hatraumah? Kri'ah Beyomanah shel Fela Szeps"

[Writing during the Holocaust: Documenting history or "documenting" the trauma? A reading of Fela Szeps's diary], *Dapim: Studies on the Shoah* 19 (2005): 95–113.

67. See, for example, David Kahane, *Lvov Ghetto Diary*, trans. Jerzy Michalowicz (Amherst: University of Massachusetts Press, 1990), 11: "In my memoirs I will stick to just the bare facts. I relate what my eyes have seen." See also Berel Lang, on the relationship between the diaries' historical and literary aspects. Lang claims that the historicity of the diary lies in the authenticity of the writer's consciousness—also when the author is mistaken or even, from a historical perspective, lying (Berel Lang, *Act and Idea in the Nazi Genocide* [Chicago: University of Chicago Press, 1990], 126–129). I would like to go a step farther and point not only to the writer's consciousness but also to traumatic points of *absence* in the writer's consciousness.

68. Diary writers were aware of the existence of destructive forces beneath the surface. See, for example, the words of Zelig Kalmanovitch, on 12 August 1943: "Trying days. There is no perceptible panic. Life follows its normal course. But the worm of extinction gnaws at the heart" (Kalmanovitch, "A Diary of the Nazi Ghetto in Vilna," 74). In a similar fashion, a schizophrenic girl describes the first manifestations of her illness: "And beneath this mask of tranquility, of normality, I was living a veritable drama" (Marguerite Sechehaye, ed., *Autobiography of a Schizophrenic Girl* [New York: Grune and Stratton, 1951], 17). See also Bruno Bettelheim, who diagnosed schizophrenia as a reaction among concentration camp prisoners (Bruno Bettelheim, *Surviving and Other Essays* [New York: Vintage, 1979], 112–124).

69. For a similar approach to illness narratives, see Shlomith Rimmon-Kenan, "The Story of 'I': Illness and Narrative Identity," *Narrative* 10, no. 1 (January 2000): 9–26.

70. Not everyone sees a contradiction or conflict between these two concepts. I will discuss this at greater length below. See Kim Lacy Rogers, Selma Leydesdorff, and Graham Dawson, eds., *Trauma and Life Stories: International Perspectives* (London: Routledge, 1999).

71. See, for example: Allan Young, *The Harmony of Illusions: Inventing Post-Traumatic Stress Disorder* (Princeton, NJ: Princeton University Press, 1995); Carol Kidron "Surviving a Distant Past: A Case Study of the Cultural Construction of Trauma Descendant Identity," *Ethos* 31, no. 4 (2003): 513–544; Amos Goldberg, "The Victim's Voice in History and Melodramatic Esthetics," *History and Theory* 48, no. 3 (2009): 220–237.

72. Cf. Dominick LaCapra: "I don't try to be orthodox as a psychoanalyst, but really aim to develop the concepts in a manner that engages significant historical problems—and for me, the Holocaust is one of the most important of these problems" (Dominick LaCapra, *Writing History, Writing Trauma* [Baltimore: Johns Hopkins University Press, 2014], 141).

73. For an excellent compilation of articles that investigate the concept of trauma from a cultural perspective, see Yochai Ataria, David Gurevitz, Haviva Pedaya, and Yuval Neria, eds., *Interdisciplinary Handbook of Trauma and Culture* (Switzerland: Springer, 2016).

74. For a more comprehensive description of their biographies, see chapters 4, 7, and 9.

75. Nussbaum also adopts the approach that language cannot be ignored in autobiographical studies. Nevertheless, she does not adopt the methodology of close reading. See Nussbaum, *The Autobiographical Subject*, 6. As Malcolm Bowie writes, "There is no way out of the twists and turns of language" (Malcolm Bowie, *Lacan* [Cambridge, MA: Harvard University Press, 1991], 48).

76. Dina Porat's introduction to the Hebrew edition of Avraham Tory's *Kovno Ghetto Diary* constitutes an example of the approach that views the primary importance of the diary in the events to which it attests. Porat outlines her editorial approach to the text in the following manner: "The reader is thus able to discover, through them, the events that struck the deepest roots—events that are, in fact, mentioned again and again in the diary. The repetitions were

retained out of faithfulness to the spirit of the original text and, for the same reason, most of the dialogues were also kept. On the other hand, most of the lengthy descriptions of [the author's] state of mind and reflections on the mysteries of the universe, fate and chance, and the nature of man—all in the flowery language of the time—were omitted, retaining only a few, in order to illustrate the writer's frame of mind" (Dina Porat, introduction to *Geto Yom Yom: Yoman Umismakhim Migeto Kovno* [Ghetto everyday: Diary and documents from the Kovno ghetto], by Avraham Tory, ed. Dina Porat [Jerusalem: Bialik Institute and Tel Aviv University, 1988], 19).

PART I

READING HOLOCAUST DIARIES

1

HOLOCAUST DIARIES

Between Life Story and Trauma

HUMANS ARE storytelling creatures. We tell stories throughout our lives—about ourselves, our families, our communities, our past, and our future. Some stories we tell aloud to others and some we tell to ourselves, within the confines of our own consciousness. Through the stories we tell about ourselves, we constitute our identities because it is through our stories that we organize the events of our lives—disparate in time and place—into a coherent form. For example, stories allow us to create a causal relationship between different events, or to make certain events central and others secondary. The story is also constantly changing—thereby changing the significance of the events in our lives. Stories have the power to situate us within our respective societies and cultures, because the building blocks of the story, such as language, figurative patterns, intertextual connotations, and even the genre within which the story is told are based on the existing practices and structures in the cultures and societies in which we live. A person may, for example, construct his or her character as a tragic or comic hero or even an antihero. Each of these choices will afford different meaning to the same events and will situate the narrator differently in relation to them, although the genre types themselves are all present within the culture. These public building blocks are, in effect, what enable us to communicate our stories to others, and what render the story—even when it is not actually communicated but remains within the narrator's head—a social, intersubjective act. Herein lies the power and appeal of the ongoing "life story" that each and every one of us tells himself or herself, in order to create identity and meaning. In the following pages, I will focus on two central aspects of narrative that will feature throughout the book.

The first aspect is time. The theoretical foundations for understanding the ability of narrative to organize time and thereby constitute identity were largely laid by Paul Ricoeur.[1] There is a correlation, claims Ricoeur, between narrative and the nature of the human experience of time.[2] Through what Ricoeur termed "emplotment," the story manages to create a synthesis of a number of distinct elements, turning them into a relatively complete continuity. In other words, the story creates a kind of coherent integration of the events in a person's life.[3] According to Ricoeur, "composing a story is . . . drawing a configuration out of a succession."[4] The narrative is not a reflection of meaning and representation that exist independently outside it and detached from the language on which it is based. On the contrary, the organizational qualities of the narrative, like the differences created by the symbolic networks of language, are what constitute identity. This is the principal force of the life story. And indeed, a successful life story, claims Charlotte Linde, is a story that succeeds in organizing the self, that is creating basic coherence. Linde stresses, in particular, the causal relationship established by the narrative. The narrative thus creates a self whose past is relevant to its present—because the present is largely an outcome of that past. The autobiographical story affords the narrator a *sense* of continuity (or perhaps a necessary illusion of continuity) and the past becomes relevant to the present that stems from it. Linde compares this temporal continuity and the relevance of the past dimension to the present while opening prospects for the future—to a musical composition played legato rather than staccato.[5]

Another aspect of the story pertains to the two domains of self it comprises—the narrating self and the narrated self. The relation between these domains is crucial to the narrative identity of the individual.

Intuitively, we generally experience ourselves as a single entity. Sometimes though, we feel that our self is composed of a number of domains that do not necessarily act in coordination or harmony with one another. We may desire something and, at the same time, recoil from it, in the knowledge that it may harm us. In many ways, the story highlights the multiplicity of the self, through the varied and sometimes contradictory elements it necessarily contains but, in the end, also enables them to exist within a single narrative framework. Beyond this, however, the story possesses a structural characteristic that gives particular prominence to such divisions within the self, as the story necessarily incorporates two domains of self—the self that experienced the events and acts in the world, and the self that is able to step away from these events and acts, observe them, consider them, and then recount them. Logically and formally, the latter self follows the former, which the latter observes from "without," as if describing another person. In narrative terms, the first self may be said to be the *protagonist* of the autobiographical story, created as its main character—acting, feeling, thinking, and experiencing—the story's central axis and center of gravity. The second self, on the other hand, is the *narrating* self that engages in the act of narration, the one that creates the story in which the protagonist self features. These two instances of the self coincide neither in situation nor in function: the narrator stands outside the event described, while the protagonist experiences or acts within the event itself. In many ways, every autobiographical story is based on this division and the constant tension between these two domains of the self.[6] Moreover, as the linguist Emile Benveniste teaches us, every time a person says "I," he or she divides in two like an amoeba. There is the self that says "I" (subject) and the self that is described (object).[7] A successful life story is one that organizes not only the human experience of time in a reasonable fashion but also the different domains of self—particularly those of protagonist and narrator. It is a story that conducts complex and intense negotiations between these two aspects to prevent them from growing too much apart and becoming alienated from one another, but also from collapsing into one another.

Over the course of the book, I will address both aspects of the self in the life stories recounted in the first person in the diaries: the narrated *protagonist* self and the *narrator* self—each of which raises a series of questions. In the discussion of the first aspect, I will ask how the autobiographical story in the diaries is organized. Is there really a continuity between the events of the narrative that enables the constitution of the protagonist self as the focus of the story? Is identity created through the means cited above—first and foremost integration and coherence of the protagonist's various temporal dimensions? Is the past relevant to the present and does it delineate prospects for the future? In the discussion of the second aspect, on the other hand, I will ask other questions, regarding the act of narration rather than the narrative it produces—questions pertaining to the manifest and hidden motivations of writers in the first person. I will ask who is really performing this act of speech and who influences it? Where do the speakers situate themselves through the act of narration and, especially, to whom does the voice that emerges really belong?

The diary, although not considered part of the classic autobiographical genre—in which individuals recount their lives in retrospect from a distance in time—is, nevertheless, a kind of ongoing story in the first person, which presents all the identity-creating characteristics of the life story and autobiography, albeit, as noted in the introduction, in a far more fragmentary fashion. This capacity of the diary may explain, in part, the prevalence of first-person writing during the Holocaust. In such a turbulent time, when all the components of identity are radically undermined, when the concepts of yesterday can no longer explain what is happening today and are unable to offer hope for tomorrow, people find it hard to understand themselves and the world, to establish order and find meaning.[8] At such a time, diary writing may help writers preserve a shred of their identity and afford a modicum of cohesion to the world into which they have been thrust. The diary weaves fine narrative threads between the fragments of the protagonist's disintegrating world. These aspects of the diary may offer a partial explanation of the assertions made by many writers, noting the importance of writing to them—to the point of near-total dependence on it. Writing in the Vilna ghetto, the Bundist Herman Kruk referred to his diary as "the hashish of my life in the ghetto."[9]

Thus far, I have presented, in brief, the "optimal" model of a life story by means of which writers constitute their narrative identities. This approach is well-suited to an "ordinary" life story, in which the events recounted do not exceed the limits of conventional human experience.[10] It is unsuited, however, to the description of traumatic events because the temporal (dis)order of the traumatic event differs completely from the linear, continuous temporality of the life story and, in effect, destroys it.[11] The act of language also loses its constitutive meaning. The traumatic event thus threatens not only the protagonist but also the narrator of the story. To explain, I will provide a general outline of the aspects of traumatic experience that undermine the foundations of narrative identity—illustrating by means of readings from diaries written at that time. It is not my intention to provide an exhaustive study or even an overview of the concept of trauma but, at most, to point to a number of characteristics pertinent to the present discussion.[12]

Trauma is an event of a total nature, during which the subject feels "intense fear, helplessness, loss of control, and threat of annihilation."[13] "Something alien breaks in on you, smashing through whatever barriers your mind has set up as a line of defense. It invades you, possesses you, takes you over, becomes a dominating feature of your interior landscape, and in the process threatens to drain you and leave you empty."[14] It is thus an event that fundamentally threatens the psychic economy. The defense mechanisms are incapable of preventing or regulating the excess of stimuli that overwhelm the psyche and thus collapse. The psyche therefore lacks the capacity to respond to them in an appropriate fashion, and is left helpless.[15] This helplessness exists on a number of planes: in the face of the devastating external events; on the plane of their psychic elaboration; and later, in light of the symptoms that appear and reappear at a compulsive and uncontrolled frequency.

At the heart of the traumatic experience is, as Dominick LaCapra put it, an "unrepresentable excess."[16] Trauma is the occurrence of a terrible event, the extreme terror of which cannot be fully represented by means of language or other symbolic systems. Any attempt to fully represent this event is doomed to failure.[17] Even when it is factually accurate, the description of the traumatic event cannot contain or fully symbolize the terrifying dimension of the experience. This is why many of the diary writers feel that they are unable to describe in words the experience they are seeking to document, even when their descriptions are accurate and detailed. The thing that escapes consciousness is not necessarily a factual detail (although, at times, facts or events may also be "erased" from memory), but something more, related to the meaning of the experience. As one of many possible examples, I cite the following passage from the diary of Avraham Lewin from Warsaw, written on 26 May 1942, toward the end of the ghetto's existence but before the deportations to Treblinka had begun:

> The blood of our children will never be erased from the Cain's forehead of the German people! It is only now that I understand Bialik's sorrow and rage in the poem "On the Slaughter." . . . If Kishinev alone could arouse such reverberations of suffering in a Jewish heart, what is happening in our hearts after the greatest tragedy we have ever known? And perhaps because the tragedy is without measure, we are entirely unable to express all of our feelings. Only if we were to be given the possibility of uprooting the greatest of all mountains, Everest, by the strength of our choked suffering, to cast it with rage and force on the head of all the Germans . . . this would be the only response worthy of our time. We have lost the ability to use words.[18]

In this entry, Lewin draws on his cultural resources to express his extreme feelings. At the beginning of the passage, he attempts to paraphrase a poem by the Jewish poet of rage, Haim Nahman Bialik (a poem that, in itself, alludes with irony to the myth of the binding of Isaac), in order to express, in words, the extreme traumatic events experienced by the Jews of Warsaw.

Since these events were both beyond the realm of the writer's own experience and outside the historical-cultural context of Jewish collective experience ("the greatest tragedy we have ever known"), they could not easily be organized and represented within the boundaries of language and culture. Bialik's poetic hyperbole, so apt in the aftermath of the Kishinev pogrom, paled in the face of the reality of the Warsaw ghetto in its last days. The events thus escape the continuity of the familiar tools of cultural expression as well. It is the inexpressibility of the horror ("our choked suffering") that affords the events their traumatic and excessive nature, that gives rise to a desire that can never be satisfied and to an imaginary, performative form of expression, bordering on the mythical, such as the act of uprooting Mount Everest (the highest mountain in the world) and casting it on the head of the Germans. Ultimately, the hyperbolic expression conveys recognition of the fact that "we have lost the ability to use words." The events elude representation and that is why it is so terrifying and painful.

This characteristic of the traumatic event creates a temporal pattern that is inherently different from the continuous and constant experience of time in the Ricoeurian life story. The continuity between the three temporal dimensions of time (past, present, and future) is forcefully disrupted, as we have seen in the above passage by Avraham Lewin. Furthermore, since the very heart of the event is that "something" that eludes the representational systems accessible to human consciousness, one might say, in a certain sense, that it never happened. In "objective" time, something terrible indeed happened, but in human time, in the conscious experience of the subject—the only kind he or she knows—it did not happen, due to its intensity.[19] There is a big black hole at the heart of the experience and in the heart of the individual who experiences it. In this sense, the traumatic event has a dense and catastrophic present but, in terms of consciousness, has no present at all—hence its destructive power. Cathy Caruth thus sums up the temporal paradox of trauma as follows: "The historical power of the trauma is not just that the experience is repeated after its forgetting, but that it is only in and through its inherent forgetting that it is first experienced at all."[20] That is to say that the forgetting inherent in the event itself creates an experience of *emptiness from the outset*, rather than a void created as a result of the absence of something that was there and disappeared. The traumatic event thus entails a basic experience of void that cannot, in itself, be fully represented and that eludes meaning. If this is true of a single traumatic event (rape, train collision, etc.), how much more so of prolonged trauma, such as that experienced by victims of the Holocaust during the course of the events themselves. The Israeli psychoanalyst Effi Ziv refers to this kind of trauma as "persistent trauma."[21] While in "ordinary" trauma, the exceptional traumatic event occurred in the past and is subsequently elaborated in the context of a more or less stable reality that may be relied on in the healing process; in the case of persistent trauma, a kind of routine and its violent unraveling are constantly intertwined. Reality itself, as an ongoing present, is perpetually unraveled and, as such creates a routine of terror, fear, and disintegration, in which the processes of unraveling temporal continuity and narrative identity receive heightened expression. These processes, as we shall see over the course of the book, are also reflected in the Holocaust diaries and are manifested in the various ways in which the texts are radically dismantled/disintegrated. Of course, these traumatic texts include other, more integrative, linear, and "optimistic" dimensions as well, but the destructive forces within them are very strong.

One of the clearest expressions of the present-less temporal pattern is the rage engendered by the sense of helplessness, as we have seen in the writing of Avraham Lewin. The other side of the same coin is numbness and apathy.[22] This was also the view expressed by the psychologist and philosopher Emil Utiz, a survivor of Theresienstadt, in 1947: "Rage and numbness were the dominant feelings among the inhabitants of the ghetto, who oscillated between them."[23] This numbness, so typical of writing at that time, reflects the neutralization of consciousness with regard to surrounding events. Unable to integrate the intensity of the events, consciousness fails in its attempt to weave them into a familiar, general context, and therefore withdraws into the realm of numbness. We have already encountered this phenomenon in Rabbi Shapira's homily concerning High Holiday prayers in the Warsaw ghetto, cited at the beginning of the book. An example of the destructive dynamic of numbness inherent in the traumatic event can be found in the diary of Pal Kovacs, a Hungarian Jew interned in the Neuengamme concentration camp. In the following passage, Kovacs describes, retrospectively, his arrival at the camp: "We arrived at Neuengamme at dawn. From that moment, we ceased to exist as human beings. No sooner had we left the railway car than I received the first kick, after which they also set a dog on me. To this day the reason is not clear. At that moment, reality penetrated my consciousness, I understood where I was and sunk into a feeling of unconsciousness, from which I have not yet awoken. I float in a dream [and] wait to wake up. But sadly, in vain."[24] Kovacs links the traumatic situation to his very humanity: "We ceased to exist as human beings." He then makes a series of paradoxical statements, pertaining to numbness, which he identifies with a state of dreaming. To fully understand the destructiveness in these statements, we must return to the distinction between "narrator" and "protagonist." These are, as I have noted, two different consciousnesses within the same persona. The existence of each, in Kovacs's case, is a paradox with regard to itself and with regard to the other.

On the one hand, the "narrator" recounts an event that he describes as inexplicable—the setting of the dog on him ("To this day the reason is not clear"). It is this inexplicable event, however, that caused reality to penetrate the protagonist's consciousness, followed by understanding ("At that moment, reality penetrated my consciousness, I understood where I was"). Rather than heightening the author's senses and sense of reality, however, this understanding plunged him into a feeling of unconsciousness in which he still found himself at the moment of writing ("and sunk into a feeling of unconsciousness, from which I have not yet awoken"). All this is described, metaphorically, as floating in a dream, waiting to wake up—in vain. In this sense, understanding reality turns into a lack of understanding and sinking into a dream. The feeling of floating occurs, however, on the level of Kovacs as a protagonist, whom he describes in the first person, from his position as a narrator, whose consciousness remains active—paradoxically allowing him to consciously recount his condition, even at the time of writing, as one who is numb, lacking consciousness and a sense of reality. Consciousness on the narrator level thus describes the disappearance of consciousness on the protagonist level.[25]

At times, numbness turns the self into an automaton. That is how Fela Szeps describes it, in her diary: "Like automatons, we go through the daily events in the camp. . . . We do everything automatically." The prisoner acts as if controlled by some external programming that neutralizes human consciousness and individual will. Szeps goes on to describe the extent of the external control exerted on the "machines": "We begin to believe and become convinced that the camp is something good, that our fate is enviable."[26] The prisoners are slowly convinced that the place designated for them by the Nazi order is the best and most suitable place for them. The automatons act, here, in a way that bypasses and neutralizes individual consciousness, to the point that it is taken over by that of the murderer, which indicates to the victims, their "natural and appropriate" place.[27]

In extreme cases, writers actually describe their very own deaths. Zalman Loewenthal, for example, a member of the Sonderkommando at Auschwitz, offers the following description of his arrival at the camp: "None of us knew what he was doing, who was doing it and what was happening with him. We completely lost our senses. We were like dead men, like robots, when they rushed us; we did not know where we were to run, why, and what was to be done. [No one] looked at anyone else. I know for a fact that none of us was alive at that time, none of us thought nor contemplated."[28] The words of psychoanalyst and poet Ruth Golan may serve as an appropriate summary of the present discussion: "If we read the trauma as a form of absence, we see that it brings up one of the impossible sentences that a living subject cannot say and mean when he says it: 'I am dead.' We can feel it again in the trauma, where a personal testimony is emptied of meaning by the subject's absence from the event that he experienced most deeply."[29]

Stopping Time

In light of the above, it is clear why diary writing is more liable to failure than any later attempt at documentation. As the first act of a textual representation of the traumatic events experienced by the writer, such writing documents the temporal distortion created by the trauma, the disruption of the continuity and motion of time as a three-dimensional present, replacing it with a massive, static present—identical, in effect, to the complete absence of the present, since it is not distinct from the past and the future. For the person who experiences the trauma, there is a basic plane on which there is no past or future but only present, and this plane is antinarrative, since narrative is based on temporal continuity.[30] This phenomenon is thoroughly described by Hanna Lévy-Hass, a Jewish communist from Yugoslavia, imprisoned in Bergen-Belsen. In an entry dated 8 November 1944 she writes:

> We have the impression that we're separated from the normal world of the past by a massive, thick wall. Our emotional capacity seems blunt, faded. We no longer even remember our own past. No matter how hard I strive to reconstruct the slightest element of my past life, not a single human element comes back to me.
>
> We have not died, but we are dead. They've managed to kill in us not only our right to life in the present and for many of us, to be sure, the right to a future life . . . but what is most tragic is that they have succeeded, with their sadistic and depraved methods, in killing in us all sense of a human life in our past, all feeling of normal human beings endowed with a normal past, up to even the very consciousness of having existed at one time as human beings worthy of this name.

> I turn things over in my mind . . . and I remember absolutely nothing. It's as though it wasn't me. Everything is expunged from my mind. During the first few weeks, we were still somewhat connected to our past lives internally; we still had a taste for dreams, for memories. But the humiliating and degrading life of the camp has so brutally sliced apart our cohesion that any moral effort to distance ourselves in the slightest from the dark reality around us ends up being grotesque—a useless torment.[31]

One of the loci in which this collapse takes place, as reflected in Fela Szeps's diary, is the body. Normally, it is specifically through the body that we perceive our identity as both changing and continuous. Despite the changes the body goes through over the years, it remains—in our consciousness—the same body, and we attribute it to ourselves. My "self" is, first and foremost, my body, a locus that captures the gaze of others when they look at me, and in which lies my consciousness. We experience our bodies as a unified continuity, from a very early stage. According to Lacan, at the age of six months infants already recognize the image of their own body in the mirror, and begin to experience this body as a unity with a center of gravity and control. The limbs and impulses that move the body thus receive a coherent dimension.[32] It is, in fact, in front of the mirror that Szeps feels tremendous alienation from her body; alienation expressed in the disintegration of the sense of continuity constituted specifically by the body. On 14 July 1943 Szeps writes: "I glance at the mirror. And maybe it really isn't me! It is the shadow of a young girl who once was: a pale, gray face, completely bloodless; a dark, tired, suffering gaze; black circles and wrinkles under the eyes. A large yellow stain on the forehead, like that of a jaundice sufferer; the lips twisted in a kind of strange contortion that purports to be a smile, exposing yellow teeth."[33] In this passage, the face breaks up into parts, each a different color (gray, black, yellow), that do not come together to form a whole human face. It is only a faded memory of a human face—a bloodless shadow, with only a contorted line in place of the smile it used to have. There is no continuity between the body in the mirror and the normal body that once was. As a locus of continuity and unity, the disintegration of the body would seem to attest to the disintegration of identity in general. This is what Szeps writes in another entry, dated 31 December 1943: "Every time I look in the mirror, I get the feeling that it is another Fela Szeps there looking at me."[34] Similar feelings are described by other diary writers, such as Avraham Lewin, who notes, in the final days of the Warsaw ghetto, in an entry dated 30 June 1942: "The Jews look like shadows, not people. Sometimes you meet someone like that, whom you haven't seen for a long time, and you are shocked: It's simply hard to recognize him. It's not the same person."[35]

Working through Trauma, or Repetition through Writing

Freud dedicated a number of essays to the process of coping with traumatic loss through representation. He identified two basic modes of coping: "working through" and "acting out" ("agieren" in German). In the course of acting out, the person who has experienced the trauma relives it repeatedly, without the ability to work through the trauma in the realms of language and action.[36] This repetition is, according to Freud, the embodiment of the death instinct, and captivates and determines the course of one's life. On the other hand, working through the loss and the basic absence it embodies enables one to disengage from complete identification with the lost object and to organize the absence into a symbolic field of language and social ritual. This effort requires constant action that repeatedly narrates and represents the event and, in so doing, seeks to acquire some form of control, if not over the event itself, then at least over its representations, thereby connecting it to the various aspects of one's life and experiences. Working through seeks to escape the compulsion to repeat inasmuch as it acts upon the trauma through new possibilities engendered by creative imagination. Freud described this dialectic of representation of that which cannot be represented, at length, in his well-known essay "Beyond the Pleasure Principle" (1920).[37] These processes of creative repetition, however, are never one-dimensional. Some have seen them as therapeutic acts but, as LaCapra has pointed out, they combine two modes of coping with trauma: working through and repetition.[38]

As autobiographical linguistic actions, the Holocaust diaries served as tools to start working through the trauma even as it was happening. Through writing, the authors reorganize their individual identities and weave the traumatic event, in a preliminary fashion, into the fabric of their lives.[39] Diary writing is, in this sense, a therapeutic act. "The pen moves slowly and with difficulty, and so does the brain. But I must write. I must pour out the stream of our sufferings, even if only before God," writes Karol Rotgeber in his Warsaw ghetto diary, and fifteen-year-old Isabelle Jesion writes: "Dear diary, when I am sad and feel abandoned, I take you up to console me."[40] In effect, the very act of writing daily diary entries, beginning with the date and sometimes the location, organizes the events within some sort of temporal framework: that of the calendar. It is not the temporal framework of human experience, based on the dimensions of past, present, and future, but the geometrical and objective framework of the calendar, in which each day exists on a linear continuum—before the next day and after the previous day. Nevertheless, the very act of writing in a diary places the writer within time.

At times, the text reveals that the act of speaking of the tragedy, in and of itself, does not necessarily express exclusively therapeutic forces. Sometimes, the writer realizes traumatic helplessness even in writing itself. For example, Yitzhak Aron, from Miory, in the Vilna district, notes in his diary, written immediately after the complete destruction of his community: "When I take up the pencil to write, it opens the terrible wound in my heart, my eyes fill with blood and I cannot write any more."[41]

Such is the diary of Calek Perechodnik, a Jewish policeman in the Otwock ghetto, who actively participated in rounding up the town's Jews during the German actions, for deportation to Treblinka. Due to an intentional act of deception by the commander of the Jewish police and an error in judgment on his own part, he even brought his daughter and wife, personally, to the collection point for deportation and saw them put on a train, the destination of which—Treblinka—he knew for certain. Naturally, these terrible events had an extreme effect on Perechodnik. The diary he later wrote in a memoir form, while in hiding, is undoubtedly one of the most shocking documents from the Holocaust period. Perechodnik experienced traumatic helplessness in the most extreme fashion and this fact permeates the entire diary. It is a diary that, in every line, describes radical helplessness that is self-aware to the point of madness. This helplessness does not remain merely on the descriptive level but also receives expression in the diary as a negative performative utterance. I would now like to cite two passages from the diary, in which the writer's traumatic situation is realized in the writing itself.

The first passage pertains to Perechodnik's expectation of resistance on the part of the Jews. As a former member of the Betar movement (part of the right-wing Revisionist Zionist movement) and a Polish patriot, the question of self-respect and the value of resistance were central to his way of thinking—evident throughout the diary. Perechodnik expresses contempt for Jewish cowardice and condemns the victims' sense of fatalism. For example, in the fourth of five episodes relating to executions, he describes how eighteen Jews from the Karczew ghetto were murdered. In the midst of the killing, the German soldier ran out of bullets. He sent a Polish boy to the police Komisariat to bring more bullets, and sat down and waited. "What did the remaining Jews do then? Did they throw themselves on him to avenge the deaths of their closest ones? They continued to lie down with their faces to the ground and waited, waited more than half an hour for the supply of bullets to arrive—obviously the bullets of deliverance. . . . [And Perechodnik concludes:] Now in Karczew near a small rise at the mill lie the remains of eighteen Jews. This grave . . . is a testimony for all time to German barbarism or to Jewish cowardice."[42]

The second passage consists of similar criticism, which Perechodnik levels at the Jews of his town, Otwock. He reconstructs his thoughts as he observed the Jews gathered in the square awaiting deportation:

> And what are you thinking about, you Jewish masses? You are passive, hopeless, silent. Unwittingly, you enact the words of the poet: the destruction of a people can be its own fault when it is plagued by despair and weakness. . . . You think about everything except about the fact that you are the descendants of Judah the Maccabee. . . . Before you, stand two hundred men with guns . . . you are eight thousand men. . . . Rise up together and in a moment you will be free. The Jewish people is cursed, too old, and lacks the strength to fight for its life. [And immediately he continues:] I am returning to my wife with five new [poison] pills.[43]

On one level, Perechodnik denounces the fatalistic helplessness of the Jews, who fail to fight for their freedom. At the same time, however, he shares that fatalism and, rather than calling for rebellion, brings his wife poison pills to facilitate her suicide. The simultaneous presence of contradictory statements is an embodiment of helplessness within the fabric of the text. In the very juxtaposition the author creates within the narrative continuity—between bringing the poison pills to his wife and his call to the Jews of Otwock to act in the spirit of Judah Maccabee (a purely imaginary appeal, of course, as it remains within the intimate, textual realm)—he casts his appeal for a proud, Jewish rebellion in a pathetic, almost parodic light.[44] The juxtaposition of the two statements realizes, within the text, the unbridgeable gaps between Perechodnik's own values and actions and, no less so, the emptiness of his words. The text itself thus realizes the basic helplessness of the trauma.

Perechodnik's consciousness is divided in two: the completely imaginary consciousness of what should have happened (a rebellion, in the spirit of Judah Maccabee), and the realistic consciousness (the suicidal will of the helpless).[45] This extreme division of consciousness, characteristic of trauma, is one of the sources of Perechodnik's suffering and is also apparent elsewhere in the diary. Toward the end of the diary, however, the gap between imagination and consciousness of reality grow even greater, until the latter becomes entirely blurred. In the subsequent entries, Perechodnik describes the diary as a "dead fetus" into which he had to "breathe life." This "child," he writes, directly addressing his wife, was not born in the pangs of birth but in the throes of death. "This child is my diary, which I believe will one day be printed, so that the entire world will know of your suffering, to your glory. . . . Now that life has been breathed in our fetus, it must be cared for and protected until it grows and becomes a living word that no power can silence."[46]

At this point, the emotive intensity of Perechodnik's rhetoric increases, as his wife Anka's senseless death is transformed into another kind of death—death during childbirth—which derives its value from the creation of new life. At the same time, another transformation takes place and the diary becomes a surrogate for his dead child. This new child-diary is expected to become immeasurably stronger as it grows, until it becomes "a living word that no power can silence."

One of the most difficult expressions of Perechodnik's helplessness throughout the diary is the need to keep silent in the face of iniquity: "And believe me that it is a skill of the highest order in this vile world. The heart bleeds and the fists clench, but silent silent you must remain."[47] It seems to me that the omnipotent language Perechodnik uses to describe words that nothing can stop (do such words exist?), in contrast to the silence that was forced upon him and tears him up from within, embodies the greatness of his loss and the paralyzing intensity of helplessness.

It is a no less interesting fact that this diary, compared to the birth of a child and arousing such great expectations, is filled with descriptions of depravity, immorality, cowardice, collaboration, terror, shame, guilt, and helplessness the likes of which are hard to find in any diaries of the period. And it is precisely on these elements that Perechodnik focuses obsessively, in a text for which he foresees immortal existence as a monument to his wife Anka's glory. It is not the birth of a child, but the birth of a monster. Once again, this embodies the gap between Perechodnik's two levels of consciousness: the level of consciousness that expresses a very clear perception of reality, and the level that seeks imaginary redemption from suffering, helplessness, loss, and guilt and, in so doing, largely denies them.

It seems, in all of this, that this text, with its exaggerated and contradictory descriptions, exhibits and realizes within it not a process of working through, but a severe and irreparable traumatic rupture.

The Spatial Metaphor of Trauma

At the beginning of the chapter, I mentioned the temporal paradox of trauma. It is worth pointing to another metaphorical field, however, to describe the structure of trauma, particularly persistent trauma: the spatial field.[48] The primary characteristic of persistent trauma, certainly during the Holocaust, is that it is all-encompassing. The fear and meaninglessness fill almost every inch of a person's world, leaving virtually no space from which to begin working through the trauma. In this sense, trauma is spatial no less than it is temporal. The total nature of the ongoing trauma of the victims of the Holocaust is also reflected in the fact that the experience of fear is two-faced—that is, it acts simultaneously upon the past and the future, on what has already happened and on what is expected to happen. This situation, in which daily life is completely filled with fear and helplessness, leaves very little in the way of an alternative, "untainted" context, in which one might work through or even discuss and contextualize the events.

The spatial metaphor is an apt illustration of the totality of the traumatic encounter that "occupies" a person's entire world, leaving no room for distinctions between "I" and "you," subject and object, past and present.[49] This blurring of distinctions essential to the constitution of identity is, in fact, an inherent part of the traumatic experience. The Holocaust diaries recount the collapse of the most basic distinctions in the human psyche—places in which, without difference, human identity cannot exist. The Bergen-Belsen diary of Hanna Lévy-Hass (2009) is, to a large extent, unique in its charting of the collapse of these fundamental distinctions of subjectivity. One of the most shocking examples cited in Lévy-Hass's diary is that of the blurring of the physical difference between "self" and "nonself," between human and animal—a kind of blurring that gives rise to great fear. The following passage relates to a young boy whose mother had just died in the camp:

> [He] couldn't kill the vermin that had settled on his body because he couldn't see them; they've burrowed deep into his skin and swarmed through his eyebrows. His chest is completely blackened by these fleas and their nests. We have never seen such a thing; we never imagined such a thing could occur.... Everyone avoids him. His brothers and sister dread his presence, his fleas, his howling.... The other night, he dragged his useless body from one bed to the other... begging people to make room for him. Everyone pushed him away in disgust.... Painful story. His case is not unique.[50]

The boundary between the world and the subject is breached in the poor prisoner described above, and the fleas burrow into his body to the point that it is impossible to distinguish between him and them. The difference between human and animal—between the human body and the parasites that nest in it—is broken and collapses. No one can tell where the boy ends and where the fleas begin. The human and the animal become a single, terrifying hybrid. He seems to have become a true manifestation of what Giorgio Agamben sees as the most horrible outcome of Nazi (very modern) biopolitics—the terrible blurring of distinction between the human and the unhuman.[51] That is why the boy arouses such fear in all who see him, including the members of his own family. Note that those who reject his pleas to share their bunks do not do so only because they are afraid of catching his fleas, but are openly disgusted by him. The encounter with the infested boy is terrifying because it embodies the terror-inducing elements that ensue from the collapse of the fundamental distinctions that govern human culture.

In another passage, Lévy-Hass describes the collapse of another kind of boundary—no less fundamental. When she describes the common showers and the gaze of the German soldiers, she observes that "sex has no meaning here."[52] Sex—not as a biological difference, but as a cognitive category that signifies the first conceptual difference—has lost its meaning. While the biological difference between men and women remains, the symbolic (gender) difference is worn away.[53]

The most radical collapse, however, is that of the distinction that defines life itself, as Lévy-Hass writes: "Death has moved in to stay. It's our most loyal tenant. . . . We end up confusing the living and the dead. Because in essence the difference between them is minimal; we are skeletons who still possess some capacity to move, they are immobile skeletons."[54] It is thus no wonder that Lévy-Hass, at the end of her diary, poses the same fundamental question we raised at the beginning of this book: "Everything we see here, everything that happens under our eyes makes us begin to question our own human qualities. A dark and heavy doubt awakens. Doubt in mankind."[55]

Another fundamental difference, typically blurred in the Holocaust diaries is described by Oskar Rosenfeld in his notebooks from the Lodz ghetto. In the act of observing others, the fundamental difference, the prerequisite for the constitution of identity—the difference between the self and the other—is erased. Rosenfeld thus describes the way in which the Prague Jews observed each other, as they awaited deportation to a destination as yet unknown to them (the Lodz ghetto): "People looked at each other without sympathy, they all had been cut down to the same level; even more, they burdened each other, seeing themselves in the other: each holding the other responsible for the specter *Jude*."[56] On one level, fundamental distinctions are blurred when the Jews of Prague, awaiting their unknown fate, are described as having lost their individuality, becoming an indistinguishable mass even in their own eyes, mere examples of the species "the Jews." On another level, they look upon each other as complete mirrors of themselves, and are unable to distinguish between gazer and gazed at, as if having overdosed on identification devoid of reality, which is constructed (reality) by making distinction. There is thus no sense of solidarity but, on the contrary, the only way to resist such a collapse of individuality is to blame the other for it, thereby paradoxically succumbing to or even reaffirming that very image.

One could cite many more fundamental distinctions that collapse in the diaries of the period but, at the closing of this chapter, I would like to return to Perechodnik's diary, and to highlight the central motif that characterizes all the relationships described in it. I refer to the blurring of the distinction between persecutor and persecuted. As noted, Perechodnik was a member of the Jewish police in the Otwock ghetto, who actively participated in the deportation of the Jews of Otwock (including his own family) to Treblinka. This put him quite literally in both positions, which may explain why the distinction between persecutor and persecuted is almost entirely blurred in almost all human relations—including those within his own family—depicted in the text that he wrote retroactively, in hiding.[57] In this diary, everyone always seems to be both persecutor and persecuted at the same time and in every given power relation. The case I would like to cite here occurs after the deportation actions at Otwock. The group of policemen involved in rounding up the Jews and sending them to their deaths plans to escape, because it is clear to all of them that the same fate awaits them as well. Perechodnik wants to join the group and speaks to its leader, Ehrlich, who rejects him brusquely. When he insists, the following scene ensues: "Wham! At that moment I received a hard blow to the face from Ehrlich, and my glasses broke. In a daze, without wondering why or what it was for, I broke into a mad run without thinking about who I was running from."[58]

This scene embodies Perechodnik's experience of the inherent dual position of members of the Jewish police, as both persecutors and persecuted. The policemen are, at one and the same time, persecuted, fleeing for their own lives, and persecutors from whom Perechodnik must flee. Although

Perechodnik is unsure exactly whom he is fleeing, it is precisely this lack of a clearly defined persecutor that seems to heighten the sense that the boundary between persecutor and persecuted has been blurred.

The traumatic encounter thus destroys the fundamental distinctions necessary to constitute the world and identity. A premise of modern (structuralist) linguistics (widely adopted in other fields in the social sciences and the humanities) is that meaning (of words and objects) derives not from identity (of the thing with itself) but, first and foremost, from difference within the symbolic system.[59] In destroying the most basic differences in the victims' consciousness, trauma gradually denies them the ability to create meaning in the world in which they exist and, consequently, undermines their sense of individual identity and their mental stability.

Trauma, and persisting trauma in particular, demolishes the most basic parameters necessary for the constitution of inner identity. It destroys temporal continuity and erases the difference between present and past, male and female, self and other, persecutor and persecuted, the body and the world, inside and outside, and so forth. The invasiveness of trauma erases identities and disrupts the symbolic orders on which they are based. It is important to stress that trauma does not erase a given difference or demolish a particular identity—national, ideological, or social—but exerts a destructive influence on the very possibility of constituting human identity as a narrative identity. In this sense, the trajectory of trauma is diametrically opposed to that of the life story. The Holocaust diaries may thus be read as a battlefield on which these two opposing forces meet—the constituting force of the life story, and the disintegrating force of trauma—in such a way as to preclude their separation from one another. The text organizes psychological and historical reality while, at the same time, reporting and even embodying its fundamental disintegration.

Notes

1. Paul Ricoeur, *Time and Narrative*, 3 vols., trans. Kathleen McLaughlin and David Pellauer (Chicago: University of Chicago Press, 1984–1988). See also Paul Ricoeur, "Life in Quest of Narrative" and "Narrative Identity," in *On Paul Ricoeur: Narrative and Interpretation*, ed. David Wood (London: Routledge, 1991), 20–33, 188–199.

2. Ricoeur, *Time and Narrative*, 1:3.

3. On the problem of coherence in life stories and especially in illness narratives, see Shlomith Rimmon-Kenan, "The Story of 'I': Illness and Narrative Identity," *Narrative* 10, no. 1 (January 2000): 9–26.

4. Ricoeur, "Life in Quest of Narrative," 22.

5. Charlotte Linde, *Life Stories* (New York: Oxford University Press, 1993), 100.

6. See Elizabeth W. Bruss, *Autobiographical Acts: The Changing Situation of Literary Genre* (Baltimore: Johns Hopkins University Press, 1976), 10–11.

7. Emile Benveniste, *Problems in General Linguistics* (Coral Gables, FL: University of Miami Press, 1971), 224.

8. In the first months of his diary, Czerniakow relates to his life story and ability to draw upon his past in order to deal with the present. See, for example, the entry dated 23 March 1940 in Adam Czerniakow, *The Warsaw Diary of Adam Czerniakow: Prelude to Doom*, ed. Raul Hilberg, Stanislaw Staron, and Josef Kermisz (New York: Stein and Day, 1979), 131. Later in the diary, Czerniakow finds it increasingly difficulty to do so.

9. Entry dated 5 July 1942, in Herman Kruk, *The Last Days of the Jerusalem of Lithuania: Chronicles from the Vilna Ghetto and the Camps 1939–1944*, ed. Benjamin Harshav, trans. Barbara Harshav (New Haven, CT: Yale University Press, 2002), 324. This brings to mind the words of Anaïs Nin who, contrary to the recommendation of her therapist, Otto Rank, continued to keep a diary: "I wanted my diary as one wants opium.... But I also wanted to save myself" (quoted in Suzette A. Henke, *Shattered Subjects: Trauma and Testimony in Women's Life-Writing* [New York: St. Martin's, 1998], 77).

10. In 1980, when posttraumatic stress disorder was first included in the American Psychiatric Association's *Diagnostic and Statistical Manual of Mental Disorders* (DSM), it was defined as stemming from events that occur "beyond the realm of normal human experience." The psychiatrist Judith Lewis Herman noted, however, that rape, sexual violence, wars, and other tragedies are in fact common and, therefore, cannot be described as "beyond the realm of normal human experience." Nevertheless, Lewis Herman claims that "traumatic events are extraordinary, not because they occur rarely, but rather because they overwhelm the ordinary human adaptations to life" (Judith Lewis Herman, *Trauma and Recovery* [New York: Basic Books, 1997], 33).

11. Augustine's discovery, according to Kleinberg, was that "the self... is constructed historically—even linearly, I would say" (Aviad Kleinberg, "Shalosh Otobiografiyot Miyemei Habeinayim" [Three autobiographies from the Middle Ages], *Alpayim* 13 [1996]: 48).

12. On the debate of definitions and the development of the concept of trauma, see Ruth Leys, *Trauma: A Genealogy* (Chicago: University of Chicago Press, 2000).

13. Herman, *Trauma and Recovery*, 33.

14. Kai T. Erikson, *A New Species of Trouble: The Human Experience of Modern Disasters* (New York: Norton, 1994), 228.

15. Jean Laplanche and Jean-Baptiste Pontalis, *The Language of Psychoanalysis* (New York: Norton, 1973), 465. Most scholars who have sought to define trauma have highlighted the experience of helplessness. Lewis Herman, for example, begins her clinical discussion of the subject, in *Trauma and Recovery*, with the words: "Psychological trauma is an affliction of the powerless" (30). Freud, too, stressed the principle of surprise that leaves the mind's defense system helpless. See Sigmund Freud, "Beyond the Pleasure Principle," in *The Standard Edition of the Complete Psychological Works of Sigmund Freud*, vol. 18, ed. and trans. James Strachey (London: Hogarth, 1955), 7–66.

16. Dominick LaCapra, *Writing History, Writing Trauma* (Baltimore: Johns Hopkins University Press, 2014), 91–94.

17. See Cathy Caruth, *Unclaimed Experience: Trauma Narrative and History* (Baltimore: Johns Hopkins University Press, 1996); Shoshana Felman and Lori Daub, *Testimony: Crises of Witnessing in Literature, Psychoanalysis, and History* (New York: Routledge, 1992).

18. Avraham Lewin, *Mipinkaso shel Hamoreh MiYehudiyah: Geto Varshah April 1942–Mai 1943* [From the notebook of a teacher at the Yehudiah School: Warsaw ghetto April 1942–May 1943] (Tel Aviv: Hakibbutz Hameuchad and the Ghetto Fighters' House, 1969), 51.

19. See Sigmund Freud, "Remembering, Repeating and Working Through," in *The Standard Edition of the Complete Psychological Works of Sigmund Freud*, vol. 12, ed. and trans. James Strachey (London: Hogarth, 1958), 145–156.

20. Caruth, *Unclaimed Experience*, 19. On the ramifications of this structure of trauma on the writing of history, see Eric L. Santner, "History beyond the Pleasure Principle: Some Thoughts on the Representation of Trauma," in *Probing the Limits of Representation: Nazism and the Final Solution*, ed. Saul Friedländer (Cambridge, MA: Harvard University Press, 1992), 143–154.

21. Effi Ziv, "Traumah Ikeshet" [Persistent trauma], *Mafteakh* 5 (2012): 55–74. See also Masud R. Khan, "The Concept of Cumulative Trauma," *Psychoanalytic Study of the Child* 18 (1963): 286–306.

22. On numbing or constriction as a clinical manifestation of trauma, see Herman, *Trauma and Recovery*, 33–73.

23. Emil Utiz, *Psychologie des Lebens im Konzentrazionslager Theresienstadt* (1947; reprint, Vienna: Continental Edition Verlag A. Sezl, 1948), 9. I thank Nitzan Lebovic for bringing this fascinating book to my attention.

24. Pal Kovacs, "Yomano shel Pal Kovacs" [The diary of Pal Kovacs], *Dapim Leheker Tkufat HaShoah* 1 (1979): 232 (3 December 1944).

25. Such statements are typical not only of prisoners in the camps (and especially Hungarian Jews, who experienced the trauma within an extremely condensed time frame) but are also common among the inhabitants of the ghettos. See, for example, the striking description offered by Hillel Seidman: "For us, Fantasy substitutes for reality, while reality recedes into fantasy. We exist uneasily between two conflicting worlds. Though the present cruelly encompasses us, yet we try to ignore it. our past world has been merciless destroyed, yet it remains alive within our collective memory" (Hillel Seidman, *The Warsaw Ghetto Diaries*, trans. Yosef Israel [Southfield, MI: Targum, 1997], 210 [11 January 1943]).

26. Fela Szeps, *Balev Ba'arah Hashalhevet: Yomanah shel Fela Szeps* [A blaze from within: The diary of Fela Szeps] (Jerusalem: Yad Vashem, 2002), 78.

27. Very similar phenomena can be observed in the *Autobiography of a Schizophrenic Girl*. In the introduction to the book, the psychoanalyst who treated her writes: "In periods of utter lethargy or in stupor when nothing is felt, an impersonal lucidity still persists, allowing him to note not only what goes around him, but his own affective state as well" (Marguerite Sechehaye, ed., *Autobiography of a Schizophrenic Girl* [New York: Grune and Stratton, 1951], x). On the subject of the automaton, see, for example, ibid., 17, 18, 58, 65.

28. Ber Mark, ed., *The Scrolls of Auschwitz*, trans. Sharon Neemani (Tèl Aviv: Am Oved, 1985), 219.

29. Ruth Golan, "The Secret Bearers: From Silence to Testimony, from the Real to the *Phantasme*," in *Loving Psychoanalysis: Looking at Culture with Freud and Lacan*, trans. Jonathan Martin (London: Karnac, 2006), 109.

30. This is how Lawrence Langer understands survivors' later, video testimonies. See Lawrence L. Langer, *Holocaust Testimonies: The Ruins of Memory* (New Haven, CT: Yale University Press, 1991).

31. Hanna Lévy-Hass, *Diary of Bergen-Belsen: 1944–1945*, trans. Sophie Hand (Chicago: Haymarket, 2009), 85–86.

32. Jacques Lacan, "The Mirror Stage as Formative of the Function of the I," in *Écrits: The First Complete Edition in English*, trans. Bruce Fink (New York: Norton, 2002), 1–7.

33. Szeps, *Balev Ba'arah Hashalhevet*, 79.

34. Ibid.

35. Havi Ben-Sasson and Lea Prais, "Twilight Days: Missing Pages from Avraham Lewin's Warsaw Ghetto Diary, May–July 1942," *Yad Vashem Studies* 33 (2005): 38.

36. Freud, "Remembering, Repeating and Working Through," 145–156. See also Sigmund Freud, "Mourning and Melancholia," in *The Standard Edition of the Complete Psychological Works of Sigmund Freud*, vol. 14, ed. and trans. James Strachey (London: Hogarth, 1957), 243–258. As LaCapra pointed out, however, working through is never complete, nor is it limited to one of these two options but is, rather, a combination of them. The question is which is the dominant mode of coping. See Dominick LaCapra, *Representing the Holocaust: History, Theory, Trauma* (Ithaca, NY: Cornell University Press, 1994), esp. 205–224; and LaCapra, *Writing History* (throughout the book). LaCapra's historical and historiographical approach to the Holocaust is largely based on these concepts.

37. Freud, "Beyond the Pleasure Principle"; Jacques Derrida shows how Freud himself engages in traumatic repetition compulsion in describing the "fort/da" game in "Beyond the Pleasure Principle." See Jacques Derrida, "To Speculate on Freud," in *A Derrida Reader*, ed. Peggy Kamuf (New York: Columbia University Press, 1991), 516–568.

38. See, for example, Maud Ellman, ed., *Psychoanalytic Literary Criticism* (London: Longman, 1994), 7. See LaCapra, *Writing History*, 50n10; Linda Anderson, *Autobiography* (London: Routledge, 2001), 79.

39. On the therapeutic need to weave trauma into a significant narrative, see Jodie Wigren, "Narrative Completion in the Treatment of Trauma," *Psychotherapy* 31, no. 3 (1994): 415–423; Kim Lacy Rogers, Selma Leydesdorff, and Graham Dawson, eds., *Trauma and Life Stories: International Perspectives* (London: Routledge, 1999).

40. Quoted in Jacek Leociak, *Text in the Face of Destruction: Accounts from the Warsaw Ghetto Reconsidered*, trans. Emma Harris (Warsaw: Żydowski Instytut Historyczny, 2004), 80, and in Alexandra Garbarini, *Numbered Days: Diaries and the Holocaust* (New Haven, CT: Yale University Press, 2006), 144.

41. Yitzhak Aron, *Mayn Klayne Tsavoe* [My little Will], Yad Vashem Archives (uncataloged, in the author's possession).

42. Calel (Calek) Perechodnik, *Am I A Murderer? Testament of a Jewish Ghetto Policeman*, trans. Frank Fox (Boulder, CO: Westview, 1996), 82.

43. Ibid., 62.

44. Ibid. See also the juxtaposition in Adam Czerniakow's entry dated 23 August 1941, which creates a sort of grotesque irony: "I write verse occasionally. A vivid imagination is needed for that, but never did I have the imagination to refer to the soup that we are doling out to the public as lunch. In the morning with Mende. He gave me a list of the deceased (Auschwitz and Buchenwald groups)" (Czerniakow, *The Warsaw Diary of Adam Czerniakow*, 271).

45. On the gap between the sense of reality and imagination in posttraumatic situations, see Edward A. Brett and Robert Ostroff, "Imagery and Posttraumatic Stress Disorder," *American Journal of Psychiatry* 142 (1985): 417–424.

46. Perechodnik, *Hatafkid He'atzuv*, 238. I have adapted the text to reflect the Hebrew edition which is far more reliable than the English or the Polish editions. See David Engel, "On the Bowdlerization of a Holocaust Testimony: The Wartime Journal of Calek Perechodnik," *Polin* 12 (1999): 316–329.

47. Calek Perechodnik, *Hatafkid He'atzuv shel Hati'ud* [The sad role of documentation] (Jerusalem: Keter, 1993), 101.

48. Cathy Caruth notes these two metaphors, albeit in a slightly different context. See Caruth, *Unclaimed Experience*, 113–114n3. See also Ruth Ginsburg, "'Whose Trauma Is It Anyway?' Some Reflections on Freud's Traumatic History," in *New Perspectives on Freud's "Moses and Monotheism,"* ed. Ruth Ginsburg and Ilana Pardes (Tübingen: Max Niemeyer, 2006), 77–92; Sue Vice, *Introducing Bakhtin* (Manchester: Manchester University Press, 1997), 218–224.

49. See, for example, Slavoj Žižek, *Looking Awry: An Introduction to Jacques Lacan through Popular Culture* (Cambridge, MA: MIT Press, 1992), 19–20. As an example, Žižek cites the work of the painter Mark Rothko. According to Žižek's interpretation, in his paintings, Rothko struggled with the barrier between "the traumatic Real" from reality, by preserving the distance between spots of color. The takeover of the space on the canvas by the "traumatic Real" led to Rothko's suicide.

50. Lévy-Hass, *Diary of Bergen-Belsen*, 103.

51. Giorgio Agamben, *Homo Sacer: Sovereign Power and Bare Life*, trans. Daniel Heller-Roazen (Stanford, CA: Stanford University Press, 1988). For Agamben, the *Musselmann* is the clearest manifestation of these modern projects of biopolitics.

52. Lévy-Hass, *Diary of Bergen-Belsen*, 101.

53. See also Oskar Rosenfeld, who, in an entry dated 7 November 1942, describes communal latrines in the Lodz ghetto, without walls or shame (Oskar Rosenfeld, *In the Beginning Was the Ghetto: Notebooks from Łódź*, ed. Hanno Loewy, trans. Brigitte M. Goldstein [Evanston, IL: Northwestern University Press, 2002], 147). On 18 January 1943, he reports the loss of the "erotic sense" among the Jews of the ghetto, particularly the "Western Jews" (156). On the other hand—and reminiscent of similar descriptions from the camps—he reports on 23 February 1943, sexual promiscuity related to material benefits and privileges, among those of "elevated social position" (159).

54. Lévy-Hass, *Diary of Bergen-Belsen*, 104. This distinction is blurred in many of the diaries from the period that describe human corpses on the ghetto streets. See, for example, Mary Berg, *The Diary of Mary Berg: Growing up in the Warsaw Ghetto*, ed. Susan Lee Pentlin (Oxford: Oneworld, 2009), 101 (10 October 1941).

55. Lévy-Hass, *Diary of Bergen-Belsen*, 113.

56. Rosenfeld, *In the Beginning Was the Ghetto*, 5. The word "Jude" appeared on the yellow badges the Jews were forced to wear.

57. A similar feeling is expressed by Baruch Milch, *Can Heaven Be Void?*, ed. Shosh Milch-Avigal, trans. Helen Kaye (Jerusalem: Yad Vashem, 2003), 76–78. Perechodnik is a clear example of what Primo Levi called "the gray zone" between murderers and victims, although Levi stresses that almost everyone—murderer and victim alike—exists within this zone. See Primo Levi, *The Drowned and the Saved*, trans. Raymond Rosenthal (New York: Vintage, 1989), 36–69, esp. 68–69. See also the memoir of Warsaw ghetto Jewish policeman Stanislaw Adler, *In the Warsaw Ghetto, 1940–1943: An Account of a Witness*, trans. Sara Chmielewska Philip (Jerusalem: Yad Vashem, 1982).

58. Perechodnik, *Hatafkid He'atzuv*, 80–81.

59. Jonathan Culler, *Ferdinand de Saussure* (Sussex: Harvester, 1976), 51.

2

READING THE DIARIES AS A CRITIQUE OF HOLOCAUST HISTORIOGRAPHY

In the introduction, we saw that Leni Yahil (1964), as well as other historians and thinkers, considered the "image of man" during the Holocaust the central question with which scholarship of the period must contend. As noted, Yahil claimed, "the main thing that prompts us to study history—even of the distant past, but certainly in the case of the Holocaust—is the problem of the figure of man. . . . It is, therefore, inconceivable that research of the Holocaust period would not focus primarily on man, evaluating human actions and behavior."[1] In reality, however, historical research has neglected this significant question.

I would like to stress that it is not that historiography of the Jews in the Holocaust has not presumed some figure of "man" in its writing. On the contrary, it presumes the existence of a certain kind of "man," as a given—without, however, making that human figure the object of its research. It is a human figure that, even in the harshest of conditions, remained whole, continuous, internally autonomous; a figure that ultimately succeeded in preserving its values and inner world against the horrors of the external catastrophe. In brief, it is a figure very different from the one that arises from the diary excerpts we have read so far.

As a point of departure for a discussion of Holocaust historiography that has focused on the victim, as compared to the position proposed in this book, I would like to make a distinction between "history of crisis" and "history of trauma."

Crisis and Trauma

The Hebrew word that denotes crisis—*mashber*—signifies a twofold phenomenon. On the one hand, as per the definition in the Even-Shoshan Hebrew dictionary, it is a "descent and low point," but it is also "the opening of the womb from which an infant emerges into the world" and, by metonymy, a birthing stool.[2] In this sense, a *mashber* is a difficult process, at the end of which comes relief and redemption through the creation of something new. This dual meaning is clearly reflected in the words of Isaiah (37:3): "for the children have come to the point of birth [*mashber*], and there is no strength to deliver them." It is a moment of *mashber*, both conceptually and literally—a "critical" time as well as a time of "crisis"; the instant at which it is determined whether the painful and difficult process will find resolution in the form of a new life. The successful conclusion of the process requires great inner strength but the reward is great, as the new life retroactively mitigates the moments of crisis, making them tolerable and worthwhile. A similar dual meaning can be found in various European languages. In English and German, for example, the words "crisis" and "Krise" denote difficulty and distress but also a turning point, particularly in the context of illness—a point that, if overcome, marks the beginning of recovery. Culturally, "crisis" is thus perceived as a paradigm of redemption.[3] In the bildungsroman, for example, the moment of crisis is also the turning point, and overcoming it moves the protagonist forward along the track of personal development—which also leads to the resolution of the plot.

As we have seen, trauma—certainly when it is as violent, all-encompassing and protracted as during the Holocaust or other situations of radical mass political violence—is an entirely different matter. It is a fundamental rupture, not a crisis. Compared to other neuroses, trauma is characterized, according to Freud, by "the evidence it gives of a far more comprehensive general enfeeblement and disturbance of the mental capacities."[4] Thus, while the time of crisis is continuous, linear, and optimistic, as it has the potential to herald new life, the time of trauma is, as we have seen and will further explore, far more complex and destructive and therefore precludes complete redemption.

Representations of the events of the Holocaust in which the figure of the victim is construed as continuous and linear, possessing extensive inner hegemony, ignore the traumatic dimensions of the event, representing it, rather, as a crisis. Indeed, the tendency to apply crisis paradigms to traumatic events is extremely widespread. Holocaust-(Zionism)-and Rebirth is, perhaps, the best known paradigm but is certainly not the only one. Holocaust-Immigration-Success is a less ideological (in the narrow sense of the word) version of the same paradigm. On another plane, the view that writing about the traumatic event—whether at the time of its unfolding or subsequently—has the capacity to redeem the writer from the trauma by creating an unaffected inner space is also an expression of the same paradigm.

There is no doubt that the crisis paradigm affords comfort and encouragement. Who would not wish to believe that human beings can withstand any circumstances, and that Jews during the Holocaust preserved their "humanity" at all times and at all costs? It helps us avert profound shocks to our personal and collective identities and, therefore, was and remains the dominant paradigm in most popular representations of the Holocaust. The considerable expansion of the concepts of heroism and resistance in popular discourse regarding the victims of the Holocaust is emblematic. According to this popular approach, nearly all victims of the Holocaust were heroes engaged, to one extent or another, in the task of "preserving their humanity"—from daily activities such as searching for food to helping others; from lighting Hanukkah candles in extreme situations and at great personal risk to organizing theaters and other cultural activities in the ghettos and, to some degree, in the camps. The crisis paradigm thus dominated and largely continues to dominate much of Holocaust discourse throughout the world. At times, this tendency received expression among the victims themselves. Iakovos Kambanellis, for example, tells how the wretched, ignominious execution of a group of Russian prisoners of war in Mauthausen quickly turned into a heroic tale, told and retold by the prisoners who would describe, in increasingly glowing terms, acts of heroism that never actually took place.[5]

The tendency to prefer the "good" story to the "bad"—or the crisis paradigm to the trauma paradigm—was not the exclusive province of the victims of Nazism or the popular imagination since that time. It also abounds in professional historical writing, particularly in representations of Jews in the Holocaust. In this sense, popular memory and professional historiography share nearly the same paradigm.

History of the Victims

Arguably, from the very beginning, historical writing on the subject of Jews during the Holocaust met the condition set by Philip Friedman in

1957: "What we need is a history of the Jewish people during the period of Nazi rule in which the central role is to be played by the Jewish people, not only as tragic victims but as bearers of a communal existence with all the manifold and numerous aspects involved. Our approach must be definitely 'Judeo-Centric' as opposed to 'Nazi-Centric.' "[6] Historiography thus sought to redeem the Jews from the objectification imposed upon them by their murderers, and to constitute them (individually and collectively) as historical subjects. This task had two important goals—not entirely distinct from one another: a historical goal and an ethical goal. To establish the field of "history of the Jews during the Holocaust," the Jews had to become subjects of their own history and not merely docile objects of the history of the Nazis, as was being written primarily in Germany and the United States. Yehuda Bauer thus described the Jews in American and European historiography as follows: "[The Jews appear] as a frog mesmerized by a snake—neither resisting nor attempting to escape; completely passive in the face of any threat. Thus, they too become part of the Nazi method. . . . I doubt that German, French, English, or American historians will deal with the fate of the victims—their responses, behavior, and lives. In this, I believe we have a role to play."[7] Such historiography, however, also considered it a moral imperative to restore Jews to the historical narrative rather than allowing them to be "eliminated" a second time, after having been physically obliterated during the course of the events themselves.[8] Had history of the Holocaust not approached the Jews as subjects, they would quite simply have disappeared from its pages.

The most complete conceptualization of the principles espoused by this historiographical school, particularly in its Israeli variant, can be found in Yehuda Bauer's reflective work, *Rethinking the Holocaust*.[9] As Bauer notes in his introduction, its main contribution to the historical interpretation of the Holocaust lies in the chapters that deal with Jewish reactions. Bauer outlines the conceptual framework within which he believes the reactions of Jewish groups during this period should be approached. The basic concepts he mentions are "resistance," "sanctification of life," and "*amidah*" (which, according to Bauer, roughly and inadequately translates "standing up against"). The first concept is taken from European national discourse, and the other two are internal Jewish concepts that developed during the Holocaust.

The "sanctification of life" (*kidush hahayim*, in Hebrew) is a concept attributed to Rabbi Yitzhak Nissenboim of the Warsaw ghetto, which reportedly reflected prevailing attitudes among Jews in the ghetto.[10] If, in the past, Jews had been required to lay down their lives during times of persecution, in order to "sanctify God's name" (*kidush hashem*), they were now required to cling to life—to sanctify it in the face of persecution intended to deny them the right to existence and to basic human dignity. Bauer notes the difficulty in translating this term and, even more so, the term "*amidah*," which encompasses numerous meanings that can only be understood from within Jewish culture, history, and tradition. This explanation and the choice of these particular concepts were meant to demarcate an immanent historical domain, with its own, unique, conceptual framework. The semantic field established by these and other concepts (such as "Jewish reaction") is one of clash or conflict between two independent subjects—the one reacting to, opposing, or withstanding the other. They allow us to describe a broad spectrum of institutional or semi-institutional activities, within the realm of Jewish experience during the Holocaust—from the organization of communities by leaders and institutions, through activities pertaining to rescue, welfare, education, culture, and religion, to uprisings and armed struggles. They provide us with the means to constitute the Jews as legitimate historical subjects, inasmuch as they acted as independent agents even in situations of extreme helplessness. The conceptual net cast over the historical events makes them more accessible to readers by applying a series of basic parameters that afford internal cohesion to the wide variety of Jewish experiences during the Holocaust.

In some cases, Bauer even tries to describe the causes of the development or lack of development of significant "*amidah*" in a given community, on the basis of its character before the war. An internal correlation is thus created between a community's past and its behavior during the Holocaust itself, thereby maintaining the principle of historical continuity.[11]

Bauer admits that historiography that focuses exclusively on active reactions to Nazi persecution distorts reality and that darker elements—such as the existence of traitors and informers within the Jewish communities, communal leaders who operated without a glimmer of hope, and so forth—cannot be ignored. In the chapters of *Rethinking the Holocaust*, he also relates to problematic and controversial figures, such as Chaim Rumkowski, head of the Judenrat in Lodz. These aspects are negligible, however, in relation to the main thrust of the chapters in which he develops the ideas of reaction, cohesion, and "*amidah*" as immanent concepts. In so doing, he constitutes the Jews as relatively autonomous and whole historical subjects, possessing internal continuity and cohesion: subjects who have managed—culturally, spiritually and, to some extent, even institutionally—to preserve their inner sense of selfhood and to "stand up against," "resist," and "react" to the Nazis and to Nazism, with courage and vitality, to their dying breaths.

This historiography, which began in the two decades that followed the war and was further developed over the course of the 1970s and 1980s, thus responded to two prevailing tendencies that it rightly saw as very problematic and that it sought to rectify: the tendency to ignore the victim's perspective and the tendency to blame the victim.[12] The first tendency is reflected in US and German scholarship on Nazism and the Final Solution, which began to gain currency during the 1960s and 1970s. In this body of research, Jewish sources were completely ignored, thereby disregarding the story of the victims and their perspective. This omission was further compounded by repeated accusations of the "passivity" exhibited by the Jews, said to have gone to their deaths "like sheep to the slaughter." More or less explicit claims of this kind were made by historians such as Raul Hilberg, Hannah Arendt, and Henri Michel. Some even attributed this "passivity" to a long-standing tradition of diaspora Jewry to avoid armed conflict, even at times of crisis. It must be noted that similar assertions were made by survivors—ghetto fighters and partisans—as well as by Zionist ideologues and propagandists. Opposite these claims, Israeli historiography, and to a certain extent also Jewish historiography in America, described vibrant and active Jewish societies that made every effort, as circumstances allowed, not to lose their dignity and not to yield, engaging in all forms of resistance—civil, cultural, religious, and in some cases, even armed.[13]

The impressive achievements of this historiography in reconstructing the reality of Jewish life, thereby preserving the Jews' memory, story, and dignity, were only possible because it presumed their existence as subjects with their own story and history.[14] It appears, however, that its premises were those of a "history of crisis" rather than of a "history of trauma."

The most basic conceptual distinction employed in this historiographical project of constituting the Jewish subject during the Holocaust as a whole and continuous subject would appear to be the distinction between "inside" and "outside"—a distinction extraneous to trauma but entirely appropriate to the crisis paradigm. Accordingly, despite the ubiquitous Nazi presence on the "outside" plane of reality, the Jewish "inside"—perceived as infinitely more decisive for the identity of the victim, is ultimately untouched. In this way, the figure of the victim remains whole and continuous—one that has not experienced fundamental ruptures and is not really helpless but retains extensive sovereignty over its "inside." Yisrael Gutman, one of the most important Israeli historians of the Holocaust, whose book on the Warsaw ghetto laid the foundations for historical writing about the Jews during the Holocaust, offers a clear example of this kind.

In an essay on the subject of "sanctification of life" in the ghetto, Gutman relates to the collective and individual fortitude that enabled the Jews in the ghettos not to lose their vitality: the will to live, the belief that the Nazis would ultimately be defeated, and the hope for a better future.[15] Part of the explanation is rooted in the ability of the Jews of the ghetto to suffer constant humiliation without allowing it to affect their inner selves:

> The Jews of Poland are subjected to grave decrees. Some of these, such as the badge of shame, forced labor, the prohibition against frequenting public places . . . are intended to humiliate the Jews, to exclude them from the society in which they live, to reduce them to the level of subhumans. . . . These humiliating decrees appear to have had little effect on the community or on individuals. . . . *In their hearts* they saw their oppressors as coarse and lowly creatures who had power on their side but were *incapable of comprehending the Jews or of harming their rich [inner] world. . . . "The greater the humiliation imposed from without, the greater the sense of Jewish pride within."* And Kaplan, apt as always, compares this situation to that of a vicious dog who fails to treat you with respect. Would you take offense? That is what makes him a dog![16]

Gutman's claim here is based, once again, on the extreme dichotomy between "inside" and "outside"—a distinction that operates on two planes. On the communal plane—the "outside," as the historical reality in which the Nazis exercise control, fails to crush the "inside," in the sense of the fundamental social and cultural values of Jewish society in the ghetto; and on the individual plane, as the reality of humiliation and persecution does not essentially undermine the rich, inner world, identity, and self-respect of each individual Jew. There are three facets to this distinction in Gutman's essay: (1) inside and outside are entirely separable from one another; (2) it is the rich, Jewish "inside" rather than the coarse, brutish Nazi "outside" that is the decisive factor for the lives of Jews in the ghetto; and (3) from the victim's perspective, the "inside" may remain undefeated by the "outside." Ultimately, the (authentic, rooted, East-European) Jews are able to preserve their identity and human dignity, despite all of the humiliation and persecution they experience.[17]

In establishing the crisis paradigm, Gutman relies on the words of Chaim Kaplan written in Warsaw at the time. The very passage he cites from

Kaplan's diary, however, demonstrates how problematic this representation of reality is. The full entry strongly implies that it should instead be read in the context of the trauma paradigm, as the paragraph in question includes an additional passage, omitted by Gutman, which further complicates efforts to characterize the figure of the victim and the relationship between the Jewish "inside" and the murderous "outside." Kaplan writes on 2 October 1940:

> Never before in our tear and blood-filled history have we encountered such a barbaric and cruel enemy. There is nothing in the world, material or spiritual, that they have allowed us, no occupation in life in which they have not singled us out for discrimination. It is a wonder that, nevertheless, we live—albeit a life of contempt and humiliation on the outside, *but our human emotions have become so inured that we have ceased to feel, and the sense of outrage that harbors in the heart of every human being does not rise up even at the most barbaric and cruel of insults.* What is this like? It is like a vicious dog who does not treat you with respect. Would you take offense? That is what makes him a dog![18]

First of all, the text clearly offers a further explanation for the invulnerability of the Jews of Warsaw—beyond Jewish pride that remains unscathed by the attacks of "vicious dogs": the Jews of Warsaw are emotionally deadened and are therefore unable to feel outrage. In other words, not only has the "outside" overcome the "inside"; it has actually destroyed it. This is another of the familiar expressions of numbness and internal death that characterize radical situations of trauma, discussed in the previous chapter.

We must also take notice, however, of the rhetorical structure of this passage from Kaplan's diary. Two opposite, even contradictory explanations are given for the same phenomenon (the Jews are not offended due to their moral superiority; they are not offended because they are emotionally dead), with no indication that the author is aware of the resulting paradoxical effect. Moreover, the final part of the passage, intended as an illustration of the first part ("What is this like?"), does not explain the first part but, in fact, contradicts it. The text is thus incoherent to the point that it is, in a formal sense, reminiscent of the discourse of madness. This part of the passage seems to me to embody the difficulties presented by explanations based on a dichotomous distinction between "inside" and "outside." It also reveals the extent to which readings rooted in the "crisis paradigm" avoid dealing with the most severe aspects of writing during the Holocaust. The avoidance is so far-reaching that the events described by historians sometimes seem to bear little resemblance to those reflected in writings from the period.[19] The terror, despair, and rage directed inward, the disintegration and helplessness that emerge from nearly every line written during the Holocaust virtually disappear, replaced mostly by descriptions of action, organization, resourcefulness, deliberation, dilemmas, and even heroism. This is evident, for example, in the words of Yehuda Bauer regarding the concentration camps. According to Bauer, in the concentration camps, "created in order to destroy man's humanity," there were many Jews who were indeed "broken, . . . yet we find within these camps many examples, albeit among a minority of the prisoners, of the preservation of human dignity [i.e., the 'inside']. It is a kind of anomalous phenomenon that, strangely perhaps, offers a glimmer of hope for humanity in general . . . *and although it pertains only to a minority, it is more important than the majority experience.*"[20]

In Bauer's opinion, the object of research and memory of Jews during the Holocaust (including the concentration camps) is the individual who "was not broken," who managed to preserve his or her identity, values, and behavior, the core of whose inner world was not ultimately destroyed. Thus, according to Bauer, the focus of attention must be the phenomenon of preservation of human dignity—as statistically limited as it may have been. In other words, Bauer's approach to the human figure in the Holocaust follows the crisis paradigm.

I am by no means suggesting that the history written in the context of this school is without value. On the contrary. Its methodological, empirical, and ethical achievements cannot be overestimated. It created a field of historical research virtually from nothing, without which we would have known little of the experience of Jews during the Holocaust or their modes of organization and action. However, in its efforts to establish the field of history of the Jews during the Holocaust, this historiographical school was not disposed to depict a different human figure—a far more complex one, fundamentally helpless at times, its "inside" invaded by the "outside"; a figure that is not necessarily continuous or linear; one that lacks complete autonomy—even over its own consciousness and will.

In an attempt to redeem the Jewish victims from objectifying historical writing, they went a step too far, in my opinion, focusing on figures in whose inner worlds the Holocaust never really happened. The fear of turning the victims—once again—into objects led to their representation as whole subjects and fully sovereign (over their inner worlds). In so doing, this historiography failed, in its fundamental patterns, to give sufficient space to the traumatic dimensions of the events.

Thus far I have dealt primarily with Israeli historiography, which indeed laid the foundations, in the early 1970s, for professional and systematic historical writing about Jews during the Holocaust. Similar emphasis on the continuity and strength displayed by victims is typical of another central approach—termed "constructivist" by Alan Mintz—in the study of Jewish texts written mostly during the Holocaust.[21] According to this approach—espoused primarily by Jewish scholars of Jewish literature and culture at US universities—the most appropriate basis for the interpretation of such texts is the cultural-linguistic context in which they were written. The constructivist model tends to focus on Eastern European Jewish literary works, understanding the ghetto diaries, for example, first and foremost (albeit not exclusively) in the context of prewar Eastern European Jewish culture and especially the Jewish languages of the period: Yiddish and Hebrew. This reading stresses Jewish cultural-linguistic continuity and ideologically focuses its attention specifically on ghetto literature, in which these characteristics are far more apparent than in the literature produced in western Europe and in the camps.[22]

In one chapter of her book *The Modern Jewish Canon*, Ruth Wisse—who may be considered a faithful representative of this approach—analyzes the phenomenon of diary writing during the Holocaust as part of the body of literature on the Holocaust in general. Wisse views these diaries as expressions of unimpaired Jewish cultural identity and thus refers to diary writing during the Holocaust as "literary resistance." She concludes her discussion of the Holocaust diarists—based, inter alia, on the diaries of Chaim Kaplan from Warsaw and Herman Kruk from Vilna—with the following words: "The ghetto diarists . . . can only try to secure their posthumous judgment through an alternative standard of victory and defeat. . . . Chaim Kaplan's last recorded words were, 'If my life ends—what will become of my diary?' Kruk continued his diary after he was taken to the Estonian labor camp Klooga. . . . Like soldiers who die for their country, these Jews obeyed the imperative to document over the imperative to live."[23] Beyond the fact that these two diarists, like other European Jews, had no control over their lives and deaths, Alexandra Zapruder's critical remark regarding this kind of pathos-laden writing is particularly apt: "There are many fragments from history that can be regarded as evidence of humanity's achievements and its progress; these diaries unfortunately do not fall into that category. . . . No celebration of the courage or grace of the writer's gesture can cover up the human fallibility and frailty that is captured within the diary's pages."[24]

Even Samuel Kassow (an adherent of the constructivist school) whose wonderful book on Emanuel Ringelblum and his activities in the Warsaw ghetto draws a complex, nuanced picture of Jewish society in the ghetto, does not escape this pitfall. Ultimately, the book focuses on the exemplary figure of Emanuel Ringelblum, who succeeded, at least in part, in rising above the terrible and traumatic helplessness that characterized most of the ghetto's inhabitants. This book too belongs to the crisis rather than the trauma genre of history.

This tendency to mitigate the traumatic and disintegrative aspects of the autobiographical texts written during the Holocaust, has been compounded by the processes of publication of these diaries, in Israel and around the world—processes that have caused the diaries to be read and received as affirmations of the assumption that "inside," the victims remained unchanged, as if nothing had happened. The best-known example—the 1955 Broadway production of Anne Frank's diary, which contributed more than anything else to the diary's dissemination—ended with a quote from the entry dated 15 July 1944, three weeks before the Frank family's hiding place was revealed: "I still believe, in spite of everything, that people are truly good at heart."[25] This sentence came to represent the optimistic message of the diary and, by synecdoche, of victims of the Holocaust in general.[26]

Often, editors even go as far as altering the texts themselves, through rewrites, edits, tendentious translations, and omissions.[27] One such example is the Polish edition as well as the English translation of the diary of Calek Perechodnik.[28] This diary is characterized by extreme anti-Polish sentiment and self-loathing. Huge efforts were thus made—both in the English translation and in the Polish edition—to soften these elements.[29] Although by no means analogous, some of the authors themselves have sought to tone down their original texts after the fact. For example, it is clear from reading Hillel Seidman's diary that he rewrote it prior to publication (in 1947).[30] A similar phenomenon can be observed in poetic texts written during the war and subsequently changed, emended, or edited for publication, whether by the authors themselves or by editors at the respective publishing houses.[31]

Ignoring the traumatic aspects of these texts, through their mitigation or redemption, thus characterizes a significant proportion of scholarly, public, and cultural discourse about the Holocaust in Israel and abroad. In my opinion, the approach to which this tendency gives rise presents fetishistic elements.

The fetishistic approach to coping with trauma was described by Slavoj Žižek, who explained the distinction between symptomatic and fetishistic coping, as follows:

> The symptom is the exception which disturbs the surface of the false appearance . . . while fetish is the embodiment of the Lie which enables us to sustain the unbearable. Let us take the case of the death of a beloved person: in the case of a symptom, I "repress" this death, I try not to think about it, but the repressed trauma returns in the symptom; in the case of a fetish, on the contrary, I "rationally" fully accept this death, and yet I cling to the fetish, to some feature that embodies for me the disavowal of this death.[32]

Fetishism is thus an expression of coping with a difficult event while denying its traumatic dimensions, by means of an object that allows one to disavow the effective rupture. It is important to emphasize that the fetish does not eliminate the traumatic event but rather helps one accept it rationally while rejecting its catastrophic nature. The fetish seeks to immediately fill the void left by the fundamental and irremediable loss. Its rhetorical structure is "Yes . . . but": Yes, I certainly recognize the trauma and the loss but, in effect, I deny their terrible and radical nature and will not truly come to grips with this traumatic dimension—including the grave and fundamental voids present in its writings and in writings about it. As José Brunner put it, the fetish entails a twofold denial: of the trauma itself and of its very denial.[33]

Fetishism may also take the form of a story or, as Eric Santner called it, in reference to the story of the Nazi period recounted in Germany after the war, "narrative fetishism": "By narrative fetishism I mean the construction and deployment of a narrative consciously or unconsciously designed to expunge the traces of the trauma or loss that called that narrative into being in the first place. . . . Far from providing a symbolic space for the recuperation of anxiety, narrative fetishism directly or indirectly offers reassurances that there was no need for anxiety in the first place."[34] Fetishistic narrative is a narrative that attempts to erase the traumatic dimension that engendered the need to tell the story in the first place. Such is the case, for example, of history of the Holocaust that ignores the fundamental ruptures in the human figure during and in the aftermath of that period. It is a story that does not seek to deal with the fundamental ruptures perpetrated "inside" by the "outside" that invades it, or with the way in which these ruptures compel us to redraw the figure of the human victim. It is a story that seeks to redeem the (autonomous, inner, and continuous) human figure of the victim almost instantly. It is thus my contention that the story of the Holocaust as a crisis story is a fetishistic narrative.

Although such fetishistic writing, which focuses on various aspects of "Jewish resistance and *amidah*," continues to be very central both in scholarship and in public discourse, it is also important to note that the past decade and a half has seen the development of a more balanced, nuanced and therefore credible historiographical approach to Jews during the Holocaust. Kassow's book on Emanuel Ringelblum, mentioned above, is a good example of this approach. Changes have also occurred in Israeli historiography. Although some have remained within the conceptual framework of "resistance and *amidah*," others have taken more interesting and less apologetic paths.[35] Some have even explored the profound failures of Jewish society during the Holocaust. For example, Lea Prais, studied the fate of some 150,000 refugee Jews who arrived in Warsaw during the war, and the failure of the Jewish community to care for them.[36]Prais devotes little attention to the inner lives of the refugees, but describes the reality of disintegration and trauma. Some of the academic research in this field, both in Israel and abroad, has begun to relate directly to the issue of individuality while drawing a far more nuanced image of the "victim" and openly challenging the "resistance and *amidah*" approach. Christopher Browning, in his book *Remembering Survival*, on the fate of the Jews in the Wierzbnik ghetto and the Starachoviece camp, claims that the Jews did have a certain degree of choice and agency, but we must also, he warns, "avoid false heroics and sanitizing censorship." He therefore claims that the concepts of *amidah* and resistance are inadequate to describe the Jews' struggle for survival, and suggests terms such as "ingenuity, resourcefulness, adaptability, perseverance, and endurance" in their place.[37]

Such a nuanced approach can also be observed in research on Holocaust diaries, which has indeed sought to address their traumatic dimension.[38] In the introduction to her excellent book on diaries written by Jews during the Holocaust, Alexandra Garbarini writes: "While I accept the basic premise that diary writing could serve as a form of resistance, I am not centrally concerned with this issue. . . . Instead, I focus on issues that may be obscured by an emphasis on resistance. Thus, in addition to writing diaries to resist German oppression, Jewish diarists write for many other reasons. . . . Thus, while diaries are not evidence of successful resistance to genocide, they are texts of struggle that document Jews' efforts to maintain a sense of an individual self, even as that possibility was being erased."[39] Garbarini examines a number of fascinating topics, such as the way in which the diaries report the reception, understanding, and analysis of information and rumors regarding the war and the persecution of the Jews; family relations; the authors' considerations regarding the manner in which the events should be represented in writing; coping with helplessness, and so on.[40] Even Garbarini, however, like Browning and others, fails to fully address the traumatic and fundamental ruptures embodied in these diaries. References to such traumatic aspects do appear in these studies, but they are somehow resolved or at least mitigated—in stark contrast to the diaries themselves, in which they are overwhelmingly dominant.[41] In this sense even these important studies do not fully adhere to what I call a history of trauma.[42]

It is astounding that there were some—even among those writing during the Holocaust itself—who expected and feared such distortions. In his ethnographic notes from the Lodz ghetto, published in *In Those Terrible Days*, Josef Zelkowicz (who perished in Auschwitz in 1944) described scenes from the homes of the Jews of the ghetto, which he visited in his capacity as a Judenrat official. His descriptions paint a grotesque and dark picture: families that had lost all sense of shame, who did not cover their nakedness and relieved themselves in public; people who had lost all hope and existed in the twilight between sanity and madness; people who stole food and money from members of their own families, and so forth. In his notes Zelkowicz actually emphasizes the rupture and the cultural, moral, and social *metamorphosis* the Jews of the ghetto had undergone. "The entire Jewish trend of thought has been totally transformed under the pressure of the ghetto," Zelkowicz writes, claiming that the ghetto is "the great negator of the civilization and progress that people nurtured for centuries" and, as such, "has swiftly obliterated the boundaries between sanctity and indignity, just as it obliterated the boundaries between mine and yours, permitted and forbidden, fair and unfair." And this blurring of boundaries had a decisive effect on human nature: "But do not think . . . that this blurring of boundaries has not claimed a price in blood and brains."[43]

This is the tone that dominates most of Zelkowicz's writing, in which he offers an alternative perspective to that of the historiography and consciousness we have seen so far, based on the concepts of *amidah*, reaction, continuity, and resistance. Zelkowicz, like many of the diary writers, observes the grave impact of the events on individuals and on society, as well as the transformation taking place on the various planes of their existence.[44] "Effect" and "transformation" are Zelkowicz's basic concepts—not "reactions," "resistance," "sanctification of life," and "amidah."

In one of his ghetto essays, Zelkowicz tells of an elderly woman who appears to embody another mode of coping with the reality of the ghetto. This old woman, in sharp contrast to all of the other figures described in his notes, expresses courage, hope, and spiritual and psychological strength: "When she speaks about herself, her son, and even her eighty-four-year-old husband who has died, her voice is solemn, strong, positive and fearless. . . . [She stands] strong as a rock in an ocean, washed by a high wave, buffeted but not swept away."[45] Zelkowiz then wonders whether this woman, "who derives her confidence from the powerful, age-old wellspring of our people,"[46] might not serve as a symbol of the fact that Jewry imprisoned in the Lodz ghetto in particular and under Nazi oppression in general, has remained steadfast in the face of all of the crises of the period, concluding:

> I would willingly posit the example of this old woman against all the unspeakable tragedies were she not eighty years old, were she not suffering from sclerosis that prevents her from coming to grips with the situation. A human being . . . who lives not in the present but in the past, and an eighty-year-old woman on top of that—this person is not a symbol of our people. In the best case, she is but a colorful rug that stands out in gleaming isolation against a mammoth heap of gray, dark rugs . . . and . . . even that colorful rug is just an old rag.[47]

Zelkowicz thus refuses to view the old woman as a heroic figure and even less so as a symbol of the steadfast *amidah* of the Jews of the ghetto. In terms of the concepts I have proposed thus far, we might say that he insists on telling the story of trauma and not the story of crisis. In this book I have sought to follow in his footsteps.

Notes

1. Leni Yahil, "Mekorot Hasho'ah Uve'ayot Mehkaran" [Holocaust: Original sources and the problems of their investigation], *Yalkut Moreshet* 2, no. 3 (December 1964): 158–159.

2. Avraham Even-Shoshan, *Hamilon Haivri Hamerukaz* [The concise Hebrew dictionary] (Jerusalem: Kiryat Sefer, 1984), 426–427.

3. On this cultural paradigm, see Leo Bersani, *The Culture of Redemption* (Cambridge, MA: Harvard University Press, 1990).

4. Sigmund Freud, "Beyond the Pleasure Principle," in *The Standard Edition of the Complete Psychological Works of Sigmund Freud*, vol. 18, ed. and trans. James Strachey (London: Hogarth, 1955), 10.

5. Iakovos Kambanellis, *Mauthausen*, trans. Gail Holst-Warhaft (Athens: Kedros, 1996), 99–100.

6. Philip Friedman, "Problems of Research on the Holocaust," in *Roads to Extinction: Essays on the Holocaust* (Philadelphia: Jewish Publication Society, 1980), 561.

7. Yehuda Bauer, *Hashlakhot Mehkar Hasho'ah al Toda'atenu Hahistorit* [The Holocaust today: An attempt at a new evaluation] (Jerusalem: The Institute of Contemporary Jewry, 1972), 11–13. Bauer was referring, in particular, to Gerald Reitlinger, Hannah Arendt, Bruno Bettelheim, and Raul Hilberg. See also Leni Yahil, "Mekomah shel Hasho'ah Bahistoryografyah HaYehudit" [The place of the Holocaust in Jewish historiography], in *Al Natzim, Yehudim Umetzilim* [On Nazis, Jews, and rescuers] (Jerusalem: Yad Vashem, 2002), 153–167, esp. 164.

8. See Yisrael Gutman, "Trumato shel Hati'ud HaYehudi Hamekori Leheker Hasho'ah" [The contribution of original Jewish documentation to Holocaust research], in *Mignizah Letziyunei Derekh Historiyim: Arkhiyonim Yehudi'im Mitkufat Hamilhamah VehaShoah* [From hidden treasures to historical landmarks: Jewish archives from the period of the war and the Holocaust] (Jerusalem: Yad Vashem, 1997), 195: "Increasingly, certain scholars in Germany and the United States tend to ignore almost entirely . . . the Jewish population itself. The Jews in these studies appear as shadowy objects, swallowed up in the flood of decrees and actions, and we learn nothing about them beyond estimated numbers of victims and names of camps. Behind the numbers, the convoys and the trains, there is no human face. We don't hear the life breath of individuals, their suffering, the challenges they face, or their longings for the future. The worn pages written by Jews during the Holocaust, rescued from the flames, are imbued with the life experiences and the expectations of the Jews who perished." See also Yisrael Gutman, *Sugiyot Beheker Hasho'ah: Bikoret Utrumah* [Issues in the study of the Holocaust: Criticism and contribution] (Jerusalem: Yad Vashem and the Zalman Shazar Center, 2009), esp. the first section.

9. Yehuda Bauer, *Rethinking the Holocaust* (New Haven, CT: Yale University Press, 2001).

10. See Yisrael Gutman, "'Kidush Hashem' Ve 'Kidush Hahayim'" [The "sanctification of (God's) name" and the "sanctification of life"], in *Ba'alatah Uvema'avak: Pirkey Iyun Basho'ah Uvehitnagdut Yehudit* [In darkness and struggle: Studies on the Holocaust and Jewish resistance] (Tel Aviv: Moreshet, Hebrew University and Sifriyat Poalim, 1985), 72–90. See also the words of Emanuel Ringelblum: "The aspiration to preserve the existence of the Jewish population is, today, an expression of *kidush hashem* [sanctification of God's name]" (Emanuel Ringelblum, *Yoman Ureshimot* [Diary and notes from the Warsaw ghetto] [Jerusalem: Yad Vashem and the Ghetto Fighters' House, 1992], 254).

11. Yehuda Bauer, *The Death of the Shtetl* (New Haven, CT: Yale University Press, 2009).

12. On this school, see Dan Michman, "Is There an 'Israeli School' of Holocaust Research?," in *Holocaust Historiography in Context: Emergence, Challenges, Polemics and Achievements*, ed. David Bankier and Dan Michman (Jerusalem and New York: Yad Vashem and Berghahn, 2008), 37–65.

13. See Gutman, *Sugiyot Beheker Hasho'ah*, 41–53.

14. For a comprehensive critique of Israeli historiography in this context, see the Hebrew edition of this book, in which I argue, primarily, that paradigmatic, methodological, and ideological constraints originating in the "Jerusalem school" of Jewish studies shaped the way in which Jews were portrayed in writing about the Holocaust: Amos Goldberg, *Trauma Beguf Rishon: Ktivat Yomanim Bitkufat HaShoah* [Trauma in first person: Diary writing during the Holocaust] (Or Yehuda: Ben Gurion University and Kinneret Zmora–Bitan Dvir, 2012), 104–130.

15. Gutman, "'Kidush Hashem' ve 'Kidush Hahayim,'" 72–90.

16. Ibid., 81; emphasis added.

17. Yehuda Bauer offers another perspective on the division between "inside" and "outside": "But if Jewish life, Jewish tradition (however one may understand it) contributed in some way to Jewish staying power, leaving them destroyed but unbroken within, providing them with a tremendous ability to live, then that is a lesson for our generation, the importance of which cannot be overemphasized" (Bauer, *Hashlakhot Mehkar Hasho'ah*, 26).

18. Chaim Aron Kaplan, *Megilat Yisurin: Yoman Geto Varshah* [Scroll of agony: Warsaw ghetto diary] (Tel Aviv: Am Oved and Yad Vashem, 1966), 350; emphasis added.

19. Mendel Piekarz points out the gap between the early writings of people such as Dvorzhetski, which still include all of the rage and terror, as opposed to their later writings, in which they rewrite and censor their earlier works (see Mendel Piekarz, "'Lehashtik o Lesaper et Ha'emet Ha'eiromah': Bein Lashon Rishon Lelashon Aharon" [To silence or to tell the bare truth: Differences between earlier and later writings], in *Sifrut Ha'edut al Hasho'ah Kemakor Histori: Veshalosh Teguvot Hasidiyot Be'artzot Hasho'ah* [The literature of testimony as a historical source of the Holocaust and three Hasidic reflections on the Holocaust] (Jerusalem: Bialik Institute, 2003), 46–88.

20. Yehuda Bauer, *Tguvot Be'et Hasho'ah: Nisyonot Amidah, Hitnagdut, Hatzalah* [Reactions during the Holocaust: Attempts to withstand, resist, rescue] (Tel Aviv: Ministry of Defense, 1983), 164–165; emphasis added.

21. See Alan Mintz, *Popular Culture and the Shaping of Holocaust Memory in America* (Seattle: University of Washington Press, 2001), 36–84.

22. Leading scholars of this school include Alan Mintz himself, in *Popular Culture* and in his book *Ḥurban: Responses to Catastrophe in Hebrew Literature* (New York: Columbia University Press, 1984), as well as David Roskies, Alvin Rosenfeld, Ruth Wisse, Samuel Kassow, Yechiel Szeintuch, and Nathan Cohen.

23. Ruth R. Wisse, *The Modern Jewish Canon: A Journey through Language and Culture* (New York: Free Press, 2000). See also supporting this view David Roskies, *Holocaust Literature: A History and a Guide* (Waltham, MA: Brandeis University Press, 2012), 43–44. Wisse's interpretation is rather surprising. Kaplan's own words in no way support the notion that he saw himself, in his writing, as a soldier in a struggle for justice; nor does the fact that Kruk took his diaries to the Klooga camp. Moreover, elsewhere, Kruk refers to his diary as the "hashish of my life"—a metaphor that may place his writing in the category of a delusional symptom. In any event, neither writer—and certainly not Kaplan, who wrote in the ghetto—chose writing over life, for the simple reason that their fate was determined by forces beyond their control or choice, regardless of their writing. Therefore, they did not die as soldiers on the battlefield. See also Garabarini's valid reservations in Alexandra Garbarini, *Numbered Days: Diaries and the Holocaust* (New Haven, CT: Yale University Press, 2006), 5.

24. Alexandra Zapruder, *Salvaged Pages: Young Writers' Diaries of the Holocaust* (New Haven, CT: Yale University Press, 2004), 9.

25. Anne Frank, *The Diary of a Young Girl: Definitive Edition*, ed. Otto H. Frank and Mirjam Pressler, trans. Susan Massotty [London: Puffin, 2007], 419.

26. See Bruno Bettelheim, *Surviving and Other Essays* (New York: Vintage, 1979), 247–257; Dina Porat, "Yomanah shel Anna Frank Umakhishei HaSho'ah" [Anne Frank's diary and Holocaust deniers], in *Hasho'ah—Hayihudi Veha'universali: Sefer Yovel LeYehuda Bauer* [The Holocaust—the unique and the universal: Essays presented in honor of Yehuda Bauer], ed. Shmuel Almog, Daniel Blatman, David Bankier, and Dalia Ofer (Jerusalem: Yad Vashem and

the Institute of Contemporary Jewry, 2001), 160–183; Sidra DeKoven Ezrahi, *By Words Alone: The Holocaust in Literature* (Chicago: University of Chicago Press, 1980), 200–204. See also Sander L. Gilman, *Jewish Self-Hatred: Anti-Semitism and the Hidden Language of the Jews* (Baltimore: Johns Hopkins University Press, 1986), 345–359.

27. Yisrael Gutman has written about this phenomenon. According to Gutman, even Ringelblum's diaries were not spared: Gutman, "Trumato shel Hati'ud HaYehudi Hamekori Leheker Hasho'ah." On distortion and censorship in Lodz ghetto diaries, see Robert Moses Shapiro, "Diaries and Memoirs from the Lodz Ghetto in Yiddish and Hebrew," in *Holocaust Chronicles: Individualizing the Holocaust through Diaries and Other Contemporaneous Personal Accounts*, ed. Robert Moses Shapiro (Hoboken, NJ: Yeshiva University Press and KTAV, 1999), 95–116; and Chajka Klinger, *Miyoman Bageto* [From a diary in the ghetto] (Merhavia: Sifriyat Poalim and Kibbutz Haogen, 1959), in which the publisher censored all of the author's harsh criticism of the Hashomer Hatzair leadership in Palestine. On the latter case, see Rinat Gorodenchik, "Brihat Tnu'ot Hano'ar MiZaglembie, 1943–1945" [The flight of the youth movements from Zaglembie, 1943–1945] (MA thesis, Hebrew University, 1986), esp. 22, 25, 27, and 53. For a conceptualization of the problem, see Amos Goldberg, "Yomanei Hasho'ah—Samkhut She'einah Medaberet Kahalakhah" [Holocaust diaries: An authority that doesn't speak appropriately], in *Kanoni Upopulari: Mifgashim Sifrutiyim* [Popular and canonical: Literary dialogues], ed. Tamar Hess, Omri Herzog, and Yael Shapira (Tel Aviv: Resling, 2007), 131–140.

28. Calel (Calek) Perechodnik, *Am I A Murderer? Testament of a Jewish Ghetto Policeman*, trans. Frank Fox (Boulder, CO: Westview, 1996).

29. See David Engel, "On the Bowdlerization of a Holocaust Testimony: The Wartime Journal of Calek Perechodnik," *Polin* 12 (1999): 316–329. See also Batsheva Ben-Amos, "A Multilingual Diary from the Lodz Ghetto," *Gal-Ed* 19 (2004): 51–74, esp. 53–58.

30. Hillel Seidman, *The Warsaw Ghetto Diaries*, trans. Yosef Israel (Southfield, MI: Targum, 1997). See, for example, an entry dated 6 September 1942 (p. 110), on the subject of an academic debate among Polish scholars, at the height of the Great Deportation, regarding the origins of Polish Jews. I am not disputing the fact that such an event took place, but there is no known description of it in this vein from the time of the action itself. There are also a number of passages clearly written after the fact. For example, there is a passage ostensibly written in the ghetto, in which Seidman refers to the exemplary behavior of Orthodox Jews even in "the various camps, Oświęcim, Buchenwald, Bergen-Belsen" (this passage appears only in the Hebrew edition, *Yoman Geto Varshah* [New York: Di Yiddishe Vokh, 1947], 215). Another salient example is the diary of Michael Zylberberg, *A Warsaw Diary* (London: Vallentine Mitchell, 1969), which presents itself as a diary, but was clearly written after the Holocaust.

31. See Yechiel Szeintuch, *Yishayahu Spiegel: Prozah Sipurit Migeto Lodz* [Isaiah Spiegel: Yiddish narrative prose from the Lodz ghetto] (Jerusalem: Magnes, 1995), 7–27.

32. Slavoj Žižek, *On Belief* (London: Routledge, 2001), 13–14. See also Slavoj Žižek, *Looking Awry: An Introduction to Jacques Lacan through Popular Culture* (Cambridge, MA: MIT Press, 1992), 34–39, in which Žižek refers to a "fetishistic split"—a kind of logic that asserts, "I know very well, but just the same . . ."

33. José Brunner, "Political Fetishism on the Left and Right in Israel" (paper presented at the "Thera-P-olitics" Psychoactive Conference, Tel Aviv University, 28 January 2008). See also references there.

34. Eric Santner, "History beyond the Pleasure Principle: Some Thoughts on the Representation of Trauma," in *Probing the Limits of Representation: Nazism and the Final Solution*, ed. Saul Friedländer (Cambridge, MA: Harvard University Press, 1992), 144–147.

35. Worth mentioning, for example, is Guy Miron's research on aspects of time, space, and identity among German Jews in the Third Reich: "'The Politics of Catastrophe Races On. I Wait': Waiting Time in the World of German Jewry under Nazi Rule," *Yad Vashem Studies* 43, no. 1 (2015): 45–76. For an extensive overview of major trends in Israeli Holocaust historiography, see Michman, "Is There an 'Israeli School' of Holocaust Research?"

36. Lea Prais, *Displaced Persons at Home: Refugees in the Fabric of Jewish Life in Warsaw, September 1939–July 1942* (Jerusalem: Yad Vashem, 2015).

37. Christopher Browning, *Remembering Survival: Inside a Nazi Slave-Labor Camp* (New York: Norton, 2010), 296–299 (quote from 297). See also Moritz Föllmer, *Individuality and Modernity in Berlin: Self and Society from Weimar to the Wall* (Cambridge: Cambridge University Press, 2013), 132–155.

38. See David Patterson, *Along the Edge of Annihilation: The Collapse and Recovery of Life in the Holocaust Diary* (Seattle: University of Washington Press, 1999), although Patterson also works within a theological-redemptive paradigm that is, to my mind, very problematic. See also Rachel Feldhay Brenner, *Writing as Resistance: Four Women Confronting the Holocaust: Edith Stein, Simone Weil, Anne Frank, Etty Hillesum* (University Park: Pennsylvania State University Press, 1994), although, as the title indicates, this book was also written, to some extent, within the conceptual framework of resistance.

39. Garbarini, *Numbered Days*, 9.

40. See also Jacek Leociak, *Text in the Face of Destruction: Accounts from the Warsaw Ghetto Reconsidered*, trans. Emma Harris (Warsaw: Żydowski Instytut Historyczny, 2004).

41. For example, Garbarini discovered a collection of diaries written by parents as letters to their children abroad, without ever being able to send these letters to them. In these diaries the parents correspond in an imaginary way (because they cannot and do not actually send the letters) with their loved ones. Garbarini's analysis (*Numbered Days*, chap. 4, 95–128) is extremely nuanced and illuminating, but she fails to discuss what it really means to correspond in such an illusionary, self-centered manner, and what effect addressing someone who will never become an actual addressee may have on one's inner self. The subheadings within this chapter are indicative of the consoling message conveyed by her analysis: "Separation and Powerlessness"; "Parenting at Distance"; "Filling in Gaps or Bridging the Divide"; "Family as a Source of Meaning and Hope."

42. On Saul Friedländer's attempt (failed, in my opinion) to represent trauma in his historical writing, see Amos Goldberg, "The Victim's Voice in History and Melodramatic Esthetics," *History and Theory* 48, no. 3 (2009): 220–237, and Alon Confino, "Narrative Form and Historical Sensation: On Saul Friedländer's *The Years of Extermination*," *History and Theory* 48, no. 3 (2009): 199–219. Dan Stone criticizes the first volume of Friedländer's *Nazi Germany and the Jews* for failing to live up to the principles that Friedländer himself had expressed in his theoretical writings (Dan Stone, *Constructing the Holocaust* [London: Vallentine Mitchell, 2003], 161–164).

43. Josef Zelkowicz, *In Those Terrible Days: Notes from the Lodz Ghetto*, ed. Michal Unger, trans. Naftali Greenwood (Jerusalem: Yad Vashem, 2002), 141.

44. See, for example, Oskar Rosenfeld, who says so explicitly: *In the Beginning Was the Ghetto: Notebooks from Łódź*, ed. Hanno Loewy, trans. Brigitte M. Goldstein (Evanston, IL: Northwestern University Press, 2002).

45. Zelkowicz, *In Those Terrible Days*, 176–177.

46. Ibid.

47. Ibid., 177–178.

3

THE DYNAMIC OF THE TEXT BETWEEN THE TWO DEATHS

A Theoretical Model for the Reading of Traumatic Texts

THIS CHAPTER is, to a large extent, the theoretical heart of the entire book. Here I propose a semiotic model for understanding the dynamic of autobiographical writing during the course of persistent, brutal, and massive trauma, as experienced by victims of the Holocaust and other events of mass violence and harsh discrimination. The model I have used is based on concepts borrowed from the work of the French psychoanalyst Jacques Lacan, which may not be intuitive to some readers, but which I have sought to make accessible even to those who are not conversant with this discourse.

As was demonstrated in the previous chapters, autobiographical writing during the Holocaust compels us to avoid the "crisis" approach, which tends toward the comfortable and reductive organization of these texts around positive principles of identity, continuity, cohesion, and autonomy. At the same time, however, we must also beware of the opposite approach, which sees the text exclusively as an embodiment of internal destruction and breakdown—a view espoused by Lawrence Langer, for example, with regard to later, video testimonies of survivors that, in his opinion, express only disintegration, melancholy, unelaborated grief, terror, and a complete halting of time.[1] As Dominick LaCapra noted, such a reading is based on a dichotomy between two extremes: at one end of the spectrum redemptive working through that violently denies the disintegrative aspects of the trauma and at the other endless, inescapable melancholy.[2] Just as every mourning process is a combination of working through and acting out, so too autobiographical texts from the Holocaust period encompass both of these aspects. There is no doubt, however, that writing as the traumatic events themselves were unfolding, at a time when reality was filled with shattering incidents and death, placed the destructive and disintegrative elements in even greater relief. Writing at such a time channels all of the disruptive forces at the expense of those that preserve and strengthen, even if it is the tension between the two that renders the very act of writing possible; a condition in which the text—along with its autobiographical protagonist and narrator—still exist.

This traumatic dynamic between the constructive and destructive forces within the text is not what poses the gravest threat, however. Within the text itself lies the twofold potential for far greater destruction, for utter devastation, when the dynamic dialectic processes come to a halt, converging in one of two catastrophic possibilities: (1) the complete disintegration of the symbolic horizon of the victim, who remains outside of it—that is, when the victim is cast out of all linguistic, social, and cultural contexts capable of explaining reality and affording meaning to his or her existence; and (2) becoming trapped in the conceptual network of the murderer, which violently dictates the victim's complete nonexistence. From the moment victims receive their identities entirely from the murderer, they begin to act like automatons programmed by the place and exclusive conceptual framework assigned to them by the murderer—simply expressed by Tamar Herman, in the Theresienstadt ghetto: "I do everything automatically."[3]

In both of these cases, the "human" (as separate consciousness) dies, even while still alive (biologically). In the first case, the "human" no longer exists, having been excluded from any social and linguistic order within and by means of which identity may be constituted and meaning may be afforded to a turbulent reality. In the second case, the "human" ceases to exist, having been completely swallowed up into the murder's order of things. From the writer's perspective, in the first case, the entire conceptual framework that affords meaning to the world has broken down, whereas in the second case, a complete identification with a master signifier dictated by the murderer has been imposed upon it. In the first case, there is an infinite gap between the writer and the structures of language and law; in the second case that gap is completely closed. Autobiographical texts written during the Holocaust thus reflect the continuous struggle of the writer and writing against these two catastrophic foci, which constantly act as destructive potentialities within the autobiographical text and constitute its catastrophic horizon.

The full realization of these destructive forces means the complete collapse of the text and the writer (as the subject of the writing and of language). Generally speaking, however, the textual fabric is woven around these "black holes" in a desperate attempt not to be swallowed up by them, while struggling to constitute an autonomous space—if only minimal—in which organization and linguistic representation is not wholly controlled by the murderer.

To describe the potential tendencies of total destruction within texts of this kind, we require a theoretical model that enables us to map the relationship between the act of writing and the "two deaths" that threaten or lie within it. The model presented below is, as was noted, based on the conceptual framework of Lacanian psychoanalytic theory.

Symbolic Death ("Second Death")

Symbolic death is referred to by Lacan also as the "second death"—that is, as opposed to the "first," natural death. Whereas the latter is an essential part of the cycle of natural existence, the former (symbolic death) is the destruction of the cycle of life itself, the death of nature.[4] In the course of this process, the symbolic fabric that constitutes what is known as "reality" unravels and is destroyed. Slavoj Žižek explains the difference: "Natural death . . . is a part of the natural cycle of generation and corruption, of nature's continual transformation, and absolute death—the destruction, the eradication of the cycle itself."[5] According to Žižek, the total annihilation that occurs with second, absolute death "is always the destruction of the *symbolic* universe"—that is of those cultural systems by means of which we constitute the world as meaningful.[6]

It is important to note that, according to Lacan, the process of symbolization already harbors the possibility of destruction of the symbolic network—the language—because it is organized, from the outset, around a traumatic kernel that cannot be symbolized. This kernel bears within it the potential for the destruction of the entire symbolic network, and the cultural constructs it supports are therefore always precarious and on the verge of collapse.

The second death can also be observed in the texts under discussion here, at moments in which it seems that the conceptual network that constitutes reality completely loses its validity and the victims find themselves outside it. This occurs, for example, when the victims' experiences and familiar historical concepts no longer help them to interpret and navigate the new reality into which they have been thrust.[7] At such times, the trauma assumes a different dimension. It is no longer a specific event, difficult to weave into a field of meaning and that, consequently, disrupts and destroys parts of the narrative, but catastrophic disintegration of the network of meaning itself and the very ability to narrate. When the shock is so great, not only is it impossible to find the appropriate words with which to represent it but language as a whole is paralyzed and the power of speech completely lost.[8]

An example of such a "death" (i.e., the exclusion of the subject from any social order, the complete breakdown of reality, the paralysis of language, muteness) can be seen in the following passage from the diary of Janusz Korczak, written in 29 May 1942. It was composed during a period of growing anxiety in the ghetto, which resulted from a wave of sudden arrests and dozens of murders, the increasing rumors and reports of the annihilation of entire communities, such as that of Lublin, and news of the existence of the Belzec death camp. In this entry, Korczak reports a minor incident that occurred in a certain shop inside the Warsaw ghetto, yet this ostensibly minor incident constitutes one of the most horrifying and dramatic moments in the entire diary:

> A small shopkeeper said to a customer with a complaint:
>
> "My good woman—these are not goods and this is not a store, you are not a customer nor I a vendor, I don't sell to you nor do you pay me because these scraps of paper are not money. You don't lose, and I don't profit. Who would bother to cheat nowadays—for what? Only one's got to do something. Well, am I not right?"
>
> If I were given a missal, I could in a pinch celebrate a mass.
>
> But I should not be able to preach a sermon to the flock in armbands. I should swallow the sentences, read a question in their eyes:
>
> "What now? And what next?"
>
> The words would stick in my throat.[9]

Upon an initial reading, the passage seems rather strange. The first part recounts a seemingly banal incident: an angry exchange between a vendor and a customer in the ghetto, wherein there existed hundreds of shops and service enterprises.[10] Korczak's reaction seems extreme—one of the most radical, perhaps the most horrendous, in the entire diary; a kind of reaction reserved for moments of true breakdown. Korczak seems to be saying that some terrible truth was revealed to him at that moment and it required immediate rectification, redemption, compassion, or atonement, and that is why he wished to pray.

The writer's initial impulse to pray—to "celebrate a mass"—is immediately suppressed, however. Korczak's reaction begins with an imaginary conditional sentence: "If I were given a missal . . ." The author then explains the obstacles he would face: "But I should not be able to preach a sermon to the flock in armbands. I should swallow the sentences, read a question in their eyes: 'What now? And what next?' "

The flow of communication Korczak imagines with the public is reversed. The words of comfort, faith, and hope he would have liked to convey were he to deliver a sermon, would have changed direction and been swallowed in his own mouth. Conversely, the direction of the question posed by the public would have flowed constantly toward him. This question too renders him mute, although it is never actually pronounced—expressed only in their eyes, exposing the meaninglessness of the words and act of the religious sermon. These obstacles condemn the realization of the imaginary impulse to deliver a sermon to failure and muteness: "The words would stick in my throat."

Ostensibly, there is a glaring lack of proportion between the real event and the drama that unfolds in Korczak's mind in reaction to it—between the trivial argument in the shop and the collapse of the religious option. What then elicits such a radical imaginary response, indicating that Korczak had witnessed a truly terrible event?

The situation that Korczak describes appears, I suggest, to touch upon the terror associated with the symbolic "second death," as it involves people trying to conduct something resembling ordinary commercial life (symbolic order) and precisely as they attempt to do so, the world breaks down. Engaging in action on the public plane—a plane that constructs reality and affords it meaning—in fact exerts an opposite action; one that reveals, at least in Korczak's eyes and in the vendor's words, that, in effect, nothing is going on, everything is a sham and an illusion: the goods are not goods, the money is not money, and the transaction is not a transaction.

At that very moment, when the illusion of reality in the Warsaw ghetto was shattered, only to reveal complete void, Korczak's entire world fell apart. The collapse of the illusion of social order results in the immediate breakdown of language. Perhaps these can be said to be two sides of the same phenomenon, whereby subjects are deprived of their entire network of concepts and familiar practices, left as "beings" outside history, social order, and, in effect, reality. Symbolic death occurs before biological death and the text disappears with the subject. Only in retrospect was Korczak able to report and attest to this breakdown. Autobiographical writing is, in its most extreme moments, an attempt to recount symbolic death and thereby overcome it, if only very partially.[11] In such situations, writing is a kind of "resurrection."

This is the nature of the symbolic death that looms over the subject at a time of radical persecution and that constitutes a source of catastrophic potential within the text itself—a potential that always activates its destructive power within the text. As was noted, however, the text also harbors a further catastrophic potentiality, linked to the crushing, choking force of the Nazi signifier—as is given manifest expression in the marking practices that the Nazis applied to the Jews; a subject I will address in greater detail in the following section.

The Jews and the Nazi Signifier

As Boaz Neumann has noted, the Nazis were obsessed with marking.[12] For this reason flags, uniforms, badges, medals, symbols, and the like were central to their modes of action. This obsession appears to have received its most quintessential expression in the ways in which the Nazis marked their victims—first and foremost the Jews. This marking, in all its forms, was a source of tremendous pressure for Jews, inasmuch as it defined them as the absolute "other," as those who do not belong to humanity or the hierarchy of the races. The Jews were perceived not as an inferior race, but as an "anti-race."

Indeed, the requirement that they wear the Jewish badge provoked grave reactions among Jews, evidence of which is provided by diaries and many other sources. Many continued to relate obsessively to the requirement until the end of the war. According to Havi Dreifuss (Ben-Sasson), in Poland "the order [to wear the badge] immediately aroused strong feelings among the Jews."[13] "The star" also plays a central role in Victor Klemperer's diary, in which it is overwhelmingly mentioned in one context or another. In his analysis of Nazi language, *The Language of the Third Reich: LTI* (*LTI* is an acronym for the Latin words *Lingua Tertii Imperii*), published in 1947, Klemperer writes: "Today I ask myself again the same question I have asked myself and all kinds of people hundreds of times; which was the worst day for the Jews during those twelve years of hell? I always, without exception, received the same answer from myself and others: 19 September 1941. From that day on it was compulsory to wear the Jewish star."[14] These words reflect the profound shock with which Jews—across borders, identities, and cultures—experienced their marking, wherever they came under Nazi rule. Marking was, in fact, an integral part of every stage of Nazi policy toward the Jews, from the early 1930s to the concentration and death camps. I believe that we can identify five central milestones in the process of marking the Jews, pointing to a clear progression, regardless of whether or not the Nazis themselves were aware of it.

The first milestone, which occurred even before the Nazis came to power, concerned the marking of "the Jew" within Nazi language—marking that constituted the Jew as an object of policy, research, and ideology. This afforded "the Jew" the status of master signifier—in differential contrast to another master signifier: "Aryan." The contrast between these two signifiers lay at the core of Nazi language from the very beginning and was a key element in its creation.[15]

A second milestone was the marking of shops and other property owned by Jews. This occurred shortly after the Nazis came to power, not by official ordinance or law but "spontaneously," during the course of boycott that began on 1 April 1933.[16] Among German Jews, some viewed this as part of a process of marking, and a sign of the beginning of the persecution of Jews in Germany. A well-known example of this is an article published by Robert Weltsch on 27 April 1933, in which he wrote: "Wear it with pride, the yellow badge." To Weltsch's mind, the import of the events was: "The Jew is marked as a Jew. He gets the yellow badge."[17] The "prophetic" significance of his words was, of course, not conscious—at that point, Jews had not yet been required to wear the identifying badge on their clothing. What Weltsch meant was that the regime had returned the Jews to preemancipation status, as Jews in the Middle Ages had sometimes been marked with a yellow badge.[18]

A third milestone was the identification of Jews on official documents, beginning in the summer of 1938. On 17 August of that year, all German Jews were required to add a conspicuously Jewish name to their names: Israel for men and Sarah for women. Victor Klemperer, for example, officially became Victor Israel Klemperer. He thus noted with bitter cynicism on 24 August 1938: "I go on working at the Dix-huitième [a book he was writing on French literature of the eighteenth century] out of pure obstinacy and without any hope or illusion. I, Victor-Israel Klemperer."[19] The trend continued when, on 5 October 1938, the order came that the passports of Jews must be marked with the letter "J."[20]

The fourth milestone—the one that elicited the gravest reactions in contemporary documents—was the marking of the Jews with the "badge of shame" on their clothing. The badge was enforced in virtually all areas controlled by the Nazis and their satellites, through ordinances that were the product of local initiatives (apart from a few exceptions, such as unoccupied France and Denmark).

The fifth milestone in the marking of the victims was the tattooing of numbers on the arms of prisoners at Auschwitz. Like the "badge of shame," the numbers were also described in the gravest terms, albeit in later testimonies of survivors.

It is important to note, in this context, that systematic marking was applied not only to Jews but also to other victims, although not in their hometowns but only upon arrival at the concentration camps, where a variety of methods of identification were used to represent the victim's "crime." A distinct color was assigned to every category of prisoner (political, criminal, homosexual, etc,), often noting national origin as well. At Auschwitz, where the practice of tattooing numbers on the prisoners' bodies was used, many of the non-Jewish prisoners—Poles and prisoners of other nationalities—were marked as well, while most of the Jews were murdered immediately upon arrival without being marked at all.[21] Nevertheless, from the perspective of Nazi marking practices, imprinting a number on the body itself expresses the most radical stage of the marking process—from the abstraction of language to the impression of an anonymous mark in the very flesh of the victim.

Some writers discerned the connection and gradual degeneration from the star ("badge of shame") to the tattooing of a number on the body. Ovadia Baruch from Thessaloniki, for example, described the moment of being tattooed at Auschwitz:

> Each of us then got a note with a number on it. The number I got was 109432. The Germans ordered us to remember the number in two languages: German and Polish. From that moment, Ovadia Baruch faded away; he disappeared and was no more! I had now become a six-digit number, a meaningless number that in one fell swoop erased the foremost marker of my identity—my name. The number 109432 is tattooed in my flesh. The imprinting of the number was done in a primitive and painful way, with considerable bleeding. More than the physical pain of the tattoo, it was the humiliation and degradation of the act. *The yellow star we were required to wear in the Baron Hirsch ghetto divided the Jews from the Greek population, but the tattooing of the number on our left forearms divided us from our names*—something we saw from the first as an attempt to break our spirits.[22]

It is noteworthy that members of the SS (*Schutzstaffel*) were also marked with a tattoo, consisting of the SS symbol—a double S in the form of two lightning bolts—and the bearer's blood type, placed near the armpit. On the significance this phenomenon beyond its practical purpose and the relationship between this and the marking of the victims, Uwe Timm wrote:

> And the SS, the Schutzstaffel, was the model for that community, bound together solely by the notion of blood and feeling itself elite, superior to all other races. SS members had their blood type tattooed on their upper arms. Although this was a sensible measure enabling a man's blood type to be instantly known if he was wounded, its deeper significance was to express blood brotherhood, an ideology that constantly returned to the arguments of blood, the family tree, breeding. It was the counterpart to the numbers tattooed on the forearms of concentration camp inmates to mark their rejection from the human community. Victims and oppressors alike were defined by numbers.[23]

Going back to the marking of the Jews, a clear trend can be identified in this process: a progression from abstract linguistic, graphic or vocal marking, pertaining to the concept of the Jew in language, to forms of marking progressively approaching the concrete body itself.[24] At first, the marking maintains metonymic distance from the subject, concerning only her property. Gradually, the metonymic distance is reduced, passing to identity cards and administrative documents, then to the clothes on the subject's body until, finally, the number is imprinted on the body itself. The gap between signifier and signified is completely eliminated, through a gradual process of concretization, whereby the signifier does not indicate a concept but the actual referent (the Jewish body). Every concrete Jew has his or her own mark.[25] The star does not signify "the Jew," but the body that wears it as a Jewish body. Ultimately, at Auschwitz, the marking becomes a physical part of the victim's body.[26] The gap between the mark and the body is reduced until it ceases to exist entirely.[27]

The reactions to the imposition of the Jewish badge found in the diaries are very grave, primarily due to feelings of shame and humiliation. Emanuel Ringelblum, for example, describes how people would "hide the armband with various ruses, behind bags."[28] According to another testimony, some Jews would avoid going out within the ghetto itself, due to the shame of the badge.[29]

The feeling of humiliation was so great that some, like Janusz Korczak, refused to wear the badge, even at the risk of severe punishment. Surprisingly and unusually (perhaps uniquely), Korczak was given the light punishment of a few days in prison. Less fortunate, according to Ringelblum's account, was a man by the name of Baruch, who refused to wear the armband and was sent to Auschwitz, "where he died."[30]

The issue of marking was a primary concern in Jewish discourse throughout the entire period—attesting to the difficulty experienced by the Jews in adjusting to it. Thus, when a rumor spread in the early days of the Warsaw ghetto that the governor-general, Hans Frank, had promised the head of the Warsaw Judenrat, Adam Czerniakow, to improve conditions in the ghetto, the example cited was, "He promised him there would be no armband," and when Czerniakow had the opportunity to discuss the condition of the Jews with the Nazi authorities, the badge was the first item on the Jews' agenda.[31] Also typical is Ringelblum's remark during the ghetto's final days in 1943, when the Germans sought to seduce the remaining Jews into believing that henceforth their situation would be normalized: "Rumor has it that the Jews will constitute 20% of all Polish production, will be able to live on the other side, will be released from the obligation to wear the armband."[32] In general, the inhabitants of the Warsaw ghetto were greatly troubled by the mark and the subject is addressed repeatedly, in many and varied contexts, in the diaries of the period.

Some wished to see the mark as a badge of honor. For example, Ringelblum tells the story of Dr. Marek Alten, deputy head of the Judenrat in Lublin: "When the badge was called the badge of shame, he responded that it is a badge of honor. He was imprisoned for three days."[33] Others saw the badge as a particular problem for assimilationists, as Chaim Aron Kaplan noted in his diary:

> In any event, the conqueror is turning us into Jews whether we like it or not. The Nazis have marked us with the Jewish national colors, which are our pride. In this sense we have been set apart from the Jews of Lodz, the city which has been annexed to the Reich. The "yellow badge" of medieval days has been stuck to them but, as for me, I shall wear my badge with personal satisfaction. I shall, however, have revenge on our "converts." I will laugh aloud at the sight of their tragedy. . . . This is the first time in my life that a feeling of vengeance has given me pleasure.[34]

The fact that the mark "succeeded" in evoking in Kaplan, for the first time in his life, a sense of satisfaction at the revenge that the Nazis exacted on the assimilationists—as if on his behalf and on behalf of the Jewish people—attests to its tremendous impact. Other entries in his diary, however, reflect a deep sense of humiliation.[35] In any event, the problem was far from being of concern exclusively to assimilationists.

Eliahu Rozanski, a member of Hashomer Hatzair in the Warsaw ghetto and later a member of the Jewish Combat Organiziation (ŻOB), wrote in the February–March 1941 issue of the underground newspaper *Neged Hazerem* (Against the stream): "Armband! How can one wear an armband! The armband seared my arm. I felt it as if I was wearing a collar around my neck. I was filled with anxiety. I couldn't fall asleep at night. I felt a constant danger in the street. I looked all around. My nerves were always on edge. What did I want? To be able to stand with my feet firmly placed on the ground and feel—this is mine!"[36]

The writer, a fervent Zionist, seeks to explain the shock and fundamental unsettlement that the armband provoked, to which end he employs considerable rhetorical and figurative tools. From his description, the mark appears to act on all physical and psychological levels, with profound consequences (it removes the ground from beneath his feet, sets his nerves on edge, keeps him awake, etc.). However, in my opinion Rozanski's most compelling assertion, is that the band sears his arm. The significance of this claim is that the armband already operates on the body itself, thus presaging the next stage of marking: the searing of a number into the victim's arm.

Very similar thoughts were expressed by Hélène Berr—a young woman from Paris, member of a wealthy and prominent family, thoroughly assimilated into French society. In an entry dated 9 June 1942, Berr writes: "I suddenly felt I was no longer myself, that everything had changed, that I had become a foreigner, as if I were in the grip of a nightmare. I could see familiar faces all around me, but I could feel their awkwardness and bafflement. It was as if my forehead had been seared by a branding iron."[37] Berr also refers to the fundamental alienation and metamorphosis she has undergone, comparing it to a mark of Cain imprinted on her body—on her forehead. The centrality of the theme of marking in Berr's diary reflects the difficulty experienced by many Jews in France at the promulgation of the new decree, as summed up by Renée Poznanski in her afterword to the Hebrew edition of the diary: "The pages written by Hélène Berr confirm, first of all, the profound impact of the change embodied in the obligation to wear the yellow star."[38]

But why did marking have such a profound impact? What was it about the Nazi marking that was so unsettling, by what process, and on which levels? It was, after all, a relatively "light" decree that did not involve material loss of rights or property, did not forcibly compel any action, did not prohibit or require any particular action in daily life, and did not in itself limit freedom. In the words of Simcha Guterman from the Płock ghetto, in an entry on the subject of the yellow star, "The decree was, after all, one which does not create any physical pain and is not tied to great monetary expenses."[39] In effect, this was the only decree that did not take from the victims but rather gave to them. It gave them a mark. Nevertheless, the reactions, as we have seen, express a profound sense of humiliation, existential alienation, and fundamental destabilization. The marking should therefore be understood as striking at a fundamental level, perhaps the most fundamental in the status of the self—well beyond its practical impact on daily life.

Moreover, according to the approach that posits an autonomous subject (i.e., a subject that existed prior to the marking and whose essence is not fundamentally shaped by it), one would have expected the Jews to reject the marking as something imposed upon them against their will and that, therefore, does not touch their essence. From this perspective, the severe and devastating pain and rupture provoked by the marking are puzzling, since only internal identity should have determined the Jews' status in their own eyes, and this identity should have, in its essence, remained resistant to every form of external marking. The marking simply declared publicly what everyone already knew: that those who bore it were considered Jews by the Nazis. If that was the entire meaning of the mark, why did it provoke such shock and pain? What was the source of its tremendous potential to wound and why did it arouse stronger reactions than any other act of persecution, including—in some cases—deportation and death? The answer must be sought on a number of levels.

First, the marking attracted annoying attention, as Hersh Wasser from the Warsaw ghetto described in his diary on 2 December 1940: "Going to the Christian quarter is also most unpleasant. Everyone stares at the Star of David."[40] There is no doubt, however, that objections to wearing the mark had a practical side, as it made life difficult and often posed a real danger. For example, Zvi Radlitzky from Lvov noted that the order came into force on 15 July (20 Tammuz), anniversary of the death of Theodor Herzl. Since the armband they were required to wear was white, with a blue Star of David on it, "there was even the impression that the Jews were proud of the blue and white band that the Germans had sought to turn into a badge of shame." "However," he continues, "all of those feelings were merely illusions that dissipated as soon as we went out into the street. If, until now, not every Jew was stopped, since not every Jew was immediately recognizable as such, now every Jew was marked and every Christian could lord over him."[41]

Even this, however, fails to explain the hardship the Jews felt with regard to the mark, since its impact was felt even when Jews were among themselves, and attempts to deal with it in a rational manner were unsuccessful, as Simcha Guterman described:

> Strach, the fisherman, stood at the bazaar and laughed at the refined people, anxious about their honor: "I am the first to wear the patch. I will wear it with honor. Shame? Let the ones who forced us to wear the patch be ashamed." . . . And yet, he did not want to be the first. As the time neared, the streets became half-empty. . . . Although everybody reiterated Strach's words and said he was right, still, when facing one's self in the mirror, one recoiled to go out with the yellow patch. . . . Everybody knew, understood, that his honor was not besmirched by this, nor marred. The human self-worth, however, protested, the person's pride protested, rebelled against shaming the human soul, the human dignity.[42]

We may presume that the irrational sense of humiliation that Guterman describes ("shaming human dignity") stems, inter alia, from the fact that—contrary to voluntary self-marking by means of which people declare and even constitute their identities, while negotiating with their surroundings—this marking was forced. Denying the possibility of negotiation regarding the mark exacerbates the sense of humiliation in the compulsion. As was noted by sociologist Erving Goffman, marking is a forced and shocking invasion of the subject's intimacy and privacy.[43] Furthermore, the fact that the Jews were marked even among themselves (very prominent in Guterman's description), that is, even when there was no need to distinguish between them and non-Jewish society, would seem to indicate that the marking did not function solely as a means of identification or a significant marker within a semiotic-cultural system. We thus begin to approach what is, to my mind, at the very heart of the terrible effect that marking had on those who experienced it. To explain this further, I will use the Lacanian concept of metonymy.

Metonymy is a *figurative device* that describes a concept or a thing by replacing it with something that is close to it in time or place. Metonymy is thus related to movement and displacement—the representation of something occurs by the movement of displacing it to something close or contiguous to it. Lacan understands metonymy in the human psyche as an ongoing process in which individuals search for the signifier—a word, a sentence, a definition, an articulation—that is best suited to them and will define their identities and satisfy their desires. The search is unending, however, because the lack of full satisfaction that we feel in our lives is not accidental but rather structural and inherent to our human nature. There can thus never be a signifier or a marker capable of perfectly representing individual identity or completely satisfying all of our wants and desires. No matter how many words we formulate or their capacity to contain or express the richness and sophistication of our personalities, any attempt to define ourselves, our identities, our desires, will always leave something out. We will always feel that even these words do not manage to fully express who we really are and what we ultimately desire. Complete identity, like complete satisfaction, is impossible. Therefore, we continue to search for further signifiers and further objects of desire that will describe more precisely our identities and satisfy our wants. This constant movement, like the constant change that flows from it, is the movement of "desire," identified in Lacanian theory with the essential human energy (like the libido in Freudian thought) that leads us in the patterns of our lives, affords us the feeling that we are alive, and causes us to desire and to long, to love, and to hate.[44] The structure of the movement of desire is, according to Lacan, metonymic, because, as Dylan Evans explains: "Metonymy [is] . . . a diachronic movement from one signifier to another along the signifying chain, as one signifier constantly refers to another in a perpetual deferral of meaning. Desire is also characterised by exactly the same never-ending process of continual deferral; since desire is always 'desire for something else', as soon as the object of desire is attained, it is no longer desirable, and the subject's desire fixes on another object."[45] This movement from signifier to signifier is both the cause and the effect of desire, as Lacan puts it: "Desire is a metonymy, even if man scoffs at the idea."[46]

This metonymic slippage is therefore essential to human existence and requires some distance so that one can move from one signifier to the other. Nazi marking, which imposed a single signifier, even affixing it to the body—actively eliminating the necessary distance between signifier and subject—halted the metonymic movement between signifiers, which is the movement of life itself. From that point on, each subject possessed only a single signifier, which eliminated and precluded passage from one signifier to another. It annihilated what Lacan calls the "chain of signifiers." In other words, the subject's constant metonymic search for signifiers of his or her changing identity and objects of desire was impeded. The search was supplanted by a unique signifier, thereby sealing the void and fundamental lack that lie at the core of human being. The Jew is no longer anything but a Jew.[47] The subject of desire, yearning, and longing, effectively ceases to exist. To the question, "What are you?" there is but one answer: "a Jew." Nothing else is relevant to the present condition and context.

This affixation blocks the essential gap between "the word" and "the self," precluding human existence in that gap into which words may be directed. The gap that arouses desires, wants, and curiosity, as well as fears, urges, and fantasies; the gap that enables the constant search for transformative identity and objects of desire, is almost entirely blocked. The subject's world under Nazism is complete and occluded, and what the Jew lacks under Nazi marking practices is lack itself. In another, not entirely unrelated context, Žižek asserts that "the unbearable absolute lack emerges at the very point when the lack itself is lacking."[48] In a situation of racial violence, this lack produces anxiety, as the theoretician Kalpana Seshadri-Crooks explains: "Thus the raced subject experiences anxiety, which is a consequence of encountering the lack of a lack. . . . According to Lacan, . . . [anxiety] appears when there is no possibility of desire, when there is a 'lack of a lack.' "[49]

It is not only the victim, however, who is terrified by the process of marking. The marking of the Jews acted upon the murderer in a similar fashion. In an article published in the Nazi weekly *Das Reich* on 16 November 1941, Goebbels described the marking of the Jews as a "thoroughly humane provision" (*äusserst humane Vorschrift*), intended to "prevent the Jew from creeping undetected into our ranks" (*kann das Jude sich unerkannt in unsere Reihen einschleichen*).[50] It is a humane provision because it facilitates the distinction between "human" and "nonhuman." The marking was intended to constitute a difference in order to enable the Nazis to identify the Jew. On 18 April 1943, however, Goebbels wrote in his diary: "I gave orders to investigate all Jews still left in Berlin. I do not want to see Jews with the Star of David running about the capital. Either the Star must be taken from them and they be classed as privileged, or they must be evacuated altogether from the capital of the Reich."[51] The sight of the marked Jews is intolerable to Goebbels. There is no other recourse but complete removal of the mark. Goebbels's words illustrate the impossible situation in which the Jews had been placed within the system of Nazi signifiers: Jews were marked in order to increase their visibility but at that point the sight of them became intolerable.

It is in this light that we should understand the observations of geographer Herbert Morgen from his travels in the "new German Eastern Areas": "As an external sign of belonging to their tribe the Jews carry . . . a yellow Star of David or a yellow triangle or something like it on their breasts and back. The general impression one receives of this human mass is appalling. And one quietly arrives at the conclusion that one is dealing here with a completely degenerate, inferior part of human society."[52]

The ordinary logic of signification is reversed here as well. It is not the characteristics of the Jews that require their marking but the marking itself that inspires fear, as if it were a particular limb or organ inherent to the Jewish body that sets Jews apart from other kinds of humans, rendering all who carry it exactly what the speaker expects to see.[53] Marking makes the fantasy unavoidably manifest and thereby arouses disgust and fear.[54]

Let us now return to the world of the victims and summarize in short their status in relation to language, between the two deaths. On the one hand, language itself, as a symbolic network that constitutes meaning, is liable to break down (that is, the symbolic, "second death"). On the other hand, victims may "choke" to death when the Nazi signifier is affixed to their bodies, thereby eliminating the necessary gap for the existence of metonymic movement of desire as the life force itself (that is, "death by the signifier"). It is my contention that in the case of radical and immense traumatic events like the Holocaust (but not only the Holocaust), the narratives recounted by the victims as the events unfold help to create a framework for traumatic experience that protects them from breaking down into one of the two more extreme possibilities—the "two deaths." Hence writing does not cure the radical disintegration of trauma that is expressed and felt in every page that was written during its overwhelming occurrence. It does, however, prevent the text and the writer from collapsing into the greater catastrophe: one of the two deaths that we have just described. The writer is not completely thrown out of the symbolic order and is not completely overpowered by the Nazi signifier. She is still within the realm of words and thus manages to maintain some of the essential distance that preserves metonymic slippage and thereby enables life.

To illustrate this, I would like to return to a passage in the diary of Fela Szeps from the Grünberg camp, addressed in a slightly different context in the introduction to the present volume. In this passage, it seems—although not stated in those terms—that Szeps effectively contrasts the task of documentation that she took upon herself with the concepts of the "second death" and "death by the signifier." In the earliest entry we have, dated 5 April 1942—Passover 5702, Szeps writes:

> There is a lot of talk here about writing a diary. Everyone thinks that there are a great deal of things that should be documented, things that don't ordinarily happen in normal life, things that we ourselves would not have believed exist in the world. Such things belonged to past ages, or were the product of the fertile imagination of story-writers. I think any of us who have read such stories have thought that were she herself to experience what the unfortunate heroines of these novels had gone through, the world would have turned upside-down, the sun and the moon would not have shone as usual, and she herself would certainly not have survived. But here, everything goes on as usual, despite the somewhat strange things that happen here, and these strange happenings are accepted with resignation, as if they were natural phenomena. Slowly, one becomes accustomed to phenomena that are out of this world, and there is nothing to write in the diary, everything seems natural.[55]

The initial impulse to document and write a diary is the product of the extreme and exceptional nature of the circumstances in which the prisoners find themselves. It is the traumatic encounter with the unfamiliar, the anomalous, and the transgressive that arouses the impulse to write. This impulse is immediately threatened by two obstacles, however. The first obstacle arises within the "normal world" perspective, from which the events appear so extreme, illusory, and impossible, that "any of us who have read such stories have thought that were she herself to experience what the unfortunate heroines of these novels had gone through, the world would have turned upside-down, the sun and the moon would not have shone as usual, and she herself would certainly not have survived." Viewed from this perspective, the reality experienced by the writer is one in which *the world infringes on its own rules.*

The first obstacle to writing—seen from the perspective of normal life—is what has been described here as the "symbolic (second) death." Szeps describes a second obstacle to writing, however: "But here, everything goes on as usual, despite the somewhat strange things that happen here, and these strange happenings are accepted with resignation, as if they were natural phenomena. Slowly, one becomes accustomed to phenomena that are out of this world, and there is nothing to write in the diary, everything seems natural."

The prisoners unquestioningly accept the symbolic order of the murderous oppressor, whereby they, as prisoners, have absolutely no right or possibility of desiring a change in their circumstances. The camp becomes the natural state of affairs for them, within which they must function as automatons. The prisoners thus exist within an extreme example of what Lacan calls "the subject who is petrified by the signifier," that is to say, the subject is incapable of creating any meaning or change of her own, by means of metonymic slippage from signifier to signifier.[56] As Colette Soler explains: "When you have a link between the signifiers . . . you have meaning"; on the other hand, "what Lacan calls a subject petrified by the signifier is a subject who doesn't ask any questions."[57] Eric Laurent further elaborates: "At the very moment at which the subject identifies with such a signifier, he is petrified. He is defined as if he were dead, or as if he were lacking the living part of his being."[58]

Such a subject can no longer desire, long, live. This is what I have called "death by the signifier," which halts the process of metonymic slippage from one signifier to another (as exemplified by the process of marking the Jews).

How, then, does Szeps contend with this twofold risk: the fear of falling into the "second death" and the sense of banality felt by the prisoners—testimony to the control exerted by the Nazi signifier over their lives? How does she navigate between the threat of being cast out of language and the inverse threat—no less dire—of being choked by the words of the murderer, affixed to the prisoners' bodies and lives? Between the feeling that "the world would have turned upside-down" and the sense that everything was, in fact, normal and routine? How does she cope with these two petrifying deaths, to be able to write her diary?

Szeps continues, "Nevertheless, the desire often arises to pick up a pencil and do something with it, to write down some of what lies deep in the heart, delving restlessly in the depths and below the threshold of consciousness. For often, only the heart, in its depths, conceals some feeling of bitterness toward that . . . and seeks some handhold to express indefinable pain, and perhaps the pencil will afford it such a handhold."[59]

Szeps realizes that a simple representation of reality is not possible and is liable to lapse into one of the two mortal silences. In this passage, however, she proposes another option—writing—of a kind that recognizes the trauma yet struggles not to sink into death or silence.

As we have explained, trauma is the encounter with the excessive dimension that escapes all structure of meaning and therefore can never be fully accessible to the consciousness of the subject experiencing the trauma. Szeps recognizes her own lack of access to the traumatic experience she is living. The pain that "lies deep in the heart," as she describes it, is immensely powerful and, at the same time, hidden and "delv[es] restlessly in the depths and below the threshold of consciousness." As such, it is inaccessible and can certainly not be represented directly. Nevertheless, despite the inability of consciousness to touch this deep pain—and perhaps because of this inability—the pain arouses a powerful desire to do something with it. Just as in the "fort/da" game, in which Freud describes his toddler grandson's mode of dealing with the trauma of losing his mother, by means of an object (the wooden spool) associated with certain signifiers (the sounds the child emitted that were interpreted by Freud as "fort" and "da," respectively), so too in the case of Szeps, the "something," as she calls it, is performed first and foremost through an object (the pencil) associated with the signifiers of the act of writing.[60] The pencil, in this case, is not merely a writing instrument, but primarily an object that enables the inaccessible pain to hold onto something. The words come as if in its wake. The pencil as an object can therefore be understood as the means by which the gap between the writer and the world is reopened, allowing the signifying chain to appear and the subject to begin again the slippage movement from signifier to signifier that rekindles desire—the life force itself.

In writing of this kind, the writer is always aware of the inaccessibility of the heart of the traumatic experience and of the incompatibility between the words (the signifiers) and reality—both internal and external. This awareness compels the writer to search constantly for new, more appropriate and accurate signifiers. In this fashion, the necessary gap between the subject and reality, as a constituting dimension through semantic-symbolic fields, is maintained. On the one hand, the world does not completely break down outside of meaning (it does not turn "upside-down" and the sun and the moon do not deviate from the laws of nature by which they are governed) and, on the other hand, the reality thrust upon the prisoners is no longer taken for granted, as a natural and legitimate state of affairs, in which the word of the Nazi oppressor is the only and last word in the prisoner's world. Writing thus succeeds in maintaining the symbolic network of language as creator of meaning, while constituting-restoring the necessary gap between subject and signifier, that is, between the psyche and the words one uses to describe and express oneself. These words no longer impose themselves violently and inexorably, as if they were an extension of the murderer's words—nor do they wholly disintegrate, casting the subject outside of them, into a world that has completely infringed its own rules. In this way, the writer remains within the framework of the trauma but is kept from falling into one of the two more catastrophic options—the two deaths.

The textual testimony of trauma, as reflected in the opening passage of Fela Szeps's diary, thus demonstrates that *trauma occurs within the symbolic world of words and not outside it*. Trauma radically undermines this world but does not destroy it completely, and should be understood in the context of the dialectic between life and death within symbolic reality. Through writing, victims seek to "frame" themselves within the trauma so as not to slide beyond it, to one of the two deaths by means of which the oppressor murders the victims symbolically even before annihilating them physically. The writing of a narrative such as the one arising from Fela Szeps's diary is thus a "life story" in the fullest sense. Beyond depicting the writer's life, the actual writing of the narrative creates and enables life, quite literally and palpably. It averts both of the two deaths that threaten victims of trauma as immense as the one experienced by the victims of the Holocaust.

However, even writing does not offer a complete safeguard against catastrophe—certainly not in the case of such severe trauma. The two deaths are always there as a potential within the text and as two powerful and active vectors of radical destruction and disintegration. The ever-present signifier of the murderer may, at any moment, infiltrate the writing of the victim and take it over as well; while the terror and excess of the trauma—the pain and fear-filled void around which Szeps's pencil revolves—may erupt all at once, inundating and sweeping writing and writer away to destruction. Writing is not victory. At most, it allows victims to constitute a limited space within which they have the possibility of symbolically struggling with those titanic forces without disappearing entirely.[61]

Notes

1. Lawrence Langer, *Holocaust Testimonies: The Ruins of Memory* (New Haven, CT: Yale University Press, 1991). With regard to the diaries, see also Langer, *Admitting the Holocaust: Collected Essays* (Oxford: Oxford University Press, 1995), and Langer, foreword to *The Diary of Dawid Sierakowiak*, ed. Alan Adelson (Oxford: Oxford University Press, 1996), vii–x.

2. Dominick LaCapra, *Writing History, Writing Trauma* (Baltimore: Johns Hopkins University Press, 2014), 151–154.

3. Tamar Herman, "Gam Kan Mutar Lahlom Vele'ehov (Yoman Migeto Terezin)" [Here too one may dream and love (A diary from the Theresien ghetto)], *Yalkut Moreshet* 47 (1989): 203 (21 October 1944).

4. A similar argument was put forward by Boaz Neumann, who claimed that the victims at Auschwitz were already ontologically dead (having died what he termed an "ontological

death"), while still biologically alive. See Boaz Neumann, *Re'iyat Ha'olam Hanatzit: Merhav, Guf, Safah* [The Nazi weltanschauung: Space, body, language] (Haifa: Haifa University, 2002). The difference between Neumann's approach and the one presented here is that Neumann views the status of the victim as exclusively dictated by the ontology of the murderer, whereas symbolic death, in the sense of being outside any meaning-imparting social order, depends not on the murderer's ontology but on the victim's language. In this context, see also Hannah Arendt, "The Concentration Camps," in *A Holocaust Reader: Responses to the Nazi Extermination*, ed. Michael L. Morgan (New York: Oxford University Press, 2001), 47–63.

5. Slavoj Žižek, *The Sublime Object of Ideology* (London: Verso, 1989), 134. On death after Auschwitz, see Theodor Adorno: "There is no chance any more for death to come into the individual's empirical life as somehow conformable with that life" (Theodor W. Adorno, "Meditations on Metaphysics," in *A Holocaust Reader: Responses to the Nazi Extermination* (New York: Oxford University Press, 2001), 43.

6. Žižek, *The Sublime Object of Ideology*, 135. This approach is identified with Lacan's later writings, from the late 1950s, beginning with the essay "The Ethics of Psychoanalysis," in which emphasis shifted from the symbolic to the Real. See ibid., 131–136.

7. See, for example, the words of the Rabbi of Piaseczno in the Warsaw ghetto, who wrote in a postscript on 18 Kislev 5703 (27 November 1942), after the Great Deportation, that he could find no historical precedents for the events at hand (Kalonymus Kalman Shapira, *Esh Kodesh* [Sacred fire] [1960; reprint, Jerusalem: Yad Vashem, 1979], 139; Nehemia Polen, *The Holy Fire: The Teachings of Rabbi Kalonymus Kalman Shapira, the Rebbe of the Warsaw Ghetto* [Northvale, NJ: Jason Aronson, 1994], 35, 132–133, 145). See also Dan Diner, *Beyond the Conceivable: Studies on Germany, Nazism, and the Holocaust* (Berkeley: University of California Press, 2000), esp. the chapters on the Judenräte.

8. This conceptualization brings to mind Lyotard's well-known metaphor of the Holocaust as an earthquake in which not only lives, buildings, roads, and so forth were destroyed but also the instruments used to measure earthquakes. See Jean François Lyotard, *The Differend: Phases in Dispute*, trans. Georges Van Den Abbeele (Minneapolis: University of Minnesota Press, 1989).

9. Janusz Korczak, *Ghetto Diary*, trans. Jerzy Bachrach and Barbara Krzywicka (New Haven, CT: Yale University Press, 2003), 58 (29 May 1942).

10. Barbara Engelking and Jacek Leociak, *The Warsaw Ghetto: A Guide to a Perished City*, trans. Emma Harris (New Haven, CT: Yale University Press, 2009), 482–529.

11. According to Žižek, symbolic death may also be momentary rather than total—contrary to the classic examples of Sade and Antigone citied by Lacan. See Slavoj Žižek, *The Metastases of Enjoyment: Six Essays on Woman and Causality* (London: Verso, 1995), 83n7.

12. Neumann, *Re'iyat Ha'olam Hanatzit*, 226.

13. Havi Ben-Sasson, "Polin Upolanim Be'einei Yehudei Polin Bitkufat Milhemet Ha'olam Hashniyah" [Poland and Poles in the eyes of Polish Jews during the Second World War, 1939–1944] (PhD diss., Hebrew University, 2005), 63.

14. Victor Klemperer, *The Language of the Third Reich: LTI, Lingua Tertii Imperii: A Philologist's Notebook*, trans. Martin Brady (London: Continuum, 2006), 155.

15. That is how it appears in *Mein Kampf*. See Moshe Zimmermann and Oded Heilbronner, eds., *Prakim Mitokh "Ma'avaki" shel Adolf Hitler* [Selections from Adolf Hitler's *Mein Kampf*] (Jerusalem: Akademon, 1994), 73. See also note 61, by the editors: "The Aryan-Jewish racial contrast . . . is accepted by Hitler as the fundamental explanation of human history."

16. The marking of Jewish shops was understood by the militants of the Nazi party as an obvious and necessary step and they exerted pressure on the leadership regarding this matter. Hitler was furious. Since he understood the tremendous importance of marking, he wished to determine its timing himself without interference. He expressed his anger at a gathering of Gauleiters on 29 April 1937. It is interesting to note the particular ferocity of Hitler's reaction in this specific speech and context, as Saul Friedländer notes: "The tone, the words, the images contained a yet unheard ferocity, the intimation of a deadly threat" (Saul Friedländer, *Nazi Germany and the Jews: The Years of Persecution 1933–39* [Frome, UK: Phoenix, 1997], 188). It was only on 22 June 1938 that the systematic marking of Jewish shops began (see ibid., 261–262).

17. Cited in Yitzhak Arad, Israel Gutman, and Abraham Margaliot, eds., *Documents on the Holocaust: Selected Sources on the Destruction of the Jews of Germany and Austria, Poland, and the Soviet Union* (Jerusalem: Yad Vashem, 1981), 44–47.

18. The source of this marking lay in the identification of Jews with prostitutes and unrestrained sexual temptation and sin in medieval Christianity. This association resulted, inter alia, in the marking of Jews with a yellow badge, which was, in many places, the mark of the prostitute. See Robert Bonfil, "The Devil and the Jews in the Christian Consciousness of the Middle Ages," in *Antisemitism through the Ages*, ed. Shmuel Almog, trans. Nathan H. Reisner (New York: Pergamon, 1988), 98.

19. Klemperer tells a number of interesting anecdotes regarding the addition of the name "Israel." For example, when he receives a letter from the Jewish community on 12 November 1939, informing him that he must add the name Israel to his listing in the telephone book, he remarks, "I haven't had a telephone for a long time, thank God." Victor Klemperer, *I Will Bear Witness: A Diary of the Nazi Years, 1933–1941*, trans. Martin Chalmers (New York: Modern Library, 1999), 319. On 26 July 1940, he tells the story of Frau Voss, who had her telephone disconnected in order to avoid adding the name Sarah, and subsequently had it reconnected (ibid., 350–351). The supplementary name was obligatory on all official documents. Klemperer thus reports on 24 February 1939 that he must sign that name at the bank (ibid., 294). On 2 August 1943, he tells of a far more serious incident: questioning at Gestapo headquarters almost cost him his life when he forgot to call himself "Victor Israel Klemperer." Victor Klemperer, *I Will Bear Witness: A Diary of the Nazi Years, 1942–1945*, trans. Martin Chalmers (New York: Modern Library, 2001), 251.

20. In so doing, the Nazis acceded to a request from the Swiss border police.

21. See Kim Wünschmann, *Before Auschwitz: Jewish Prisoners in the Prewar Concentration Camps* (Cambridge, MA: Harvard University Press, 2015), 209–210. See also United States Holocaust Memorial Museum, "Tattoos and Numbers: The System of Identifying Prisoners at Auschwitz," *Holocaust Encyclopedia*, http://www.ushmm.org/wlc/article.php?lang=en&ModuleId=10007056, last modified 2 July 2016.

22. Yigal Shahar, *Ho Madre: Sipur Ahavah Be'auschwitz* [Ho Madre: A love story in Auschwitz] (Jerusalem: Yad Vashem, 2002), 45–46; emphasis added.

23. Uwe Timm, *In My Brother's Shadow: A Life and Death in the SS*, trans. Anthea Bell (New York: Farrar, Straus and Giroux, 2005), 54.

24. This brief overview shows how the marking of the Jews accompanied the radicalization of their persecution in two ways: (1) In general, each new type of marking was instituted in close proximity to pivotal changes in anti-Jewish policy (although not every transition was accompanied by distinctive marking) and perhaps even reflect those changes: the April boycott marked the beginning of the Nazi persecution of the Jews in Germany; the administrative changes regarding official documents were part of the radicalization of anti-Jewish policy in

late 1938, culminating in the *Kristallnacht* attacks; and the "badge of shame" requirement was one of the first orders issued in occupied Poland, perhaps even presaging the establishment of the ghettos. It is interesting to note that immediately after one of these pivotal events—*Kristallnacht*—Heydrich, at a meeting of the Nazi leadership, proposed marking the Jews with special badges, but the idea was eventually rejected by Hitler. See Friedländer, *Nazi Germany and the Jews, 1933–39*, 282–283. (2) With a number of reservations, it can be said that these five stages parallel—albeit not precisely from a chronological perspective—the (cumulative) stages in the development of Nazi anti-Jewish policy: linguistic marking occurred when Nazi activities against the Jews were primarily of a propagandistic nature; the marking of property coincided with economic persecution and dispossession; marking on official documents paralleled the revocation of civil rights and the implementation of policies designed to encourage Jewish emigration; marking with the "badge of shame" accompanied the process of ghettoization; and marking of the body was a precursor to murder itself, which occurred at Auschwitz and other camps.

25. This was best described by David Kahane in the Lvov ghetto: "From that day on the Jew ceased to be a human being; instead, he became '*A Jude*' no. 1, 2, 3" (David Kahane, *Lvov Ghetto Diary*, trans. Jerzy Michalowicz [Amherst: University of Massachusetts Press, 1990], 48).

26. An interesting fact worth noting is that even before the law was enacted by one of the central Nazi authorities, a number of civilian and military authorities had already begun, of their own initiative, to mark the Jews. Thus, for example, the Jews of Lodz, Rzeszow, and Woloclavek—followed by the Jews of the Kalisz district—were required to wear a distinctive mark from the very outset, by local orders, without prior coordination with the various authorities. This attests that the marking of the Jews (as their internment in ghettos) existed as a latent fundamental pattern in the Nazi code. Central orders, however, in the area of the General Government, were not late in coming. On 23 November 1939, in an order issued by the governor-general Hans Frank, the Jews were required to wear a white armband bearing a star of David. The order gave no reason for the requirement but, according to Yisrael Gutman, "the measure . . . succeeded more than anything else in bringing about the isolation of the Jews" (Yisrael Gutman, *The Jews of Warsaw 1939–1943: Ghetto, Underground, Revolt*, trans. Ina Friedman [Bloomington: Indiana University Press, 1982], 29).

27. In many ways, this process parallels the restriction of Jewish living space—a process culminating in the gas chambers, as noted by Neumann, *Re'iyat Ha'olam Hanatzit*, 91–92.

28. Emanuel Ringelblum, *Yoman Ureshimot* [Diary and notes from the Warsaw ghetto] [Jerusalem: Yad Vashem and the Ghetto Fighters' House, 1992], 64. (This entry does not appear in the English edition.)

29. Quoted in Philip Friedman, "The Jewish Badge and the Yellow Star in the Nazi Era," *Historia Judaica* 17 (1955): 63.

30. Emanuel Ringelblum, *Notes from the Warsaw Ghetto: The Journal of Emanuel Ringelblum*, trans. Jacob Sloan (New York: Schocken, 1974), 105.

31. Ringelblum, *Yoman Ureshimot*, 89 (this entry does not appear in the English edition); see also p. 93.

32. Ibid., 414. See also Tamar Lazerson's description of her passage to the Aryan side: "The yellow star on one's chest and gloom in one's heart . . . the brigade, the Germans, the ghetto—was all behind me and slowly sunk into the past. The yellow star was no longer on my chest" (Tamar Lazerson-Rostovsky, *Yomanah shel Tamara: Kovno 1942–1946* [Tamara's diary: Kovno 1942–1946] [Lohamei Hageta'ot: The Ghetto Fighters' House and Hakibbutz Hameuchad, 1976], 123 [1 April 1945]).

33. Ringelblum, *Yoman Ureshimot*, 80.

34. Entry dated 30 November 1939, Chaim Aron Kaplan, *Scroll of Agony: The Warsaw Diary of Chaim A. Kaplan*, trans. and ed. Abraham I. Katsh (Bloomington: Indiana University Press, 1999), 78–79. Many of the references to this subject in Ringelblum's diary also relate to assimilationists.

35. See, for example, the entries from 30 January 1940 (p. 110), 13 May 1940 (p. 152), 27 June 1940 (p. 165), 17 November 1940 (p. 225), 26 November 1940 (p. 227), and others, in ibid.

36. See Josef Kermisz, ed., *Itonut Hamahteret* [The underground press], vol. 2 (Jerusalem: Yad Vashem, 1980), 87. It is interesting that at each and every stage of marking, there were those who already felt the next stage. Thus, as noted above, Robert Weltsch, in Germany, saw the social stigmatization as embodying the marking with the yellow star, and Eliahu Rozanski felt that the marking with the armband "seared" his arm.

37. Hélène Berr, *The Journal of Hélène Berr*, trans. David Bellos (New York: Weinstein Books, 2008), 56.

38. Renée Poznanski, afterword to *Yoman* [Diary], by Hélène Berr (Ben-Shemen: Modan, 2010), 274.

39. Simcha Guterman, *Leaves from Fire*, trans. Mindle Crystel Gross (Charleston, SC: Self-published by Yaakov Guterman, printed by CreateSpace, 2015), 146.

40. Hersh Wasser, "Daily Entries of Hersh Wasser," *Yad Vashem Studies* 15 (1983): 212.

41. Zvi Radlitzky, "Reshimot Miyemei Hakibush HaGermani BeLvov (Lemberg) 1941–1943" [Notes from the days of the German occupation in Lvov (Lemberg) 1941–1943], *Yalkut Moreshet* 21 (1976): 9.

42. Guterman, *Leaves from Fire*, 147.

43. Erving Goffman, "On the Characteristics of Total Institutions," in *Asylums: Essays on the Social Situation of Mental Patients and Other Inmates* (New Brunswick, NJ: Aldine Transaction, 2009), 1–124.

44. The Lacanian concept of "desire" does not refer to erotic desire, although it is not entirely detached from it. Desire is a kind of pervasion of primal erotic energy into all areas of life, while neutralizing its manifestly erotic dimension somewhat.

45. Dylan Evans, *An Introductory Dictionary of Lacanian Psychoanalysis* (London: Routledge, 1996), 117.

46. Jacques Lacan, *Écrits: The First Complete Edition in English*, trans. Bruce Fink (New York: Norton, 2002), 439. See also ibid., 428–429.

47. On the relationship between signifier and signified in creating the subject, see Julia Kristeva, *Desire in Language: A Semiotic Approach to Literature and Art* (New York: Columbia University Press, 1980), 127–128: "[A] language is not a system; it is a system of signs, and this vertically opens up the famous gap between signifier and signified, thus allowing linguistics to claim a logical, mathematical formalization on the one hand, but on the other, it definitely prevents reducing a language or text to one law or one meaning. . . . [A] subject of enunciation takes shape within the gap opened up between signifier and signified."

48. Slavoj Žižek, "I Hear You with My Eyes," in *Gaze and Voice as Love Objects*, ed. Renata Saleci and Slavoj Žižek (Durham, NC: Duke University Press, 1996), 108.

49. Kalpana Seshadri-Crooks, *Desiring Whiteness: A Lacanian Analysis of Race* (London: Routledge, 2000), 45.

50. Josef Goebbels, "Die Juden sind schuld," *Das Reich*, 16 November 1941, 1–2. Similar justifications appear in other Nazi texts and in some of the orders themselves. See sources cited

in "The Yellow Badge: A Shibboleth in Nazi Europe," *Wiener Library Bulletin* 8, nos. 5–6 (September–December 1954): 40, 42.

51. Josef Goebbels, *The Goebbels Diaries 1942–1943*, ed. and trans. Louis P. Lochner (New York: Doubleday, 1948), 335.

52. Originally appeared in *Zeitschrift fur Geopolitik* 18 (March 1941): 139; quoted in Max Weinreich, *Hitler's Professors* (New York: YIVO, 1946), 94.

53. See Diner, *Beyond the Conceivable*, 108.

54. The Jewish badge is, in a sense, a signifier that is not a signifier, inasmuch as it would appear to fail to meet the most basic criterion of signification, that the sign "stands for something else." See Umberto Eco, *Semiotics and the Philosophy of Language* (Southampton, UK: Macmillan, 1984), 8. In the case of the Nazi mark, the signifier is affixed to the "something else" that it is supposed to signify—the Jewish body—as a superfluous duplication of it.

55. Fela Szeps, *Balev Ba'arah Hashalhevet: Yomanah shel Fela Szeps* [A blaze from within: The diary of Fela Szeps] (Jerusalem: Yad Vashem, 2002), 23.

56. Jacques Lacan, *The Seminar of Jacques Lacan, Book XI: The Four Fundamental Concepts of Psychoanalysis*, ed. Jacques-Alain Miller, trans. Alan Sheridan (New York: Norton, 1998), 203–215.

57. Colette Soler, "The Subject and the Other (II)," in *Reading Seminar XI*, ed. Richard Feldstein, Bruce Fink, and Maire Jaanus (Albany: State University of New York Press, 1995), 48.

58. Éric Laurent, "Alienation and Separation (I)," in *Reading Seminar XI*, ed. Richard Feldstein, Bruce Fink, and Maire Jaanus (Albany: State University of New York Press, 1995), 25.

59. Szeps, *Balev Ba'arah Hashalhevet*, 24.

60. Sigmund Freud, "Beyond the Pleasure Principle," in *The Standard Edition of the Complete Psychological Works of Sigmund Freud*, vol. 18, ed. and trans. James Strachey (London: Hogarth, 1955), 14–17.

61. For a more extensive discussion of this topic, see Amos Goldberg, "Trauma, Narrative, and Two Forms of Death," *Literature and Medicine* 25, no. 1 (2006): 122–141.

PART II

FROM AUTOBIOGRAPHICAL TIME TO DOCUMENTATION TIME

Victor Klemperer's Diary

4

THE LIFE STORY OF VICTOR KLEMPERER

PART II is dedicated to the reading of the diaries kept by Victor Klemperer in Dresden during the Nazi years focusing on the temporal experience, as reflected during the course of the protracted traumatic event. As we shall see, the autobiographical structure of time that underlies these diaries underwent a fundamental disruption but was reorganized in a very different way in the context of documentary writing. In order to understand the disruptions in Victor Klemperer's life story during the Nazi period, and the way in which the story took shape in his diaries, we must first devote a few words to the course of Klemperer's life prior to this period, as he himself described it—primarily in the diaries he kept from age sixteen and in the autobiography he wrote during the years 1939–1942.[1]

Klemperer saw his life story as a process of formation and realization of his German identity. This teleological trajectory largely dictated the course of his life and the way in which he perceived himself, both professionally and personally. In many ways, Klemperer represents a typical assimilationist German Jew of the turn of the nineteenth century and the first half of the twentieth century, whose own history and that of his family is marked by the constant progression toward full assimilation in German society and culture.

The youngest of eight children (four boys and four girls), Victor Klemperer was born in 1881 to Henriette and Wilhelm Klemperer in Landsberg an der Warthe (now Gorzow Wielkopolski, Poland). His father, Rabbi Dr. Wilhelm Klemperer, a Jew of Czech origin, served as the rabbi of two small communities. In the community of Bromberg (now Bydgoszcz, Poland) his liberal views led to conflict with the Orthodox congregation, as a result of which he left to become second preacher (*zweiter Prediger*) at the Reform congregation in Berlin. The move to Berlin was a milestone in the life of the family. Beyond the broadening of their horizons and the abundance of new educational and cultural opportunities in the big city, the move from the small, conservative community of Bromberg to the radical, liberal congregation of Berlin marked the family's virtual detachment from Jewish tradition and the wholesale adoption of German identity. "Here the longing for Germanness found its most radical expression," Klemperer wrote in retrospect in his autobiography.[2]

Worship at the Reform synagogue in Berlin resembled that of the Protestant church. For example, services were held on Sundays and in German; during prayer, men and women sat together and the men did not cover their heads; the Jewish bar mitzvah was replaced with the Christian confirmation (*Einsegnung*) ceremony, held on Easter Sunday, for boys and girls age fifteen or sixteen; and so forth. It goes almost without saying that basic components of Jewish religious practice, such as the dietary laws and the Sabbath, were not observed at all.

Perceiving conversion as an admission ticket to Christian society, all the boys in the Klemperer family eventually converted to Christianity and married non-Jewish women (the girls remained Jewish and married Jewish men). Two of Klemperer's brothers were physicians (his eldest brother Georg was considered one of the foremost doctors in Germany at that time, and was even summoned to the Soviet Union to treat Lenin), and the third was a successful lawyer.

In 1906, Klemperer married Eva Schlemmer, a Christian, and in 1912 converted to Protestantism. In 1915 he volunteered—enthusiastically, it should be noted—for service in the German army, and fought for about six months on the French front. He subsequently served a further two years as a military censor in Kaunas and in Leipzig.

After considerable deliberation and a number of stints as a journalist, Klemperer finally decided to pursue an academic career, specializing in post-Revolution French literature—a decidedly unusual choice in Germany at a time when anti-French sentiment prevailed. Although the subject of his dissertation was the German Romantic novelist Friedrich Spielhagen, his postdoctoral thesis (*Habilitation*) focused on Montesquieu, and virtually all of his academic publications were in the field of French literature. In 1919, he was appointed professor of Romance languages at the Technische

Hochschule—a second- or third-tier academic institution as far as the humanities were concerned—in Dresden.[3]

Being awarded this professorship was a significant milestone in Klemperer's journey toward Germanness. Heide Gerstenberger characterized it as follows: "[The new position] afforded not only material security and social status. For Klemperer, it was a confirmation of his belonging to Germanness."[4]

Indeed, despite his attraction to the writers of the French Enlightenment,[5] Klemperer saw himself, in all of his academic endeavors, first and foremost as a German—a liberal, certainly, but one whose national affinity sometimes verged on chauvinism. The cornerstone of Klemperer's philosophical-cultural approach to literature was the idea of *Völkerpsychologie* ("peoples' psychology").[6] This idea, as understood by Klemperer, was based on the premise that culture, and more specifically the literature and language of each people, is an expression of its unique essence and a reflection or embodiment of the "spirit of the nation."[7] The origins of this approach, which exerted considerable influence on the development of linguistics and cultural and anthropological studies, were thoroughly liberal. The Jewish scholars Heymann Steinthal and Moritz Lazarus sought to establish a theoretical framework in support of the idea that the "nation" is not a matter of blood but of collective psychology created through the profound commonality of culture and language. Klemperer's adoption of this theory as a cornerstone of his academic research reflects his fundamentally liberal identity but also his identification with certain national-chauvinistic aspects of the *Völkerpsychologie*,[8] which stressed essentialist national elements in culture and literature rather than seeking to understand them in terms of historical development.[9] In light of the different psychologies of peoples, Klemperer believed that the peoples of the Germanic and the Romance lands had very little in common. He also doubted the ability of members of one people to substantially and profoundly understand the literature of another people. Large parts of his work are dedicated, explicitly or implicitly, to the hierarchical differences between the essences of Germanic and Romance cultures.[10]

As noted, Klemperer—like his teacher, Karl Vossler (and unlike many other German Romanists of the time)—belonged to the liberal wing of German Romance studies. His academic interest in the thinkers of the French Revolution and his attempts to bring French literature closer to German consciousness were certainly an expression of this. He believed that this body of literature was underrated in German academia and by the German cultural establishment, due to the long-standing political hostility between Germany and France. Nevertheless, and despite the fact that even when he claimed German intellectual and cultural superiority he sought to avoid drawing explicit political conclusions, some of his basic conceptions were close to prevalent right-wing conservative views in Germany, which, to a certain extent, were not very distant from Nazi racial theory and perhaps even helped pave the way for its acceptance.[11] Thus, although he did not identify with the political right—primarily because it was tainted with anti-Semitism—some of his nationalist and cultural views are surprisingly close to those espoused by that camp.[12] A telling indication that Klemperer was not all that far removed from ultranationalist views is his surprising reaction to a lecture given by a colleague on the topic "Race Hygiene and National Health": "fragmented, pastoral pathetic, not exactly original, at best patched together, but nevertheless impressive."[13] Klemperer himself sensed this problematic affinity. On 19 July 1937, for example, he asserts: "I myself had too much nationalism inside me and am now punished for it."[14] And in his book *Language of the Third Reich*, devoted to an analysis of the Nazi language, he ruminates on the connection between his national-cultural approach and Nazism: "I deliberated with shame whether I had played a role, perhaps even a leading one, in this movement."[15] Although he exonerates himself in the lines that follow, the very fact that he raised the question attests to his awareness of the disturbing affinity between his views on culture and Nazi ideology.

It is also worth noting that Klemperer believed, as German conservatives always had, that Protestantism (to which he had converted) was an integral part of the German essence and spirit. Gerstenberger put it as follows: "*Völkerpsychologie*, that is, the idea that members of a given people are imbued with a single spirit and therefore share an identical essence, formed the basis of his historical-literary inquiry."[16]

Klemperer's life story was thus marked by the progression toward complete assimilation, and had been, from his perspective, a success.[17] On several occasions in his diary he notes with pride that two members of the family (he and his brother Georg) were accorded entries in the *Brockhaus Encyclopedia* (*Brockhaus Enzyklopädie*).[18] He also took great pride in the musical accomplishments of his famous cousin, the conductor Otto Klemperer.[19] His conviction was confirmed by the fact that on 23 November 1932—only a few months before the Nazis came to power—he was asked by the Continental News Agency to write an article on the subject "What Awaits German Scholarship in the Year 1933," to be published on 1 January 1933.[20] The course of this life story was cut short, however, by the Nazis' rise to power.[21] Klemperer's standing at the university plummeted, and in 1935 he was dismissed.[22] His financial situation gradually worsened and many of his friends abandoned him. In early 1934 the Teubner publishing house revoked its contract with him, and at a certain stage he was barred from libraries, which cut him off from the source materials for his research.[23] During the war he was forced to move to the *Judenhaüser* ("Jews' Houses"), to which all the Jews of Dresden were confined, while his own home was let for a pittance to a former acquaintance. His freedom of movement, as a Jew, was also very limited.

From the moment the Nazis came to power, Klemperer was exposed to the violence of the regime. Increasing numbers of friends and acquaintances were sent to the concentration camps and disappeared, while reports of deaths and suicides abounded within his circle. During the war years, the violence reached Klemperer himself. He spent eight very difficult days in prison—due to a one-time infringement of the blackout regulations—and like other Jews suffered violent, terrifying searches of his home by the Gestapo.[24] During these years he was also pressed into forced labor, including work in a munitions factory. He suffered hunger for extended periods of time and once, in his desperation, even stole food from his neighbor at the *Judenhaus*—something of which he was very ashamed.[25]

The deportations of Jews from Germany began in late 1941. Klemperer did not know the fate of the deportees for certain until almost the end of the war, but in early 1942, he began to hear chilling rumors about the murder of German Jews transported to Riga.[26] He later tells of the harsh conditions in Poland and Theresienstadt and the horrors of the camp at Auschwitz, although he was unaware of the specific nature of the camp as a giant, Europe-wide extermination site.[27] Generally speaking, Klemperer was well aware that the mass murder of Jews was under way, and lived in (justified) fear that he too could be sent to the East at any moment.[28] By virtue of his marriage to Eva (an "Aryan"), his own record as a war veteran, and a good deal of luck—without which no Jew could have survived during this period—Klemperer was among the very small minority of Jews who were not deported from Germany.[29] Nevertheless, on 13 February 1945, he too was slated for deportation to the East, according to the order he received. On that day, however, the massive bombings of Dresden by the Allies began and reduced the city to rubble. Under cover of the ensuing chaos, Klemperer and his wife escaped to a village in southern Bavaria, where he lived under a false identity for the final months of the war, until liberation.

Although Klemperer's suffering was terrible, "objectively" speaking, the events that he experienced were nowhere near the horrors to which Jews in Poland and the Soviet Union were subjected. At the same time, he endured blatant violence, unbearable material and emotional personal loss, and lived—practically and consciously—in close proximity to death, which, from a certain point onward became a real, concrete, and daily threat. Alongside the experiences of loss and fear of death, however, Klemperer also experienced a tremendous ideological and psychological blow. His conceptual world, the course of his life, and his self-perception were fundamentally undermined. His belief in *Völkerpsychologie* and his perception of the essence of Germanness—the two pillars of his personal and intellectual identity—were shattered.

At the end of the war, Klemperer decided to remain in Dresden, which fell in the Soviet occupation zone and eventually became a part of East Germany. Judging by the diaries of the war years, his hatred of Communism was no less intense than his hatred of Nazism, and this choice was probably the product of a mixture of opportunism, local identity, and postwar ideology. In any event, he integrated well into East Germany's Communist order and enjoyed a level of academic prestige of which he could only have dreamed before the war.[30]

Victor Klemperer was an obsessive autobiographer.[31] He began to keep a diary at age sixteen and wrote diary entries on a regular basis from that point almost to the time of his death. During the course of the year 1932, his diary writing reached an impasse, due to a deep personal crisis—precipitated, inter alia, by his wife Eva's depression, his own lack of professional satisfaction, and a sense of financial insecurity—and he considered abandoning it.[32] It is thus possible that the Nazi rise to power—an event that brought about a change in the nature of the diaries—saved him from silence.

Klemperer did not intend to publish the diaries from the Nazi period as they were, although at a certain point during that period, he considered publishing excerpts (after careful editing) as a third part of his autobiography.[33] He eventually rejected the idea and it was only after German unification, many years after his death, that his second wife Hadwig decided to allow the diaries to be published. They were significantly abridged (only 1,500 of some 4,500 pages of the original text were included) and published in 1995.[34] They immediately became best sellers in Germany. Within a short time, more than 140,000 copies were sold and Klemperer became a cultural icon. German television even produced a drama series based on the diaries, broadcast in prime time. It is important to note that Klemperer's diaries also enjoyed success outside of Germany. The English translation of diaries from the Nazi period received enthusiastic reviews in the United States and the United Kingdom, which also led to the publication of an English translation of Klemperer's old work, *LTI*, first published in German in 1947.[35] The tremendous success enjoyed by the diaries from the Nazi period and the great interest in the figure of Klemperer himself led to the publication of his postwar diaries.[36]

In this context, it is interesting to take note of the editing of Victor Klemperer's diaries. As Paola Traverso has pointed out, surprisingly, the 1,500 or so pages of the diary selected for publication end in June 1945—not at the end of the war (8 May) nor at the end of that year, but rather upon the conclusion of the Klemperers' arduous journey home from Bavaria, to which they had escaped following the Allied bombings in February 1945.[37] The commercial version of the diaries thus ends with the words: "In the late afternoon, we walked up to Dölzschen [the Dresden suburb where they had made their home]."[38] In other words, having lived through hell and withstanding all the tests he encountered, at the end of the story the hero returns home, in the spirit of the ancient Greek romances, as if nothing had happened: his faith remains unaltered, his love for the homeland unshaken, and even his home remains as it was—still standing, awaiting his return.[39] The subsequent entries, which describe the difficulties with which returning home was fraught, as well as Klemperer's joining of the East German Communist Party, shed ironic light on this idyllic "ending." Klemperer's entries from July 1945 to the end of that year were, however, published separately from the diaries of 1946–1959.[40]

Klemperer and his diaries have been the subject of lively historical and academic debate in Germany, the United States, and elsewhere, mainly regarding the source of their appeal and the extent to which they have contributed to the image and historical understanding of the period.[41] It is interesting to note that Klemperer has aroused relatively little interest in Israel, even in academic circles.[42] A small portion of the diaries from the Nazi period was published in Hebrew in 2004.[43]

As noted at the beginning of this chapter, the chapters that follow address the disruption of concepts of time in the diaries of Victor Klemperer, primarily with regard to relations between these concepts and the construction of narrative identity.

Notes

1. Victor Klemperer, *Leben sammeln, nicht fragen wozu und warum: Tagebücher 1918–1932,* 2 vols. (Berlin: Aufbau, 1996) (henceforth Weimar Diaries); and Victor Klemperer, *Curriculum Vitae,* 2 vols. (Berlin: AtV, 1996).

2. Klemperer, *Curriculum Vitae,* 1:41.

3. Beginning in the late eighteenth century and largely due to the influence of the nationalist philosopher Johann Gottlieb Fichte, the rise of German nationalism led to the marginalization of Romance studies in Germany. See Peter Jacobs, *Victor Klemperer: Im Kern ein deutsches Gewächs* (Berlin: AtV, 2000), 124. After the initial excitement over the appointment had worn off, Klemperer became increasingly frustrated at the institution's inferior academic status.

4. Heide Gerstenberger, "Meine Prinzipien über das Deutschtum und die Verschiedenen Nationalitäten sind ins Wackeln gekommen wie di Zähne eines alten Mannes," in *Im Herzen der Finsternis: Victor Klemperer als Chronist der NS-Zeit,* ed. Hannes Heer (Berlin: Aufbau, 1997), 14.

5. In his introduction to the English edition of Klemperer's diary, the translator, Martin Chalmers, accords far greater weight to this fact than it deserves, citing it as a decisive component of Klemperer's identity and world view—as a liberal universalist who identified, above all, with the values of the French Revolution. See Martin Chalmers, preface to Victor Klemperer, *I Will Bear Witness: A Diary of the Nazi Years, 1933–1941,* trans. Martin Chalmers (New York: Modern Library, 1999), vii–xxi. (Note: All of the references to Klemperer's diaries in this and the following chapters are to Chalmers's translation, with the exception of passages that do not appear in the English editions, which I have translated directly from the German.) On the distortion in this view, see below.

6. Sometimes this term is also translated as "folk psychology" but in this book I will translate it as "peoples' psychology" throughout.

7. According to Uriel Tal, the exponents of *Völkerpsychologie,* as developed by Lazarus and Steinthal, "were opposed to the mythological, romantic conception of the *Volksseele* [soul of the nation]" (Uriel Tal, *Christians and Jews in Germany: Religion, Politics and Ideology in the Second Reich, 1870–1914,* trans. Noah Jonathan Jacobs [Ithaca, NY: Cornell University Press, 1975], 182). In Klemperer's work, however, the concepts of *Völkerpsychologie* and *Volksseele* are not that distant from one another. For a very critical analysis of Klemperer's cultural conceptions, see Paola Traverso, "Victor Klemperers Deutschlandbild: Ein jüdisches Tagebuch," *Tel Aviver Jahrbuch für deutsche Geschichte* 36 (1997): 307–344.

8. Traverso notes the playing down of these elements in the diary during the process of Klemperer's acceptance. She attributes this, inter alia, to the tendency to portray the victims and survivors of the Holocaust as saints. Denise De Costa presents a similar argument with regard to the construction of the figure of Etty Hillesum. De Costa cites the example of the photograph of Hillesum used on the cover of a collection of essays on her writing. The cigarette she was holding in the original photograph was "retouched" out of the picture, as if it were unworthy of a representative figure like Hillesum to smoke or to hold a cigarette in such a provocative manner (Denise De Costa, *Anne Frank and Etty Hillesum: Inscribing Spirituality and Sexuality* [New Brunswick, NJ: Rutgers University Press, 1998], 18–20). In a similar vein,

the Hebrew translation of Hillesum's diary does not include a passage in which she refers to having had sex with two men during that period. This omission was pointed out by Hanan Frenk, who suggested that it may be explained in light of our normative expectations of a "victim" of the Holocaust (Hanan Frenk, "God Is Not Accountable to Us," *Haaretz*, 13 December 2002, http://www.haaretz.com/jewish/books/god-is-not-accountable-to-us-1.25464, accessed 13 April 2017).

9. Originally, this approach stressed the spirit of the nation as a "bridge . . . between historical tradition and suprahistorical transcendence" (see Tal, *Christians and Jews*, 182). See also Walter Zwi Bacharach, "Jews in Confrontation with Racist Antisemitism 1879–1933," *Leo Baeck Institute Year Book* 25 (1980): 199.

10. See Traverso, "Victor Klemperers Deutschlandbild."

11. According to Ingrid Belke, the concepts of "folk psychology" were a product of the idea of the nation-state and particularly of the culturally homogeneous German nation-state with Prussia at its core. See Ingrid Belke, introduction to *Moritz Lazarus und Heymann Steinthal: Die Begründer der Völkerpsychologie in ihren Briefen*, ed. Ingrid Belke (Tübingen: Mohr, 1971), xiii–cxlii, esp. xxxvi and cxxiv. See also George L. Mosse, *Toward the Final Solution: A History of European Racism* (New York: Harper and Row, 1980), 65. Etienne Balibar explicitly identifies *Völkerpsychologie* with racism. See Etienne Balibar, "Is There a 'Neo Racism'?," in *Race, Nation, Class: Ambiguous Identities*, by Etienne Balibar (trans. Chris Turner) and Immanuel Wallerstein (London: Verso, 1991), 17–28.

12. See Bacharach, "Jews in Confrontation with Racist Antisemitism," 198–200, in which he writes about the founder of this school of thought, Moritz Lazarus. According to Bacharach, despite his declared liberalism, "Lazarus raised an argument which did not differ much from 'spiritual racism.' This attitude has rightly been called 'a form of spiritual chauvinism.'" See also Taverso "Victor Klemperers Deutschlandbild," 318–339.

13. Klemperer, Weimar Diaries, 1:320.

14. Klemperer, *I Will Bear Witness, 1933–1941*, 230.

15. Victor Klemperer, *The Language of the Third Reich: LTI, Lingua Tertii Imperii: A Philologist's Notebook*, trans. Martin Brady (London: Continuum, 2006), 122.

16. Gerstenberger, "Meine Prinzipien," 17.

17. On the connection between the ideas of the school of "people's psychology" and the movement for Jewish emancipation in Germany, see Matti Bunzl, "*Völkerpsychologie* and German-Jewish Emancipation," in *Worldly Provincialism: German Anthropology in the Age of Empire*, ed. H. Glenn Penny and Matti Bunzl (Ann Arbor: University of Michigan Press, 2003), 47–85. It is worth noting that in this essay, Bunzl rejects the idea of an affinity between the *Völkerpsychologie* approach and chauvinist-racist nationalism.

18. In the entry dated 10 May 1938; in the long entry on his time in prison—23 June to 1 July 1941 (in his description of the fifth day); and in the entries on his return from Munich to Dresden—26 May to 10 June 1943.

19. He reacts angrily to the assertion of a colleague with Nazi leanings that Jews lacked creativity and had not produced any "real musician"—belittling Otto Klemperer in the process (see the entry dated 17 June 1934, p. 72).

20. See letter to Victor Klemperer from the Continental News Agency, Berlin 1932, Nachlass Klemperer, Victor (1881–1960)/5, Briefe, Sächsische Landsbibliothek—Staats und Universitätsbibliothek Dresden (SLUB), Mscr.Dresd.App.2003, 426. I do not know whether Klemperer acceded to this request or what he wrote, but the very fact that he was asked to do so is symbolic of the cruel abruptness with which the course of his life was interrupted and

turned upside down soon afterward; a course that had been constructed up until that point with a clear affinity to "German Scholarship."

21. For a full and detailed account of this life course and its shattering, see Arvi Sepp, *Topographie des Alltags: Eine Kulturwissenschaftliche Lektüre von Victor Klemperers Tagebüchern 1933–1945* (Antwerp: University of Antwerp, 2008), 151–162.

22. The official cause given for Klemperer's dismissal was "lack of interest" in his field of research. The cause was crucial, as it allowed him to continue to receive some form of stipend throughout the period.

23. Klemperer's correspondence with his publisher, Teubner, is touching. In a letter dated 24 January 1934, Teubner informed him that the fourth volume of his history of literature would not meet with success within the borders of the Reich, "for reasons I need not explain to you." In a letter dated 15 February 1934, he suggests that Klemperer look for a publisher in France or Switzerland and, in so doing, might expand his readership. He regrets that he cannot help him in this endeavor, as it would be interpreted by the foreign publisher as expressing a lack of confidence in the book. When Klemperer insists and asks Teubner to wait, as the situation may yet change, the publisher graciously replies that he does not see things that way but that Klemperer was, of course, entitled to view things differently. In his final letter, dated 14 August 1935, Teubner states explicitly that he is unable to publish a book by a "non-Aryan" author. And that is where the correspondence ends. See correspondence with Teubner, Nachlass Klemperer, Victor (1881–1960)/5, Briefe, Sächsische Landsbibliothek—Staats und Universitätsbibliothek Dresden (SLUB), Mscr.Dresd.App.2003, 465–469.

24. The searches were often accompanied by humiliating violence against Klemperer and his wife Eva. A diarist from the Lvov ghetto offered the following observations on this intolerable phenomenon: "The searches continue, accompanied by acts of theft. It is, however, our daily bread and I can therefore say that it is nothing special. A friend told me that lately he has been visited four times and each time they have diminished his possessions. It is not an isolated incident. Some people experience such visits on a daily basis and even a few times a day. It is a wonder people can stand it. I'm not talking about the material aspect but the moral aspect. But I have stopped wondering" (11 December 1941) (Bella Gutterman, ed., *Bevo Ha'emah: Yehudei Lvov Tahat Hakibush Hagermani: Dapei Edut Yuni 1941–April 1942* [Days of horror: Jewish testimonies from German-occupied Lemberg 1941–1943: Testimonies from June 1941 to April 1942] [Tel Aviv: The Institute for the History of Polish Jewry and the Diaspora Research Center, 1991], 158).

25. See entry dated 6 June 1942. Victor Klemperer, *I Will Bear Witness: A Diary of the Nazi Years, 1942–1945*, trans. Martin Chalmers (New York: Modern Library, 2001), 68.

26. See entry dated 13 January 1942 (ibid., 5). He tells of the mass murder of Jews in Kiev and Romania in the entry dated 29 December 1942 (ibid., 180).

27. See, for example, the entry dated 17 October 1942 (ibid., 155).

28. See, for example, the entry dated 16 September 1942 (ibid., 146).

29. On "mixed" couples (*Mischehe*), see Marion Kaplan, *Between Dignity and Despair: Jewish Life in Nazi Germany* (New York: Oxford University Press, 1998), 74–93; Nathan Stolzfus, *Resistance of the Heart: Intermarriage and the Rossenstrasse Protest in Nazi Germany* (New York: Norton, 1996). In February 1945, 198 registered Jews remained in Dresden, of a total of 1,265 who had resided in the city at the end of 1941, before the deportations to Riga, Theriesenstadt, and Auschwitz. See Chalmers, preface to Klemperer, *I Will Bear Witness 1933–1941*, xxi, n2.

30. The diaries from late 1945 and from the Communist period were published later. The first of these appeared in 1997, under the title *Und so ist alles schwankend: Tagebücher Juni bis*

Dezember 1945; and the second in 1999, under the title *So sitze ich denn zwischen allen Stühlen: Tagebücher 1945–1959*. On Klemperer during the Communist period, see Steven E. Aschheim, "Comrade Klemperer: Communism, Liberalism and Jewishness in the DDR. The Later Diaries 1945–59," *Journal of Contemporary History* 36, no. 2 (2001): 325–343.

31. As I have already noted, besides the diaries Klemperer wrote two books of an autobiographical nature, both based largely on his diaries. The first of these is his partial autobiography, *Curriculum Vitae*, which covers the period until 1918. It was written during the years 1939–1942 but published only in 1989. The second work is his book, *LTI* (*The Language of the Third Reich*), which analyzes Nazi language. The book has the appearance of a linguistic study but, as Klemperer himself notes in the introduction, it is not scientific in the strict sense of the word. It is based primarily on his experiences and on the diaries he kept between 1933 and 1945. *LTI* was published in 1947.

32. See, for example, the entry he wrote on Sunday, 24 April 1932: "I no longer have any joy in the diary nor do I have the peace of mind for it. Why should I waste this time? I don't go back and read it; no one does. At some point, it will be burned. A diary requires introspection. I am happier when I can work and read without self-awareness." (Weimar Diaries, 2:750; see also the entry of 14 May 1932 [ibid., 751]).

33. See entry dated 21 November 1942. Klemperer, *I Will Bear Witness, 1942–1945*, 168.

34. Victor Klemperer, *Ich will Zeugnis ablegen bis zum letzten*: vol. 1, *Tagebücher 1933–1941* (Berlin: Aufbau, 1995). According to the editor, newspaper clippings pasted into the diaries were excluded, as were repetitive entries. Pasting newspapers clippings was a common practice in diaries; see, for example, the editor's note to the Hebrew edition of Adam Czerniakow's diary, *Yomanei Geto Varshah* [The diaries of the Warsaw ghetto] [Jerusalem: Yad Vashem, 1970], xxx, on the entry dated 20 August 1941, where he states that here the writer attached two pages of the *Warschauer Zeitung* to prove a point he made in the text. This is the edition I have used, checking samples against the manuscripts preserved in the SLUB archive (Mscr.Dresd.App. 2003, 134–139). Based on these samples, the published edition would appear to be entirely reliable.

35. Klemperer, *I Will Bear Witness 1933–1941*; Arvi Sepp, "The Reception of Victor Klemperer's Diaries 1933–1945 in Contemporary American Holocaust Scholarship," in *Tales of the Great American Victory: World War II in Politics and Poetics*, ed. Diederik Oostdijk and Markha G. Valenta (Amsterdam: VU University Press, 2006), 131–142; Klemperer, *The Language of the Third Reich*.

36. In 1996, Klemperer's diaries from the Weimar period were published, as well as the entries written in Soviet-occupied Dresden in late 1945. In 1997, an abridged version of the diaries from the Nazi period appeared in didactic format, for the benefit of "young readers" (*Das Tagebuch 1933–1945, Eine Auswahl für junge Leser*) and, in 1999, Klemperer's diaries from 1945–1959 were published. There is no doubt that this is an extremely impressive autobiographical corpus, which has afforded its author far greater fame than his academic works or his German cultural criticism. Victor Klemperer, an anonymous scholar of literature and culture, passed away without knowing that he would become the most famous chronicler of the Nazi period.

37. See Traverso's article ("Victor Klemperers Deutschlandbild") on the reception of Klemperer's diaries in Germany, in which she explains the construction of the figure of the pure, innocent victim, devoid of all moral and other flaws.

38. Klemperer, *I Will Bear Witness, 1942–1945*, 514.

39. Mikhail M. Bakhtin, "Forms of Time and of the Chronotope in the Novel: Notes toward a Historical Poetics," in *The Dialogic Imagination: Four Essays*, ed. Michael Holquist, trans. Caryl Emerson (Austin: University of Texas Press, 1981), 86–110. Compare this to the

story of Primo Levi's homecoming (Primo Levi, *If This Is a Man/The Truce*, trans. Stuart Woolf [London: Abacus, 2004], 379–380), which ends with the author's dream attesting to the fact that he had, in fact, never left Auschwitz.

40. Victor Klemperer, *Ich will Zeugnis ablegen bis zum letzten*: vol. 1, *Tagebücher 1933–1941*; vol. 2, *Tagebücher 1942–1945* (Berlin: Aufbau, 1995); and the entries for the second half of 1945 in *Und so ist alles schwankend: Tagebücher Juni bis Dezember 1945* (Berlin: AtV, 1996).

41. In addition to the works I have already cited on Klemperer's diaries (Heer's *Im Herzen der Finsternis*, dedicated entirely to the diaries), I would like to note Omer Bartov, *Germany's War and the Holocaust* (Ithaca, NY: Cornell University Press, 2003), 192–215; and Walter Ze'ev Laqueur, "Three Witnesses: The Legacy of Viktor Klemperer, Willy Cohn and Richard Koch," *Holocaust and Genocide Studies* 10, no. 3 (1996): 252–266.

42. Two exceptions are Steven Aschheim, *Scholem, Arendt, Klemperer: Intimate Chronicles in Turbulent Times* (Bloomington: Indiana University Press, 2001); and recently, Guy Miron, "'Lately, Almost Constantly, Everything Seems Small to Me': The Lived Space of German Jews under the Nazi Regime," *Jewish Social Studies* 20, no. 1 (2013): 121–149; See also Miron, "'The Politics of Catastrophe Races On. I Wait': Waiting Time in the World of German Jewry under Nazi Rule," *Yad Vashem Studies* 43, no. 1 (2015): 45–67. Other Israeli scholars have quoted from Klemperer's diaries only incidentally. Saul Friedländer, who makes extensive use of diaries from that period in the two volumes of his monumental history of the Holocaust, made Klemperer one of the books' main protagonists. See Saul Friedländer, *Nazi Germany and the Jews: The Years of Persecution 1933–39* (Frome, UK: Phoneix, 1997); Friedländer, *Nazi Germany and the Jews: The Years of Extermination 1939–1945* (London: Weidenfeld and Nicolson, 2007). It is also worth noting that the German historian Susanne Heim delivered a lecture on Klemperer at a conference held at Yad Vashem, in Jerusalem: Susanne Heim, "The German-Jewish Relationship in the Diaries of Victor Klemperer," in *Probing the Depths of German Antisemitism*, ed. David Bankier (New York: Berghahn, 1999), 312–325. Interestingly, a review of Klemperer's *LTI* was published in Israel, in 1950: Raphael F. Aronstein, "Hineh Hayehudi Klemperer" [Here is the Jew Klemperer], *Orlogin* 1 (1950): 226–234. I am grateful to Roi Nathan for bringing this review to my attention.

43. Victor Klemperer, *Yomanim 1933–1945 (Mivhar)* [Diaries 1933–1945 (A selection)], ed. Ilana Hammerman, trans. Tali Kunes (Tel Aviv: Am Oved, 2004).

5

THE DISRUPTION OF LIFE-STORY TIME IN THE KLEMPERER DIARIES

September 1944 was a relatively calm month for the remaining Jews of Dresden. The deportations had stopped, incidents of blatant violence had decreased, and Germany's defeat seemed certain. On 14 September, Klemperer found the peace of mind to write a sort of reflective summary of past events. The entry begins with encouraging reports of the Allies' progress on the various fronts. In this context, he describes how his friend and neighbor at the Jews' House, Neumark, found a newspaper from 1943, in which a series of reports all point to the military and political collapse of Germany. After noting some of the more dramatic developments, such as the fall of Stalingrad—an event that seems "remote as a fairy tale" (*Märchenferne*) to him,[1] he writes the following:

> But something else made a greater impression on us—it was the same for both Neumark and myself—the impotence of memory to fix all that we had so painfully experienced in time. When—insofar as we remembered it at all—had this or that happened, when had it been? Only a few facts stick in the mind, dates not at all. One is overwhelmed by the present, time is not divided up, everything is infinitely long ago, everything is infinitely long in coming; there is no yesterday, no tomorrow, only an eternity. And that is yet another reason one knows nothing of the history one has experienced: The sense of time has been abolished; one is at once too blunted and too overexcited, one is crammed full of the present. The chain of disappointments also unfolded in front of me again.... Ever since Stalingrad, since the beginning of '43 therefore, I have been waiting for the end. I remember asking Eva at the time: Do you think it is *a* defeat, or do you consider it to be *the* defeat, the

> catastrophe? That was in February '43. . . . After that I was a factory slave for fourteen months.[2]

The collapse of personal time occurs—judging by this entry in Klemperer's diary—specifically toward the end of the Nazi period, when "objective" historical time seems to accelerate toward resolution and change.[3] Scientific, "geometrical" time, calendar time with a "before" and an "after" collapses on the most basic level. The facts, reflects Klemperer, may register on a certain level but dates vanish completely.[4] However, the order of subjective time, based on the three dimensions—past, present, future—also collapses.[5] There is no yesterday and no tomorrow, only an eternal and constant present.[6] The gap between fictional time and objective, historical time is erased as well, and the fall of Stalingrad is an event that is as far removed from the writer as a fairy tale from reality. As a result of this, Klemperer doubts the validity of the documentation project he has taken upon himself, because his ability to understand the events he seeks to document in his diary has also diminished. Ultimately, historical time collapses into subjective time, and the question of whether Stalingrad is a real turning point concludes, ironically, from the perspective of fourteen months as a factory slave. Klemperer thus remains—as he himself asserts—entirely helpless, since time no longer serves as a suitable conceptual framework for the organization of human experience.[7]

This passage represents the dialectic of diary writing, in all its difficulty. On the one hand, it reveals the various aspects of the collapse of time in Klemperer's diaries. On the other hand, at the moments of writing themselves, we must presume that some part of the temporal experience has been restored. Were that not the case, writing itself—which naturally entails a more or less linear temporal order—would be entirely impossible.[8] The dramatic moments of destruction are thus described within the narrative but from an entirely different perspective—distinct from that of the time of their occurrence, when narrative was not possible. Something of the order of human time that allows writing itself is restored. This dialectic between the temporality of trauma and the temporality of writing is the subject of this chapter.

The Present: Standing Time

On 6 August 1942, Klemperer wrote in his diary: "Habituation: A couple of weeks have passed since the murder of Joachimsthal, a couple of months since the house searches here. And already I am living in a state of dull-witted placidity. Habituation: On Tuesday another transport leaves Dresden for Theresienstadt; and already it appears to me, appears to Jewry here as a matter of course."[9] Klemperer reports here, in a concentrated fashion, a number of the most frightening elements in the lives of Dresden's Jews: arbitrary murders, deportations to Theresienstadt, and violent, humiliating house searches by the Gestapo and their unpredictable consequences. Despite the radical nature of the events, they leave Klemperer feeling "dull-witted." On a personal level, the constant presence of the fear of death became an ordinary matter, while on a collective level, the deportation process was practically taken for granted—the natural state of affairs and thus, ostensibly, no longer a source of terror. On the one hand, such a mechanism helps to defend the psyche against a surfeit of terrifying events and stimuli. At the same time, however, it is an expression of the present engulfing consciousness, therefore unable to perceive—on the basis of a "normal" past or future—the terrible abnormality of the deportation. Nazi eternity co-opted the Jews' sense of time, and became a habit that precludes all expectation of change.

An earlier entry, dated 20 April 1939—a few months after *Kristallnacht* and before the outbreak of the war, reflects a similar feeling. The entry was written in a period when German Jews did not yet face the threat of imminent death on a daily basis, although anti-Jewish legislation and violence had already reached unprecedented levels. It is specifically in this context that Klemperer writes: "Each day as wearing as the next. We are dulled by so much tension." Indeed, this feeling of standing time, of the present endlessly, grindingly repeating itself, and the experience of empty apathy and dulled senses recur numerous times throughout the diaries.[10] Various forms of the word "*Stumpf*"—apathy—appear hundreds of times. Feelings of dullness and apathy, alongside the inverse feelings of terror, can be found in all of the Holocaust diaries, virtually without exception.[11] The extent to which apathy is linked to trauma in Klemperer's diary can be deduced from the fact that expressions of numbness and apathy appear particularly at critical junctures of crisis: in 1933, in the wake of Hitler's rise to power; in 1938, with the intensification of anti-Jewish policies, which Klemperer experienced firsthand; and in 1942 and 1943—the years of the deportations of the Jews of Dresden. During these periods, Klemperer frequently expresses numbness and apathy.[12] Numbness, the expressions of which are spread over time, functions within the story in two opposing directions: on the one hand, it is an expression of trauma and part of it; on the other hand, it is also—ostensibly, at least—a defense mechanism that enables one to survive the trauma.[13]

The diary entry quoted above, dated 20 April 1939, stresses that the reason for the dulling of the senses lies not in the absence of events but, on the contrary, in the enormous tension created by the events. It is important to remember that the events in question were no ordinary occurrences but events of great historical significance, some of which are listed at the beginning of the entry: celebrations of Hitler's birthday, Germany's annexation of Bohemia, Italy's occupation of Albania, Roosevelt's message, the British naval concentration at Malta, and the impending war. All of these things produced intolerable tension, which, paradoxically, gave rise to the sensation of time standing still. Klemperer's apathy and numbness were, in fact, the result of the intolerable intensity of emotion produced by the surfeit of events. It is precisely the rapid progression of historical time—with all the threatening potential it entails—that flattens the writer's experience of subjective time. To the author, time is almost dead.[14]

The standing still of time is reflected in this entry also in the manner in which the Jews of Dresden speak about the harsh events: "People often here with whom conversations always run along the same track."[15] What this means is that time stands still not only on the plane of reality but an identical process occurs on the verbal plane as well. Despite the increasing severity and frequency of events, the conversations about them repeat themselves. They move along a fixed internal track, in a kind of repetition compulsion. One might say that these conversations are the antithesis of processes of working through the events because the repetition they offer occurs in a pure form, entirely independent of the experience and without reinterpreting it or forming new options by which to view reality.[16]

Contrary to many other passages, the internal organization of which closely follows the daily chronology, this entry summarizes eleven days of narrative flow, and its organizing principle is the progressive restriction of perspective and focus—from events in Greater Germany, through Klemperer's circle of acquaintances, to the couple's daily routine. It is also a restriction of time—from political time to social time and, ultimately, to domestic time. This restrictive movement is framed by two clearly biographical references: one to Hitler's birthday, publicly celebrated throughout the Greater Germany he had founded (its "creator"—*Der Schöpfer Grossdeutschlands*—in Klemperer's words); and the other to his own autobiographical (and intellectual) writing with which he was preoccupied at the time and that was "burying" him—as he put it. This movement between two biographies—one (Hitler's) divine and the other (his own) mortal—is the movement of the text to death and standing time.

Standing time—death—is already fully present here, although it is not concrete or evident. It is still a secret. So it appears, from another biography mentioned in the text: that of the judge Moral, a Jewish judge who had recently been dismissed from his position and had his assets blocked. "Moral, completely depressed . . . very old and gone to seed. There is some secret about the man, something broken inside him. Why his whole life long, in 40 years of service, never more than District Court Judge in small places."[17] Klemperer recounts two things about the judge: that he has some secret about him, which Klemperer seems to reveal as the secret of death, and that, looking back at his life, he (or Klemperer) sees it in a negative light. In Moral's case, death has not yet been fully realized but is present as a secret within him. Its effects are already visible: he is broken and withered, and his past—viewed from within his secret—appears extremely dismal: forty years as a "District Court judge in small places." The trauma here tarnishes the past as well. A few months later, on the night between 1 and 2 October, Moral commits suicide.[18] Six months later, on 20 May 1940, Klemperer writes: "I envy Moral a hundred times a day."[19]

Death is thus present and has an effect but is still hidden. A few lines earlier, Klemperer refers to another place where death is hidden: in the newspapers. Reports of execution of traitors, "who question the Führer, we follow you! atmosphere," appear in small print.[20] Klemperer encounters this truth of death within himself in exactly the same fashion, remarking: "So the small print runs daily through my head: Will they beat us to death? But really only in small print and by the way." The presence of death is certain but not yet evident. Only later will death become evident and omnipresent.

The Paradox of the Past in Traumatic Situations

The present dimension as the fulcrum of time in the developing life story is fundamentally disrupted. Consequently, the past is also affected. Diaries written in the camps, and sometimes even in the ghettos, openly and directly describe the erasure of the past and the collapse of the order of time. We have just seen how Moral's past is completely devaluated by him. In the Grünberg camp, Fela Szeps recounts: "The deportations . . . I am not certain of it, but it seems to me that when it finally sunk in, it caused a kind of internal rupture. My heart was inundated but would not burst. Home, parents, everything went up in smoke, as if it had never existed."[21] Not only is the present marred; the past is erased as if it had never happened!

As we have seen, Klemperer's diary also includes moments in which the temporal order collapses, but these are not always explicit and narrated directly, as in the camp diaries. At times, this destructive process takes place—even when very real—within a less evident stratum of the text. The Nazi period and especially the war years fundamentally undermined the natural place of the past in Klemperer's life story. This occurred on a number of planes. On the most basic level, the past can no longer serve as a point of reference for making sense of the present, because the present is experienced as unprecedented.[22] Klemperer reiterates this idea a number of times. On 27 January 1934, for example, he writes that, in the past, he and Eva could never have imagined living under a quarter of the difficulties they were now experiencing. The impossibility of learning from the past and the irrelevance of the past recur in various contexts throughout the diary. On 8 May 1942, for example, he writes: "The last war was such a decent business." However, the feeling that the past is irrelevant to understanding the present does not mean that the past does not play a significant role in the story. On the contrary, the past often acts as a powerfully destructive force that disintegrates retroactively and, in so doing, disintegrates the present as well.

One of Klemperer's most explicit assertions regarding his attitude to his past can be found in the entry dated 21 May 1940, on the eve of the Klemperers' involuntary move to the Jews' House. As part of the policy of intensifying the decrees and restrictions imposed on the Jews in Germany with the outbreak of the war, Jews were forced out of their homes and concentrated in "Jews' Houses" (*Judenhäuser*). As a result of this policy, the Klemperers had to leave the home they had purchased and renovated only a short time before in the Dresden suburb of Dölzschen and move to the Jews' House on Caspar David Friedrich Strasse in Dresden. The coerced move took place just as the Nazis had won swift victories on the French front. The two events—the Klemperers' move to the Jews' House and the defeat of France—become intertwined in the diary, drawing a particularly bleak picture. As if it were not enough that the collapse of the French front had put an end to any hope of bringing down the Nazi regime and had sealed their fate as Jews in the Third Reich, along came the order to move to the Jews' House, signifying not only the very fact of being expelled from their home but also the shattering of the dream of a house of their own—one that the couple had only recently fulfilled, at great financial and emotional cost.

The description of the move is grotesque. While the Klemperers are packing up their things and preparing for the forced move, the new tenant—an acquaintance by the name of Berger—is already there, remodeling the house he had just rented for a pittance, with the intention of turning it into a greengrocer's shop.

In preparation for the move, the Klemperers must decide what they are taking and especially what they are not taking. The difficult and crowded conditions at the Jews' House mean that they can only take a small portion of their belongings. The most significant decision for Klemperer concerns his books and writings—a decision he charges with broader significance: "Since Friday in the midst of the chaos of the move and myself more actively involved in it than ever before. It's a matter of getting rid of all ballast. We can take very little with us, most has to go into storage. Every day the French collapse makes a bigger impact on the move. The victory of Hitler's Germany seems certain. And since that means every prospect of us returning to our old hearth disappears, I should like to extend the concept of ballast to almost everything I own and am virtually ravaging my past." What is so striking in this passage is the way in which the constraints of reality that prevent Klemperer from taking most of his belongings to his new home cause him to turn against his own past. The realistic ballast of the things that he cannot take with him become a metaphoric ballast representing his own past which he wants to destroy, as if responding to the eradication of his future by the Nazis in an analogous fashion—with his own destruction of his past.[23]

This self-destruction is a typical way of coping with the helplessness that lies at the heart of the traumatic experience. In describing the final stage in the formulation of Freudian trauma theory, Jean Laplanche and Jean-Baptiste Pontalis stress the dimension of helplessness. In the face of an attack of fear from without that the ego is unable to regulate, it prefers to create its own "instinctual," internal anxiety, in order to gain control, as it were, over the situation. Laplanche and Pontalis conclude that "The ego is attacked from within . . . just as it is from without."[24]

Note, however, that later in the passage, Klemperer lists the things he is keeping as icons of hope and faith: a number of issues of *Uhu*, in which "there is a breath of freer time" and "a kind of dix-huitième spirit"—that is, the spirit of the French Enlightenment. In the end, he also takes all of the material he needs for the autobiography he is writing, which indicates an effort to preserve his past and hold on to it in order to constitute a future of hope and maintain the human order of time. Klemperer's active attitude to his past thus oscillates between destruction and preservation.

Childhood Memory: The Obscene Father-of-Enjoyment

The dynamic of time in Klemperer's diaries is complex. The past is not always ravaged by the narrator who thereby obtains some control over his life story. At times, the past is charged with redoubled destructive force and devastates his world without any attempt at control by the narrator. In some way, the past is tarnished by the trauma and, as such, returns to the present and shapes it.[25] This process can be demonstrated through childhood memories, as recounted in Klemperer's diaries.

In some autobiographical writing, particularly posttraumatic, the narrator's childhood memories are significant. The childhood past is perceived in this literature as an autonomous world—protected, open, and looking toward the future. From the protected basis of the past, the future is constructed chronologically—as opposed to the predetermined future of the catastrophe.[26] In Klemperer's diaries from the Nazi period, inverse processes occur.

Childhood memories do not abound in Klemperer's diaries. For this reason, however, the dramatic contrast between the memories that appear in the Weimar diaries and those that appear in the diaries from the Nazi period is all the more evident. During the Weimar period, Klemperer's childhood memories are generally "positive"—that is, they create the foundations of a primal place that is safe and protected and provides hopeful prospects and aspirations.[27] In the diaries from the Nazi period, on the other hand, many if not most of the memories are accompanied by very difficult feelings of fear, guilt, shame, and rejection.[28] These feelings are especially apparent in those parts of the diary in which Klemperer collects every significant event from his childhood that he recalls for use in his autobiography.[29] These are particularly dark memories.[30]

The entry dated 9 October 1938 (Klemperer's fifty-seventh birthday) is illustrative in this context. In the entry, Klemperer touches upon a number of subjects. After noting his particularly fatalistic mood (*allerfatalste*) on his birthday and recalling a troubling and depressing correspondence with relatives who had left Germany, he dedicates a few lines to Jewish reactions to the Munich Agreement, and then goes on to describe, at length, a visit with his sister Margarete (Grete) who was not well at the time.[31]

> All the Judeans write delightedly about the peace that has been preserved . . . they do not see that our fate is thereby sealed. Otherwise it would perhaps have been the death of us; this way of our Negro slavery has been made eternal. Only Grete thinks the way we do. . . . Every person probably has a few details in his mind, emotionally loaded trifles, which overshadow everything else. With Grete it is the story of how on a journey Father ordered a chocolate for himself and only a glass of beer for her, a girl of about fifteen. The antipathy to Father gradually intensifying into hate increasingly preoccupies her (I also remember the apple cake, which he ate by himself, to accompany his pills, while everyone else watched).

At the beginning of the entry—as in many others—Klemperer refers to the sealed fate of the Jews, a fate of slavery worse than death (we must remember that this entry was written even before *Kristallnacht*). Klemperer implicitly assumes here, as elsewhere, that Nazism will last for a very long time, to the point that the "Negro slavery" imposed upon them seems eternal (*äternisierte Negersklaverei*).

The focus of the story now passes to Grete, and the narrator once again appears to detach himself from his narrative. He begins with a generalization—"Every person probably has a few details in his mind, emotionally loaded trifles"—apparently intended to lend force to his sister's story. This is followed by Grete's reminiscence, to which Klemperer adds his own memories, in parentheses, further validating his sister's difficult feelings.[32] The common theme of the two stories is the father's egotism: reserving all enjoyment for himself and not allowing his children to partake.

In this story, the world of childhood is marred, but primarily the figure of the father as a figure of identification is marred.[33] This differs from the "good" autobiography, as seen in other stories, mostly in the Weimar diaries (as we shall see below). Here, in a story told in 1938, the father figure is twisted and hard. It is not the authoritative and protective father who constitutes childhood that is open to the future and enables, even retroactively—after or during the course of the harsh events—the use of such a childhood as an anchor for an autobiographical story with some dimension of therapeutic continuity, as in Saul Friedländer's post-Holocaust autobiography, for example.[34] Nor is it a father figure (as in Hamlet) who returns to instruct the son to repair the damage caused by his death. In the above passage, Klemperer's real father returns in this entry in the form of the Freudian primordial father from *Totem and Taboo,* the "obscene father-of-enjoyment" who reserves all enjoyment for himself (women in Freud, chocolate and apple cake in Klemperer); a father who is the all-powerful protagonist of the destructive fantasy that there was, at one time, at least one man (the father) who possessed all power and all enjoyment exclusively—the fantasy that denies the subject (the son) any path of his own to enjoyment.[35]

"Hitler's rise to the status of Führer resurrected this omnipotent, mythical, obscene father, and destroyed the legislation that represents the authority of the dead father [from Freud's *Totem and Taboo*]," argues Jean-Gérard Bursztein.[36] It is therefore interesting that Klemperer's own father is tinted here with the colors of this cruel father figure of enjoyment that dominated Germany at that time. And we must remember that this was in the period following the Munich Agreement, when Hitler appeared to be getting everything he wanted, while taking pleasure in the misery of others without suffering any consequences.[37] Klemperer's father figure would thus appear to have been in a way recast in his diary in the image of the cruel regime. The significance of this is that the autobiographical past (the story of his childhood and the figure of his father) was contaminated by the traumatic present.[38]

This father figure is very different from the ones described in the Weimar diaries. The differences can be defined by comparing this story to one with similar components, recounted in an entry dated 6 August 1927. In this entry, Klemperer describes how his father, who was in conflict with his community over his liberal tendencies, went to Berlin to look for work in the assimilationist liberal community there, better suited to his own radical assimilationist views:

> It seems that Father had just been hired in Berlin. This was an even greater liberation for him than it would have been for me to work as a lecturer in Berlin, because he broke free from Orthodoxy and moved to a Reform congregation. "Everything went well, thank God—Wilhelm," he wrote in a telegraph he sent to Mother after his trial sermon. And the "thank God" was so typical of him. I believe that sometimes he truly believed [in God] and always wanted to believe and considered it a proper thing. And now, secret shopping with Mother in Bromberg. She bought some pork in a Christian shop (in Bromberg!).... Nearly 40 years have passed since then—the passage to Germanness has always remained, for me, the loftiest thing.[39]

Here too the protagonist is the father, who seeks to fulfill his most ardent desires. While in the previous story, written during the Nazi period, the father's desires were perceived as selfish and denying enjoyment to the other members of the family—in this story, the distant father (away in Berlin) establishes a new law (Reform in place of Orthodox) that allows the entire family access to enjoyment. By virtue of his desires, the mother may now satisfy her own desires (for pork) for the whole family. The entire affair signifies, for the young Victor, a new direction and identity: toward Germanness.

It is interesting to note that the earlier story (1927) appears in the context of a reaffirming and encouraging message, in light of the anti-Jewish atmosphere in Germany at that time. The later story, on the other hand, is evoked by analogy to the anti-Jewish stance of the Nazi regime. The father figure in the earlier story enables Klemperer to struggle for his identity—and even demands it—whereas the father figure in the later story embodies Klemperer's capitulation to the Nazis who sought to deny him his identity and even his life. This parallel between the way in which past memories are shaped and the political reality in the diary writer's present, assumes a teleological nature in 1942, the year of deportations and terror, when the diary changes character entirely.

In late 1941, the situation of the Jews in Germany in general and in Dresden in particular took a turn for the worse, and this is very evident in Klemperer's diaries. Beginning in September of that year, the Jews were required to wear the "badge of shame," a decree Klemperer described as the most terrible that had befallen the Jews of Germany. In October, deportations of Jews from Berlin and elsewhere began. Many of the deportees, especially those sent to Riga and Minsk, were murdered as soon as they got off the trains. Rumors of this reached Klemperer's ears and he reports on them in the diary. This wave of deportations ended in January 1942. In that same month, some one thousand of Dresden's Jews received deportation notices, but their deportation was postponed due to the intervention of the factory owners who desperately needed working hands and as a result of problems that had arisen in the process of deporting the Jews from the Reich, in general. The deportations resumed in the spring, and by the end of the year, nearly all of the Jews of Dresden had been deported. There was an overriding atmosphere of terror and fear. Arbitrary arrests, extremely violent house searches by the Gestapo and suicides became a matter of daily routine. At the same time, food rations were cut drastically, especially for Jews, and Klemperer suffered hunger all the time. This was coupled with a general feeling of uncertainty regarding the fate of the deportees and those who had not yet been deported, and—of particular interest to Klemperer—the fate of mixed couples. Klemperer's (entirely justified) existential feeling throughout this period was that his life lay in the balance and he could die, be murdered, or deported at any moment.

By the summer of 1942, the Final Solution had been implemented in full force throughout Europe, and the Jews of Dresden clearly felt this. Alongside the deportations to Poland and to Theresienstadt, there were a series of inexplicable murders and incarcerations of acquaintances and relatives of some of the residents of the Jews' House on Caspar David Friedrich Strasse. Klemperer knew most of them and was even on friendly terms with some. One of the murdered men, Paul Kreidl, was in fact one of Klemperer's closest friends. The presence of violent death was felt everywhere, at all times.

At that time childhood memory appears in the diary as a nightmare. On 27 July 1942, Klemperer recalls his childhood nightmares that had now become reality: "When I was young I often had a nightmare in which I was going to be executed, and now the nightmare is very likely to come true. I can see a room with gallows and chair before me." At this stage, the gap between present and past collapses. The dream of the past is the reality of the present.[40]

Childhood thus not only fails to function within Klemperer's autobiographical story as a protected reserve from within which he may write and restore some form of continuity to his life story but, in fact, penetrates reality in such a way as to create a shocking distortion of the temporal order. The entry dated 17 August 1937 (before *Kristallnacht* and the war) illustrates this dynamic in another context:

> In the *Stürmer* (which is displayed at every corner), I recently saw a picture: two girls in swimming costumes at a seaside resort. Above it: "Prohibited for Jews," underneath it: "How nice that it's just us now!" [Wir jetzt wieder unter uns sind!] Then I remembered a long forgotten incident. September 1900 or 1901 in Landsberg. In the lower sixth we were 4 Jews among 16, in the upper sixth 3 among 8 pupils. There was little trace of anti-Semitism among either the teachers or the pupils. More precisely none at all. . . . So on the Day of Atonement—Yom Kippur—the Jews did not attend classes. The next day our comrades told us, laughing and without the least malice (just as the words themselves were also only uttered jokingly by the altogether humane teacher), Kufahl, the mathematician, had said to the reduced class: "Today it's just us." [Heut sind wir unter uns.] In my memory these words took on a quite horrible significance: to me it confirms the claim of the NSDAP [Die Nationalsozialistische Deutsche Arbeiterpartei—The Nazi Party] to express the true opinion of the German people. And I believe ever more strongly that Hitler really does embody the soul of the German people [*Volksseele*], that he really stands for "Germany" and that he will consequently maintain himself and justifiably maintain himself. Whereby I have not only outwardly lost my Fatherland. And even if the government should change one day: my inner sense of belonging is gone.

Klemperer recounts two incidents: one in the present—about a picture he had recently seen in the *Stürmer*; and the other in the past—about the "altogether (*durchaus*) humane" mathematics teacher Kufahl. Neither of the incidents, however, possesses independent meaning. The picture in the *Stürmer*, although it occupies all of the terrain (it is "displayed at every corner") is not that threatening or even that significant in and of itself, which is why it is not the focus of Klemperer's story. Nor is the second incident, the one from the past, significant in itself. When it occurred, he ascribed no importance to it and certainly not anti-Semitic significance.

In retrospect, however, the earlier incident gains new meaning and becomes very significant. It is an event that undermines Klemperer's identity because it seems to attest to the fact that Hitler is not merely a passing episode but embodies the essence of the German nation. It is incontrovertible "evidence" in the discussion that Klemperer conducts with himself throughout the diary whether true Germanness is the one that Hitler represents or the one that he represents. It now becomes clear to him, looking back, that it is Hitler who represents true Germanness and not only is he (Klemperer) utterly excluded from that Germanness but he is doomed to be persecuted by it.

The first incident thus presents a paradox. On the one hand it is indeed a terrible and meaning-laden event that acquires destructive power over the author but, on the other hand—as an anti-Semitic incident—it never happened. When the incident with the mathematics teacher occurred, in 1900 or 1901, it lacked all anti-Semitic significance and, therefore, as an anti-Semitic event, it never happened. It was merely a harmless, amusing episode. Klemperer stresses just how much it "never happened," since there was not a trace of anti-Semitism anywhere in the school—neither among the students nor among the teachers. Only in retrospect, within the framework of the story, does the incident assume its ostracizing, offensive, and destructive significance, to become a real event in his life. What this means is that although the first incident preceded the second, which merely duplicates it—at the same time, the second incident came "first," because it is in fact the second incident that constituted the first as a destructive and terrifying event. Thus, the normal order of time between present and past—crucial to the course of the life story—collapses. The present tarnishes the past, which returns to the present to demolish Klemperer's place as a Jew within the social order.[41]

This discussion brings us to one of the central issues in Klemperer's diaries: the undermining of his German identity. Identity is the part of consciousness, psyche, and behavior itself that allows one to perceive oneself as a person on the continuum of time. Narrative identity, as explained in chapter 1, links a person's past to his or her present and enables the person to hope for the future. Klemperer's life story and identity received a terrible blow during the Nazi period and was profoundly disrupted, as we will see below, because the fundamental beliefs on which he built his life were undermined and perhaps even collapsed. The present was disconnected from the past, and the past was undermined in light of the present. Either way, the continuity created by narrative time drastically disintegrated, leaving Klemperer disoriented and helpless.

The Crisis of German Identity and Political Ideology

Like very many German Jews during the Nazi period, Klemperer felt that his German identity—previously so desirable in his eyes—had been radically shattered. At the same time, as we have seen, he also experienced a crisis in his historiosophical approach. Not only was blood—not language or culture—the determining factor for national belonging, but the German essence he had believed so superior suddenly showed a particularly cruel face. Consequently, his identity as a German was radically challenged. Moreover, a Jewish identity in which he had no interest was now forced upon him. With great rapidity, a sweeping change came over his conceptual world, which thus seemed to lose its meaning for him. In the 1930s and 1940s the old value system was cast in a particularly dubious—and even cruel and grotesque—light, suddenly interrupting the course of Klemperer's life toward Germanness. Within a short time, Klemperer's conceptual world and belief system were fundamentally undermined, seeming to lose their validity. A deep rupture was created between his past and present selves. The diary entries from this period express great confusion with regard to this crisis, and Klemperer's assertions in the matter include a number of inconsistencies and internal contradictions that reflect his inner turmoil and confusion.

On 3 May 1943, for example, he tells of a conversation at the Jews' House with a friend, who called Klemperer's baptism "comedy" and argued that Zionism was, in fact, the true response to the situation. Klemperer takes exception to this, and contends, as he does on other occasions, that Zionism itself is a form of Nazism.[42] On 11 May he revisits the subject in relation to a book he is reading—*Tohuwabohu*, by the Zionist author Sammy Gronemann—which interests him greatly. Immediately after noting this fact, he adds that he is now fighting the hardest battle for his Germanness: "I must hold onto this: I am German, the others are un-German. I must hold onto this: the spirit is decisive, not the blood. I must hold onto this: On my part Zionism would be a comedy—my baptism was not a comedy."

Klemperer thus feels that he is fighting the battle for his life story. Zionism, as a Jewish national identity, which he has opposed all his life, poses the most immediate threat to his identity. He therefore states, in no uncertain terms, in this passage and practically throughout the diary, that he views it as a movement that resembles Nazism. At the same time he tries with all his might to hold on to his German identity and to the most significant act he has performed in his life toward acquiring that identity: baptism.

In the diary, however—as the genre allows—there are also many passages that imply the opposite, such as the entry dated 27 October 1937: "I no longer believe in any political change, nor do I believe that a change would be of any help to me. Neither in my circumstances nor in my feelings.—Contempt and disgust and deepest mistrust with respect to Germany can never leave me now. And yet in 1933 I was so convinced of my Germanness." And on 27 March 1942, he writes: "What shakes me . . . is the precariousness of my position as a German"; immediately adding: "Nevertheless: I *think* German, I *am* German—I did not give it to myself, I cannot tear it out of myself."

Sometimes, the narrator allows another character in the diary to represent one of the two voices in the dilemma of identity. Thus, during the course of his work as a forced laborer together with the remaining Jews in Dresden, a debate arises regarding the meaning of Jewishness and Germanness. Surprisingly, Klemperer represents the "Jewish" side; he feels that a chasm has opened up between him and his Germanness, contrary to the position taken by Feder—another Jew—who, despite everything, has stuck to his German identity. Klemperer sums up the argument: "Feder, the student of Lamprecht, was defending my books, my life's work against myself."

This confusion has been described very convincingly by many readers, although they have differed in their interpretations. Steven Aschheim identifies in Klemperer what he calls "multiple identities" but, ultimately, sees Klemperer—beyond all of his ruminations—simply as a liberal.[43] Omer Bartov, on the other hand, considers Klemperer a German intellectual, a typical product of German *Bildung* and one who is able, from his position, to document both sides: the Jewish and the German.[44] Hans-Joachim Petsche summarized Klemperer's identity as follows: "A German nationalist, liberal, cosmopolitan anti-Zionist, anti-Bolshevik, anti-Communist, Jew, perhaps even a Communist? Apparently first and foremost a German Jew whom the Germans turned into a Jew who never again wanted to be one of the losers and nevertheless found himself yet again on the losing side. Could anyone possibly develop less of a clear personality than Klemperer? Neither entirely German nor entirely Jewish, neither a proper liberal nor a proper Communist. His fate is not representative and he is not a typical hero. Klemperer was both anxious and arrogant."[45] For the purposes of this discussion, beyond the uncertainties of Klemperer's identity in and of themselves, it is important to note the ways in which they are embedded in the rhetorical and narrative structures of his diary. Close reading of a number of relevant, key passages in the diary may serve to illustrate the complexity of the matter, both in terms of the act of writing and in relation to the rhetorical means that constitute the narrative. The rupture between past and present strongly manifests itself on both levels, and Klemperer's narrative identity is caught in deep crisis.

The entry dated 9 October 1938 deals with various aspects of the Klemperer family's collapse, and mentions three authority figures. In this entry, as we have seen, Klemperer's fantasy regarding his father is evoked by analogy to the political reality of Nazi Germany.[46] On both planes, the figure is an obscene one who keeps all enjoyment for himself while, at the same time, denying enjoyment to the author. In the same passage, however, another father appears alongside Klemperer's biological father and Germany's political father (Hitler)—a dual father figure of political ideology: "Voltaire and Montesquieu." This reference comes at the end of a passage that begins with the author mentioning his birthday and, as noted, deals mostly with the disintegration of the family. The passage concludes as follows: "Whatever may happen politically, inwardly I am definitively changed. No one can take my Germanness away from me, but my nationalism and patriotism are gone forever. My thinking is now completely a Voltairean cosmopolitanism. Every national circumscription appears barbarous to me. A united states of the world, a united world economy. This has nothing to do with cultural uniformity and certainly nothing at all to do with Communism. Voltaire and Montesquieu are more than ever my essential guides." Although not stated explicitly, the role of the ideological fathers in this passage can be read in direct relation to its central theme—the lamented disintegration of the Klemperer family, scattered across the globe. Voltaire and Montesquieu, in their cosmopolitan approaches, offer an ideological basis for an alternative family story, one that is not necessarily bound to a single homeland—Germany.[47] This serves as a kind of rectification for the aberration in the story of the Klemperer family, many of whose members have left Germany, thereby abandoning the path set out by their father on his way to Germany and Germanness. The longing he expresses is a response to the sadly, ironic remark he made on 13 June 1934, in light of his nephew's immigration to the United States: "We want to set up a Klemperer colony there"; and to his observation on 23 January 1944: "Father was born in the Prague ghetto. His sons were important men in Germany. His grandsons are in England, America, Sweden.[48] His great-grandsons have Swedish and American blood and will know nothing of him."

It is important to note that, in chronological terms, the cosmopolitan solution intimated in an entry dated 1938 does not appear to have rectified the aberration in the Klemperer family story, as it continues to disturb him even in 1944. The invocation of the new "fathers," Voltaire and Montesquieu, however, was intended to save the Klemperer family story in a much broader sense. What is at stake is the assertion "I am German" that Klemperer fought for years to make his own, which embodies his story on nearly every level. On the one hand, he was forced to struggle with his exclusion from German society, which defined him, against his will, as a Jew. On the other hand, as we have seen, he had to cope with the monstrous manifestations of Germanness that went against everything he believed in. On 18 May 1942, for example, he declares his disappointment at the fact the German people are not the chosen people, as he had believed.

Nevertheless, Klemperer continued to insist that he was a true German. He repeats this over and over again. On 21 July 1935, he describes a conversation, during the course of which he declared: "I am German forever, German 'nationalist.' . . . The Nazis are un-German." On 30 May 1942, in a conversation with Marckwald, he considers the problem faced by the entire assimilated generation—it is impossible to return, nor is Zionism a solution as far as he is concerned. Therefore, "Perhaps it is not at all up to us *to go, but rather to wait*: I am German and am waiting for the Germans to come back; they have gone to ground somewhere."[49] Alongside such statements, however, Klemperer also expresses the understanding that he is not free to decide his identity, unilaterally. In point of fact, it is determined by powerful, external factors. On 16 April 1941, he concedes: "Once I would have said: I do not judge as a Jew. . . . Now: Yes, I judge as a Jew, because as such I am particularly affected by the Jewish business in Hitlerism, and because it is central to the whole structure, to the whole character of National Socialism." That is to say that Klemperer is aware of the fact that the definition of the unique identity of Hitlerism depends upon Jews and that Jewish identity is therefore forced upon him against his will and against his past feelings.[50] He thus finds himself in a situation in which his self-perception is not supported by the social and political structure, and he must recognize that. And indeed, the insight that his Jewish identity is forced upon him and controlled by the role assigned to him by Nazism is repeated a number of times in the diary.

However, opposite the political structure dictated by definitions of race that deny him his Germanness, Klemperer presents, in the spirit of *Völkerpsychologie*, the language that compels his German identity. On 28 January 1943, for example, he writes: "Belonging to a nation depends less on blood than on language.... But all the elements of culture which one absorbs consciously or unconsciously, are carried along by the river of language.... If I have grown up in a language, then I am under its spell forever; I can in no way, through no act of my will, withdraw from the nation whose spirit lives in it and no stranger's command can detach me from it." His identity, which ties him to his fate, thus comprises both his present external image in the eyes of the Nazis, as a Jew, and the language into which he was born and in which he was raised, as a German.[51] Klemperer tries to resolve this antagonism in the passage on Voltaire and Montesquieu.

The narrative assertion "I am German" is largely contingent upon another question with which Klemperer grapples: "What is Germanness?" Prior to the Nazi period, Klemperer had clear views on this matter. He believed in the idealistic principles of *Völkerpsychologie*, whereby every people has its own transcendent essence—the soul of the nation, embodied in the manifestations of its historical and cultural development. Klemperer saw Germanness as the greatest of all national spirits, inasmuch as it is based on individual fulfillment and the realization of individual potential.

Klemperer was puzzled by the concrete manifestations of the spirit of the German nation during the Nazi period—so different from everything he believed in. From the perspective of that time, the essential characteristics of Germanness appeared to be cruelty, collectivism, and deprivation of freedom. His past views and the present political reality were constantly colliding, severely rupturing his narrative identity. Thus, as early as 25 April 1933, he writes: "And all my faith in national psychology—where has it gone? Perhaps the current madness is indeed typically German"; and on

21 July 1935, he declares: "My principles about Germany and the various nations are beginning to wobble like an old man's teeth."[52]

In a certain sense, Voltaire and Montesquieu, the new "fathers," indeed help him to overcome these obstacles and to narrate a new life story that constitutes and supports a cosmopolitan identity at the expense of national identity and nonnationalist German cultural identity. Moreover, since Klemperer had put all of his academic energy into the study of French literature—giving considerable weight to Voltaire and Montesquieu—he succeeds, in this passage, in retroactively constituting his past as a scholar of the writers of the French Enlightenment, in whose footsteps he was following. This retroactivity acts as a kind of bridge and healing. The continuation of the story, however, provides a number of reasons to suspect that the retroactively erected bridge to the past is not only a connective and identity-constituting bridge, but also the embodiment and replication of the problem of identity and his painful breach with the past.

First of all, this entry, dated October 1938, is the only time in the diary that these two "fathers"—Voltaire and Montesquieu—are mentioned as the author's ideological forebears. Up to this point they appear only in the context of academic papers on which Klemperer was working at the time. In effect, this is the last time the two philosophers are mentioned until the end of the Nazi period. Furthermore, this passage—perhaps the most famous in Klemperer's diaries, quoted countless times as an expression of his humanist and universalist approach—is actually quite unusual and unrepresentative of the diaries as a whole.

Of all the passages in which Klemperer discusses German identity, there is no other in which he explicitly expresses such a radical proposal for the neutralization of the formative powers of the national framework. What is more, this is the only passage in which he makes a clear distinction between Germanness and German nationalism, and the only one in which his considerations on identity focus on his cosmopolitan consciousness rather than on his Germanness—while his declaration that no one can take his Germanness from him is incidental. In other words, it is a radical exception within the narrative statement: while the focus of all the other passages is the statement "I am German," here the focus is the statement "I am cosmopolitan." This uniqueness raises the suspicion that within the narrative framework of the diary, this statement functions as a false narrative statement.

The emotivity of the language, as revealed in a close reading of this passage, also points to the fact that, ultimately, the entry leaves the author without ideological fathers. Although he declares that "inwardly I am definitively changed" (*ich bin innerlich endgültig verändert*), the passage is formulated not as a retroactive testimony to inner change that has actually taken place but as a caricature of a political manifesto. Contrary to Klemperer's usual, moderate, prosaic style, the phrases here are short, absolute and filled with pathos: "*No one* can take my Germanness away from me"; "My nationalism and patriotism are gone *forever*"; "My thinking is now *completely* a Voltairean cosmopolitanism"; "*Every* national circumscription appears barbarous to me"; "This has . . . *nothing at all* to do with Communism."

On one level of the text, the narrator acquires the power to constitute his identity, but this power is immediately revealed to be a caricature on another level. This is clearly a case in which, as Paul de Man argued, what the text actually does is far more important than what it says about what it does.[53] The exaggerated rhetorical investment in categorical declarations overturns them, making them sound almost like self-parody. They express the tremendous effort invested in an artificial and failed attempt to create a new ideology and identity.[54] Practically, identification with them cannot recuperate his life story, and that is why these fathers are not mentioned again in the diary.

It goes without saying that a single quote cannot epitomize the complexity of Klemperer's identity—but if we ascribe some particular meaning or status to Klemperer's last direct reference in the diary to the subject of identity, a very different picture than the one portrayed in the previous entry emerges. On 15 January 1945, Lewinsky, one of Klemperer's Jewish friends who had remained in Dresden, reported that Nuremberg had been heavily bombed. Lewinsky was outraged, in the spirit of the Nazi press, at the "British terror raids" that had destroyed cultural treasures and churches. Klemperer angrily responds: "I asked him whether he knew who had destroyed the synagogue in Nürnberg and the Tower of London, whether he knew how many factories in Nürnberg were working to keep the war going. I told him I began to see red if I just heard the words 'German culture.'" Klemperer does not merely justify the massive bombing of the city of Nuremberg for practical reasons or revenge. He adds a remark that reveals his views on German culture in general and casts doubt on the validity of his distinction between German culture and German nationalism, on which he sought, with such certainty, to base his German identity in 1938. It thus seems that the French ideological fathers also fail to create sustainable continuity between the past and the present, and they too keep all of the understanding for themselves.

Nazi Control over the Future

Once the sense of temporal continuity has unraveled, when the present is trapped within itself and the past disintegrates, burying the writer beneath it, we can expect there to be no sense of future—that is, as consciousness expecting and hoping in the present for what will occur in the future. And indeed, in the diary, many statements attest to the absence of a future, related to the devastating belief that the Nazi regime will last forever and the lack of hope in the possibility of its collapse or destruction in the near or distant future. At the same time, however, the diary also contains many expressions of expectation and hope for the future.

Contradictory statements appear from the very beginning of the Nazi period. On 20 April 1933, less than two months after the Nazi rise to power, Klemperer writes: "I almost believe now that I shall not see the end of this tyranny. And I am almost used to the condition of being without rights." A few days later, on 25 April, he quotes from remarks he has heard from Jews: "There is no salvation." On 4 November 1934, on the other hand, he approvingly cites the words of an acquaintance who does not believe that it will go on for much longer (but he immediately adds that these words of encouragement only help for a moment).[55] Of course, such statements are not unique to Victor Klemperer. Willy Cohn of Breslau, for example, writes on 24 June 1933: "We have gotten used to not thinking much about the future."[56]

In later entries, the pendulum continues to swing back and forth. On 3 May 1939, for example, after having declared that, contrary to the position he presents to friends, he himself is without hope, Klemperer asserts: "But all ifs and thinking about the future are pointless now." On the other hand, in the final entry for 1939, four months after the outbreak of the war, he concludes that although their situation has worsened in comparison to the previous year, he feels much better because in the previous year everything had been at a standstill (note: this is the most immediate expression of temporal collapse) and now there is movement. He therefore declares without hesitation: "I am now convinced that National Socialism will collapse in the coming year." He thus continues to oscillate between the two extremes until the end of the period.

How then should these contradictory statements be understood? Can one type of statement be considered a more faithful and authentic reflection of Klemperer's feelings, or are both feelings equally faithful and authentic? Or perhaps the question should be: how do the different statements function within the text and how do they restore or undermine the author's life story?

I believe the latter question to be the more apt and what we see are, in fact, two aspects of the perception of time experienced by Klemperer. Looking at it in this way, we may identify two distinct levels within the text. One level is very realistic: Klemperer feels that the future leads to catastrophe and death. The other level is more imaginary: the future with which he would like to identify is one in which Hitler is defeated and his own nightmare comes to an end. This future is not based on any political timetable, in the context of which it might appear possible as a concrete reality, and is therefore experienced as an imagined and wishful option.[57] And indeed, after a number of disappointments, Klemperer himself expresses the fear that his belief in Hitler's downfall is merely a fantasy with no basis in reality. On 14 October 1940, he writes: "Is it not perhaps autosuggestion, if I keep on knocking it into my head: Hitler is losing the game? The present state of play could not be more opaque."

What is interesting is that Klemperer is not aware that the opposite extreme of autosuggestion—that of utter despair—is no more realistic or sober. Proof that his negative analysis is inexorably linked to his subjective state can be found in the fact that he does not change his position even after the German army has suffered a series of defeats. On 1 January 1943, for example, after the defeat of the German army in North Africa and on the eve of its collapse in Stalingrad, he tells how he has lost his ability to imagine a different future:[58]

> Herbert Eisenmann reported a proclamation by Hitler to the soldiers at the front and to the people. In this year of 1943 he will achieve a "clear final victory." Eisenmann senior again expressed the opinion that the regime will collapse in March.—Frau Eiger . . . paid us a New Year's visit. To her and Lewinsky I maintained categorically that the regime is close to breaking down—so categorically that I almost talked myself into it. But in my heart of hearts I am quite without hope. I am no longer capable of imagining how I could ever live without the star [badge] as a free man again and in tolerable financial circumstances.[59]

In this story, two figures represent diametrically opposed views of the future: Hitler is convinced that he will bring complete victory within the year and

Eisenmann is certain that the regime is on the verge of collapse. Outwardly, Klemperer identifies with the position presented by Eisenmann. In his heart of hearts, however, he identifies with Hitler's perspective, which makes it impossible for him to imagine himself in the future as a free man. This mechanism of identification is far more decisive than realistic reports from the battlefields of Europe and North Africa. Indeed, it seems that the more time passes, the more pessimistic Klemperer becomes, as a single perspective takes control of his view of his future—the perspective of the most terrible other: the Nazi. The cruel other decisively influences his perception of the future, and on one occasion, Klemperer takes note of this, almost explicitly. On 2 September 1938, during a period of increasing radicalization of anti-Jewish policy and a strengthening of Germany's international standing (following a series of achievements—most importantly the annexation of Austria, the Sudeten crisis, reinforcement of the alliance with Italy and a change of the balance of power within the alliance, in Germany's favor), he writes: "I no longer believe in these predictions of collapse. . . . I am gradually beginning to believe as firmly in the unshakability of the NSDAP *as if I were a sworn supporter*. . . . Thus are our hearts very dejected, each day a little more" (emphasis added). This tendency is also evident much later, in 1944—a year in which it was already clear to everyone (including Klemperer himself) beyond a doubt that the war had been decided in favor of the Allies. Thus, on 8 June, when he hears word of the Allied landing at Normandy, he writes: "I can hardly imagine living to see the end of this torture, of these years of slavery." These words are similar in spirit to the difficulty described by Primo Levi in the far more difficult circumstances of the concentration camp: "We all said to each other that the Russians would arrive soon, at once; we all proclaimed it, we were all sure of it, but at bottom nobody believed it. Because one loses the habit of hoping in the Lager."[60]

We thus complete a full circle. The past, the present, and the future are not the same in Klemperer's diary as they are supposed to be structured in a "life story" as theorized by Paul Ricoeur. In his book *Time and Narrative*, and in a further series of articles, Ricoeur claims that there is a correlation between narrative and the nature of the human experience of time.[61] Ricoeur's model is grounded in the Augustinian theory that human time is a threefold present.[62] According to Augustine, the past and the future have being in the human experience only inasmuch as they subsist in the conscious present—the past in the form of memory and the future in the form of expectation or hope. The present itself, on the other hand, exists as the "attention" of consciousness as it transfers events from the future (as expectation) to the past (as memory). Following Augustine, Ricoeur claims that the congruence between this conception of time and narrative time is virtually complete and that is why narrative enables the creation of continuous and dynamic identity. The epistemological and structural point of departure of this temporal system is the primary, immediate existential experience of the present—which, as noted, comprises three dimensions. In Klemperer's diary, however, as I have shown, this system is completely disrupted. The past in the present does not function as memory, the future in the present does not function as expectation or hope, and the present is not a kind of attention to reality that enables the motion of time but primarily an infinite eternity of numb and apathetic repetition.

Nevertheless, there is one plane on which the temporal systems appear to endure, but it is a plane on which the future rather than the present serves as the Archimedean point of departure. And although, as we have seen, the future—that is, expectation occurring in the present—practically ceases to exist in Klemperer's diaries, there is at least one area in which it seems to exist as a time-constituting dimension: "Studying, as if I were completely certain of tomorrow! It is the only way to keep one's chin up," writes Klemperer on 19 August 1942.[63] In other words, the future dimension exists in direct relation to Klemperer's intellectual activities but, as he notes, its existence depends on a certain kind of "as if." This imagined dimension that comes into being in relation to his intellectual pursuits—and especially, as we shall see, in the context of the task of documentation that he has taken upon himself—is the subject of the next chapter.

Notes

1. The feeling that reality is a fairy tale is also present in the diaries of camp prisoners. See Renata Laqueur Weiss, "Writing in Defiance: Concentration Camp Diaries in Dutch, French and German. 1940–1945" (PhD diss., New York University, 1971), 67. See also, for example, the June 1942 testimony of an anonymous prisoner from Slovakia who escaped from Majdanek: Livia Rothkirchen, *Hurban Yahadut Slovakia: Te'ur Histori Bete'udot* [The destruction of Slovak Jewry: A documentary history] (Jerusalem: Yad Vashem, 1961), 166–167; and Fela Szeps, *Balev Ba'arah Hashalhevet: Yomanah shel Fela Szeps* [A blaze from within: The diary of Fela Szeps] (Jerusalem: Yad Vashem, 2002), 23. See also David Patterson, "The Collapse and Recovery of Time in the Holocaust Diary," *Modern Jewish Studies Annual* 9 (1994): 133n17.

2. Victor Klemperer, *I Will Bear Witness: A Diary of the Nazi Years, 1942–1945*, trans. Martin Chalmers (New York: Modern Library, 2001), 357.

3. This discrepancy between historical and subjective time toward the end of the war is mentioned in other diaries as well. See, for example, Hanna Lévy-Hass, *Diary of Bergen-Belsen: 1944–1945*, trans. Sophie Hand (Chicago: Haymarket, 2009), 48–49 (entry dated 30 August 1944).

4. In general, we may discern two temporal systems: one pertaining to dates, within which a given date can be placed before or after another—that is, "objective" time; and the other to perceptions of the past, present, and future in the human experience. At a certain point, for Klemperer, the two temporal systems appear to have collapsed. Similarly, Pal Kovacs, a Hungarian Jew interned at the Neuengamme camp, reports a debate between the prisoners at the beginning of 1945—whether a new year had begun for them or whether the new year would only begin after liberation, as some claimed. Kovacs, "Yomano shel Pal Kovacs" [The diary of Pal Kovacs], *Dapim Leheker Tkufat HaSho'ah* 1 (1979): 242.

5. Three-dimensional time on which Augustine, and subsequently Ricoeur, based the human experience of time as narrative time. See Paul Ricoeur, *Time and Narrative*, 3 vols., trans. Kathleen McLaughlin and David Pellauer (Chicago: University of Chicago Press, 1984–1988).

6. When Yitskhok Rudashevski is forced to leave his apartment and move to the Vilna ghetto, he writes (6 September 1941): "I think of nothing: not what I am losing, not what I have just lost, not what is in store for me" (Yitskhok Rudashevski, *The Diary of the Vilna Ghetto, June 1941–April 1943*, trans. Percy Matenko [Jerusalem: The Ghetto Fighters' House, 1973], 32).

7. For such tendencies in postmodern literature, see Ursula K. Heise, "Chronoschisms," in *Chronoschisms: Time Narrative, and Postmodernism* (Cambridge: Cambridge University Press, 1997), 11–76.

8. Marguerite Sechehaye, a psychiatrist who edited the diary of a schizophrenic girl, makes precisely this point: Sechehaye, *Autobiography of a Schizophrenic Girl* (New York: Grune and Stratton, 1951), xi.

9. Awareness of a "pseudo-normal" reality that affords the illusion of stability and security also appears in the diary of Herman Kruk from the Vilna ghetto. Following the first wave of murders, in late 1941, the ghetto enjoyed a long period of "calm." See, for example, the entry dated 22 March 1942 in which Kruk describes a children's recital, during the course of which the words of Y. L. Peretz, "Oh, don't say the world is lawless!" were declaimed (Herman Kruk, *The Last Days of the Jerusalem of Lithuania: Chronicles from the Vilna Ghetto and the Camps 1939–1944*, ed. Benjamin Harshav, trans. Barbara Harshav [New Haven, CT: Yale University Press, 2002], 243). In the Theresienstadt ghetto, this was the essence of existence—"life as if," as Egon Redlich put it in his diary. This is also the title chosen for the printed edition of Redlich's diary: Egon Redlich, *Hayim Ke'ilu: Yoman Egon Redlich Migeto Terezienstat (1943–1944)* [Life as if: The diary of Egon Redlich from the Theresienstadt ghetto (1943–1944)] (Lohamei Hageta'ot: Hakibbutz Hameuchad and the Ghetto Fighters' House, 1984).

10. This theme recurs in many of the diaries. For example, Hanna Lévy-Hass writes in the extreme conditions of the concentration camp: "The horror that surrounds us is so great that the brain becomes paralyzed and completely incapable of reacting to anything that doesn't stem directly from the nightmare *we are presently living through* and that is constantly before our eyes" (Lévy-Hass, *Diary of Bergen-Belsen*, 60 [entry dated 8 September 1944]; emphasis added). And this is how Lévy-Hass begins her diary at Bergen-Belsen: "My whole being seems paralyzed and with each passing day I feel more apathetic about the world outside, less suited to life as it is now" (ibid., 37). An eternal present or the lack of a present are two facets of the same phenomenon.

11. I will cite only a few of the countless examples: On 5 October 1942, Miriam Chaszczewacki, in reference to a kiss from a boyfriend remarks: "It made no impression on me. Is it possible because my thoughts are on the situation? Or because all feelings are now gradually withering away" (quoted in Stefania Heilbrunn, *Children of Dust and Heaven* [Pacific Palisades, CA: Remember Point, 2012], 135). On 4 July 1943, Zelig Kalmanovitch reports: "This week there was considerable agitation, but one no longer becomes excited. The tragic events have no more effect. The final day is being awaited" (Kalmanovitch, "A Diary of the Nazi Ghetto in Vilna," in *YIVO Annual of Jewish Social Science*, vol. 7 [New York: YIVO, 1953], 57). On 25 April 1942, Sara Fiszkin writes: "I feel nothing and care about nothing" (Sara Fiszkin, "Yomanah shel Sarah Fishkin" [The diary of Sara Fiszkin], *Yalkut Moreshet* 2, no. 4 [1965]: 31). As the Warsaw ghetto burns, Calek Perechodnik declares: "The hospital burned for more than twenty-four hours, and all the sick inside burned alive. Their cries were heartrending, but the time had passed when one took heart the adversity of fellow creatures" (Calel [Calek] Perechodnik, *Am I A Murderer? Testament of a Jewish Ghetto Policeman*, trans. Frank Fox [Boulder, CO: Westview, 1996], 157). On 30 June 1944, an anonymous boy from the Lodz ghetto asserts: "We are suffering as no living creature has suffered before, despite the lack of normal human feelings that distinguishes us" (*Yomano shel Na'ar Almoni MiLodz* [Diary of an anonymous boy from Lodz], Yad Vashem Archives, O.33/1032). Avraham Lewin writes on 24 May 1942: "Our hearts are petrified and empty" (Lewin, *Mipinkaso shel Hamoreh MiYehudiyah: Geto Varshah April 1942–Mai 1943* [From the notebook of a teacher at the Yehudiah School: Warsaw ghetto April 1942–May 1943] [Tel Aviv: Hakibbutz Hameuchad and the Ghetto Fighters' House, 1969], 52). Janusz Korczak tells of a particularly shocking incident: "A young boy, still alive or perhaps dead already is lying across the side-walk. Right there three boys are playing horses and drivers; their reins have gotten entangled. They try every which way to disentangle them, they grow impatient, stumble over the boy lying on the ground. Finally one of them says: 'Let's move on, he gets in our way.' They move a few steps away and continue to struggle with the reins" (Janusz Korczak, *Ghetto Diary*, trans. Jerzy Bachrach and Barbara Krzywicka [New Haven, CT: Yale University Press, 2003], 58).

12. 21 March 1933; 25 April 1933; 30 April 1933; 17 June 1933; 9 November 1933. Subsequently, he rarely mentions dullness/numbness or apathy, returning to these themes only in 1938: on 29 June 1938; 2 October 1938; 22 January 1939. This is followed by another hiatus—until 1942, when the subject becomes one of the diary's central themes, up to the end of 1943: 11 May 1942; 2 July 1942; 12 July 1942; 30 August 1942; 6 September 1942; 21 September 1942; 9 October 1942; 13 November 1942; etc. Toward the end of the war, the subject arises again, beginning in September 1944 and very frequently during the course of 1945.

13. Lori Daub and Nanette C. Auerhahn, "Knowing and Not Knowing Massive Psychic Trauma: Forms of Traumatic Memory," *International Journal of Psychoanalysis* 74 (1993): 287–302.

14. See also Willy Cohn's diary entry dated 20 May 1940, in which he describes the German advance in France and concludes, "Everything happens at such rapid pace," while nothing changes for him—he does not even know where his eldest son is, and that is the fate of millions, he adds. Willy Cohn, *Kein Recht, Nirgends: Tagebuch vom Untergang des Breslauer Judentums, 1933–1941* (Cologne: Böhlau, 2006), 797–798.

15. Remarks on recurring conversations, expressing standing time, appear throughout the diary. See, for example, entries from 25 April 1933, a short time after Hitler came to power, and 26 July 1942, at the height of the deportations. I have found no similar observations in the diaries prior to the Nazi period. The significance of this and the extent to which it is directly

related to the trauma itself may be inferred from the fact that in 1942, the year of the deportations, hunger, and terror, Klemperer makes at least eight references to it—more than in any other year (on 7 May, 14 June, 2 July, 17 July, 26 July, 30 August, 29 October, 6 November). One can also find these very same expressions in Willy Cohn's diary of Breslau. See, for example, as early as 8 September 1933: "Actually one hears [in conversations] always the same things" (Cohn, *Kein Recht, Nirgends*, 75).

16. Sidra DeKoven Ezrahi identified two types of representation after the Holocaust: the one frozen, striving to indicate the event itself, and the other a constant, dynamic process of interpretation. Despite the dangers posed by the latter option, DeKoven Ezrahi believes that it offers the possibility of releasing memory trapped in the compulsion to repeat the trauma. See Sidra DeKoven Ezrahi, "Representing Auschwitz," *History and Memory* 7, no. 2 (1996): 121–154.

17. In a previous entry, dated 14 March 1939, Klemperer reports a "standing" conversation with Moral: "Moral was here on the afternoon of the eighth: the same old conversations and fears, nothing new." It is also interesting to note that we find a similar structure (citing someone else expressing regrets about his past) in a far more extreme situation—following the deportations of October 1941—in the diary of Avraham Tory, who quotes a bitter remark by the head of the Judenrat, Elchanan Elkes: "It wasn't worthwhile living for more than sixty years in order to witness a day like this!" (Avraham Tory, *Surviving the Holocaust: The Kovno Ghetto Diary*, ed. Martin Gilbert, notes by Dina Porat, trans. Jerzy Michalowicz [Cambridge, MA: Harvard University Press, 1990], 55).

18. Klemperer hears the news on 8 October and writes about it on the 9 October, his fifty-eighth birthday.

19. The living envying the dead is a recurrent theme in the diaries of the period. See, for example, the words of Hersh Wasser, in the Warsaw ghetto, on 26 May 1942, some two months after the deportations had begun: "The attitude toward death is quite casual. I venture to say that the dead are object to envy. Nobody really has the courage to die but the general opinion is that the dead have already passed through their vale of tears. . . . The living envy the dead" (Hersh Wasser, "Daily Entries of Hersh Wasser," *Yad Vashem Studies* 15 [1983]: 271). In this context, it is interesting to note an expression used by Herman Kruk, in an entry dated 4 April 1943. Wandering around the ghetto, Kruk discovered three vials of poison: "I grabbed them like a drowning man grabs a razor" (Herman Kruk, *Togbuch fun Vilner Geto* [Diary from the Vilna ghetto] [New York: YIVO, 1961], 495). Poison is the final salvation that one grabs as if it could save one from death.

20. The blind religious belief in Hitler was one of the things that annoyed Klemperer the most. See the chapter "I Believe in Him [Hitler]" (*Ich glaube an ihn*): Victor Klemperer, *The Language of the Third Reich: LTI: Lingua Tertii Imperii*, trans. Martin Brady (London: Continuum, 2006), 97–111. The issue also arises in other diaries, although sometimes admiringly or secretly sharing the belief. See, for example, Meir Busak, "Yamim Aharonim Bamahaneh Hagermani Brnenetz (Pirkei Yoman Milifnei 40 Shanah)" [Final days at the German camp of Brnenec (Diary excerpts from 40 years ago)], *Yalkut Moreshet* 41 (June 1986): 182.

21. Szeps, *Balev Ba'arah Hashalhevet*, 42 (Hanukkah 1942). See Milch, *Can Heaven Be Void?*, ed. Shosh Milch-Avigal, trans. Helen Kaye (Jerusalem: Yad Vashem, 2003), 204: "If I could only fall asleep for a few months and wake up after it's all over, a different man oblivious to the past."

22. Very many of the diarists expressed the feeling that the present is unprecedented. David Roskies writes of the ghetto diarists that, until 1942, they felt that they could still evoke archetypes from Jewish literature of destruction, in the sense of "déjà vu" (David Roskies,

Against the Apocalypse: Responses to Catastrophe in Modern Jewish Culture [Cambridge, MA: Harvard University Press, 1984], 220–224. This is certainly true of some of the writers. The Rabbi of Piaseczno, for example, in his homily for Hanukkah 1941, notes a number of terrible historical precedents. Nearly a year later, however, he expressed the following reservations: "Only until the end of the year 5702 [summer of 1942] was it the case that such sufferings were experienced before. However, as for the monstrous torments . . . which the malevolent, monstrous murderers invented against us . . . there has never been anything like them" (Kalonymus Kalman Shapira, *Esh Kodesh* [Sacred fire] [1960; reprint, Jerusalem: Yad Vashem, 1979], 139; Nehemia Polen, *The Holy Fire: The Teachings of Rabbi Kalonymus Kalman Shapira, the Rebbe of the Warsaw Ghetto* [Northvale, NJ: Jason Aronson, 1994], 35, 84, 132–133, 145). See also Moshe Flinker, *Young Moshe's Diary: The Spiritual Torment of a Jewish Boy in Nazi Europe*, trans. Geoffrey Wigoder (Jerusalem: Yad Vashem, 1965), 28 (30 November 1942); and Patterson, "The Collapse and Recovery of Time in the Holocaust Diary," 130. Other writers felt this sense of the present as being entirely without precedent at an even earlier stage. As early as 2 October 1940, Chaim Kaplan, for example, writes: "But never before in our history drenched in tears and blood, did we have such a cruel and barbaric enemy" (Chaim Aron Kaplan, *Scroll of Agony: The Warsaw Diary of Chaim A. Kaplan*, trans. and ed. Abraham I. Katsh [Bloomington: Indiana University Press, 1999], 202; see also 129–130). Dr. Israel Milejkowski, writing in the Lodz ghetto, viewed the phenomenon of the ghetto itself—unrelated to the deportations—as an anomaly in Jewish history (quoted in Alan Adelson and Robert Lapides, eds., *Lodz Ghetto: Inside a Community Under Siege* [New York: Viking, 1989], 149). Klemperer too held a similar view at a relatively early stage of the persecution. According to Eliezer Schweid, all of the Jewish testimonies—from the very beginning of the Nazi occupation—display awareness of the exceptional nature of the events. He notes, however, that these are expressions of feelings of extreme suffering, expressed during the course of the events themselves. See Eliezer Schweid, "Hadilema Hakiyumit Vehamusarit shel Hahitnagdut Hamezuyenet Bageto" [The existential and moral dilemma of armed resistance in the ghetto], in *Kedushat Hahayim Veheruf Hanefesh: Kovetz Ma'amarim Lezikhro shel AmirYekutiel* [Sanctity of life and martyrdom: Studies in memory of Amir Yekutiel], ed. Isaiah M. Gafni and Aviezer Ravitzky (Jerusalem: The Zalman Shazar Center, 1992), 281.

23. Parting from property often means parting from a past. See the observations of the Sonderkommando Zalman Gradowski, regarding precious ornaments, in Ber Mark, ed., *The Scrolls of Auschwitz*, trans. Sharon Neemani (Tel Aviv: Am Oved, 1985), 180.

24. Jean Laplanche and Jean-Baptiste Pontalis, *The Language of Psychoanalysis* (New York: Norton, 1973), 469. See also the first part of Calek Perechodnik's diary (Perechodnik, *Am I A Murderer?*).

25. In many of the diaries, we find the opposite phenomenon: a powerful sense of nostalgia. Nostalgia too gives expression to the destructive detachment from the past—in another way. See, for example, Milch, *Can Heaven Be Void?*, 55–72 . "Every word, and anything else that reminded me of my former life and my family upset me and made me cry" (169). Similarly, Perechodnik, *Am I A Murderer?*, at the beginning of the diary. For a general description of the phenomenon in relation to the epistemology of narrative, see Donald Polkinghorne: "At times it is a discordant experience, as whem we think of the past with regret or nostalgia, making present what can no longer be changed or returned to" (Donald Polkinghorne, *Narrative Knowing and the Human Sciences* [Albany: State University of New York Press, 1988], 129).

26. See Richard N. Coe, *When the Grass Was Taller: Autobiography and the Experience of Childhood* (New Haven, CT: Yale University Press, 1984). This kind of relating to the past

fulfills a prominent therapeutic function in the autobiographies of Saul Friedländer and Aharon Appelfeld. See Saul Friedländer, *When Memory Comes,* trans. Helen R. Lane (New York: Farrar, Straus and Giroux, 1979); Aharon Appelfeld, *The Story of a Life: A Memoir,* trans. Aloma Hallter (New York: Schocken, 2004).

27. In the Weimar diaries, Klemperer relates to the memories collected in the diary as to "paper soldiers" that he cut our and placed in a chest in his childhood, in order to be able to play with them again (see entry dated 15 August 1931). See also Walter Nowojski's assessment of Klemperer's attitude to his memories: Walter Nowojski, afterword to Klemperer, *Leben sammeln, nicht fragen wozu und warm: Tagebücher 1918–1932* (Berlin: Aufbau, 1996), 773–774.

28. See, for example, the following entries: 15 December 1933; 23 December 1933; 12 May 1934; 20 December 1934 (although here the possibility of fixing the past arises); 17 August 1937; 23 September 1937; 9 October 1938; 27 July 1942; 30 December 1942; 24 February 1943; 11 October 1943; 23 March 1945.

29. A detailed study of Klemperer's autobiography, *Curriculum Vitae* (2 vols. [Berlin: AtV, 1996]), is beyond the scope of the present discussion. I will, therefore, limit myself to a brief observation. The image of Klemperer's childhood in the *Curriculum Vitae* is largely based on the childhood memories he extracted from the diaries of the Weimar and Nazi periods. It is difficult to say what the autobiography would have looked like had it been written before the Nazi period. It is especially difficult to imagine the colors in which he would have painted his childhood. Nevertheless, it is clear that in its present form, the autobiography presents a rather dismal childhood. Some of the dynamics that appear in the diary (which will be addressed below) can also be found in the autobiography. Indeed, it seems that the trauma acts upon past events as well, retroactively tarnishing Klemperer's childhood.

30. 23 December 1933; 13 May 1934; 23 September 1937. The childhood memories of Janusz Korczak also deal mostly with death and sorrow. See Korczak, *Ghetto Diary,* esp. 10–11. Here, too, it is difficult to imagine how the memories would have been recounted in other circumstances but it seems that the atmosphere of the ghetto and the problems Korczak dealt with largely shaped his descriptions of the past. In this matter, Korczak himself had a clear opinion. He writes: "Reminiscences hinge on our immediate experience. Reminiscing, we lie unconsciously. This is an obvious fact and I mention it only for the benefit of the most primitive reader" (ibid., 40). See also the memoirs of Noemi Szac-Wajnkranc, written in hiding. Szac-Wajnkranc begins her memoirs with a series of cherished childhood memories. At the center of all of these memories, however, lie a number of disheartening experiences: how her parents thought her very ugly as a child; how she once got lost "and then instead of rejoicing [at my return], I got a spanking from you, Father." Her husband ironically refers to the place in which they met as an "unlucky" place, and both later recall their first fight. See Noemi Szac-Wajnkranc, *Halaf im Ha'esh: Reshimot al Geto Varshah Shenikhtevu Bemahbo* [Gone with the fire: Notes on the Warsaw ghetto written in hiding (Jerusalem: Yad Vashem, 2003)], 19–20.

31. For many who wrote diaries during the Holocaust, birthdays (as well as year-ends) often served as a point of departure for reflections on the subject of time. For example, Rudashevski writes, on 10 December 1941: "It dawned on me that today is my birthday. Today I became 15 years old. You hardly realize how time flies. It, the time, runs ahead unnoticed and presently we realize, as I did today, for example, and discover that days and months go by, that the ghetto is not a painful, squirming moment of a dream which constantly disappears, but is a large swamp in which we lose our days and weeks" (Rudashevski, *The Diary of the Vilna Ghetto,* 103–104). See also Rose Jakobs, *Yomanah shel Na'arah Bemahbo Bishnot Hasho'ah* [Diary of a girl in hiding during the Holocaust] (Israel: privately printed, 2002); and Mary Berg, *The Diary of*

Mary Berg: Growing Up in the Warsaw Ghetto, ed. Susan Lee Pentlin [Oxford: Oneworld, 2009], 98–101 [10 October 1941]). Particularly poignant are the words of a little girl in Theresienstadt on her birthday, quoted by Egon Redlich: "Last year, news came on my birthday that my father had died, this year they put my grandmother on a transport, also on my birthday. What will happen next year? What kind of disaster will take place?" (Egon [Gonda] Redlich, *The Terezin Diary of Gonda Redlich*, ed. Saul Friedländer, trans. Laurence Kutler [Lexington: University Press of Kentucky, 1992], 60 [27 July 1942]).

32. Again, as in the previous passage, the narrative structure is progressively restrictive, beginning with a general observation on the nature of human memory, proceeding with what appears to be the focus of the story—his sister's hatred toward their father—and concluding with Klemperer's own memories, confined within parentheses, which support Grete's feelings, to some extent. The author's hesitancy in revealing his own memories (in parentheses), in the context of the autobiographical genre, where the signified is always the "I," reverses the intranarrative hierarchy. In my opinion, Klemperer himself is the main character, while Grete plays a secondary role, similar to that of most secondary characters in autobiographical narrative—to help define the main character. This is, of course, the main function of secondary characters in general. See Joseph Ewen, *Milon Munahei Hasiporet* [A dictionary of narrative fiction] (Jerusalem: Akademon, 1978), 49.

33. A similar father figure arises from Korczak's reminiscences written in the ghetto, See, for example, Korczak, *Ghetto Diary*, 29–36. Later, Korczak recounts a series of terrible dreams, one of which includes an inverse, beneficent figure—his father, pushing cake into his mouth. Korczak awakens in a sweat and "at the most crucial point" (ibid., 72).

34. See Sidra DeKoven Ezrahi, "See under: Memory: Reflections on When Memory Comes," *History and Memory* 9, nos. 1–2 (1997): 364–375.

35. This father figure appears already in Freud, in *Totem and Taboo*. There, Freud outlines, on the collective-historical plane, the figure of a primordial father, ostensibly very similar to the Oedipal father who acts on the plane of subjective development. The two figures in fact differ from one another in two decisive senses. First, the Oedipal father—the father of the Law—has one wife, like any other man. His enjoyment is, therefore, limited from the outset. The primordial father, on the other hand, controls all of the women and his enjoyment is complete. Second, the prohibition against enjoyment that the Oedipal father imposes on the son—the prohibition against sexual involvement with the mother—is perceived as an external prohibition, thereby the possibility that were the external obstacle (the father) to be removed, the son could then attain full enjoyment. In the story of the primordial father, however, the murder of the real father by the sons did not resolve anything. Access to enjoyment was even more blocked than before, because the dead father returned in a far more terrifying form: as the "name of the father." According to the Lacanian interpretation, the myth of the primordial father can be a corrective myth, on condition that it is treated as a neurotic fantasy. If, however, we are convinced that there was indeed, at one time, a subject that could attain complete enjoyment, then the path to partial enjoyment—that is to the existence of desire and, hence, to the existence of the vital subject—is blocked. See Slavoj Žižek, *Looking Awry: An Introduction to Jacques Lacan through Popular Culture* (Cambridge, MA: MIT Press, 1992), 23–25.

36. Jean-Gérard Bursztein, *Hapsikho'analizah shel Hanatzizm: Masah al Heres Hatzivilizatzyah* [The psychoanlysis of Nazism: An essay on the destruction of civilization], trans. Miriam Meir (Tel Aviv: Resling, 2004), 42.

37. With regard to the obscene father-of-enjoyment, see, for example, Tory, *Surviving the Holocaust*, 425 (16 July 1943).

38. This father figure appears in such an explicit fashion only once but it seems that like other decisive stories in Klemperer's diaries—it is precisely because they are important junctures of meaning that they materialize only once in the diary and are immediately hidden again beneath the surface. Later in the chapter, I will discuss the case of another unusual passage that expresses a significant truth—only once. We may, however, already cite as an example the story of his opportunistic oath of loyalty to the Führer; an oath he was forced to take in November 1934, in order not to lose his job as a member of the academic staff at the Technische Hochschule in Dresden. This problematic event is reported in the entry dated 20 November 1934, and is mentioned again in the diaries only on 16 July 1936. There, Klemperer shows painful awareness and understands the extent to which this failure limits his moral ability to judge the German opportunism around him. The affair is never mentioned explicitly again, although it is clear that this incident was very significant for him and it is inconceivable that it did not have a long-term effect on the nature of his "life story." In light of other similar cases, this memory might have been expected to surface again in the diaries, yet it does not. For example, in the entry dated 1 January 1939, he tells of a driver who complained about the situation in Germany, and remarks that everyone complains and then immediately says "Heil Hitler!"—as if he had forgotten that he himself had opportunistically pledged his loyalty to the Reich and the Führer. See also the entry dated 10 April 1938, and dozens of others. Klemperer's silence is, of course, no indication of the story's marginal significance. In fact, it is also mentioned in the *Curriculum Vitae,* written after 1939, also in the context of his inability to judge what he always saw as opportunism on his father's part (Klemperer, *Curriculum Vitae,* 1:42). Like this story, revealed in the diary only for the blink of an eye despite its momentous significance, so too the story about Klemperer's father is laden with meaning and is therefore, in my opinion, a constitutive father-figure narrative, stated in the passage in question and reiterated throughout the diary in various ways. A hidden "sin" of this kind can be found in many of the Holocaust diaries, surfacing only rarely but present throughout. In Yitskhok Rudashevski's diary, for example, hovering above the text like a shadow is the sin of having abandoned his grandmother to a certain fate during a deportation action, while the rest of the family went into hiding. See Rudashevski, *The Diary of the Vilna Ghetto,* 44–45. Perhaps that is why he is sensitive to the morally impossible situations in the ghetto, such as when a hungry woman steals food (see ibid., 67–68 [17 October 1942]).

39. The most vivid account appears in Klemperer, *Curriculum Vitae,* 1:44. This is one of the most exuberant childhood stories in the *Curriculum Vitae,* which—as noted above—is generally characterized by a dark mood where Klemperer's childhood is concerned.

40. On the contraction of time, see Freud's "Wolf Man": Sigmund Freud, "From the History of Infantile Neurosis," in *The Standard Edition of the Complete Psychological Works of Sigmund Freud,* vol. 12, ed. and trans. James Strachey (London: Hogarth, 1958), 7–122.

41. For an illuminating analysis of this Nazi sense of "wir unter uns" ("it's just us"), see Peter Fritzsche, *Life and Death in the Third Reich* (Cambridge MA: Harvard University Press, 2008), 65–75.

42. See, for example, the entry dated 3 June 1934.

43. Steven E. Aschheim, *Scholem, Arendt, Klemperer: Intimate Chronicles in Turbulent Times* (Bloomington and Cincinnati: Indiana University Press and Hebrew Union College, 2001).

44. Omer Bartov, *Germany's War and the Holocaust* (Ithaca, NY: Cornell University Press, 2003).

45. Hans-Joachim Petsche, "Victor Klemperer—ein Missverständnis?," in *Victor Klemperers Werk: Texte und Materialien für Lehrer,* ed. Karl-Heinz Siehr (Berlin: AtV, 2001), 248.

46. At this stage, despite the family's collapse, there has been no erosion, as yet, of the concept of family itself, that is, of the possibility of belonging to a family. At Auschwitz, this final bastion collapsed as well. The Sonderkommando Zalman Gradowski writes: "The intoxication of family life fades instantly, and one is left with the deep pain of a surgical operation, immediately on disembarking from the train" (Zalman Gradowski, "Writings," in *The Scrolls of* Auschwitz, ed. Ber Mark, trans. Sharon Neemani [Tel Aviv: Am Oved, 1985], 194). It is a surgical operation for the removal of the very sense of family.

47. This feeling is already apparent in the entries from the beginning of the Nazi period. On 20 April 1933, for example, he writes: "I simply am not German and Aryan, but a Jew and must be grateful if I am allowed to stay alive." This runs counter to the claim of Nathan Stolzfus that, ultimately, Klemperer saw himself as a true German. Klemperer's statements on the subject are, in fact, quite varied. See Nathan Stolzfus, *Resistance of the Heart: Intermarriage and the Rossenstrasse Protest in Nazi Germany* (New York: Norton, 1996), 544. Jean Améry also pointed out the necessity of social context for the creation of identity, especially for the intellectual: "A special set of problems in connection with the social function or nonfunction of the intellect arose for the Jewish intellectual of *German educational and cultural background*. No matter to what he turned, it did not belong to him, but to the enemy. . . . The German-Jewish Auschwitz prisoner . . . could not claim German culture as his possession, because his claim found no sort of social justification" (Jean Améry, *At the Mind's Limits: Contemplations by a Survivor on Auschwitz and Its Realities*, trans. Sidney Rosenfeld and Stella P. Rosenfeld [Bloomington: Indiana University Press, 1980], 8).

48. See also the entry dated 6 March 1936, in which he writes with sadness of the dispersal of his family over the face of the globe.

49. On "waiting time" see Guy Miron, "'The Politics of Catastrophe Races On. I Wait': Waiting Time in the World of German Jewry under Nazi Rule," *Yad Vashem Studies* 43, no. 1 (2015): 45–76. For an extensive analysis of the "time dimension" in German Jewish experience during the Holocaust, see Miron, "The 'Lived Time' of German Jews under the Nazi Regime," *Journal of Modern History* (forthcoming).

50. In a number of places, Klemperer remarks that the Jewish people is an invention of Hitler. See, for example, 28 July 1942.

51. Although it is true that this approach derives from *Völkerpsychologie*, the feeling was shared by other German Jews. See, for example, Hannah Arendt, "What Remains? Language Remains," in *The Portable Hannah Arendt*, ed. Peter Baehr (New York: Penguin, 2000), 3–22.

52. In a previous paragraph in the same entry (as noted above), he declares his loyalty to nationalist Germanness in a conversation with Herr Kaufmann: "I am German forever, German 'nationalist'. . . . The Nazis are un-German." As a narrator, however, he places this declaration in an ironic light, concluding: "That was on 17 July; we felt ill all day on the eighteenth."

53. Paul De Man, *Allegories of Reading: Figural Language in Rousseau, Nietzsche, Rilke and Proust* (New Haven, CT: Yale University Press, 1979). See further Linda Anderson, *Autobiography* (London: Routledge, 2001), 49.

54. For more on the distinction between utterance and enunciation, see the discussion in chapter 1.

55. Oscillation between belief in the nightmare coming to an end and denial of such a possibility is typical of many—perhaps most—of the diaries. See, for example, Shulamit Roethler, "Miyomanah shel Metta Lande" [From the diary of Metta Lande], *Edut* 6 (1991): 85–96. Although considering how historical changes come about, Lande notes: "I, for one, cannot imagine that this will ever end and that we will come through it."

56. Cohn, *Kein Recht, Nirgends*, 55 (*Man gewöhnt sich daran, nicht weit zu denken*).

57. In these two perspectives we see the gap between "symbolic" and "imaginary" identification—a distinction made by Jacques-Alain Miller. At first the subject identifies with the place from which he or she is observed. In Klemperer's case, the gaze is destructive rather than constitutive because he is being observed by the Nazis. The second identification, on the other hand, is entirely imaginary, as we identify with the image of what we would like to be—in this case, someone with future. Reality, however, does not support this image. See Slavoj Žižek, *The Sublime Object of Ideology* (London: Verso, 1989), 105.

58. In a slightly different context, the theme of the eradication of all prospects for the future of the Jews is addressed, in the imperative, by a Gestapo inspector to one of the transportees: "No miracles will happen for you, don't delude yourselves" (8 September 1942). The Nazi prohibition against imagination and hope also appears elsewhere. For example, when the rabbi of the community of Dortmund delivered words of comfort at a funeral in the 1930s and called upon those present to look toward a better future, he was taken to the local police station, where the officers said to him: "How dare you, dirty Jew, tell your people that they should hope for a better time to come?" (quoted in Michael Marrus, "Killing Time: Jewish Perceptions during the Holocaust," in *The Holocaust: History and Memory: Essays Presented in Honour of Israel Gutman*, ed. David Bankier et al. [Jerusalem: Yad Vashem, 2001], 12–13).

59. See also Adam Czerniakow's efforts to publicly pretend that things are fine: Adam Czerniakow, *The Warsaw Diary of Adam Czerniakow: Prelude to Doom*, ed. Raul Hilberg, Stanislaw Staron, and Josef Kermisz (New York: Stein and Day, 1979), 376–377, 382 (entries from 8 and 19 July 1942).

60. Primo Levi, *If This Is a Man/The Truce*, trans. Stuart Woolf (London: Abacus, 2004), 177.

61. Ricoeur, *Time and Narrative*, vols. 1–3. See, for example, Paul Ricoeur, "Life in Quest of Narrative," in *On Paul Ricoeur: Narrative and Interpretation*, ed. David Wood (London: Routledge, 1991), 20–33, and Ricoeur, "Narrative Identity," ibid., 188–199; Ricoeur, *Time and Narrative*, 1:3.

62. Augustine, *Confessions*, trans. Henry Chadwick (Oxford: Oxford University Press, 2008), book X, 179–220.

63. Yitskhok Rudashevski also tells how reading in the ghetto is his greatest pleasure, as books unite him to freedom (see Rudashevski, *The Diary of the Vilna Ghetto*, 106 [entry dated 13 December 1941]). Oskar Rosenfeld too remarks on the pleasure of reading (Rosenfeld, *In the Beginning Was the Ghetto: Notebooks from Łódź*, ed. Hanno Loewy, trans. Brigitte M. Goldstein [Evanston, IL: Northwestern University Press, 2002], 146–147 [4 November 1942]). Janusz Korczak, on the other hand, writes: "Reading as relaxation begins to fail. A dangerous symptom. I am distracted and that itself worries me. I don't want to sink into idiocy" (Korczak, *Ghetto Diary*, 76). In the diary of Tamar Lazerson-Rostovsky from the Vilna ghetto, reading and studying actually represent the absence of hope and a future (see Lazerson-Rostovsky, *Yomanah shel Tamara: Kovno 1942–1946* [Tamara's diary: Kovno 1942–1946] [Lohamei Hageta'ot: The Ghetto Fighters' House and Hakibbutz Hameuchad, 1976], 83 [1 August 1943]).

6

FROM AUTOBIOGRAPHICAL TO DOCUMENTARY DIARY

In this chapter, I will suggest that in the wake of the breakdown of autobiographical temporality, as described in the previous chapter, a new temporal order emerged, deeply connected to the documentary character of the Nazi-era diary. Before reaching this conclusion, however, the chapter will take a rather long detour. The first parts of the chapter are dedicated to depicting the radical transformation that Klemperer's diaries underwent—from the personal-autobiographical to the documentary—the far-reaching ramifications of which will be described at length. Only in the last part of the chapter will I return to the issue of temporality, to suggest that this radical shift in the meaning of the diary also afforded it a new temporal structure, which, I would argue, is what made writing so precious to Klemperer. Let us begin, however, with the basic change in the nature of Klemperer's Nazi-era diary.

Klemperer's Documenting Diary

On 8 April 1944, Klemperer reports a conversation with Stühler—another resident of the Jews' House—in which he explained the purpose of writing the diary:

> "I shall bear witness."
>
> "The things you write down, everybody knows, and the big things, Kiev, Minsk, etc., you know nothing about."
>
> "It's not the big things that are important to me, but the everyday life of tyranny, which gets forgotten. . . ."

Stühler, a little later: "I once read that fear of something is worse than the event itself. How I dreaded the house search. And when the Gestapo came, I was quite cold and defiant. And how our food tasted afterward! All the good things, which we had hidden and they had not found."

"You see, I'm going to note that down!"

Klemperer explicitly states that the purpose of the diary is to bear witness—not to the "big things," but to everyday life under the tyranny of the Nazi regime. As such, his testimony deals directly with the private and intimate domain—his own and that of his surroundings. Nevertheless, the purpose of his writing is not autobiographical in the narrow sense because, ultimately, he describes events that tells us far more about the period than about the individuals caught up in it. His testimony regarding everyday life documents an aspect of tyranny that may be forgotten, as he himself points out.[1] Contrary to autobiographical diary writing, which tries to convey impressions and sights of the present without any need for justification or a declared purpose, documentary diary writing ascribes considerable weight to the future dimension. It is the thought of future oblivion that compels the author to write. The "I" as a witness serves as a kind of window into the "Zeitgeist," recounting it through what the writer has seen and experienced in order to transmit it to the future reader—to the addressee.[2] The focus of the writing (what happened to "me," what "I" saw) is thus an interim phase on the way to the object of documentation (history) and is intended for future readers. In this sense, documentary writing creates temporal continuity between the present and the future.

Beyond documenting everyday life, Klemperer takes two further tasks upon himself in his diary: documenting Nazi language and documenting public sentiment toward the regime, its policies, and its actions. These two tasks are indicated in the diary by means of specific technical terms. The first is referred to as "LTI" (which stands for the Latin "Lingua Tertii Imperii," that is, "Language of the Third Reich") and the second as "vox populi" ("voice of the people," in Latin).[3]

These further documentary tasks also constitute a certain continuity in his writing, as they stem, in many ways, from his previous views. Two central elements of *Völkerpsychologie* are the belief in language as the most significant field for the comprehension of private and collective consciousness and reality, and the belief that each people possesses a typical collective consciousness. At the same time, these tasks also served as conscious and intentional preparation for future writing about the Third Reich, on the subject of which Klemperer deliberated in the diary throughout the war period. He had considered writing a comparative linguistic study of three revolutions—the French, the Communist, and the Nazi—but eventually decided to document events to serve as the basis for two works: one on Nazi language and the other the final part of his autobiography. Writing "as the basis for" largely determines the documentary nature of the diary and, once again, stresses the future dimension.

The documentary task that Klemperer undertakes is laden with meaning for him. It is a role (*Aufgabe*) he must not betray.[4] Writing, for Klemperer, is also heroic: "I shall go on writing. That is *my* heroism. I will bear witness, precise witness!" Klemperer wrote these words on 27 May 1942, after having sent his wife Eva to deposit pages from the diary in their hiding place, while describing the danger this entailed for both of them.

Documentation also sustained him existentially throughout the period. On 24 January 1944, for example, he writes: "Yesterday morning, depressed atmosphere because of Eva's condition, filled up by diary." The extent to which his writing served him as a life preserver, in every sense, is demonstrated by the entry dated 26 July 1942, also written at a time when Klemperer felt the noose tightening around his neck. After a number of his acquaintances and friends from the Jews' House had been murdered—including Frau Voss's brother Joachimsthal, who was murdered for no apparent reason—there was no longer any logic that supported his own prospects of survival. He therefore felt that his chances of survival were fast disappearing. Like him, Joachimsthal was married to an "Aryan." Like him, he owned no property—a possible reason for murder. He also served in World War I, worked in the armaments factory, and was on the list for the last transport. Klemperer was thus directly exposed to the complete arbitrariness of Nazi murder and, naturally, terribly frightened by this—a state of mind he described in the diary. Toward the end of the entry, however, he writes about what saves him, nonetheless: "Again and again I save myself by turning to what is now my work, these notes, my reading. I am not only cold in the face of all the ghastliness, I also take a certain delight in curiosity and its satisfaction: 'So you can also bear personal witness to that, you have also experienced that. Yet another addition to the Curriculum or the *LTI*!' And then I feel brave, because I dare to make a note of everything." Documentation is so important to Klemperer that, for its sake, he is knowingly prepared to risk his life and the lives of others—that of his wife Eva, to whom he entrusts the task of conveying the manuscript to its hiding place; those of the people mentioned in it; and that of their friend Annemarie, who hides the diary in her home. At times he even wonders, in the diary, whether the risk is morally justified. On 27 September 1944, for example, he writes: "My diaries and notes! I tell myself again and again: They will not only cost me my life, if they are discovered, but also Eva's and that of several others whom I have mentioned by name, had to mention, if I wanted them to have documentary worth. Am I entitled, perhaps even obliged, to do so, or is it criminal vanity?" Nevertheless, he continues to write. On 29 January 1945, he mentions yet again the documentary value of the diary as a response to Eva's claim (justified to Klemperer's mind) that he should not have used names, thereby risking the lives of those mentioned in the diary. His role as witness and documenter was thus one for which he was prepared to pay an enormous price.

The Shift from the Autobiographical to the Documentary and Back

This documentary aspect of the diary is not a given. It is, in effect, a significant shift, practically a reversal, compared to the diaries he had kept since the age of sixteen (and those he continued to keep after the war, until close to his death, in 1960). Beyond the marked changes in content and tone—from a melancholy diary to one in which the feeling of terror predominates—there is a complete shift in the role and function of the diary.

As we have seen, the role of the diary during the Nazi period was one of historical documentation. Klemperer defined the role of the diary he wrote before the Nazi period, however, in very different terms, as the following passage from 3 September 1929 demonstrates: "Just to gather life. Impressions, insights, things read, seen, everything. Without asking what for and why; will it become a book or a memoir or nothing; does it amount to my memoirs or does it spoil like a poor photographic plate. Don't ask, just gather. And when it comes out—along with the paper soldiers from the chest."[5] In this type of autobiographical writing, the dominant temporal dimension—as witnessed by the above passage—is the present, which the writing seeks to capture and preserve or, in Klemperer's words, "to gather" (*sammeln*). The future final form this gathering will assume is irrelevant, and the value of the writing does not depend upon it.[6] It is immaterial, he says, whether the writing will ever amount to a coherent story or whether it will remain like the negative image on a spoiled photographic plate. Diary writing must absorb and convey impressions, insights, experiences, and so forth.

Although the present is the most fundamental temporal dimension in Klemperer's diary writing prior to the Nazi period, the past and the future are not completely absent but, rather, converge upon and are subordinate to it, as in the Ricoeurian-Augustinian "threefold present" conception of time. Thus, in the final sentence in the above passage, Klemperer evokes the paper soldiers of his childhood, which he used to cut out and keep in a chest in order to play with again later but which were eventually lost—and even considered calling his memoirs, in the event of their publication, "Paper Soldiers."[7] In so doing, he envelops the present in the past, in the form of a childhood memory that is subordinated to it and serves as an interpretive image, along with the future that emerges from it as an open prospect.[8]

The focus of writing is, according to this passage, the "I," and especially the "self-reflective I"—the one that perceives, understands, and reads. In another entry, dated 1932, Klemperer gives greater weight to the reflective dimension, albeit by negative implication: "It [diary writing] requires affording meaning to oneself. I am far happier when I am working or reading, without awareness."[9] Writing thus demands constant introspection and is of an existential nature. And indeed Klemperer's earlier diaries consciously and intentionally focus on the private and professional spheres. Gathering and reflection are the writing's central characteristics, and the dominant presence of the "I" as an existential protagonist is almost self-apparent. The role of the narrator is limited to reflection and minimal mediation that is as unobtrusive as possible.

The transition from autobiographical to documentary diary that occurred gradually following the Nazi rise to power is not an easy one for Klemperer, and seems to demand apologetic clarifications on the writer's part, regarding the unworthy (i.e., historical) content that finds its way into the diary.[10] The shift from the autobiographical to the documentary would appear to be related—even before it becomes a "role" or "heroism"—to a sense of sin or betrayal. On 21 February 1933, shortly after the Nazis came to power, Klemperer already writes in this vein: "For something like three weeks now the depression of the reactionary government. *I am not writing a history of the times here. But I shall nevertheless record my embitterment,* greater than I would have imagined I was still capable of feeling. It is a disgrace [the German *Schmach* also connotes humiliation], which gets worse with every day that passes. And there's not a sound from anyone and everyone's keeping his head down, Jewry most of all and their democratic press."[11] Some three months later, he concludes the entry dated 15 May 1933, dedicated in large part to "history" rather than to events in his personal life, as follows: "Of the National Socialists' criminal and insane acts I only make a note of what somehow touches me personally. Everything else can be looked up in the newspapers." On 1 August 1934, when powerful historical events (St. Bartholomew's Eve, the murder of Dollfuss in Austria, etc.) find their way into the diary, he writes: "It is not my intention here to register individual historical facts. Only this feeling of holding one's breath."

Klemperer feels that the content of his writing in the diary is changing practically against his will and that the object of observation is no longer the "I." "History" forcefully invades the "private" and, to Klemperer's mind, this requires some sort of explanation. He does not want to document the history of the period, but due to the invasive nature of the historical events he is unable to prevent them from creeping into his text, where they occupy an increasing amount of space. At this initial stage, the justification for their inclusion in the diary lies in the intensity of the events, which have a decisive impact on his feelings and his mood—and as such have a legitimate place in the diary, which still makes a desperate effort to focus on the "I" of the writer. This development is imposed on the diaries and Klemperer is unable to resist it. He can only observe the change and document the tremendous historical forces invading his diary, while expressing his discomfort with the act of documentation itself.

Klemperer's attempts at justification only appear, however, for the first year and a half. Gradually, he willingly assumes the role of documenter and witness that has been forced upon him, and documentary writing becomes a "role" (*Aufgabe*) and "heroism" (*Heldentum*). As we shall soon see, this role also has a restorative value for Klemperer. At the same time, his discomfort is not completely assuaged and it continues to emerge from time to time, mainly toward the end of the Nazi period, but in the opposite direction.

On 1 May 1945, in the Bavarian village of Unterbernbach (the Klemperers' final stop on their flight from Dresden), when Klemperer feels that their situation is relatively safe, he reports on the hearty meat meals they have been enjoying. Their good fortune is due to the fact that the villagers have been slaughtering pigs every day, in order to prevent them from falling spoil to the Russians. Klemperer finds it necessary, however, to add the following: "It is not very elevated of me to mention every single meal, but my picture of the times would be untruthful if I did not do so."

Just as at the beginning of the Nazi era, here again toward its end, we encounter an untypical apologetic ars-poetic statement by Klemperer. This time he apologizes for describing, in the diary, every meat meal he enjoyed so immensely after so many years of hunger. He feels that it is not decent to portray, in the diary, his personal fascination with the meat, and therefore adds an apology—that this is the only way to be true to the documenting mission he has taken upon himself. This apology indicates that some change has taken place in his writing, for which Klemperer feels he should apologize.

I would suggest that what we witness here is, in fact, the hesitant return of the "I-protagonist" to the diary, gradually supplanting the historical events. The detailed references to food are in keeping with this tendency and are no less concerned with Klemperer's personal desire for food, after the long years of hunger, than with the historical circumstances: the chaos of the collapsing regime and the Russian advance. They place Klemperer's desire at the center of the narrative and, in so doing, announce the return of the personal and the private as such. The "autobiographical" seeks, albeit hesitantly and beneath the surface, to regain independent status within the diary, but still needs to be excused in terms of historical and documentary discourse. In other words, the "I-protagonist" seeks to regain the center stage but still needs the permission of the "I-witness." It is precisely in this shift, however, that the power of the "I-witness" becomes apparent. Contrary to the "apologies" of the early Nazi period, in which it was the "autobiographical" that allowed the "documentary" to enter the diary—toward the end of the Nazi period, it is in fact the "documentary" that allows the "autobiographical" to return to the diary. Klemperer excuses this return as stemming from his duty to documentary accuracy.

These ars-poetical apologies effectively demarcate the story of the Nazi period, creating a kind of narrative boundary within the diaries and differentiating an independent narrative segment from Klemperer's life story, the limits of which are drawn by his gestures of apology for moving between the autobiographical and documentary: the first for passing from the autobiographical to the documentary and the second for returning to the autobiographical.[12] And if the boundaries of a story have bearing on the meaning of the story has a whole, we might say that Klemperer's story of the Nazi period is the story of the "sin" of moving from the autobiographical to the documentary.[13]

One of the most interesting expressions of this passage can be found in the sense of apathy and numbness that sometimes accompany it.[14] Numbness is not only documented in the writing, but is often also a necessary condition for it. On a number of occasions, Klemperer refers to this kind of experience as "cinema"—that is, a situation in which he dissociatively and dispassionately observes the difficult events that befall him, as if he were a viewer, watching a scene on a cinema screen.[15] Confronted with invasive and inexorable terror, the documenter develops radical emotional distance—as if the feeling protagonist (the autobiographical "I") makes way for the cold analysis of the documenter.

On 12 July 1942, prior to one of the deportations, Klemperer writes, with regard to their neighbor Frau Voss's mother, who had been slated for transport: "Around midday we are going to visit her mother in the Henriettenstift home. I am curious to take a look at this old people's home twenty-four hours before its evacuation. More curiosity and a kind of sense of duty as a chronicler than pity."

In this harsh passage, Klemperer displays (along with remarkable candor) unusual callousness. He is going to visit the condemned, not out of a sense of pity or compassion or in order to comfort them, but out of the pure curiosity of a chronicler.[16] Klemperer creates a clear contrast between these two qualities—curiosity and compassion—thereby intimating that documentation is a form of insensitivity to the suffering of others, even when that suffering presages his own future.[17] The experiential detachment from events stands at the base of the ability to observe and record. Klemperer essentially admits that he is simultaneously present and not present. He is present as a narrator, driven by curiosity, but as a protagonist who experiences the event together with the other characters, he is effectively not present. It would appear that in the case of a traumatic event, in order for the documenting narrator to survive, the protagonist—as the one who experiences the events—must be considerably reduced, if not eliminated entirely.

Thus, during the course of the Nazi era and in the context of documentation, the power of the documentary narrator gradually increases, eventually attaining primacy over the protagonist experiencing the events.[18] During that time, the main figure of the diary becomes the narrator "I," who observes, records, documents, and narrates, rather the protagonist "I" whose inner life dominates Klemperer's pre- and post-Nazi-era diaries. *Consequently, during this period, real power—all but lost by the protagonist (the real helpless Klemperer persecuted by the Nazis)—passes over to the documenting narrator (who at least has the power to tell the story). And this, in my opinion, is what makes diary writing itself so powerful.*[19] Documentation appears to change the hierarchy between narrator and protagonist, while—no less importantly—maintaining the necessary distance between them. Therein lies its tremendous performative power.

Documentary writing thus affords the writer power and a degree of control. It also, however, exposes the writer to new, no less severe dangers. I would like to examine this dialectical dynamic by means of a long diary entry relating to the eight days in which Klemperer was held in police custody, from 23 June to 1 July 1941, for a one-time oversight in obeying the blackout regulations. The disproportionately harsh punishment was because he was a "non-Aryan"—a fact that was as clear to him as it was to the prison guards, increasing his anxiety that he might be turned over to the Gestapo upon completion of his sentence. Klemperer summarized his experiences a few days after his release and return home, under the heading "Cell 89, June 23–July 1, 1941." This is undoubtedly the most difficult period described in the diary but it was, as Klemperer explains, divided in two: the first four days and the last four days. The dramatic change was wrought by a guard who acceded to his request and, on the fourth day, brought him paper and a pencil. When he received the pencil, Klemperer felt that a significant change had occurred and that the second half of his imprisonment was beginning. His world—or so it seemed to him at first—was suddenly transformed. His comparison between the first four days and the last four days offers considerable insight into the significance of documentary writing and a rare testimony to the power and weakness of writing in a traumatic situation.

Reading the pages of the diary that document the time he spent in jail, and particularly those pertaining to the first four days, it is clear that emptiness was Klemperer's main problem. He says so explicitly, and the words *Nichts* (nothingness) and *Leer* (emptiness) appear dozens of times throughout his account. Note, however, that the emptiness is experienced, first and foremost as the absence of an object.[20] When he compares his relatively clean cell to the dungeons of the past, when prisons were filthy, strewn with straw and vermin, he comes to the surprising conclusion that the prisoners of old were actually better off: "Was the romantic medieval dungeon really any more cruel? Perhaps one suffered less because the torment was greater. Straw and rustling rats and spiders, which one could observe, were, after all, a distraction from the self, the outside world, not the utter bareness, the abstract space of the cell, the naked idea of imprisonment. I had to break free of this idea of emptiness." The terrifying emptiness in Klemperer's condition does not stem, at first, from the absence of self. On the contrary, the "self" is the only thing that exists in the cell. What is entirely absent is an external object of any kind.[21] In this sense, according to Klemperer, the stronger the external stimulus, the less one suffers.[22] The absence of an external object effectively means the collapse of "reality" as a meaningful symbolic order.[23]

This collapse of "reality" external to the self takes shape, as it were, within the prison experience. Klemperer feels that he is in a world where there is no real law but only arbitrariness masquerading as law. Klemperer encounters this (lack of) order immediately on arrival, when he is ordered to hand over his glasses and his books. When he protests, based on his knowledge of prisoners' rights, the reply is "We make the rules here." From this particular case, Klemperer extrapolates to the wider sphere of his life and reaches a general conclusion—expressed most clearly in his prison notes: "There is no law in Germany anymore, only arbitrary power, there is also no equality anymore before arbitrary power." Thus, in Klemperer's world, the encounter with reality occurs in a place where the organizing network of the law does not exist, and this is, of course, one of the reasons that the encounter is so raw and traumatic.[24] In his prison experience, Klemperer therefore approaches what I have called "symbolic death," in which the subject is fundamentally excluded from all differential systems, such as language and law, capable of establishing his or her status and position as such.[25]

Internal collapse soon follows, and the first four days in prison, as he describes them, are unbearable. An example of this is the process that occurs when his wife, Eva, visits him in prison. The results of the visit are catastrophic for him, and his condition rapidly deteriorates. Initially, he considers that for the first time they will be apart on their anniversary, 29 June. Then, in a series of thoughts and confessions that examine their lives together in retrospect, the positive image he had previously held of them as a couple breaks down. He feels, contrary to what he has always believed, that he has been an inconsiderate and selfish husband, who has repressed his wife and been insensitive to her needs. He feels the need to confess all of his sins to her and, at a certain point, appeals to her directly in the diary, in the second person, in the style of confessional literature. As he does so, he lists his sins one by one, finally declaring that he does not believe in the possibility of forgiveness, because the past cannot be changed and because he does not believe he has a future.[26] He also concludes that he has no right to expect empathy and understanding for his actions. His emotional world, at least as far as his relationship with Eva is concerned, collapses following the visit. On this level,

Klemperer very accurately describes his situation when he mutters over and over to his wife: "I am helpless." Thus, as we have seen in the previous chapter, even the past collapses in the face of present and he cannot imagine any future of consolation.

On the fourth day of his imprisonment, however, a fundamental change occurs. A decent guard, upon Klemperer's request, brings him a pencil and paper. It seems to him that redemption has come and, with it, an end to his suffering: "At that moment my life was just as much transformed as when the prison door slammed shut. Everything was lighter again, indeed had become almost light. Suddenly I realized that at midday of this Friday I would have the whole first half of my sentence behind me. Only another four days, and what was so terrible about them, now that I could occupy myself in almost accustomed manner?"[27] The first thing that returns to him upon receiving paper and a pencil stub is the sense of time—albeit not yet the temporal order of the life story, that is, the relation between the three dimensions of human time (past, present, and future). For the moment, he merely reenters the objective dimension of time and regains his perception of the relativity of the four remaining days until his release. Incidentally, however, as he reacquires his initial bearings within "objective" time, a new dimension of time enters the prisoner's life: hope-bearing future time. By means of the pencil, Klemperer reconstitutes himself as a person who is not detached from the temporal plane—in other words, he reconstitutes himself as a historical creature.

In Klemperer's case, all of this happens simply by virtue of the return of the object (the pencil) to his life, even before he writes a single letter. What is more, he delays the writing itself at first, preferring to take pleasure in the idea of possessing a writing instrument and the potential it entails. These things in themselves were enough to repair the sense of collapse he had expressed only a day earlier: "All morning long I did not need to use the pencil at all, simply making plans, the simple consciousness of possessing it filled me entirely. The remorse of the previous day had become much lighter, in fact it had disappeared entirely; in four days we would be together again—a great deal could be made better after all, extenuating circumstances and forgiveness were not worthless after all, and yesterday I had perhaps painted myself in colors that were too dark. Even after the midday meal, the pencil still remained unused for a while." Only in the late afternoon does he take up the pencil and ceremoniously write his first line: "On my pencil I climb back to earth from the hell of the last four days." The pencil restores

Klemperer to earth—to symbolic reality and to the world of human beings. It appears to be a dramatic turning point.

From the moment he actually begins to write, however—not merely taking pleasure in possessing the object and in the potential it represents—comes the fall, and redemption no longer seems so certain. Again, he loses his sense of time, which suddenly comes to a standstill. His self-image is also shattered, once again. When he tries to pass the time by playing word games, he remembers only a handful of famous people whose names begin with the letter "A," and wonders: "Had imprisonment so numbed my memory, was the knowledge contained in my head so modest?"

The status of the pencil is thus paradoxical: it both rescues Klemperer from his despair and leaves him there. Klemperer himself wonders, in retrospect, to what extent the pencil improved his condition.[28]

> The pencil really had made a profound difference to me. On Friday I had spooned up my midday meal for the first time without feeling completely full, afterward I had missed smoking for the first time, and in the evening I had laid down to sleep feeling real hunger and already tormented because I was unable to smoke. And the cell had smelled worse than before, and its walls had pressed in on me more than before. *I had certainly clambered up out of hell on my pencil—but not as far as earth itself, only as far as limbo.* I had only been liberated to the point where I felt the absence of complete freedom more strongly than when I was completely trammeled. If a few hours were more filled, the gaps between them yawned all the more emptily. (emphasis added)

The pencil thus brings about a fundamental change, but it is a change of an unusual sort—one that impels both movement and countermovement at the same time. It arouses both appetite and hunger; the desire to engage in the old habit of smoking and the distress at the inability to do so. It fills the time and empties it again; comprises both presence and absence. The pencil restores the "object" to Klemperer's world, but acts as a missing object. In other words, it evokes the concept of an object for which the writer longs (food, pipe, space, freedom, etc.), but these are experienced as lost objects and therefore provoke deep distress and pain. It rescues the subject from despair and plunges him back into the void—into limbo.[29] The description of time in this passage is particularly interesting, because it demonstrates how receiving the pencil actually exposed radical discontinuity in the experience of time: "If a few hours were more filled, the gaps between them yawned all the more emptily."

Let us return for a moment to Klemperer's "limbo." I would suggest that this limbo represents the traumatic zone between the two deaths discussed at length in chapter 3 (and as noted there, a similar process can be observed in the diary of Fela Szeps)—between impending biological death and symbolic death, which places the subject outside language, law, and human society. As Slavoj Žižek explains: "The place 'between two deaths', a place of sublime beauty as well as terrifying monsters, is the site of *das Ding*, of the real-traumatic kernel in the midst of symbolic order. This place is opened by symbolization/historicization. . . . As soon as 'brute', pre-symbolic reality is symbolized/historicized, it 'secretes', it isolates the empty, 'indigestible' place of the Thing."[30] The process of writing constitutes some sort of symbolic order in the midst of the brute and terrible reality that strikes at Klemperer. Due, however, to the extraordinary nature of the period, he is also exposed, at the same time and with terrible intensity, to absence—to the traumatic Thing (*das Ding*).[31] Therefore, unlike in "normal" circumstances, the mechanisms of sublimation, mediation, and mitigation of the symbolic structuration fail, and the traumatic erupts and threatens to destroy both writing and the subject who has just constituted himself by it. Writing transfers him from the natural to the symbolic plane, but could, with the very same movement, destroy them both (the subject and the symbolic plane).[32] Limbo is the place between these two deaths—the symbolic and the biological—and that is where Klemperer remains suspended between heaven and earth.[33] Indeed, just as his release approaches, his fear is further heightened, as Klemperer himself notes: "It [the fear] was so strong that the pencil did not help me at all."[34]

The paradoxical movement of writing that occurs in such a traumatic period may thus be summarized as follows: it restores the object and the symbolic organization of the subject's world but, at the same time, also negates them; it revives the subject and restores the subject's sense of time but may also plunge the subject back into the fear that lies between the two deaths.

However, the difficulties posed by documentation—as reflected in Klemperer's diary—do not end there. What the writer discovers is that, in some way, documentary writing also subverts itself. It entails necessary displacement—betraying the total nature of the traumatic event.[35] As noted, Klemperer wrote this long entry after his return home, based on the notes he had taken in prison itself. Klemperer ends his lengthy description with the following observation, in which he relates to the declaration with which he began his record, that is, that the days of imprisonment were, for him, an extraordinary experience—a shockingly real and total experience.

> Then, spreading out my notes [written in prison], I began this record. The further I got with them, the more my experience, my suffering dwindled away. No half measure, a fearfully whole thing, I think I called it at the beginning. And what was it in the end, what torments did I report? How can it be compared with what is experienced by thousands upon thousands in German prisons today? Everyday life in prison, no more, a bit of boredom, no more. And yet I feel that for myself it was one of the most agonizing times of my life.

Klemperer's disappointment is evident. Writing, as entering the public sphere of the language that organizes the experience, betrays the one-time, harsh experience.[36] It renders his own experience comparable to that of others—a comparison that dwarfs it to the point that all that remains is everyday life and a little boredom.[37] It is here that Klemperer stumbles upon the failure of his documentary aspiration, as formulated with regard to his future *Curriculum Vitae*: "This feeling, the sheer dread of being strangled in the dark, I must put *that* down in the Curriculum." In his prison notes, he discovers that this goal can never be realized. Indeed, as time passes and the trauma intensifies, the question begins to emerge in the diary: How well does the documenter understand the object of his documentation? This question first appears on 25 September 1937, and is repeated throughout the diary. It reaches its most articulate form in the entry dated 5 July 1942, written at the height of the period of the deportations from Dresden and the violent and frightening house searches carried out by the Gestapo.

At the beginning of the entry, Klemperer describes the fear of waiting for the Gestapo searches, and the hardships and hunger they are suffering. He concludes with the following words: "I would now like to express the motto of the Curriculum as follows: We know nothing of the distant past, because we were not there, we know nothing of the present, because we were there. Only from the past that we have experienced ourselves can we gain a little—very little that's certain—knowledge through later recollection."[38] In the face of all-pervasive death and collapse, in the face of the urn that reminds him again and again of his impending death, and in face of the thoughts of nothingness that terrify him, Klemperer formulates his task in writing—product of the failure of the documenting consciousness to understand the history it experiences. He thus intimates that he is writing for the future, in the hope that the text will be deciphered and its full significance will, in retrospect, come to light. Despite this self-awareness, the fact remains that he himself cannot be completely conscious of the object of his writing, which he does not understand. It is in the context of this lack of understanding that the writing takes place, without knowing whether he will ever completely comprehend what he has written. At such times, Klemperer's diary documents the paradox of documentation. The motto of such writing is that we do not understand what we are documenting and only the future may be able to explain it.[39]

It is interesting to note that very similar things were written by Gustawa Jarecka in September 1942, in the radical situation following the Great Deportation from Warsaw of the summer of that year, during the course of which nearly all of the ghetto's inhabitants were sent to Treblinka. After months of terror, frustration, and rage in the face of the annihilation of the Jewish community of Warsaw, Jarecka was asked to write the story of the Deportation for the Ringelblum Archive. She prefaced her factual account with a kind of existential introduction on the feeling of one who documents murder. Inter alia, she notes: "One can lose all hopes except the one—that the suffering and destruction of this war will make sense when they are looked at from a distant, historical perspective."[40]

In this sense, the significance of writing about terror and its documentation—for Klemperer in Dresden and for Jarecka in Warsaw—lay in the hope that those moments of terror might have meaning in the future.

The New Temporality of Documentation: A Past of a Future That Was Never Present

It seems that we can now summarize the essence of the connection between documentation and the traumatic experience: The subject renounces (by necessity) the present in favor of the future. The present—as existential experience—shrinks and almost disappears. The present may be resurrected in the future, restoring the symbolic order, but then it will exist only as the past of an imagined future and will always be a past that never entirely existed as present.

The point of departure and target of documentation is not the present as in the Ricoeurian life story, but the future. What motivates the writing and affords it meaning is the hope that the diary will be passed on to others.[41] Logically, this transmission precedes the writing, and the understanding of the text, the meaning that it will carry, will become clear only in the future.[42] The text will be redeemed (in the Benjaminian sense) only in the future and, therefore, takes the future perfect tense ("will have been")—the present does not fully exist for the documenter but will exist only in the future.[43] Its appearance resembles the return of the repressed, as Lacan wrote: "What we see in the return of the repressed is the effaced signal of something which only takes on its value in the future, through its symbolic realization, its integration into the history of the subject. Literally, it will only ever be a thing which, at the given moment of its occurrence, *will have been.*"[44]

The tenses are thus completely reversed. The future precedes the present in Klemperer's diary and, in this sense, the writer "dies" in existential terms in the present, in order to be resurrected in the future.[45] In light of this, we may understand the interesting entry dated 27 September 1944, in which Klemperer summarizes his feelings toward the end of the Nazi period:

> And again and again: I have published nothing for twelve years, been unable to complete anything (*nichts*), have done nothing (*nichts*) but record and record. Is there any point to it . . . ? The English, the Gestapo, the angina, my sixty-three years. And if it is completed, and if it is successful, and if I "survive through my work"—what is the point of it all for me? I have so little talent for faith, in fact none at all; of all possibilities nothingness (*Nichts*) appears to me, as far as the individual personality is concerned, and that is all that counts, because what do I care about the "universe" or the "nation" or anything else that is not I myself?—nothingness (*Nichts*) appears to me the most likely. And I recoil from that alone, not from the "eternal judge," in whatever shape. But I am only writing all this down (which goes through my head every day, several times a day) *because I do not want to send away an empty page. And immediately afterwards I shall go on working, i.e. reading and taking notes. Not because I am so full of energy, but because I am unable to do anything better with my time.* (emphasis added)

Klemperer, here, deals with "nothingness" (*Nichts*) or absence—of individual personality, which is, in his words, "all that counts."[46] In this encounter with nothingness, the writing is subtracted from its essential positive meaning.[47] Klemperer only fills this absence, this emptiness on the page, he says, because he does "not want to send away an empty page."[48] The transmission of the diary that requires him to write in order not to leave the pages empty, is a point of transition from the death of writing, as we have seen, to the meaning of testimony given later, in the future, by means of which it will exist in retrospect. In the act of documentation he recognizes the basic nothingness of his existence, in order to continue to live afterward—perhaps to "survive," as he himself puts it—within his writing.[49]

It is time to draw together the various threads of this discussion. At the beginning of the chapter we saw that the transition from the autobiographical to the documentary is accompanied by apologies, as Klemperer feels that he has betrayed the classic self of first-person writing. We also saw, in Klemperer's diary, two distinct approaches to the future: one filled with despair that denies the very possibility of a future, and one optimistic that expresses complete confidence in its existence. The first approach often stems from catastrophic events, while the second tends to be associated with the act of documentation. Perhaps now, we may understand why.

The reorientation toward subjectivity based on testimony and documentation must, somehow, first "kill" the subject of autobiography within the writing.[50] It must shrink greatly and perhaps even "die" as an autobiographical "present present." It is therefore permeated with numbness and apathy and even misunderstanding of what is actually documented—that it might be able to document and thereby ensure the possibility of "resurrection" in the future. The autobiographical subjectivity that focuses on the present can no longer exist and thus transforms itself to a new kind of documenting subjectivity focused on the future, hence its paradoxical nature: simultaneously existing (the writing is there) and not existing (since it lacks a present present). Perhaps this is the reason that Klemperer's war diary bears the mark of apology at the beginning and at its end.

Klemperer feels that his reorientation toward the future, at the cost of destroying the present, is a kind of betrayal. It is a betrayal of the idea of the present-based modern individual and his or her linear continuity—two elements that, as we have seen, form the basis of autobiographical writing in its Augustinian and Ricoeurian sense. In renouncing the present that binds together human linear continuity, a documenter such as Klemperer involuntarily betrays modern thought, which Foucault described as having a strong present consciousness—a mode of thought to which Klemperer faithfully adhered until the Nazi period. Jürgen Habermas claims, with regard to modernism, that "the new value which is now accorded to the ephemeral, the momentary and the transitory, and the concomitant celebration of dynamism, expresses precisely the yearning for a lasting and immaculate present.... Modernism is a 'yearning for true presence.'"[51] If so, then the documenting self—which constitutes itself precisely within numbness and can therefore never exist as "true presence"—is experienced as betrayal requiring an apology. It is, however, the writer's only way of surviving somehow: "writing him/herself to death" within documentation, specifically in order to enable future meaning and out of a belief in its existence—even if this existence will only be realized and thereby constitute the writer in the distant future.[52] It is a paradoxical subjectivity that must die in order to exist.

The need to "kill" the present creates a strange kind of dual voice: on the one hand, the continuity of life is cut off, the linearity of Klemperer's life story collapses, and as a direct result, the diary fills with expressions of despair regarding his chances of surviving the war—also and especially, as noted, when the signs of the approaching storm increase. At the same time, however, writing is the main locus in which Klemperer functions consistently as if the future is assured; something he repeats numerous times in his diary.[53]

Thus, in an entry dated 11 May 1942, Klemperer begins with a description of his miserable circumstances and explicitly notes that contrary to Nazi time, which gallops ahead, his own time ebbs away as his situation deteriorates from day to day and from year to year. He adds that he cannot imagine very far ahead with regard to his financial circumstances and that any thought beyond the immediate future is pointless. In his situation, the experience of the future, as expectation occurring in the present, is meaningless. Toward the end of the entry, however, when referring to documentary writing in preparation for his future works—the *Curriculum Vitae* and the *Language of the Third Reich*—his tone changes dramatically: "In the background there is always the thought of the Curriculum and LTI. . . . I read and take notes as if I were certain of both and of the next ten years."

In conclusion, we have seen that there are two parallel temporal systems in Klemperer's diary, and two fundamentally distinct types of future. One temporal system, which focuses on the living present, is the linear life story, the collapse of which almost inevitably provokes, in Klemperer, a growing sense of despair. In this existential temporal system, the future is, on the whole, not experienced and, in effect, does not exist.

In the temporal system of the act of documentation, on the other hand—at the heart of which lies the future that exists at the expense of the present—only the future might "decipher" what is written in the present. It is a system entirely based on the structure of "retrospect," but it is mostly within this system that Klemperer manages to feel a degree of existential certainty.[54]

The watershed between the two temporal systems is the expression "as if" ("as if I were certain of both and of the next ten years"). The "as if" subtracts the future from the existential experience of expectation based on logical continuity and a structural framework such as the Ricoeurian life story, and creates it (the future) as an imaginary prospect that precedes the present and constitutes it.[55] This "as if" requires a reader to whom the words are addressed—it demands the existence of an Other, because the reader acts like an analyst in Lacanian transference. There, in the imagination of the analyzed, the analyst functions as "the one who already knows," thereby setting the therapeutic process in motion.[56] Similarly, diarists believe that although they themselves do not fully understand the events—they or others will, in the future, understand what is written today in a state of uncertainty and lack of understanding.[57] The reader who exists in the future will, *retrospectively*, constitute the writer who—as present consciousness—lacks full, real, and certain existence in the presence. The temporal order of the diary is therefore that of a "future perfect" in which the writer is always dependent on the future reader to construct her retroactively in the tense of "will have been."

Notes

1. Avraham Tory from the Kovno ghetto offers another explanation of the act of documentation: "General, large-scale events will remain in people's memory. But singular episodes such as the sufferings of an individual are bound to be forgotten" (Avraham Tory, *Surviving the Holocaust: The Kovno Ghetto Diary*, ed. Martin Gilbert, notes by Dina Porat, trans. Jerzy Michalowicz [Cambridge, MA: Harvard University Press, 1990], 437–438). Fela Szeps writes: "I want our petty desires to be known, that people should know our thoughts, our feelings" (Fela Szeps, *Balev Ba'arah Hashalhevet: Yomanah shel Fela Szeps* [A blaze from within: The diary of Fela Szeps] [Jerusalem: Yad Vashem, 2002], 31–33 [28 June 1942]).

2. Many of the diarists stress that their experience is typical and representative of the events of the period. See, for example, Yitzhak Katzenelson, "Pinkas Vittel" [Vittel notebook], in *Ktavim Ahronim 5700–5704* [Last writings 1940–1944] (Tel Aviv: Hakibbutz Hameuchad, 1956), 180 (21 July 1943); Calel (Calek) Perechodnik, *Hatafkid Ha'atzuv Shel Hateud* [The sad role of documentation] (Jerusalem: Keter, 1993), 11–13 (omitted from the English edition). In this sense, the literature of the victims is synecdochical—that is, individual stories representing the event as a whole. As noted in the introduction, Holocaust diaries were usually written for a general, universal readership: "Literature does [speak to man in general] even in the apparent discretion of a private journal" (see Georges Bataille, *Death and Sensuality: A Study of Eroticism and Taboo* [New York: Walker, 1962], 188).

3. Both concepts, related to Klemperer's espousal of *Völkerpsychologie*, also express its breakdown. The German language is no longer the same language and the spirit of the German people is no longer the spirit of individualism, as he had previously thought.

4. See, for example, the entry dated 16 June 1942.

5. Victor Klemperer, *Leben sammeln, nicht fragen wozu und warum: Tagebücher 1918–1932*, 2 vols. (Berlin: Aufbau, 1996) (henceforth Weimar Diaries), 2:571.

6. See entry dated 14 May 1932 (Weimar Diaries, 2:751–752), in which it is very clear that he constantly struggles with the question of whether the diary has a purpose (that is, the prospect of publication), come what may, and tries to wrap up pieces of the present that they might be read in the future.

7. See entry dated 15 August 1931.

8. On this kind of open temporality, see Wendy J. Wiener and George C. Rosenwald, "A Moment's Monument: The Psychology of Keeping a Diary," in *The Narrative Study of Lives*, vol. 1, ed. Ruthellen Josselson and Amia Lieblich (Newbury Park, CA: Sage, 1993), 30–58.

9. Weimar Diaries, 2:748 (24 April 1932).

10. In many of the diaries, we find "apologies" of various kinds, which express a degree of recognition of the fact that writing is the product of some fundamental loss and ultimately serves as a surrogate for that which has been lost. For Herman Kruk, writing appears together with the feeling that he is going to be a victim. Rather than fleeing, as he might have, he decides to write a diary (see Herman Kruk, *The Last Days of the Jerusalem of Lithuania: Chronicles from the Vilna Ghetto and the Camps 1939–1944*, ed. Benjamin Harshav, trans. Barbara Harshav [New Haven, CT: Yale University Press, 2002], 46–47 [23 June 1941]). In the diary of an anonymous boy from Lodz, the author writes that he had tried a number of times to begin keeping a diary but only now had he been successful. The writing begins after a terrible incident that aroused strong feelings of guilt and self-loathing in him—when he steals bread from his sister, whom he is looking after following their parents' deaths. It is only after his sister's death and the collapse of his role as a replacement father that he is able to write (see *Yomano shel Na'ar Almoni MiLodz* [Diary of an anonymous boy from Lodz], Yad Vashem Archives, O.33/1032). Zelig Kalmanovitch begins his diary with an apology, repeated many times throughout the diary—for having delayed writing. In the very first entry, he apologizes for having begun a year too late (Zelig Kalmanovitch, "A Diary of the Nazi Ghetto in Vilna," in *YIVO Annual of Jewish Social Science*, vol. 7 [New York: YIVO, 1953], 10–12). For Yitzhak Aron, from the Vilna district—as for Calek Perechodnik—writing was a surrogate for impossible revenge against the murderers; renunciation of a settling of accounts that could never be (Yitzhak Aron, *Mayn Klayne Tsavoe* [My little Will], Yad Vashem Archives [uncataloged, in the author's possession]). What all of these "apologies" and their connection to writing appear to have in common is the need to compensate for the radical helplessness entailed by the experience of loss. As Judith Lewis Herman claims, feelings of guilt afford the illusion of control—as if one could have acted otherwise (see Judith Lewis Herman, *Trauma and Recovery* [New York: Basic Books, 1997], 53–54).

11. Victor Klemperer, *I Will Bear Witness: A Diary of the Nazi Years, 1933–1941*, trans. Martin Chalmers (New York: Modern Library, 1999), 4; emphasis added.

12. The phenomenon of closing a thematic circle opened at the beginning or end of a notebook or a diary, or at the end of a significant period, is common to many diaries. The way in which Calek Perechodnik, for example, concludes his memoir/diary is very similar to the way in which he began (see Calel [Calek] Perechodnik, *Am I A Murderer? Testament of a Jewish Ghetto Policeman*, trans. Frank Fox [Boulder, CO: Westview, 1996]). In another manner, Etty Hillesum's opening and concluding sections of her wartime diary (before Westerbork) are dominated by sexual imagery that embody the state of helplessness in which she finds herself. James Boswell concludes his London journal (1762–1763) as he began, in order to afford the book a kind of closure. The diary opens with his departure from Edinburgh, taking his leave from the mountainous landscape, and concludes with his taking his leave from the church (St. Paul's) in London. See Elizabeth W. Bruss, *Autobiographical Acts: The Changing Situation of Literary Genre* (Baltimore: Johns Hopkins University Press, 1976), 68.

13. In effect, Klemperer's diary writing in the years prior to the Nazi rise to power faced a crisis and perhaps even collapse. On more than one occasion, he considered giving up diary writing altogether (see, for example, entries from 24 April and 14 May 1932). It is therefore possible that the events actually saved his diary, although he himself found the change in its nature hard to accept.

14. The narrator's emotional detachment from the event, even when describing a personal experience, is one of the clinical manifestations of trauma. For example, a rape victim offered the following description: "I left my body at that point. I was over next to the bed, watching this happen.... I dissociated from the helplessness. I was standing next to me and there was just this shell on the bed.... There was just a feeling of flatness. I was just there. When I repicture the room, I don't picture it from the bed. I picture it from the side of the bed. That's where I was watching from." A World War II combat veteran describes a similar experience: "Like most of the 4th, I was numb, in a state of disassociation, There is a condition . . . which we called the two-thousand-year-stare. This was the anesthetized look, the wide, hollow eyes of a man who no longer cares. I wasn't to that state yet, but the numbness was total. I felt almost as if I hadn't actually been in battle" (quoted in Herman, *Trauma and Recovery,* 43). In an interview I conducted in another context, at Yad Vashem, with Mr. Rudolph Tessler, a native of Hungary and an Auschwitz survivor, he repeatedly characterized the manner in which he had related to the events he had experienced with the phrase "I was numb" (recording in the author's possession). Dissociation is also recognized as a symptom of schizophrenia, described as follows by Marguerite Sechehaye, in her introduction to *Autobiography of a Schizophrenic Girl*: "This renders clearer the intrinsic nature of schizophrenia which consists in a dissociation of an affectivity deeply disturbed by the loss of contact with life from an intelligence remaining intact and acting as a motion picture camera to record whatever comes within range of the lens" (Marguerite Sechehaye, *Autobiography of a Schizophrenic Girl* [New York: Grune and Stratton, 1951], xi).

15. The concept appears many times in the diary and stems, inter alia, from Klemperer's passion for the new, cinematic medium. See, for example, the long entry describing his imprisonment, between 23 June and 1 July 1941, addressed at length below.

16. Saul Friedländer relates, in similar contexts, to the appropriate distance between historians and the events they describe: Saul Friedländer, "Trauma, Transference and 'Working Through,'" *History and Memory* 4 (1992): 39–55. Distance in historical writing on the Holocaust, as an ethical problem, is largely at the heart of an exchange of letters between Friedländer and Martin Broszat: "Martin Broszat/Saul Friedlander: A Controversy about the Historicization of National Socialism," *Yad Vashem Studies* 19 (1988): 1–47.

17. A prime example of the fact that documentation was indeed perceived as a kind of indifference to the suffering of others can be found in the diary of Yitskhok Rudashevski, who was sent by his youth club to document the history of one of the courtyards on Shavler Street, in the Vilna ghetto. He thus writes on 22 October 1942: "I got a taste of a historian's task. I sit at the table and ask questions and record the greatest sufferings with cold objectivity. I write, I probe into details, and I do not realize at all that I am probing into wounds, and the one who answers me—indifferent to it: two sons and a husband taken away—the sons Monday, the husband Thursday.... And this horror, this tragedy is formulated by me in three words, coldly and dryly"; and on 5 November: "Today we also went to Shavler 4 with the questionnaire for investigating the ghetto. We did not get a good reception. And I must sadly admit that they were right. We were reproached for having calm heads. 'You must not probe into another person's wounds, our lives are self-evident.' She is right, but I am not at fault either because I consider that everything should be recorded and noted down, even the most gory, because

everything will be taken into account" (Rudashevski, *The Diary of the Vilna Ghetto*, 73, 84). And Janusz Korczak writes: "To describe someone else's pain resembles thieving, preying upon misfortune, as if there were not enough of it as things are" (Janusz Korczak, *Ghetto Diary*, trans. Jerzy Bachrach and Barbara Krzywicka [New Haven, CT: Yale University Press, 2003], 40–41).

18. The passage of the dominant role from the protagonist to the narrator is related to the passage from the narrative itself as a textual product to the act of narration that is the realm of the narrator.

19. Like Freud's grandson who, helpless as he was at the prospect of losing his mother, managed to gain a degree of control over the situation by repeating it, staged as a game in which he would throw an object away from himself, while exclaiming "o-o-o-o." This interpretation, suggested by Freud himself (in "Beyond the Pleasure Principle," in *The Standard Edition of the Complete Psychological Works of Sigmund Freud*, vol. 18, ed. and trans. James Strachey [London: Hogarth, 1955], 4–17), does not fully exhaust the semiotic process entailed in this story, although it does express a very significant aspect of it. See Kaja Silverman, *The Subject of Semiotics* (New York: Oxford University Press, 1983), 71.

20. Renata Laqueur Weiss, "Writing in Defiance: Concentration Camp Diaries in Dutch, French and German, 1940–1945" (PhD diss., New York University, 1971), 68.

21. When Yitskhok Rudashevski goes to explore new areas added to the Vilna ghetto, he feels "pleasure" at first, in "seeing new places," which he explains as follows: "What a pleasure! A simple emotion of a prisoner, who has found another new corner in his cell. He examines it and is pleased for the moment: to discover something new lying in his cell." The feeling is immediately replaced, however, by one of pervasive "unfriendliness": "Cold mud confronts them from every little corner" (Yitskhok Rudashevski, *The Diary of the Vilna Ghetto, June 1941–April 1943*, trans. Percy Matenko [Jerusalem: The Ghetto Fighters' House, 1973], 68 [18 October 1941]).

22. In Lacanian terms, this paradox can be explained as resulting from the fact that Klemperer's condition is a terrible regression to a state of being without meaning, when the self is experienced by the subject in a raw and immediate fashion, outside of and detached from signifiers of real objects in the world. See Jacques Lacan, *The Seminar of Jacques Lacan, Book XI: The Four Fundamental Concepts of Psychoanalysis*, ed. Jacques-Alain Miller, trans. Alan Sheridan (New York: Norton, 1998), 209–213. See also Silverman, *The Subject of Semiotics*, 169–171.

23. See, for example, Perechodnik, *Am I a Murderer?*, 137–138.

24. I will discuss this further in the third part of the book, which focuses on the diary of Chaim Kaplan in Warsaw.

25. Symbolic death also releases nature from its own laws. Thus, Korczak no longer trusts the thermometer and the scales he uses in the ghetto, but suspects them of lying. In other words, in the world of the Warsaw ghetto, the laws of nature are irrelevant, and the ghetto acts on a plane that has broken free of those laws (see Korczak, *Ghetto Diary*, 73).

26. Such sentiments are echoed by Calek Perechodnik, in his diary; "To be exact, this is a confession about my lifetime, a sincere and true confession. Alas, I don't believe in divine absolution. . . . I don't ask to be absolved" (Perechodnik, *Am I A Murderer?*, xxi).

27. The moment of acquiring the possibility of writing is often described as a very significant time. Pal Kovacs, for example, begins his diary in the Neuengamme camp with the following words: "An incredible thing has happened. I managed to obtain pencil and paper" (Pal Kovacs, "Yomano shel Pal Kovacs" [The diary of Pal Kovacs], *Dapim Leheker Tkufat HaSho'ah* 1 [1979]: 231).

28. Indeed, Klemperer relates to the pencil but hardly mentions the paper and never the act of writing—focusing on the object rather than on the action or the space in which it takes place. For Fela Szeps, as well, the concrete pencil is far more present than the writing itself: "Nevertheless, the desire often arises to pick up a pencil and do something with it" (Szeps, *Balev Ba'arah Hashalhevet*, 24). So too Korczak.

29. Primo Levi also uses the term "limbo" to describe the period of time between liberation from Auschwitz and return to life (Primo Levi, *If This Is a Man/The Truce*, trans. Stuart Woolf [London: Abacus, 2004], 328, 335).

30. Slavoj Žižek, *The Sublime Object of Ideology* (London: Verso, 1989), 135.

31. The Thing (*das Ding*) is the object in the order of the real: what is "beyond the signified" and outside the symbolic network itself. It is therefore unimaginable and the encounter with it extremely traumatic. See Jacques Lacan, *The Ethics of Psychoanalysis*, trans. Dennis Porter (New York: Norton, 1992), 54–55, 125.

32. Jorge Semprún described the danger in writing memoirs from the concentration camp as follows: "Like a luminous cancer, the account I was wresting from my memory, bit by bit, sentence by sentence, was devouring my life" (Jorge Semprún, *Literature or Life*, trans. Linda Coverdale [New York: Viking, 1997], 194).

33. In the concentration camps, a prisoner could experience death while still living. See Jorge Semprún's bitterly cynical remark regarding Wittgenstein's assertion: "'Death is not an event in life. Death cannot be lived,' wrote that idiot Wittgenstein" (ibid., 193). See also Jean Améry, *At the Mind's Limits: Contemplations by a Survivor on Auschwitz and Its Realities*, trans. Sidney Rosenfeld and Stella P. Rosenfeld (Bloomington: Indiana University Press, 1980), 1–20 (esp. 15–20). In this context, it is worth noting Boaz Neumann's distinction between "He is dead" (ontologically) and "He is going to die" (biologically): Boaz Neumann, *Re'iyat Ha'olam Hanatzit: Merhav, Guf, Safah* [The Nazi weltanschauung: Space, body, language] (Haifa: Haifa University, 2002).

34. A similar phenomenon occurs in Klemperer's diary toward the end of the war. There too, it is just before the defeat of Nazi Germany and his liberation from the terror of the Nazi regime that his feelings of fear and despair reach new heights.

35. Jean Laplanche and Jean-Baptiste Pontalis, *The Language of Psychoanalysis* (New York: Norton, 1973), 33, 465–469.

36. See also Jacques Derrida, "Shibboleth," in *Midrash and Literature*, ed. Geoffrey H. Hartman and Sanford Budick (New Haven, CT: Yale University Press, 1986), 307–334.

37. The reason may have to do with the "easy" circumstances of Klemperer's experience, but Imre Kertész expressed similar feelings with regard to Auschwitz, albeit in retrospect: "That is in part how I came to realize: even in Auschwitz, it seems, it is possible to be bored—assuming one is privileged. . . . That boredom, together with that strange anticipation: I think that is the impression, approximately, yes, that is in reality what may truly denote Auschwitz—purely in my eyes, of course" (Imre Kertész, *Fatelessness*, trans. Tim Wilkinson [London: Vintage, 2004], 119).

38. According to Cathy Caruth, this lies at the heart of Freud's *Moses and Monotheism*—the unrealizable urge to document events from within. See Cathy Caruth, *Unclaimed Experience: Trauma Narrative and History* (Baltimore: Johns Hopkins University Press, 1996), 11–13.

39. Korczak too was aware of the writer's limited ability to understand the text that he himself had written—all the more so the reader: "I have read it over. I could hardly understand it. And the reader? No wonder, that the memoirs are incomprehensible to the reader. Is it possible to understand someone else's reminiscences, someone else's life? It seems that I ought to

be able to perceive without effort what I myself write about. Ah, but is it possible to understand one's own remembrances?" (Korczak, *Ghetto Diary*, 77).

40. As translated in Joseph Kermish, ed., *To Live with Honor, to Die with Honor: Selected Documents from the Warsaw Ghetto Underground Archives* (Jerusalem: Yad Vashem, 1986), 704. On the author and date of the document, see Samuel Kassow, *Who Will Write Our History? Emanuel Ringelblum, the Warsaw Ghetto, and the Oyneg Shabes Archive* (Bloomington: Indiana University Press, 2007), 5–6. See also Stefan Ernst's reflection from 1943, written while in hiding on the Aryan side of Warsaw: "The struggle to save myself is hopeless.... But that's not important. Because I am able to bring my account to its end and trust that it will see the light of day when the time is right.... And people will know what happened.... And they will ask, is this the truth? I reply in advance: No, this is not the truth, this is only a small part, a tiny fraction of the truth.... Even the mightiest pen could not depict the whole, real, essential *truth*." Quoted in Saul Friedländer, *Nazi Germany and the Jews: The Years of Extermination 1939–1945* (London: Weidenfeld and Nicolson, 2007), iii.

41. In a certain sense, this is how Lejeune understands the perception of time in every diary. See Philippe Lejeune, *On Diary*, ed. Jeremy D. Popkin and Julie Rak, trans. Katherine Durnin (Manoa: University of Hawai'i Press, 209), 334. See also Julie Rak, "Dialogue with the Future: Philippe Lejeune's Method and Theory of Diary," introduction to Lejeune, *On Diary*, 16–26.

42. The future orientation is often comforting, but comes at the expense of the existential experience of the present. See, for example, Kruk, *The Last Days of the Jerusalem of Lithuania*, 468–469 (3 March 1943). The future orientation can also be perceived as an accusation demanding an apology. Yehoshua Moshe Aronson, for example, tries to explain to (accusing) future readers why the Jews did not rebel (Aronson, *Alei Merorot* [Leaves of bitterness] [Bnei Brak: private publication, 1996], 122–123). Zalman Gradowski also explains to an anonymous reader how the prisoners had reached a state of inhumanity (Gradowski, "Writings," in *The Scrolls of Auschwitz*, ed. Ber Mark, trans. Sharon Neemani [Tel Aviv: Am Oved, 1985], 177).

43. Benjaminian redemption is not the culmination of a teleological process but the sudden stopping of time at the moment in which the past realizes its ethical and political potential in the present. See Walter Benjamin, "Thesis on the Philosophy of History," in *Illuminations*, ed. Hannah Arendt, trans. Harry Zohn (New York: Schocken, 1969), 253–264. See also Žižek, *The Sublime Object of Ideology*, 128–140.

44. Jacques Lacan, *The Seminar of Jacques Lacan, Book I: Freud's Papers on Technique, 1953–1954*, ed. Jacques-Alain Miller, trans. John Forrester (New York: Norton, 1988), 159.

45. The present does not exist because it exceeds the limits of consciousness and is open to countless interpretative possibilities, all of which collapse before it. Therefore, this present does not exist in our consciousness and, as future, is unraveled. In this, the documentation project resembles the postmodern novel, according to the analysis of Ursula K. Heise. See Heise, "Chronoschisms," in *Chronoschisms: Time Narrative, and Posmodernism* (Cambridge: Cambridge University Press, 1997), 65–75.

46. Kurt Rosenberg also describes his life as "living in the nothingness" (*leben in das Nichst*): Kurt F. Rosenberg, *"Einer, der nicht mehr dazugehört": Tagebücher 1933–1937*, ed. Beate Meyer and Björn Siegel (Göttingen: Wallstein, 2012), 282 (23 March 1935).

47. And on 31 December 1944, he writes: "The best means for that [avoiding thoughts of death] is immersion in study, to behave as if the accumulation of material had a real purpose." In this context it is worth noting the expression Klemperer repeats numerous times throughout the diary, with regard to writing itself: *Vanitas vanitatum*, "vanity of vanities."

48. On a similar feeling in the diaries of prisoners in the camps, see Laqueur Weiss, "Writing in Defiance," 38–39.

49. A radical and shocking illustration of this situation can be found in the statements of witnesses who returned from the shooting pits of Ponar, after having been shot but not killed. When they returned to the ghetto, Kruk took their testimonies and recorded them in his diary. One of the witnesses describes his experience standing in front of the executioners, as follows: "I was calm because I didn't really exist any more. . . . Only my body was standing there, waiting indifferently for the bullet" (quoted in Kruk, *The Last Days of the Jerusalem of Lithuania*, 224 [4 March 1942]). Yet it was important to him (to the witness), as the meaning of life, to transmit this testimony. In another sense, Kruk refers to the ghetto as "dead" before the Aktion.

50. A similar approach to the writing of trauma, albeit to later, retrospective writing, can be found in Jorge Semprún's *Literature or Life* (*L'Ecriture ou la vie*—perhaps better translated "Writing or Life"; the title itself attests to the fact that the two options are mutually exclusive). For example: "I posses nothing more than my death, my experience of death, to recount my life, to express it. . . . I must make life with all that death. And the best way to do this is through writing, Yet that brings me back to death, to the suffocating embrace of death. That's where I am: I can live only by assuming that death through writing, but writing literally prohibits me from living" (Semprún, *Literature or Life*, 163).

51. Jürgen Habermas, "Modernity: An Unfinished Project," in *Habermas and the Unfinished Project of Modernity: Critical Essays on The Philosophical Discourse of Modernity*, ed. Maurizio Passerin d'Entrèves and Seyla Benhabib (Cambridge, MA: MIT Press, 1997), 40. See also Michel Foucault, "What Is Enlightenment?," in *The Foucault Reader: An Introduction to Foucault's Thought*, ed. Paul Rabinow (New York: Pantheon Books, 1984), 32–50, esp. 39–40.

52. Tamar Herman writes in Theresienstadt on 1 November 1944: "The only escape from my situation is work and constant activity. To that I must devote myself and live in the hope that I may one day be able to look back on today from afar and everything will look not quite so terrible" (Tamar Herman, "Gam Kan Mutar Lahlom Vele'ehov [Yoman Migeto Terezin]" [Here too one may dream and love (A diary from the Theresien ghetto)], *Yalkut Moreshet* 47 [1989]: 205).

53. See, for example, 10 August 1933; 6 October 1934; 17 January 1942; 17 March 1942; 11 May 1942; 29 May 1942; 26 July 1942; 24 October 1942.

54. As I have noted, the future gaze is very important to diarists. On the binding of the notebook he used, the Auschwitz Sonderkommando Zalman Gradowski wrote the following invitation-imperative: "Take interest in this document which contains very important material for the historian" (Gradowski, "Writings," 173). There were other writers, however, who were certain that future readers would not believe them—leading to a further paradox of documentation: the documentation of that which appears to be patently unbelievable. For example, another Auschwitz Sonderkommando, Zalman Loewenthal, who recorded his actions and went to the trouble of burying his writings along with those of others, for future generations, wrote: "hundreds of years later [they] will not believe this; we are certain of this" (Zalman Loewenthal, "Writings," in Mark, *The Scrolls of Auschwitz*, 235). In this, as in other such cases, Holocaust diarists cast doubt even on the capacity of future readers to "decipher" their writings and experiences. These moments of doubt are indeed also moments of great despair. However, even the sheer ability to imagine that someone in the future will read these texts and try to "decipher" them—even unsuccessfully—has the power to reestablish the "retrospect" temporal structure. See also Pal Kovacs, a Hungarian Jew deported to the Neuengamme camp,

who addressed the following words to his loved ones, in a diary entry dated 31 January 1945: "Will we yet read this diary together?" (Kovacs, "Yomano shel Pal Kovacs," 248).

55. To better understand the difference between this temporal order and that of Augustinian-Ricoeurian autobiography, which focuses on the present, cf. Karl Joachim Weintraub, *The Value of the Individual: Self and Circumstance in Autobiography* (Chicago: University of Chicago Press, 1978), 23–24. For the purposes of this discussion, we may consider Weintraub's approach representative of classic autobiographical theory.

56. "And since the 'I' of this récit only constitutes itself through the credit of the eternal return, he does not exist. He does not sign prior to the récit qua eternal return. . . . It is the eternal return that signs and seals" (Jacques Derrida, *The Ear of the Other: Otobiography, Transference, Translation*, ed. Christie McDonald, trans. Peggy Kamuf and Avital Ronell [Lincoln: University of Nebraska Press, 1988], 13).

57. That is how I understand the dialogue that Korczak demands from his autobiographical writing: "I talk to people a lot. . . . I converse only with myself. Writing a diary or a life story I am obliged to talk, not to converse" (Korczak, *Ghetto Diary*, 95–96).

PART III

THE JEWISH SELF UNDER NAZI DOMINATION

Chaim Kaplan's Warsaw Diary

7

CHAIM KAPLAN AND HIS DIARY

PART III focuses on the wartime diary of the Warsaw Jew Chaim Aron Kaplan. Kaplan's diary, written in Hebrew, covers the period from the Nazi invasion of Poland on 1 September 1939, when Kaplan was age fifty-nine, until 4 August 1942, a few days before he was deported to Treblinka. The following chapters discuss the complex relations that the diary reveals between the writer, a Jewish victim; Nazism; and the Nazis, his persecutors (in other words, between the Jewish "I" and the Nazi "Other").[1]

Kaplan's war diary was a continuation of the diary that he had begun keeping in 1933. Prior to the war the diary had, from Kaplan's point of view, fulfilled a dual function. First and foremost, the diary provided him with a means of free expression, as someone who had always felt himself to be a loner and even hostile to the world around him. In 1936, for example, Kaplan writes that "The diary has become my daily bread. I have virtually no true friends and comrades."[2] Elsewhere he confides that "After all, I have in my world no comrade closer and more intimate than it."[3] Yet already at this early stage Kaplan stresses an important secondary element of his diary, its documentary nature: "The diary indeed reflects only my personal life, yet I am, however, part of the surroundings and contend with the conditions of life, and my personal life conveys something of life in general."[4]

Kaplan's prewar diary covers a diverse range of aspects of the author's life, including his extramarital affair, his yearning for his children in Palestine, his countless personal feuds (many of which ended up in court) and daily educational matters in the school that he founded, in addition to the dramatic political events unfolding in Poland, Germany, and Palestine. Yet as we saw in Klemperer's diary and as is evident in many other Jewish diaries of the period, with the outbreak of war the diary's focus and character are transformed. From a journal focusing mainly on the writer's intimate and personal spheres, it becomes an overtly historical-documentary document. From this point on, Kaplan's gaze is directed almost exclusively outward. Abraham Katsh, who wrote the preface to the printed edition of Kaplan's diary, noted: "Until the outbreak of the world war the diary serves primarily the personal sphere . . . but from the tense months of the summer of 1939, with the impending storm of war, the nature of the diary underwent a blatant change. Chaim Aharon Kaplan abandons the individual sphere."[5] Indeed, Kaplan regarded documentation to be a sacred mission. On 16 January 1940 he writes as follows:

> I don't know if there is anyone else who keeps a daily record? The conditions of life that surround us do not facilitate such literary work. I am one of the fortunate people whose pen never ceases to flow even during these deranged times. Anyone who does this takes his life into his hands, but this does not frighten me. I feel within me that these are momentous times and that I have a responsibility, I have an inner awareness that I am engaged in a national duty, an historical duty, and that I am not at liberty to discard it. I do not edit what I write. The momentary reflex shapes my writing. Perhaps this gives it value. I am somehow convinced that Providence has sent me on this mission. My records will serve as historiographical material for the future historian.[6]

Nevertheless, as is true of all first-person narratives, the war diary too is not only a historical document but also reveals the writer's life story. Events are always observed from a subjective perspective, and the diary includes a good number of descriptions of his personal experiences, as well as his feelings and emotional and intellectual responses to events. Although he did not seek to focus his writing on these elements, they are all inherently integrated into his narrative. Thus Kaplan reveals through his descriptions his inner world and his point of view, which find expression in virtually every line. Despite the diary's clearly stated tendency toward documentation, the Polish scholar Jacek Leociak rightly calls it an "intimate diary," and in this respect Kaplan's journal is indeed a life story.[7] Yet in fact, like most other Holocaust diaries the diary presents not only a "life story" but also an account of the disruption and sometimes even the disintegration of life. It portrays how the life of an Eastern European, Zionist Jewish intellectual, thoroughly immersed in both ancient and modern Hebrew and European culture, was disrupted by the Nazi occupation, and paints a picture of his lifelong struggles to establish and confirm this identity, even during this period. In this respect it is a "life story," underscoring the act of narration that facilitates life. As such, the diary was of tremendous existential value to Kaplan: "The diary is my life, my comrade, my ally. Without it I would be lost. I pour into it my discourse and all my heart's feelings until I gain some relief. When I am angry and my blood boils, when I am filled with resentment and inner agitation I drag myself toward the diary and am immediately inspired by the God of creativity, although I doubt whether the work of recording I do deserves to be called 'creation' . . . the main thing is that I find emotional rest therein and that's good enough for me."[8]

Who Was Kaplan?

Kaplan was born in 1880 in Horodysze (also Gorodishche) near Baranowicze in Poland (at that time part of the Russian empire today in Belarus). His family members possessed a strong Jewish consciousness and spoke Hebrew well. He received his initial education in a *heder* (the traditional Jewish educational institution), and went on to study at the Mir yeshiva and the Vilnius pedagogical seminary. In adulthood Kaplan abandoned his religious belief but remained loyal to Jewish tradition, in which he was extremely well versed, as a vibrant national culture. Although he was not a religious man he observed some of the precepts (yet did not refrain from writing in his diary on the Jewish New Year), frequently attended synagogue, made an effort to study the Jewish religious texts regularly, and frequented religious circles.[9]

Kaplan was a zealot of the Hebrew language. Upon arriving in Warsaw in 1900 he founded and ran a private school in which he introduced the method of "Hebrew in Hebrew," namely, the teaching of the Hebrew language using this tongue itself, rather than teaching it as a foreign language. Hebrew was taught with a modern Sephardic pronunciation.[10] The diaries he kept during the 1930s testify to his interminable educational, ideological, financial, and legal struggles to maintain the school. These educational innovations sparked fierce debate, but this did not deter Kaplan from pursuing them, believing that they would play an essential role in the rebirth of Hebrew spirit and culture. He was involved in contemporary Jewish Warsaw cultural discourse, and published a large number of articles, critiques, and feuilletons in the Jewish press and periodicals of the period. A collection of his articles was published in 1937 in Poland under the title *Pezurai* (in Hebrew).[11] During the twenties and thirties several more of his works appeared, including a number of Hebrew grammar books, works presenting the Bible in the light of modern scholarship, a Passover *Hagada* with modern interpretation, and a book of games for teachers and counselors.[12] Almost all his writing addresses topics of Jewish culture and education.

Kaplan was an ardent Zionist, leaning to the right, although he was not affiliated with any particular party. Among the Zionist leaders, he particularly admired Nahum Sokolow. During the interwar years Kaplan participated in the activities of the Zionist Organization in Warsaw and encouraged his two children, Leon and Zipora, to emigrate to Palestine. For many years he considered taking this step himself. As a profoundly nationalist Jew he yearned to live in the Land of Israel, yet feared that he might not endure the hardships of life there. He visited Palestine in June 1935 as a tourist, and was favorably impressed by the enterprise of national regeneration, in particular its cultural aspects. However, he remained apprehensive about uprooting himself and about the challenges of making a new start in the country, in which despite all his intentions he felt a stranger.[13] He eventually returned to Warsaw and remained there, devoting himself to the struggle for Jewish education based on the Hebrew language and inculcating Jewish cultural values within modern and progressive educational frameworks.

As mentioned, Kaplan began writing his diary in 1933 and continued it during the war years. His diaries were smuggled across to Warsaw's "Aryan" section in 1942: sensing that his end was near, Kaplan entrusted the diary to one of his students, who passed it into the hands of a Pole named Wytzek (who assisted Jews during the Holocaust) for safekeeping. After the war a number of the diary copybooks were handed over to the Jewish Institute in Warsaw and to Abraham Katsh, head of the Jewish Studies Institute at New York University.[14]

Incomplete versions of the wartime diary in several languages appeared many years later. It was first published in English in 1965 (edited and translated by Abraham Katsh), followed by several further editions, the latest of which was published by Indiana University Press in 1999.[15] The English editions were highly bowdlerized by the editor and translator Katsh.[16] The diary appeared for the first time in Hebrew in 1966, titled *Scroll of Agony: A Warsaw Ghetto Diary*. This edition includes almost all the diary entries (only a few highly personal ones were omitted) from 1 September 1939 to 4 August 1942, apart from those dated March 1941 to February 1942. Some of these entries were published previously in the periodicals *Yalqut Moreshet* and *Betsaron*.[17] The diary has also been published in German, French, Danish, and Japanese translations.

Kaplan wrote his diary entirely in Hebrew and resolutely composed a new entry almost every day. As such, it provides extensive coverage of processes and events that occurred in Warsaw, alongside attempts to interpret these occurrences and reports of his and other Jews' feelings and responses to them. It covers the entire period of occupation up to Kaplan's deportation to Treblinka in August 1942. The diary is at once an exceedingly important historical document concerning the lives of the Jews under Nazi occupation in Warsaw and an autobiographical testimony that can improve our understanding of the world of the writer-individual in the face of these events.

Despite his somewhat disparaging attitude toward Kaplan as a person, the historian Emanuel Ringelblum, who led the clandestine documentation project in the Warsaw ghetto known as Oyneg Shabes, already during the war years accorded the diary recognition as a historical document of major importance. Reviewing the documentation activity conducted in the Warsaw ghetto, Ringelblum notes:

> The Hebrew diary of the author and Hebrew teacher Kaplan contained thousands of pages in which were to be found a wealth of reports on all that occurred in Warsaw on a daily basis. Kaplan was not a person of wide horizons, yet all that befell an average Warsaw Jew, his suffering and experiences, the desire for revenge that pulsated in his heart, all these were faithfully reflected in the diary. The diary's importance lies precisely in the fact that its writer was an ordinary man. On more than one occasion I asked Kaplan to hand the diary over to us for safekeeping and I guaranteed that we would return it once the war had ended. He grudgingly agreed that we should copy the diary, but the task of copying was plagued by many hardships. A part of the diary remained in the *Oyneg Shabes* archive, while the complete manuscript was lost along with its author, who was taken to the Umschlagplatz.[18]

It appears that Ringelblum was mistaken in his assessment of Kaplan's talent as a writer: neither was he mediocre nor were his horizons limited. Indeed, historian Saul Friedländer characterizes him as "usually more farsighted than any other diarist."[19] As will be discussed further below, the mutual lack of appreciation between Ringelblum and Kaplan most likely resulted from their differing political stances. As luck would have it, Ringelblum's surmise with regard to the diary's fate was also proved wrong, and the work survived. Since the war, the diary has come to be one of the major historical sources regarding the life of the Jews in Warsaw during the Nazi occupation, and is mentioned by virtually every study of Polish Jewry focusing on this period.[20] Likewise, scholars of literature frequently refer to the diary, presenting it as an example of elegiac and poetic yet profound and analytical prose writing during the Holocaust, a text that is at once self-conscious and aware of its surroundings.[21]

While Kaplan's writing is rich and multifaceted, in the following chapters I seek to examine his work from the perspective of the text's stance and that of the subject encompassed therein toward the Nazi as their (big) "Other." By (big) Other I mean the ones who controlled the life and death of the Jews, who sealed their fate, passed the laws, determined policy, and controlled language—the ones who determined reality and the rules by which it was organized. The Jews were complete subjects to their rule, which thus shaped their inner self. It follows that the Nazis at once played a major role in shaping the Jews' self and at the same time were their oppressors and murderers. What, then, was the extent of the Nazis' influence on the Jews' language, their self-perception, their identity, and their effect on the inner world of the Jews? To what extent did they influence their story? Where should this influence be located? Although not couched in these exact terms, Chaim Kaplan was preoccupied with these questions when writing his diary, and they are among the diary's focal points, as will be demonstrated in the next two chapters.

Notes

1. Following Lacan's notion of the "Other," which indicates the authoritative place in which the symbolic order is produced. According to Lacanian theory the subject's attitude toward the Other is extremely complex. On the one hand, the Other is the ultimate extraneousness, but on the other hand the subject bares a structural dependence to the Other and unavoidably identifies with him. See, for example,Jacques Lacan, *The Seminar of Jacques Lacan, Book XI: The Four Fundamental Concepts of Psychoanalysis*, ed. Jacques-Alain Miller, trans. Alan Sheridan (New York: Norton, 1998), 203–216; Bruce Fink, *The Lacanian Subject: Between Language and Jouissance* (Princeton, NJ: Princeton University Press, 1995).

2. Diary entry dated 11 April 1936 (Archive of the Jewish Historical Institute in Warsaw, ZIH 302/218) (henceforth Kaplan Diary). Kaplan expresses his sense of loneliness on numerous occasions throughout the diary, and indulges in a good deal of self-pity. On 13 March 1937, for example, he writes: "It seems to me that no-one is as lonely as I in life." His hostility to his fellow humans is unmistakable and his diary is studded with expressions such as "villain," "garbage," wicked Galician," and "stupid Galician." It appears that he did not enjoy a warm relationship with his children either. He respects few of the people whom he mentions in his diary. In an entry dated 20 March 1937 he discerns that his attitude toward others is influenced by two opposite poles of self perception, fluctuating between an attitude based on a feeling of "I am the best," and a sense that he himself is worthless and insignificant.

3. Kaplan Diary, 14 December 1938 (ZIH 302/218).

4. Ibid., 11 April 1936 (ZIH 302/218).

5. Abraham I. Katsh, introduction to Chaim Aron Kaplan, *Megilat Yisurin: Yoman Geto Varshah* [Scroll of agony: Warsaw ghetto diary] (Tel Aviv: Am Oved and Yad Vashem, 1966), 11. The following review is based on these sources, on Katsh's introduction to the English edition of the diary (Chaim Aron Kaplan, *Scroll of Agony: The Warsaw Diary of Chaim A. Kaplan*, trans. and ed. Abraham I. Katsh [Bloomington: Indiana University Press, 1999], 9–17), and primarily on his diaries from the years 1936 to 1939, which have not been published and are kept in the archive of the Jewish Historical Institute in Warsaw. See also a concise and excellent review in Jacek Leociak, *Text in the Face of Destruction: Accounts from the Warsaw Ghetto Reconsidered*, trans. Emma Harris (Warsaw: Żydowski Instytut Historyczny, 2004), 72–73; and Abraham I. Katsh, "Kaplan, Chaim Aron," in *Encyclopaedia Judaica*, ed. Michael Berenbaum and Fred Skolnik, vol. 11, 2nd ed. (Detroit: Macmillan Reference, 2007), 774–775.

6. All of the references to Kaplans's wartime diary are based on the original Hebrew text. Where available, I have used Abraham I. Katsh's English translation (Kaplan, *Scroll of Agony*), adapting it, as necessary, to render it more faithful to the original Hebrew. On Kaplan's perception of his historical mission, see Alexandra Garbarini, *Numbered Days: Diaries and the Holocaust* (New Haven, CT: Yale University Press, 2006), 22–57. See also Alvin Rosenfeld, *A Double Dying: Reflections on Holocaust Literature* (Bloomington: Indiana University Press, 1980), 40–44.

7. Leociak, *Text in the Face of Destruction*, 15. For the definition of "Life Story," see chapter 1.

8. Entry dated 14 November 1941 ("Hayim Ahron Kaplan" file, Moreshet Archive D.2.470).

9. Kaplan Diary, see the entries dated 20 September 1936 (ZIH 302/218) and 20 August 1936 (ZIH 302/218). This kind of hybrid and "fluid" identity was very common in interwar Poland, despite the sharp ideological rifts. This is very well reflected, for example, in the autobiographies written by Jewish youth in Poland. See Shandler, *Awakening Lives: Autobiographies of Jewish Youth in Poland before the Holocaust* (New Haven, CT: Yale University Press, 2002).

10. He lived in Nowolipki st. 20 in Warsaw (see his Yad Vashem "page of testimony," which was filled by his son-in-law Benjamin Gesundheit), http://db.yadvashem.org/names/nameDetails.html?itemId=6687639&language=iw. There were obviously other Hebrew schools in Poland but they were, for the most part, branches of the Tarbut network. Kaplan's school was completely private and did not belong to any network. See Miriam Eisenstein, *Jewish Schools in Poland 1919–1939* (New York: King's Crown, 1950), esp. chap. 4. See also Kamil Kijek, "Was It Possible to Avoid 'Hebrew Assimilation'? Hebraism, Polonization and Tarbut Schools in the Last Decade of Interwar Poland," *Jewish Social Studies* 21, no. 2 (2016): 105–141.

11. Chaim Aron Kaplan, *Pezurai: Mehkarim, Reshimot Ufelyetonim: Kol Kitvei Hamehaber Bitkufat Hashanim 1900–1936* [My scatterings: Studies, articles, and feuilletons: The author's complete writings during the years 1900–1936] (Warsaw: Va'ad Hayovel, 1937).

12. Chaim Aron Kaplan, *Sefer Hamis'hakim Hasha'ashuim Vehahit'amlut: Sefer Ezer Lehorim, Lemorim Uletalmidim* [The book of games, quizzes and exercises: A reference book for parents, teachers, and students] (Warsaw: Limud, 1922); Kaplan, *Haggadah shel Pesah: Hotza'ah Omanutit Umada'it, im Be'ur Ivri Hadash* [Passover Haggadah: An artistic and scientific edition with new Hebrew explanations] (Warsaw: Limud, 1924); Kaplan, *Dikduk Halashon Veshimushah* [The grammar of the language and its usage] (New York: Hebrew Publishing, 1926); Kaplan, *Amei HaTanakh: Tziurim Histori'im Mihayei Amei Hamizrah* [The peoples of the Bible: Historical portraits from the lives of the peoples of the East] (Warsaw: Limud, 1926).

13. He arrived at Haifa on 30 June 1935 together with his wife Toibe. Both were registered as emigrants (Central Zionist Archive s104\578\2). His arrival was reported on 5 July by the

Doar Hayom newspaper. A month later, the newspaper reported that "The pedagogical writer C. A. Kaplan has started working as a pedagogical director at the Safra school" (*Davar*, 7 August 1935). Eventually he quit his job and returned to Poland later that year.

14. Several of the copybooks were lost. One is kept at the Moreshet archive, the Polish family retains some of them, and others are kept at the archive of the Jewish Historical Institute (ZIH) in Warsaw. A copy is also kept at the Washington Holocaust Museum.

15. The English version (Chaim Aron Kaplan, *Scroll of Agony* [New York: Macmillan, 1965]) does not include the entries from March 1941 to February 1942. In addition, extensive sections of the published years have been omitted. The subsequent English editions, the first of which was published in 1973 (New York: Collier Books), include the entries dated March to October 1941. The entries dated October to April 1942 are missing from these editions as well. The Indiana University Press 1999 edition is similar to the 1973 edition.

16. On the very common phenomenon of bowdlerization in Holocaust diaries, see Engel, "On the Bowdlerization of a Holocaust Testimony: The Wartime Journal of Calek Perechodnik," *Polin* 12 (1999): 316–329; Amos Goldberg, "Yomanei HaSho'ah—Samkhut She'einah Medaberet Kahalakhah" [Holocaust diaries: An authority that doesn't speak appropriately], in *Kanoni Upopulari: Mifgashim Sifrutiyim* [Popular and canonical: Literary dialogues], ed. Tamar Hess, Omri Herzog, and Yael Shapira (Tel Aviv: Resling, 2007), 131–140.

17. The entries written between April 1941 and May 1942 were not included in the printed edition, but are kept in the Moreshet archive (D.2.470). Several of that year's entries appeared in Hebrew in the following periodicals: *Yalqut Moreshet* 3 (December 1964): 7–22 (prior to the publication of the printed edition); *Bitzaron* 53, no. 1 (254) (October–November 1965): 7–18; *Bitzaron* 69, no. 5 (28) (April–May 1969): 15–17, 39. The choice of material in each of these publications appears to be tendentious in the sense that few entries expressing Kaplan's despondency or aggression toward institutions or people in the ghetto are included. I have yet to find an answer to the question of why the entries for this year were included in neither the printed edition of 1966 nor the English-language editions.

18. Emanuel Ringelblum, *Ktavim Ahronim: Yahasei Yehudim-Polanim* [Last writings: Jewish–Polish relations], vol. 2 (Jerusalem: Yad Vashem, 1994), 19.

19. Saul Friedländer, *Nazi Germany and the Jews: The Years of Extermination 1939–1945* (London: Weidenfeld and Nicolson, 2007), 41.

20. See, for example, Friedländer, *Nazi Germany and the Jews, 1939–1945*; Yisrael Gutman, *The Jews of Warsaw 1939–1943: Ghetto, Underground, Revolt*, trans. Ina Friedman (Bloomington: Indiana University Press, 1982); Dalia Ofer, "Everyday Life of Jews under Nazi Occupation: Methodological Issues," *Holocaust and Genocide Studies* 9, no. 1 (1995): 42–69; Barbara Engelking and Jacek Leociak, *The Warsaw Ghetto: A Guide to a Perished City*, trans. Emma Harris (New Haven, CT: Yale University Press, 2009); Alon Confino, *Foundational Past* (Cambridge: Cambridge University Press, 2012).

21. Rosenfeld, *A Double Dying*, 40–44; Sidra DeKoven Ezrahi, *By Words Alone: The Holocaust in Literature* (Chicago: University of Chicago Press, 1980), 102–103.

8

THE JEWS AND NAZI "LAW"

On 8 January 1940, Chaim Kaplan asserted in his diary: "Nazism cancelled all law and justice; in particular, with regard to the Jews who have been excluded from all legal jurisdiction. . . . When one born of a 'low race' is brought before Nazi justice, he is judged not on the basis of the law that applies to everyone, but on the basis of 'judicial sentiment.' "[1] This notion is anything but unusual in the diary. Unlike most other Warsaw Jewish diarists, Kaplan was obsessed with understanding the Nazis and Nazism. He was haunted and preoccupied by their evil and wanted somehow to decipher it. The Nazis, their relation to the law, and the way in which this affected their attitude toward the Jews are thus among the most frequently recurring themes in his wartime diary, in which they appear hundreds of times. This chapter will examine, in political-psychoanalytic theoretical terms, the ways in which Nazi law is referred to in Kaplan's diary.

The standing of the "law" in Nazi Germany and its attitude toward the Jews was paradoxical and confusing. On the one hand, there were judicial, administrative, and enforcement systems in Nazi Germany and all of the areas under German occupation. There was even a formal pretense of continuity between the judicial system in Nazi Germany and the one that preceded it, in the Weimar Republic—as the Weimar Constitution was never abrogated and the previous civil and criminal codes continued to exist during the Nazi period, albeit with significant adaptations.[2] The legislative, judicial, and enforcement authorities continued to operate throughout the period, and the administrative and bureaucratic apparatuses throughout the Reich acted on the basis of numerous laws, decrees, and regulations. In fact, as Raphaël Lemkin (one of the first jurists to deal with the subject of Nazi Germany, and the originator of the term "genocide") notes, the endless promulgation of sweeping and draconian laws that penetrate every aspect of life is the very essence of the totalitarian regime.[3]

So too was the case with regard to the persecution of the Jews and even their extermination. An endless barrage of laws, regulations, ordinances, and decrees emerged in Germany and in all territories under German occupation. The exclusion of Jews from society; the theft of their property; the revocation of their rights; their concentration in ghettos, "Jews' Houses," and other places; their exploitation as slave laborers; their deportation to the camps; and their eventual murder were all "regulated." In that sense everything was "legal."

Nevertheless, it is very hard to speak of the Third Reich as a law-abiding state, or of the radical crimes committed within this framework as legal acts.[4] Such assertions not only arouse indignation and strong moral condemnation, but are fundamentally flawed. Alongside the judicial system in Nazi Germany, there operated powerful political institutions of the Nazi Party and terror institutions that enjoyed extraterritorial status vis-à-vis the judicial system and took precedence over it, in any case of conflict: the SS, the SD, the Gestapo, and all of the terror institutions that operated on their authority. These institutions, which wielded immense power, operated their own "penal" system—dealing with anyone perceived as an "enemy of the state," and groups considered inferior or destructive from a racial or eugenic perspective. "I am totally indifferent to whether a legal clause opposes our actions," Himmler declared at the founding of the Academy for German Law in 1936.[5] These terror apparatuses were responsible for the greater part of Nazi crimes, and the civil legal system collaborated with them or stood aside.

Moreover, the Nazi legal and administrative system itself was based on a number of fundamental principles that withdrew the state of law from the category of "law"—that is, not merely law in the purely formal sense of the word, but a rational authority that regulates relations between citizens or subjects and the authorities, in an egalitarian manner and on the basis of justice (natural or positive).[6] On 28 February 1933, following the Reichstag fire, an article of the Weimar Constitution was evoked, enabling the promulgation of emergency decrees in order to safeguard public security. A state of emergency thus came into force. The temporary and limited state of emergency, however, quickly became the normative, all-encompassing legal state and, in effect, the central regulatory principle in Germany itself and throughout the Reich, allowing virtually any crime to be committed under the aegis of "constitutionality."

A further principle that was structurally bound to the "state of emergency" principle was the "Führer principle" (*Führerprinzip*), which, according to legal scholar Diemut Majer, stood "at the heart of National Socialist ideology."[7] This principle saw, in the Führer, a figure entirely beyond the law and unrestricted by it. The Führer's authority was not bound by legal, religious, or other norms, and from March 1933, his orders became supreme law. All of the judicial and administrative institutions adapted to the Führer's will and his direct, indirect, and even imagined orders. The Führer principle was supplemented by a further, closely related legal principle: the Volkist principle of racial inequality. The entire judicial system was thus organized on a racial basis, relating to the national community (*Volksgemeinschaft*)—at one with and embodied in the person of the Führer—as the source of legal authority. All those who were not considered part of the national community were, therefore, effectively perceived as outside the law.

These principles created the formal basis for the functioning of Nazi Germany as a totalitarian state in which, as Hannah Arendt put it, the active principle was not the law but rather total terror. This state terror did not derive its authority from the force of justice or reason but served as the direct executor of a supreme and eternally valid law—the law of history and nature itself, which drives the struggle between the races in the spirit of social Darwinism. The duration and validity of such a law lies beyond any human law, and only endless terror is consonant with it and constitutes its practical realization. Arendt thus asserts that "lawlessness is the essence of tyranny [and], terror is the essence of totalitarian domination."[8] The concentration camp was the embodiment of this terror in its purest form. The totalitarian terror state, however, which sometimes hid behind an appearance of law, effectively permeated every stratum of German society and every corner of the Reich.

Following Arendt but in psychoanalytical terms, Jean-Gérard Bursztein describes Nazism as a political perversion, at the heart of which lies the radical and unprecedented rejection of the symbolic law that is the basis for every social connection. According to Bursztein, Nazism promised the return of the primordial obscene father (to whom Freud referred in *Totem and Taboo* and to which we alluded in our discussion of Klemperer) in the figure of Hitler. This obscene father is not bound by any limitation and embodies the promise to the German people to overcome separateness and structural splits in order to return to primal unity in the form of national community (*Volksgemeinschaft*), thereby restoring the subject's strong but unrealistic and impossible fantasy of direct access to full and endless enjoyment.[9]

The Jews in Nazi Law

The Jews were the primary victims of this ideological and political method, first in Germany and, later, throughout Europe. In the power struggles between the German army and the terror apparatuses—first and foremost the SS and the civil administration operated by Party officials—over control in the occupied areas in Poland, the terror apparatuses won the upper hand.[10] What this meant was that Jews and Poles in these areas were left outside any law. Immediately following the invasion, the Nazis declared that a "harsh racial struggle" would be conducted in Poland, which would not recognize any "legal restrictions," and that is indeed what happened.[11] The Polish elite was liquidated, Polish national institutions crushed, and broad "experiments" in racial demographic engineering—involving the transfer of entire populations—turned tens and hundreds of thousands into refugees in their own country.

The terror unleashed against the Jews was far worse. Warsaw, the city of Chaim Kaplan, was emblematic. Upon entering the city, in September 1939, the Nazis immediately imposed a reign of terror. Jews were abducted for day labor, during the course of which they were humiliated and suffered violent abuse. Any Jew walking in the street risked sadistic, violent attacks, sometimes lasting hours at a time. German soldiers would often target ultra-Orthodox Jews, violently cutting off their beards while humiliating them. At the same time, the widespread theft of Jewish property began—some by order of signed decrees and some simply by looters. In his memoirs, the engineer Henryk Brysker documented the response faced by anyone who dared to complain to the Germans of property taken without legal justification or written authorization: "The Gestapo man to whom the complaint was addressed would respond with a blow of his revolver butt to clear the complainant's head of any notion that the German rulers might be pilferers or thieves."[12]

After a short while, the initial outburst of violence subsided a little, replaced by a system of laws, decrees, and regulations, which deprived the Jews of virtually all means of support. Bank accounts were frozen, businesses transferred to Aryan hands, Jews dismissed from nearly all of their places of employment. As part of their cruel, colonialist project, the Germans sought to establish a regime of slavery in Poland, to provide for the economic needs of the Reich. The Poles were relegated to the role of slaves, while the Jews were denied even that status. They were completely excluded from all of the central economic spheres and were left without means practically overnight. The Jews of Warsaw and the General Government (the governorate of German-occupied areas of Poland) were inundated with decrees that choked every possibility of support. Subsequently, the Jews of Warsaw were confined to the ghetto, along with some 150,000 refugees, in terrible conditions of hunger and poor sanitation that resulted in the spread of disease and a mortality rate of 20 percent during the two years of the ghetto's existence.

Jews were thus placed outside the law in a number of senses. Every thug could do as he pleased with the Jews, robbing or assaulting them, while the Jews were unable to resist and had no recourse to the law, because the law in the General Government—and especially anti-Jewish legislation—was based on racial principles that denied Jews the protection of the law as well as their other rights. Above all, however, a considerable portion of the authority over the Jews was assigned to the security apparatuses (such as the SS, the SD, the Security Police, and the Gestapo), which were, as we have noted, structurally outside the realm of the law.[13]

The Jews in the General Government were formally subject to the "law," in the sense that the policies against them were conducted by means of decrees and regulations and within the legal framework meticulously set out by the head of the General Government—lawyer Hans Frank. In practice, however, as asserted by Mark Mazower, for example, they were outside all law.[14] For them, the law—in the sense of an order that organizes relations between people and between people and institutions, in a rational, consistent, and (more or less) egalitarian and predictable fashion, based on certain principles of justice—did not exist.

The Jews were outside the law in a deeper sense, however: they lacked symbolic status within the social and political network constituted by the Nazis in Europe. Indeed, a report prepared by the Polish underground in October 1939 reads: "From the first days of September to the present, the fate of the Jews in the occupied territories is a lone path of suffering, humiliation, persecution, and expropriation of property. . . . From a legal perspective, the Jews are the object of special laws and are, in effect, outside the law."[15] Jurists within the Warsaw ghetto worked on a precise and detailed description of the ways in which legal concepts and juridical thought were collapsing and losing their validity and meaning in the context of Jewish life in the ghetto, under Nazi occupation. Such is the case of the diary of Stanislaw Adler, a lawyer who worked in the legal department of the Jewish police.[16]

Warsaw ghetto diarists such as Adam Czerniakow and Emanuel Ringelblum—to the extent that they relate to the Germans, almost never question the rationale behind their actions. Others, such as Janusz Korczak or Rachel Auerbach, hardly speak of the Germans at all. Chaim Kaplan, on the other hand, engages from the very start in observing and trying to understand the mechanisms of the Nazi occupation and its attitude toward the Jews, and in investigating the ideological and psychological motives of the agents of the Nazi regime.[17] He was thus keenly aware of the paradoxical state of the law under Nazi occupation and describes, in detail, the grave ramifications of this reality for Jewish subjects and their ontological and epistemological status.

Even before the war, in the wake of *Kristallnacht* in Germany, Kaplan, who lived in Warsaw, understood that the Nazis have no real affinity with the law. When the Nazi senior jurist Hans Frank (who, as noted, would become head of the General Government in occupied Poland less than a year later) visited still-independent Poland on 15 December 1938 and lectured on the principles of law in Nazi Germany, Kaplan remarked: "Nazism and law—are there two greater opposites than these? The entire essence of Nazism is the rule of power. What does this have to do with law? In Germany there is no justice, only tyranny."[18] With the beginning of the Poland Campaign, this issue became crucial for Kaplan himself.

In the very first days of the war, even before the capture of Warsaw, Kaplan reaches the conclusion that the Nazi's goal with regard to the Jews is far-reaching. On 6 September, the day before the head of Polish propaganda, Colonel Umiastowski, announced that the Germans were at the gates of Warsaw, and some three weeks before the city's fall, Kaplan declares: "In a day or two, we will be handed over to a robber and a murderer, to a cruel barbarian, one of whose goals in life is to eradicate the Jewish race from under the heavens."[19]

This is a very unusual declaration at such an early stage of the war. It is not based on any encounter with the Germans or experience of living under German rule, as it is only the sixth day of the war and the Nazis had not yet reached Warsaw. Nor does it stem from the prior experiences of the Jews in Germany or in the areas annexed by Germany, as Nazi policies toward the Jews at this point were limited mainly to isolation, despoliation, and expulsion. Although members of the Nazi leadership often used expressions of extermination with regard to the Jews, there was not yet, at this time, any concrete plan for their annihilation.[20] Kaplan's assertion is thus based on full confidence in the seriousness of Nazi rhetoric—particularly Hitler's—and an understanding of the structure of Nazi logic with regard to the Jews.

The historian Saul Friedländer described Kaplan as "usually more far-sighted than any other diarist."[21] Indeed Kaplan understood from the earliest stages that the Nazi violence against the Jews was a structural matter—the (non-)status of the Jew within the structure of Nazi reality.[22] The acts of violence indicate not only the Nazi intention to persecute the Jews but also that the Jew has no place in their vision of the world or the symbolic framework they have constituted and within which they act: *the Jew is outside symbolic law.* Kaplan understands that the Nazi goal is not only to get rid of the Jews or to murder them, but to eradicate them as a race "from under the heavens."[23] He understands that the Nazi interest lies not in individual Jews (numerous though they may be), as he frequently notes in his diary, but in negating the place of the Jewish race within the symbolic framework they had constituted. He understands that in the "new world" the Nazis are striving to create, there is simply no place for the Jews—who are outside the order of things. With the beginning of the occupation this understanding receives confirmation.

At a very early stage, Kaplan discovers that, contrary to their image, the Nazis are not men of law and order.[24] He points to this discrepancy many times, throughout the diary, but already on 5 October 1939, he describes the devastating results of the "legal" status of the Jews.[25] Following a detailed description of acts of theft and abuse, he concludes: "There is no end to the abuse we suffer. They plunder merchandise in every shop—'legally' in the open and illegally in secret. Our resources are depleting, we are becoming more impoverished by the hour. But material ruin is not the main thing; it is rather the suffocating atmosphere, the recognition that you are a nonentity, that you are prey and spoil to every thug and to every ruffian." In this passage, Kaplan's attention is focused not on the material consequences of the theft and abuse—"material ruin is not the main thing"—but on something far more basic that he is not yet able to define precisely—"the suffocating atmosphere, the recognition that you are a nonentity."

At this point, Kaplan describes the theft of Jewish property, including plunder by "legal" means, as a kind of ruffianism. Its effect on the Jews, however, is to plunge them into a depressing and dispiriting state of helplessness.

The choking metaphor and the expression "nonentity" (*hadal ishim* in Hebrew—one who ceases to be counted among men) indicate a kind of nullification that has not yet been stated explicitly but is keenly felt, already at this stage, as far more significant than material loss.

The Nazis' fundamental attitude to the law continues to trouble Kaplan, and especially the status of the Jews in Nazi law. The topic arises in relation to border adjustments between Germany and the Soviet Union, and the possibility that parts of Poland with Jewish populations might come under Soviet jurisdiction.[26] In this context, Kaplan compares Soviet repression to Nazi repression. He thus writes on 13 October 1939:

> The first victims of Russian Bolshevism were the Jews, and the Jewry of Russia, too, has been driven from the earth. There are no signs of Jewishness at all in Russia. Yet nevertheless . . . there is plunder on the one hand and plunder on the other, but the Russians plunder one as a citizen and a man, while the Nazis plunder one as a nonentity Jew. . . . The Nazi is a sadist, however. His hatred of the Jews is a psychosis. He flogs and derives pleasure from it. The torment of the victim is a balm to his soul, especially if the victim is a Jew.

Comparing the two forms of repression, Kaplan reaches a conclusion he expresses in a play on words that contrasts the Russians who "plunder one as a citizen and a *man*," and the Nazis who "plunder one as a nonentity [*hadal ishim*—non-*person* in Hebrew] Jew." The Soviets discriminate against the Jew as a member of society ("a citizen") and, therefore, as a subject ("a man"). The Nazis, on the other hand, see the Jew as one who is outside every social system ("a Jew"), and is therefore denied humanity (*hadal ishim*—"a non-person"). Kaplan thus recognizes that the Jews, despite the extensive legislation concerning them, are outside of all law and, as such, are excluded—in their own, internal perception as well—from the realm of the human. They are objectively nonpersons (*hadal ishim*). Furthermore, he recognizes that the Nazi attitude toward the Jews is based on boundless sadistic pleasure.

Nearly a year later, on 3 August 1940, Kaplan expresses the (mistaken) belief among the Jews that the Russians are about to enter Warsaw: "Conclusion: the entry of the Bolsheviks has become almost a certainty." Although he knows that the Jews will not have an easy time under Communist rule, he stresses: "Here the danger of annihilation hangs over us. Here we have ceased being human . . . we have been excluded from all legal protection. But under the aegis of the Reds, we will once again be human."

In other words, above and beyond Kaplan's earlier observation that the Jews are effectively outside the framework of the law—in ironic contrast to the laws, regulations, and decrees with which they are inundated—he now expresses, in the clearest possible terms, the effect of "being outside the law," and not only from the Nazi perspective but *in the eyes of the narrator himself*: "we have ceased being human." Only the Jews' return to the world of the law, under Soviet rule, will restore them to the status of subjects.[27] It is important to note that in December 1938, after *Kristallnacht* and a worsening of the situation of the Jews of Germany but before the Nazi invasion of Poland, Kaplan still believed that German Nazism and Soviet Communism embodied similar phenomena, as far as the Jews were concerned.[28] He now recognizes the difference, understanding that a fundamental change has taken place, beyond economic persecution and repressive, discriminatory legislation. The law no longer organizes the Jews' public status (in a legal, philosophical, and psychoanalytical sense) on the basis of reciprocal relations between them and the sovereign power, imposing responsibilities and granting rights. In effect, the Jews no longer have a place in the social and political networks—not even an inferior place that affords minimal social and political protection. The Nazi "laws" now place Jews entirely outside human society, denying them recognition as subjects of the law.[29]

Parenthetically, I would add that Jews elsewhere in Europe had also recognized the fundamental change the concept of law had undergone, as Hélène Berr, for example, writes in September 1942, in Paris: "Those laws are illegal from start to finish, a mere product of their whims; those laws are nothing more than a pretext for making arrests, that's their only aim, not to legislate or regulate anything at all."[30]

The grave ramifications of this (il)legal status for individuals and for their relations with others are also documented in Kaplan's diary. For example, on 12 October 1939, he writes: "Even in our poverty, in our misery, and in the low state we were in until now, we were not accustomed to such shameful and humiliating orders. We are ashamed to look at one another, as if we were impure or lepers!"[31] The Jews themselves internalized the Nazi position that objectively excluded them from the law and the social order and, as such, rendered them "nonpersons." That is why they were ashamed to look at one another. Every glance reaffirmed their existential feeling that they were no longer a part of human society, but impure and lepers—groups traditionally excluded from the social order. Kaplan therefore repeatedly states, as for example, on the eve of the establishment of the ghetto, on 25 October 1940: "We will be like a leper colony, the scum of the human race, *in our own eyes as well*."[32]

"Everything Is Forbidden to Us, and Yet We Do Everything"

Thus far we have seen that Kaplan reached the conclusion that Jews are outside Nazi law and realized that, in the course of this process, Jews may lose their sense of being part of the social human order even in their own eyes. The Nazis are thus perceived as acting in a confused and disorderly fashion. For example, on 24 February 1940, Kaplan notes that there is "chaos" in the ranks of the occupier, who is unable to boast of his order but, on the contrary, only of "exemplary disorder." However, the diary also presents another perception of Nazi "law" regarding the Jews and its ramifications for Jewish self-image. According to this approach, the Nazi attitude to the Jews was methodical and consistent, and based on a full and absolute legal system, without loopholes or exceptions. Kaplan thus writes on 25 October 1940, on the eve of the establishment of the ghetto: "[The] Nazi method against the Jews is always complete and absolute." He therefore finds it hard to believe that the ghetto that is being created will be open.[33] Similarly, according to jurist and ghetto Jewish Police officer Stanislaw Adler: "Legal reasoning had undergone 'simplification' during the Nazi occupation. To the question 'Is it permissible?' the routine reply of the lawyer was now: 'No, it is not permitted.' And to the question 'What is the danger?' there was only one reply: 'Death by shooting.' "[34]

One of Kaplan's most quoted phrases in this context, repeated a number of times in the diary, is: "Everything is forbidden to us, and yet we do everything."[35] Ostensibly, this is a positive expression of the Jews' ability to continue to exist and engage in vibrant activity, despite the fact that "legally," everything is forbidden. Indeed, this is how Yisrael Gutman interprets Kaplan's words: "Like Ringelblum, Kaplan views the disregard of German orders (concerning the requirement that foreign currency be handed over to the authorities, secret production in workshops, and the smuggling of food into the ghetto) as a line of spontaneous resistance, typical of Polish Jews—inured to hard and trying times."[36]

There is undoubtedly a lot of truth in this interpretation but I believe the phrase "Everything is forbidden to us, and yet we do everything" deserves closer examination.

Stanisław Różycki, an inhabitant of the ghetto who wrote some very important essays on it, referred in an essay, "This Is the Ghetto! A Report from 20th Century Inferno," to this very phrase but turned it on its head: "Precisely because nothing is permissible, everything is possible. . . . When you are beyond the law . . . then the slave has no rights even to breathe fresh air. That is why the slave . . . today does all that tomorrow may be punishable by death . . . throwing off the remainders of our conscience and ethics."[37]

Kaplan's understanding of this saying is a bit different. He begins his entry of 1 August 1940 with the words: "The Jewish people have always lived in material and spiritual straits. Our enemies have always engulfed us to destroy us. Yet Jewish creativity never ceased throughout all the days of our exile." The Jews, he continues, have a conspiratorial tradition of creativity and existence: "Every nation, in its time of misfortune, has conspirators [!] who do their work in secret. In our case an entire nation has been raised on conspiracy. . . . We have a special term for this concept: Marranos [*anusim*]."

It is in this context that the phrase "Everything is forbidden to us, and yet we do everything" appears: "In these days of our misfortune we live the life of Marranos [*anusim*]. Everything is forbidden to us, and yet we do everything. Every Jewish occupation is under a ban, yet nevertheless we somehow support ourselves; true, we do it with grief, but we do survive. Public social life has been stopped, but something can still be done in secret."[38] If so, contrary to the passages in which Kaplan compares Soviet and Nazi persecution of the Jews—where the difference is between placing legal restrictions on Jews and excluding them entirely from the framework of the law—in this equation, Jews are described as wholly enveloped by the law, leaving them virtually no space free from its orders and bans. From this perspective, Kaplan sees a parallel between the lives of Jews during the Nazi period and traditional Jewish behavior under conditions of repression and harsh legal restrictions throughout history. According to this analogy, the Jews of the Nazi period, like those of previous eras, continued to pursue a "conspiratorial" tradition of existence and creativity in the shadow of occupation.[39] The comparison to *anusim* (a term associated primarily with the crypto-Jews of the Iberian Peninsula after 1391) intimates a liminal status of clandestine identity, unsupported by public "law." It presumes that the "inside" can remain unharmed, even when it is not recognized by the "outside" (such as the law). This is, however, a "solution" that leaves profound scars.

Indeed, Kaplan himself feels, as witnessed in the passage quoted above, that extolling the "*anusim* strategy" of the Jews of Warsaw is problematic. The difficulty becomes more apparent later in the entry, in Kaplan's description of a cultural meeting at the Zionist soup kitchen, as an example of the kind of activity that attests to Jewish vitality—everything is forbidden to them, yet they do everything. He concedes that "Gatherings of this sort don't enhance knowledge, but the custom persists, and that is the important thing"—highlighting the continuity, if only formal, of the Eastern European Jewish tradition of cultural and political gatherings. At the same time, however, he also describes the wretchedness of the meeting, adding: "Everyone sat with bowed heads . . . almost as if we were ashamed to look one another in the face." Once again we see the victims' own sense of shame; those present felt that they had not done anything significant, that they had not succeeded in overcoming the system of repression that was choking them.

How can this feeling of wretchedness be explained? At first glance, it seems obvious that an explanation should be sought in the context of normal life before the war. In contrast to the political gatherings held in ordinary times, this meeting was a mockery, more noteworthy for what it was not than for what it was, embodying the loss of meaning of public institutions—emptied of content, leaving only the private sphere and the sense of personal shame. Personal shame supplanted the discussion and debate of the public sphere because the latter had effectively ceased to exist.[40] Although this explanation accentuates the change experienced by the inhabitants of the ghetto, it still relates to the consciousness of normal life as the yardstick for evaluating new events. We may also look at things from another perspective, however.

Based on an analysis by Levinas, Giorgio Agamben offers the following explanation of shame:

> To be ashamed means to be consigned to something that cannot be assumed. But what cannot be assumed is not something external. Rather, it originates in our own intimacy; it is what is most intimate in us (for example, our own physiological life). Here the "I" is thus overcome by its own passivity, its ownmost sensibility; yet this expropriation and desubjectification is also an extreme and irreducible presence of the "I" to itself. It is as if our consciousness collapsed and, seeking to flee in all directions, were simultaneously summoned by an irrefutable order to be present at its own defacement, at the expropriation of what is most its own. In shame, the subject thus has no other content than its own desubjectification; it becomes witness to its own disorder, its own oblivion as a subject. *This double movement, which is both subjectification and desubjectification, is shame.*[41]

In the present case, it may be precisely this paradoxical movement—in which the victim declares, by the very fact of his subjective existence (the Zionist meeting), his own disorder (reflected in the terrible wretchedness of the meeting)—that gives rise to the sense of shame.[42] It would thus appear that in a situation in which "Everything is forbidden to us, and yet we do everything," the subject will experience disintegrative shame of this kind.

The phrase is repeated a number of times throughout the diary, as an expression of Jewish vitality.[43] As time goes by, however, Kaplan begins to see some sort of a different truth in this expression and in what it symbolizes. He realizes that such a position, which is completely outside the law, does not constitute his status as a subject and does not afford him life but, on the contrary, denies it to him. The (Nazi) law here stands in opposition to life itself, to the point that it is almost insurmountable—contrary to the notion that "everything is forbidden to us, and yet we do everything." Kaplan thus writes on 16 May 1942, some two months before the mass deportations to Treblinka: "Life in the ghetto is stagnant and frozen. . . . Whatever we do we do illegally; legally we don't even have permission to exist. . . . Our lives—if this can be called living—have taken on their inert, monotonous forms and no changes occur in them. The only ones who bring some activity into the sordid life of the ghetto are the killer and his friend death." Toward the end of the ghetto's existence, Kaplan understands, on the one hand, that there is no real escape from Nazi "law" but, on the other hand, that it is not a law that orders life but rather one that leads to death.[44] In the words of Avraham Lewin, written in the Warsaw ghetto on 3 July 1942, less than three weeks before the mass deportations: "Jews have one right in Germany," a German Nazi minister once said: "to die."[45] Therefore, life under Nazi law is not really life. Ironically, the only things that accord life a modicum of vitality are murder and death.

Shockingly, Kaplan also draws his own conclusions from this fact in the diary's final entry, dated 4 August 1942, a few days before his murder. The entry was written at the height of the mass deportations to Treblinka, at a time when the status of the Jews of Warsaw as existing "outside the law" had reached its horrifying and cruel culmination. Kaplan weighs his possibilities of escape, and since he has no money to pay a bribe or get a factory job—something he believes would have offered a chance of survival, at least for a while—he also considers the possibility of hiding, eventually rejecting that as well: "My only salvation is hiding. This is an outlaw's life, and a man cannot last very long living illegally." With this realistic assessment, that life entirely outside the law is not possible under the Nazi occupation, Kaplan concludes his diary and his life.

In short, Kaplan describes the paradox and impossibility of Jewish existence at once outside the law and under its total domination. He also grasps, however, at a very early stage, that the status of the Nazis in relation to the law is twofold: on one level, they are the legislators but, on the other, they too exist outside or beyond the law—on the opposite side. For example, in an entry dated 22 January 1940, Kaplan tells about a manhunt the Germans were conducting for someone by the name of Kott, wanted for murder on political grounds. The Nazi press that had released the story, blamed the Jews, although Kott was, in fact, a Christian, according to the Nazi racial laws. Kaplan remarks: "But the addled conquerors go along their merry way. This time they paid no attention to the rule they themselves laid down."[46] The Nazi method is thus paradoxical: legislators are not bound by their own laws. In this sense, the Nazis are a clear embodiment of the obscene, sadistic father of *Totem and Taboo*; the cruel figure who is above laws and is identified with perverted and boundless enjoyment.

The Law and Sadistic Pleasure

In Kaplan's diary, as we have seen, Jews are—paradoxically—both outside Nazi law and utterly controlled by it. In a certain sense, this is a variation on the model presented in chapter 4. In the Nazi world, it is hard for Jews to find the appropriate distance from the law. The Nazis either affix the law to them—to their very bodies—with no breathing space ("Whatever we do we do illegally; legally we don't even have permission to exist"), or place them entirely outside the concept of law ("We are outside all law"). This duality is the duality of Nazi persecution and annihilation, characterized throughout by exemplary order and the appearance of strict adherence to the law, alongside manifestations of complete lawlessness and sadistic cruelty.[47]

Indeed, the idea of Nazism as utterly lawless sadism, not for rational, utilitarian ends, but in order to derive endless pleasure from the suffering of others, is very dominant in Kaplan's diary. Thus, on 14 January 1940, he writes: "[The Nazis are] our archenemies . . . tyrants and oppressors, who are commanded and ready to trample us for their sadistic appetites and to annihilate us to the very last one. . . . From where will our help come?"[48] On 6 September 1940, Kaplan explicitly notes that, ultimately, the cruel economic exploitation of the Jews is undertaken not for the sake of profit—that is not for rational, utilitarian ends—but for the sheer pleasure of the torment itself: "A normal murderer, who does what he does for the sake of lucre, kills and flees. . . . Not so a murder afflicted by the disease of sadism. He derives particular pleasure to watch the death throes of his victim. And more than he takes pleasure in his money, he takes pleasure in his suffering." This is also how Kaplan explains the establishment of the ghetto, in an entry dated 2 November 1940: "Our torments give him physical pleasure, and he needs nothing further." After the closure of the ghetto, he notes (26 November 1940): "The ghetto was executed with terrifying sadism, the essence of which is hard for a healthy person to understand."[49]

The entry of 24 October 1940 is illustrative in this context. It was written during the chaos of the creation of the ghetto, and focuses on the utter lack of law, reason, and order that characterized the process. This lack drives Kaplan and—so he reports—all of the Jews of Warsaw mad. There is confusion everywhere and it is still unclear what the boundaries of the ghetto will be and whether it will be an open or a closed ghetto. Orders and counterorders, rumors and counterrumors give rise to anxiety and chaos.

On one level, the difficulties are clear and concrete or, in the words of the historian Yisrael Gutman: "The despair of the masses is understandable; they feared for their homes and livelihoods."[50] As we have seen in other contexts, however, Kaplan was of the opinion that "material ruin is not the main thing."[51] What appears to trouble Kaplan no less than the other hardships and misfortunes (such as isolation, humiliation, detachment, uprooting, etc.) is the lack of logic and method (i.e., law) in the process of establishing the ghetto. In other words, the establishment of the ghetto proves, once again, that the law no longer exists for the Jews.

Kaplan begins with a description of the influx into the ghetto, in which he finds—yet again and from another perspective—an illustration of the Jewish condition: "The streets of Warsaw are filled with carts loaded with belongings and family members. So long as poverty can be locked in the innermost places, people forget it exists; but when it is brought outside it awakens disgust and loathing." What is incredible is that the "poverty" to which Kaplan refers is not only the result of Nazi policies, which had deprived Jews of virtually all of their possessions during the first year of occupation, but also reflects the unintentional internalization of the antisemitic viewpoint, employing traditional and Nazi anti-Jewish rhetoric: even in Kaplan's eyes, the Jews arouse disgust, loathing, and repulsion. He immediately explains, however, in a very lengthy passage, that "this pitiful phenomenon, which is not only the fruit of pathological hatred . . . that only addle-brained psychopaths afflicted with the disease of pointless hatred . . . thieves, robbers, and bandits . . . in short a band of evildoers, are capable of enacting such unjust and wicked laws."

In the same breath, Kaplan links psychopathic sadism ("addle-brained psychopaths") and lawlessness ("thieves, robbers, and bandits") and legislation itself ("a band of evildoers . . . capable of enacting such unjust and wicked laws"), as emblematic characteristics, in his opinion, of the Nazi attitude toward the Jews. This view brings together and even identifies Nazi psychopathic pleasure with Nazi law regarding the Jews. In Kaplan's diary, they are two sides of the same coin.

Jean Améry, following Georges Bataille's interpretation of sadism, offers an explanation of this duality that coincides with Kaplan's approach, as reflected in his diary. Améry writes as follows: "For Georges Bataille, sadism is to be understood not in the light of sexual pathology but rather in that of existential psychology, in which it appears as the radical negation of the other . . . by negating his fellow man, who also in an entirely specific sense is 'hell' for him, he wants to realize his own total sovereignty. The fellow man is transformed into flesh, and in this transformation he is already brought to the edge of death; if worst comes to worst, he is driven beyond the border of death into Nothingness."[52] Sadism, according to Bataille, is the transformation of a subject into flesh—an object. "Radical negation of the other" is, to a large extent, the goal of Nazi law with regard to the Jews, as Kaplan well observed. Furthermore, according to Agamben, Nazi law structurally denied Jews their very humanity: "When referring to the legal status of Jews after the racial laws, the Nazis also used a term that implied a kind of dignity: *entwürdigen*, literally to 'deprive of dignity.' The Jew is a human being who has been deprived of all *Würde*, all dignity: he is merely human—and, for this reason, non-human."[53] In other words, just as the Jews were objects, as victims of Nazi sadism, so too with regard to Nazi law, they were objects rather than subjects of the law. Sadism and law are thus not contradictory elements of Nazism but two aspects of the same phenomenon—both of which, afforded the Nazis, like the Freudian obscene father-of-enjoyment, immense pleasure at the expense of their victims' endless suffering.[54] Kaplan was well aware of this in his diary.

In this vein, we may also understand Kaplan's words later in the entry: "And 'the world' sits silent?! . . . O Leader of the city, where are you? But He Who sits in Heaven laughs[!]"[55] Since the law in its protective sense no longer exists for Jews, because Nazi "law" proved to be total sadistic pleasure, Kaplan appeals to the "world" and to the God of Israel to enforce their law. In both cases, however, he was to be bitterly disappointed. "The world" (Kaplan places it in distancing quotation marks) is silent. His appeal to God, as "Leader of the city"—one supposed to impose order in the world, leads to even greater disappointment: "He who sits in Heaven laughs."[56] It emerges that even the Jewish God is on the Nazis' side, laughing and deriving pleasure as they do. He too has ceased being the God of the law, to become the God of complete and obscene enjoyment.[57]

The Nazi Voice to the Jewish Ear

To the connection between law, enjoyment, and sadism we must add a further element discussed by Kaplan, and that is "voice," because, as the psychoanalyst theoretician Mladen Dolar rightly asserts, "[It is] the voice that commands and binds. If there is to be a covenant, there has to be a voice."[58] As we will soon see in Kaplan's diary, there are indeed close and complex connections between law (and its absence) and voice (and its absence).

In the entry dated 24 October 1940, discussed above, Kaplan describes the atmosphere of "chaos" on the eve of the closing of the ghetto and the confusion regarding the division of the streets between Jewish and Polish Warsaw: "At every hour, new changes are made regarding one area or another." He then returns to the discrepancy that has long troubled him: "The conqueror's reputation for order is undeserved. Everything he does bears the seal of disorder"—there are no rules or norms that can give a sense of stability amid the chaos; disorder prevails. He then concludes: "And an additional doubt is gnawing at us: Will it be a closed ghetto? . . . A closed ghetto means gradual death. An open ghetto is only a halfway catastrophe. . . . *The conqueror himself sits silently . . . [!] When will there be an end to this torment?!*"[59] We see here the way in which chaotic reality becomes a fundamental inner torment due to the silence of the Nazi authorities. On one level, the silence of the Nazis is hard to bear, as they are the only ones with the authority to clear up the confusion regarding the nature of the ghetto: open or closed—that is a place open to the "Aryan" part of the city, which thus still allows minimal economic activity, or a closed, giant prison for the Jews of Warsaw. The Nazis, however, refuse to provide the vital information they have. The future thus remains uncertain and chaotic.

The difficulty, however, seems to extend much further, as this silence is typical of many of Kaplan's descriptions, in which the Nazi voice is absent from his accounts of events (see below). Even in the descriptions of severe cruelty that abound in the diary, the component of voice is often missing—as if the Nazi abuse is inflicted in complete silence. In light of this, I would suggest that this torment, related to the silence of the "conqueror," may also be understood on a structural and functional plane. Nazi silence not only denies the Jews essential information but also empties their world of the sovereign voice of the law that affords it some sort of rational order, in which the subject may find place and belonging. In their silence, the Nazis would appear to have denied the Jews this necessary structural function, no less than they denied them vital information regarding the nature of the ghetto.

This function is related to what Louis Althusser termed "interpellation"—that is the law's hailing of the subject, thereby constituting him or her as such within the symbolic order of society. The voice in this case may be crucial. The following (famous) passage from Althusser's essay is worth quoting at length, in this context:

> I shall then suggest that ideology "acts" or "functions" in such a way that it . . . "transforms" the individuals into subjects . . . by that very precise operation which I have called *interpellation* or hailing, and which can be imagined along the lines of the most commonplace everyday police (or other) hailing: "Hey, you there!"
>
> Assuming that the theoretical scene I have imagined takes place in the street, the hailed individual will turn round. By this mere one-hundred-and-eighty-degree physical conversion, he becomes a *subject*. Why? Because he has recognized that the hail was "really" addressed to him, and that "it was *really him* who was hailed" (and not someone else). . . . Verbal call or whistle, the one hailed always recognizes that it is really him who is being hailed.[60]

According to Althusser's example, the hailing voice is necessary for the constitution of the subject. It happens when the representative of the authority calls you personally as a worthy part of the social order. At this very moment you lose some of your individual freedom and uniqueness, as you have to abide by the social rules that call for you through the voice of the policeman. He stresses that this process can occur by means of a verbal call or a whistle but the individual must hear (literally or metaphorically) the other's hail, understand that it is meant for him, and respond to it. In this sense, killing may also constitute interpellation. That is to say that when the law executes a prisoner, or even when a police officer shoots an escaped criminal in the name of the law, an Althusserian interpellation takes place. The criminal is killed as a subject who is defined by the law as "deserving death"—specifically "hailed" and assigned a place. The person is not simply murdered arbitrarily but, rather, called to death for a particular reason. Even if that person is "deserving death," it is as one who has been sentenced to death. In this case, the very act of killing may be seen as interpellative "hailing," which affirms the relationship between the subject and the law.

A murder scene that Kaplan describes in his diary stands in stark contrast to the Althusserian situation. The event takes place in the ghetto's final days, some two weeks before the beginning of the mass deportations. During this period, the Nazis eliminated many of their Jewish collaborators in the ghetto, and it is probably in this context that the incident occurred. On 25 June 1942, Kaplan describes the murder of a woman—in all likelihood a Jewish collaborator:

> In the past few days death has begun to stroll about in the streets of the ghetto even during the daytime. A military car drives into Orla Street in a great hurry. An officer and a very splendid lady get out of it. When they alight, the officer stretches out his hand to the lady and takes leave of her. The lady walks on ahead; the officer lingers behind her. Not many moments pass when a shot is heard. The officer aimed his gun at the lady, and she falls to the ground and dies. A woman is killed in broad daylight in the sight of hundreds of passersby and the thing makes no impression. There are various rumors about the reason for this incident, but they are beside the point at the moment.[61]

Kaplan describes a murder in which the murder loses its symbolic status as a shocking crime. It becomes a neutral datum, a purely biological fact ("the thing makes no impression"). Murder loses the quality that makes it such—it loses its murderousness.[62] Like the murder described by Robert Antelme under different circumstances: "[The SS man] Fritz has shot him, two shots, while we were walking. Nobody turned his head. Nothing even of the solemnity of crime nor of its secrecy."[63] This erosion of the consciousness of murder manifests itself as two sides of the same coin—in the description of the Jewish perspective and in the description of the Nazi act.

Particularly striking, from the Jewish perspective, is the thick presence of death, which is taken for granted; a living, anthropomorphized presence (it "has begun to stroll about in the streets of the ghetto even during the daytime"). Death is the normative situation, while the actual murderer is merely a chance embodiment of it. The murder evokes no response from the inhabitants of the ghetto because there is nothing unusual about it. It has lost its shocking, human dimension. The indifference may, however, be due to the way in which the act of murder is committed by the Nazi side, as perceived by Kaplan.

The behavior of the Nazi officer reflects a lack of recognition of the life of a Jew, as a human being who is protected by some law, as someone who is part of the symbolic order.[64] Contrary to Althusser's police officer who hails a civilian, the Nazi officer does not hail the woman he kills, does not cause her to turn toward him. He simply murders her, shooting her in the back. The murder does not take place as part of an interpellation instigated by the law toward an individual.[65] It is random and lawless. The hailing voice is completely absent. The Jewish woman was not called to her death by the law because—at least from Kaplan's perspective, as narrator of the incident—she was not killed pursuant to any law.[66]

In Kaplan's account, the Nazi officer did not actually murder the woman, as the act of murder never took place. The description is circumstantial: "a shot is heard" (in the passive voice—but no one actively fired the shot); the officer aims his gun at the woman and she falls (but again, he did not shoot her).[67] The end result is that the "woman is killed." Use of the word "killed" rather than "murdered," combined with the objectless passive form (killed by whom?) further strengthens the feeling that, in reality, no one actually committed murder. Kaplan's concluding phrase, "There are various rumors about the reason for this incident, but they are beside the point at the moment," lends even greater weight to this feeling. And again, the entire incident unfolds—with the exception of the gunshot—in complete silence.[68]

However, just as the Nazi voice is absent from the descriptions of the horrors, it is often traumatically and impossibly present. In such cases, the voice expresses only the sadistic, obscene enjoyment that subverts all law, and is no less of a torment than silence.

An example of the fact that the Nazi voice is the voice of psychopathic, sadistic, exposed, and traumatic madness can be found in an entry dated 3 February 1940. In this entry, Kaplan addresses "the nature of Nazism." He understands that it represents an unprecedented phenomenon and, therefore, "Descriptive literary accounts cannot suffice to clarify and emphasize its real quality." Furthermore, only the victim of the Nazis "who has bared his back to the lashes of its whips . . . might be able to give a true description of this pathological phenomenon called Nazism," characterized by "sadistic cruelty," "warped sensibility," and so forth.

He then tries to illustrate what he found so hard to define: "Let a few recent facts attest to its nature." He goes on to describe four incidents that reveal the sadistic, arbitrary, and lawless nature of the Nazis in their relation to the Jews. The first three are horrifying and violent but it is the fourth incident, to which Kaplan testifies in the first person and calls "an event of little [practical] consequence," that leaves the strongest impression on him.

Kaplan tells of a German patrol passing through the crowded, frozen streets of Warsaw. "One of them immediately thundered at the hundreds of passersby to get out of the way. Everyone fled and the path cleared in an instant. They did not have the chance to beat anyone, but Nazi coarseness left an indelible impression on all sensitive souls who witnessed the event." According to Kaplan, this incident was more illustrative of the Nazi sense of "lordship" (*Herrentum*) than acts of blatant violence.

What distinguishes this story and seems to have made such an impression on Kaplan is the fact that he heard the arbitrary and frightening voice of "lordship" even without its immediate violent effect. What he heard was the voice of psychopathic and hysterical sadism that destroys every law—the most tangible voice, the voice of violence itself.[69]

Perhaps this is why the Nazi regime itself was identified, and continues to be identified with voice/sound: the sound of marching, the voices of Nazi leaders and, above all, the voice of the Führer—which Yaron Jean calls an "arch-voice."[70] Hitler's voice is often described as possessing erotic force and, according to Jean-Gérard Bursztein, embodied "the lost object that was finally found," that is, full and final pleasure. It is the meaningless voice that constitutes the perverted order of Nazi Germany, as described, for example, by Goebbels: "He [Hitler] calls himself the drummer. He is the medium chosen for this purpose, to reestablish the old order solely by the power of his voice."[71]

Mirroring this voice another voice appears in Kaplan's diary, announcing the disintegration of law and meaning. It is not the law-destroying, sadistic, and perverted voice of the Nazis but its mirror image: the voice of the prophet of catastrophe, embodied by Kaplan's friend Hirsch.

The "Real" Voice

As noted above, Kaplan's writing during the war tends more to generalization than to description of specific cases (contrary to his diary of the 1930s). Most of the diary is written in the first or third person plural and is often anonymous ("you hear in a whisper"). Very few characters breach the wall of anonymity. The most prominent of these is Reb Hirsch, who first appears in the diary, in an unusually complete fashion, in the final days of the ghetto (and the diary), prior to and during the course of the mass deportations.[72] These are days of escalating terror, fear, and death. It is interesting that he is characterized primarily by his voice.

During the course of May 1942, terrifying reports arrived in the ghetto from the East and the Lublin area, where the Belzec death camp was already in operation.[73] During this period, the Gestapo carried out extensive killings in the ghetto. The fear of death that swept over the ghetto also pervaded Kaplan's diary. The fear stemmed primarily from the fact that no reason, order, or method (e.g., no law), could be discerned in these murders, and each person felt slated for death. Kaplan thus writes on 30 May:

> You are certain that the death sentences have already been drawn up; it is merely a matter of awaiting your turn—your turn to die. Perhaps it will come tonight, perhaps in a few more nights, but you will not escape your fate. It is a mental state that drives you mad and shatters your nerves.... The worst part of this ugly kind of death is that you don't know the reason for it.... The lack of reason for these murders especially troubles the inhabitants of the ghetto. In order to comfort ourselves we feel compelled to find some sort of system to explain these nighttime murders. Everyone, afraid for his own skin, thinks to himself: If there is a system, every murder must have a cause; if there is a cause, nothing will happen to me since I myself am absolutely guiltless.

The murders in the ghetto are entirely unsystematic, devoid of any method or rule or law from which one might deduce who deserves to live—even on the basis of the most warped criteria—and who deserves to die. This impossible situation drives the ghetto's inhabitants to madness. It seems to imply that everyone "deserves" to die, without any reason or justification. In the face of the Nazis' chaotic silence, the Jews devise—in a wholly phantasmic manner—a rationale (and law), which the murders express and enforce. Everyone understands that it is mere fantasy but no one wants to recognize it as such. Only one man gives voice to the terrible truth: "But my friend Hirsch, who is a very clever Jew, thinks differently. The system is a lack of system.... They go to the files, indiscriminately draw out a card, and whoever is picked, is picked: he is destined to die. Hirsch's opinion has earned him many enemies. People do not want to die without cause." It comes as no surprise that the voice that indicates the true state of affairs makes many enemies, although—and perhaps because—he confirms what everyone already knows: that the world, as a reality based on law and order and one that enables life, no longer exists for the Jews, and that the arbitrary law of terror is the only "law" that exerts complete control over their lives and is, therefore, already leading them to their deaths. They are all slated for death.

As Alexandra Garbarini notes, Kaplan creates a fascinating story out of the figure of Reb Hirsch—one that appears only toward the end of the diary. Hirsch's voice is distinct from Kaplan's but, at the same time, it is a voice that is clearly very close to Kaplan's heart.[74] He calls him "my Hirsch" and it seems as if he would like to assume the voice as his own.[75] In the end, however, and although Hirsch's voice is the voice of truth, it is irrelevant—it has no place or existence in the world of the ghetto. Thus, Kaplan writes on 16 June 1942: "My Hirsch is screaming like a crane." The expression "screaming like a crane" illustrates the irrelevance of Reb Hirsch's words for the inhabitants of the ghetto. It also demonstrates the extent to which Hirsch is characterized by his voice.

In an entry dated 2 July 1942, immediately prior to the Great Deportation, it becomes even more apparent that Reb Hirsch's power resides in his voice and that this voice cannot be heard or even serve as a source of identification and encouragement for Kaplan. In this entry, Kaplan tells of rumors and evaluations spreading throughout the ghetto that the Nazis are on the verge of defeat, and the Jews' circumstances are about to improve. Once again, however, reality proves them wrong: "Suddenly we have awakened. It was but a dream." Meanwhile, reports of the Nazi advance toward Palestine reach the ghetto, and all are absorbed by this concern—concern for the Jews of Palestine, and because many had hoped to be saved in an exchange of German citizens in Palestine for Polish Jews. "As we sat together . . . discussing our worries, Hirsch suddenly appeared, *and his voice was like thunder*" (emphasis added). Reb Hirsch tells them that a hundred Jews have been murdered by the Gestapo, adding: "You're worried about Palestine? Worry about your ghetto! The days of your life are numbered and counted."

The figure of Reb Hirsch, who "suddenly" appears, is again characterized by his voice: the tangible voice of thunder (sound without meaning)—that proclaims the lack of method and reason, the collapse of reality, and death. Opposite the voice of the ghetto inhabitants, including Kaplan, engaged in idle chatter, Reb Hirsch appears as the voice of the prophet speaking from within the void itself; a voice that no hopeful fantasy can silence. Reb Hirsch's voice is not that of Kaplan, the empathetic chronicler, party to the fanciful talk of the Jews of the ghetto. It is the voice of the prophet announcing the near and certain end of the Jews of Warsaw—an end that, in symbolic terms, has already come—from the moment they were excluded from all rule and law.[76]

Notes

1. Chaim Aron Kaplan, *Megilat Yisurin: Yoman Geto Varshah* [Scroll of agony: Warsaw ghetto diary] (Tel Aviv: Am Oved and Yad Vashem, 1966), 135.

2. Moshe Zimmermann, foreword to Michael Stolleis, *The Law under the Swastika: Studies on Legal History in Nazi Germany*, trans. Thomas Dunlap (Chicago: University of Chicago Press, 1998), esp. viii. See also Stolleis, *The Law under the Swastika*, 1–25.

3. Raphaël Lemkin, *Axis Rule in Occupied Europe* (Washington, DC: Carnegie Endowment for International Peace, 1944), ix.

4. On the demise of the rule of law in Nazi Germany, see at length Michael Burleigh, *The Third Reich: A New History* (London: Pan Macmillan, 2001), 149–215.

5. Ibid., 192.

6. On the status of the law in Nazi Germany, see Saul Friedländer, *Nazi Germany and the Jews: The Years of Extermination 1939–1945* (London: Weidenfeld and Nicolson, 2007), 10.

7. Diemut Majer, *"Non-Germans" under the Third Reich* (Baltimore: Johns Hopkins University Press, 2003), 10. See also Ian Kershaw, *Hitler: A Biography* (New York: Norton, 2008), esp. 320–357.

8. Hannah Arendt, *The Origins of Totalitarianism* (Cleveland: World, 1958), 464 and, more broadly, 460–468.

9. Jean-Gérard Bursztein, *Hapsikho'analizah shel Hanatzizm: Masah al Heres Hatzivilizatzyah* [The psychoanlysis of Nazism: An essay on the destruction of civilization], trans. Miriam Meir (Tel Aviv: Resling, 2004), 27–65. The constitution of the human subject in psychoanalysis, certainly in Lacanian psychoanalysis, is associated with the law. The first law in this formation process is the law that proceeds from the Oedipal drama, by means of which the "name of the father" separates the child from the mother. The "father" (or paternal function) says "no" to the child's desire for union with the mother, creating the first law that distinguishes between permitted and forbidden—the taboo of incest. In the prohibition against the child's merging with the mother and the frustration of his oceanic feelings toward her, this primordial, symbolic law effectively frustrates direct access to the endless pleasure to which man aspires. From the moment the mother is forbidden to the child—difference and separation from the Other, from the world, and from the self, becomes inevitable and irreparable. Complete union becomes impossible and exists only as yearning for the lost Eden. At the same time, the lack created by the law gives rise to the desire that seeks surrogate love objects, by means of which this structural lack may be compensated for or filled—always only partially—during the course of one's life.

10. According to Bursztein, this was because the Jews, more than any other people or community, symbolized the "law." The Jews are the people of the law.

11. Christopher Browning, *The Origins of the Final Solution* (London: Arrow, 2005), 24.

12. Quoted in Yisrael Gutman, *The Jews of Warsaw 1939–1943: Ghetto, Underground, Revolt*, trans. Ina Friedman (Bloomington: Indiana University Press, 1982), 9.

13. On the judicial system in Nazi Germany and the German-occupied territories, see Majer, *"Non-Germans" under the Third Reich*. On the philosophy of the state of emergency, see Carl Schmitt, *Political Theology: Four Chapters on the Concept of Sovereignty*, trans. George Schwab (Cambridge, MA: MIT Press, 1985); Schmitt, *The Concept of the Political*, trans. George Schwab (New Brunswick, NJ: Rutgers University Press, 1976); Giorgio Agamben, *State of Exception*, trans. Kevin Attell (Chicago: University of Chicago Press, 2005).

14. Mark Mazower, *Hitler's Empire: How the Nazis Ruled Europe* (New York: Penguin, 2008), 98, 246–249. Maurycy Allerhand, a Jewish professor of law at Lvov University, describes an encounter with Professor Polanski, a lecturer in law during the Bolshevik period and mayor of Lvov under the Germans. Polanski asked Allerhard how he was, and when the latter said he was studying the law books of the General Government, the former replied: "Such study is unnecessary, as these laws now are not binding." This account reveals an awareness of the non-binding (for the legislator!) nature of Nazi law. See Bella Gutterman, ed., *Bevo Ha'emah: Yehudei Lvov Tahat Hakibush Hagermani: Dapei Edut Yuni 1941–April 1942* [Days of horror: Jewish testimonies from German-occupied Lemberg 1941–1943: Testimonies from June 1941 to April 1942] (Tel Aviv: The Institute for the History of Polish Jewry and the Diaspora Research Center, 1991), 44.

15. Quoted in Andrzej Żbikowski, "Yahasei Yehudim Vepolanim Tahat Hakibush Hagermani" [Jewish–Polish relations under German occupation during World War II], *Dapim: Studies on the Shoah* 22 (2008): 185.

16. Stanislaw Adler, *In the Warsaw Ghetto, 1940–1943: An Account of a Witness*, trans. Sara Chmielewska Philip (Jerusalem: Yad Vashem, 1982), e.g., 80, 110, 122, 133–134, 180. See also Svenja Bethke, "Crime and Punishment in Emergency Situations: The Jewish Ghetto Courts in Lodz, Warsaw and Vilna in World War II—A Comparative Study," *Dapim: Studies on the Holocaust* 28, no. 3 (2014): 173–189.

17. On this unique aspect of Kaplan's diary, see David Engel, "'Will They Dare?' Perceptions of Threat in Diaries from the Warsaw Ghetto," in *Holocaust Chronicles: Individualizing the Holocaust through Diaries and Other Contemporaraneous Personal Accounts*, ed. Robert Moses Shapiro (Hoboken, NJ: Yeshiva University Press and KTAV, 1999), 71–82. Other diaries, such as that of Avraham Lewin (*Mipinkaso shel Hamoreh MiYehudiyah: Geto Varshah April 1942–Mai 1943* [From the notebook of a teacher at the Yehudiah School: Warsaw ghetto April 1942–May 1943] [Tel Aviv: Hakibbutz Hameuchad and the Ghetto Fighters' House, 1969]), ascribe satanic motives to the murderers. In the Lodz ghetto, on the other hand, due to its hermetic isolation and almost complete lack of contact with the Germans in everyday life, they are practically absent from the narrative.

18. Archive of the Jewish Historical Institute in Warsaw, ZIH 302/218 (henceforth Kaplan Diary).

19. Kaplan, *Megilat Yisurin*, 12. All of the references to Kaplan's wartime diary are based on the original Hebrew text. Where available, I have used Abraham I. Katsh's English translation (Chaim Aron Kaplan, *Scroll of Agony: The Warsaw Diary of Chaim A. Kaplan*, ed. and trans. Abraham I. Katsh [Bloomington: Indiana University Press, 1999]), adapting it, as necessary, to render it more faithful to the original Hebrew.

20. For example, Hitler spoke in this vein in a speech before the Reichstag (Yitzhak Arad, Israel Gutman, and Abraham Margaliot, eds., *Documents on the Holocaust: Selected Sources on the Destruction of the Jews of Germany and Austria, Poland, and the Soviet Union* [Jerusalem: Yad Vashem, 1981], 132–135). Kaplan was familiar with this speech and quoted from it, both at the beginning of the period (1 September 1939) and toward the end of the diary when reports of mass murder in Belzec and Lublin reached the ghetto (see, e.g., 2 February 1942; see also 2 April 1942 and 7 April 1942 [although probably 17 April; see Alexandra Garbarini, *Numbered Days: Diaries and the Holocaust* (New Haven, CT: Yale University Press, 2006), 188n126]). Himmler, however, wrote in May 1940: "'I hope completely to erase the concept of Jews through the possibility of a great emigration of all Jews to a colony in Africa or elsewhere.'... Concerning the systematic eradication of the ethnic composition of eastern Europe, Himmler

concluded: 'However cruel and tragic each individual case may be, this method is still the mildest and best, if one rejects the Bolshevik method of physical extermination of a people out of inner conviction as un-German and impossible'" (quoted in Browning, *The Origins of the Final Solution*, 69–70).

21. Friedländer, *Nazi Germany and the Jews: 1939–1945*, 41.

22. On the cultural processes that constructed this position, see Alon Confino, *A World without Jews: The Nazi Imagination from Persecution to Genocide* (New Haven, CT: Yale University Press, 2014).

23. Kaplan thus preceded Abba Kovner who, in his well-known manifesto of 1 January 1942, revealed the Nazis' true intentions (see Dina Porat, *The Fall of a Sparrow: The Life and Times of Abba Kovner*, trans. Elizabeth Yuval [Stanford, CA: Stanford University Press, 2010], 57–75). Kaplan may only have meant what he wrote in a general sense, not yet imagining the actual fulfillment of his prophecy. Nevertheless, it is an unusual statement at so early a stage. It is worth noting Kaplan's disbelief when the first reports of murder by gas reached the ghetto, in February 1942 (see, for example, the entry dated 23 February 1942). It is also interesting to note that the expression "eradicate from under the heavens," used by Kaplan with regard to the future of the Jewish people, appears in the Bible in reference to the elimination of sinners, especially Amalek, by God or by divine order. The rhetoric identifying the Nazis with Amalek is thus implicitly reversed. See Genesis 6:17; Exodus 17:14; and Deuteronomy 7:24, 9:14, and 25:19. The only time the expression is used in reference to Israel, in the Bible (there too as a divine prerogative), it appears in the negative: "And the Lord did not say that He would blot out the name of Israel from under heaven" (2 Kings 14:27).

24. I use the terms "law" and "order" as if they refer to the same phenomenon because, in Kaplan's diary, the breach of both marks the breach of universal norms (at least where the Jews are concerned), on the basis of which the Germans conduct their policies toward the Jews. Law and order are expressions of methodical procedure in the sphere of public conduct—of "the law" as a theoretical concept necessary for human existence.

25. See, for example, entries dated 15 October 1939; 8 November 1939; 11 November 1939; 26 January 1940; 16 February 1940; 24 February 1940; 10 September 1940; and 24 October 1940.

26. According to the original pact between the Soviet Union and Germany, the eastern part of the city of Warsaw, up to the Vistula, was supposed to have been included in the Soviet occupation zone. In the end, the map of the division of Poland was changed by mutual agreement. See Gutman, *The Jews of Warsaw*, 10–11.

27. Similarly, Reuven Ben-Shem wrote, in the Warsaw ghetto: "The Poles and the peoples of Europe are also suffering. None of this is, however, anything more than suffering at the hands of a savage occupier who indeed flouts all of the laws of occupation but there are, nonetheless, limits to his actions. This is not the case with the Jews. For them there is no law whatsoever and, therefore, one who harms them is not punished; and, therefore, everything that is done to them is permitted and justified. We have been excluded from the category of human beings and placed in the category of animals whom it is laudable to kill. You killed a Jew? It's as if you killed an animal. There is no law and no judge" (Reuven Ben-Shem, "Mitokh Yoman Geto Varshah 1941" [From a diary of the Warsaw ghetto 1941], *Yalkut Moreshet* 25 [1978], 39). See also Peretz Opoczynski, *Reshimot* [Sketches from the Warsaw ghetto] (Tel Aviv: The Ghetto Fighters' House and Hakibbutz Hameuchad, 1970), 232–250.

28. Kaplan Diary, 3 December 1938 (ZIH 302/218).

29. Similarly, Zvi Radlitzky wrote, in the Lvov ghetto: "From the very first days, Jews were placed outside the law" (Zvi Radlitzky, "Reshimot Miyemei Hakibush HaGermani BeLvov

(Lemberg) 1941–1943" [Notes from the days of the German occupation in Lvov (Lemberg) 1941–1943], *Yalkut Moreshet* 21 [1976]: 9).

30. Hélène Berr, *The Journal of Hélène Berr*, trans. David Bellos (New York: Weinstein Books, 2008), 131 (18 September 1942).

31. Such expressions are by no means exceptional, as discussed in the next chapter.

32. Kaplan, *Megilat Yisurin*, 374; emphasis added.

33. Ibid.

34. Adler, *In the Warsaw Ghetto*, 153.

35. See the words of Mary Berg: "It is forbidden to print newspapers uncensored by the Nazis, to sing national songs, to attend religious services . . . in brief, it is forbidden to live!" (Mary Berg, *The Diary of Mary Berg: Growing Up in the Warsaw Ghetto*, ed. Susan Lee Pentlin [Oxford: Oneworld, 2009], 83 [31 July 1941]).

36. Yisrael Gutman, afterword to Emanuel Ringelblum, *Ktavim Ahronim* [Last writings], vol. 2 (Jerusalem: Yad Vashem, 1994), 335.

37. Marta Markowska, ed., *The Ringelblum Archive: Annihilation—Day by Day* (Warsaw: Karta Centre, 2008), 118–119.

38. The comparison to "Marranos" (*anusim*) appears a number of times in Kaplan's diary. See also Jacek Leociak, *Text in the Face of Destruction: Accounts from the Warsaw Ghetto Reconsidered*, trans. Emma Harris (Warsaw: Żydowski Instytut Historyczny, 2004), 215–216. Other diarists, such as David Kahane of Lvov, rejected this analogy. See David Kahane, *Lvov Ghetto Diary*, trans. Jerzy Michalowicz (Amherst: University of Massachusetts Press, 1990), 54.

39. Kaplan cites a historical concept although he is aware of the fact that historical concepts had lost their meaning and historical continuity had been disrupted, severed even linguistically. On this subject, see Dalia Ofer, "Everyday Life of Jews under Nazi Occupation: Methodological Issues," *Holocaust and Genocide Studies* 9, no. 1 (1995): 42–69.

40. I refer to the public sphere in the Habermasian sense. See Jürgen Habermas, *The Theory of Communicative Action*, trans. Thomas McCarthy (Boston: Beacon, 1984–1987).

41. Giorgio Agamben, *Remnants of Auschwitz: The Witness and the Archive*, trans. Daniel Heller-Roazen (New York: Zone Books, 1999), 105–106; emphasis added. See the entire chapter on shame (87–135).

42. It is not without relevance in this context to note that in certain senses, internal Jewish cultural activity served Nazi purposes. It created a false sense of freedom that served them well. Thus, for example, the German Komissar of the Warsaw ghetto, Heinz Auerswald, wrote to Hans Frank that, in his "view," the principle that "has turned out most advantageously was to allow the Jews maximum freedom to regulate their own affairs inside the district. The entire communal administration lies in their hands. . . . When deficiencies occur, the Jews direct their resentment against the Jewish administrations and not against the German supervisors. Added to that is the widest freedom accorded to the Jews until now in so-called cultural activities. They have theatres, variety shows, coffee houses, etc. The Jews have opened public schools and to a considerable extent developed the trade school system. All of these measures have produced a certain reassurance which is necessary, if their economic capacity is to be exploited for our purposes" (quoted in James E. Young, *Writing and Rewriting the Holocaust* [Bloomington: Indiana University Press, 1988], 34; see also Young's remarks there). In an entry dated 5 November 1942, Oskar Rosenfeld tells of the resumption of concerts in the Lodz ghetto, on instructions from the chief of the Nazi administration of the ghetto, Hans Biebow (Oskar Rosenfeld, *In the Beginning Was the Ghetto: Notebooks from Łódź*, ed. Hanno Loewy, trans. Brigitte M. Goldstein [Evanston, IL: Northwestern University Press, 2002], 147). Saul

Friedländer's assessment of the Jewish cultural association (*Kulturbund*) in Germany in the 1930s seems relevant here: "Singer's Kulturbund fitted Nazi needs. . . . It foreshadowed the Nazi ghetto, in which a pretense of internal autonomy camouflaged the total subordination of an appointed Jewish leadership to the dictates of its masters" (Friedländer, *Nazi Germany and the Jews: 1939–1945*, 65–66).

43. See, for example, entries dated 2 October 1940 and 26 December 1940.

44. Similarly, Primo Levi wrote about Auschwitz: "To sink is the easiest of matters; it is enough to carry out all the orders one receives, to eat only the ration, to observe the discipline and the work of the camp. Experience showed that only exceptionally could one survive more than three months in this way" (Levi, *If This Is a Man/The Truce*, trans. Stuart Woolf [London: Abacus, 2004], 96). See also Viktor Frankl, *Man's Search for Meaning*, part 1, trans. Ilse Lasch (Boston: Beacon, 2014), 5. Similar assertions can also be found in writings from the ghettos. See, for example, Gutterman, *Bevo Ha'emah*, 166. The writer recounts that, for Jews, the penalty for any infraction is death: "Of course, no punishment—and for Jews there is, in effect, only one punishment, the death penalty—can prevent infractions or disobedience of German orders, because the conditions that the Germans have created are such that without breaking the regulations they issue, existence is impossible."

45. Havi Ben-Sasson and Lea Prais, "Twilight Days: Missing Pages from Avraham Lewin's Warsaw Ghetto Diary, May–July 1942," *Yad Vashem Studies* 33 (2005): 44.

46. Similarly, on 27 May 1942, Kaplain complains that even in the courthouse, the law has no validity.

47. This duality is brilliantly represented in Jonathan Littel's novel *The Kindly Ones*, trans. Charlotte Mandell (New York: Harper, 2009).

48. The question "From where will our help come?" is taken from Psalms 121:1: "I lift up my eyes to the mountains: from where will my help come?" (Robert Alter, *The Book of Psalms: A Translation and Commentary* [New York: Norton, 2007]). Kaplan does not cite the biblical reply: "My help is from the Lord, maker of heaven and earth."

49. See also entries dated 16 February 1940; 18 March 1940; 3 May 1940; 29 July 1940; 17 November 1940; 26 November 1940; 2 January 1941; 3 January 1941; 14 February 1941; and many others.

50. Yisrael Gutman, *Yehudai Varshah 1939–1943: Geto, Mahteret, Mered* [The Jews of Warsaw 1939–1943: Ghetto, underground, uprising] (Tel Aviv: Yad Vashem, the Institute of Contemporary Jewry, and Sifriyat Poalim, 1977), 66. (The sentence does not appear in the English edition of Gutman's book.)

51. Entry dated 5 October 1939.

52. Jean Améry, *At the Mind's Limits: Contemplations by a Survivor on Auschwitz and Its Realities*, trans. Sidney Rosenfeld and Stella P. Rosenfeld [Bloomington: Indiana University Press, 1980], 35. See also Georges Bataille, *Death and Sensuality: A Study of Eroticism and Taboo* (New York: Walker, 1962), 149–196. A shocking expression of the treatment of human beings exclusively as objects ("flesh") can be found in the Nazi attitude to the corpses of their murdered victims. Peretz Opoczynski describes such a case of sadistic abuse in the Warsaw ghetto: "The mad sadists forced the undertakers to heave the bodies up and down, to stand them on their heads, lie them down and bend them over. This desecration of the dead went on for nearly two hours, to the sound of the savages' sarcastic, bestial laughter" (Opoczynski, *Reshimot*, 238).

53. Agamben, *Remnants of Auschwitz*, 68.

54. On this connection between total law and sadistic pleasure, see Jacques Lacan, "Kant with Sade," *October* 51 (1989): 55–75. Lacan himself linked the categorical imperative and

sadism to Nazism and the destruction of European Jewry in *The Seminar of Jacques Lacan, Book XI: The Four Fundamental Concepts of Psychoanalysis*, ed. Jacques-Alain Miller, trans. Alan Sheridan (New York: Norton, 1998), 275.

55. Kaplan uses similar terms in reference to the Nazis, on 18 March 1940: "The enemy laughs at our thoughts."

56. "Leader of the city," following *Genesis Rabbah* 39, 1.

57. See a similar distinction in Renata Saleci, "I Can't Love You Unless I Give You Up," in *Gaze and Voice as Love Objects*, ed. Renata Saleci and Slavoj Žižek (Durham, NC: Duke University Press, 1996), 198.

58. Mladen Dolar, "The Object Voice," in Saleci and Žižek, *Gaze and Voice as Love Objects*, 25. His discussion follows Lacan's theory of the voice, inspired by Theodor Reik's analysis of the shofar. See Lacan's seminar on anxiety (22 May 1963, unpublished), cited in Dolar, "The Object Voice." See also Theodor Reik, "The Shofar," in *Ritual: Psychoanalytic Studies*, trans. Douglas Bryan (New York: Farrar, Straus, 1946), 221–361; and Slavoj Žižek, *The Metastases of Enjoyment: Six Essays on Woman and Causality* (London: Verso, 1995), 54–57.

59. Emphasis added. Kaplan expresses a similar idea toward the end of the diary, during the tense period before the mass deportations, when rumors began to arrive regarding the fate of Polish Jewry. In this context. he writes on 25 June 1942, with regard to the Nazis: "Whatever happens or is done is cloaked in total silence."

60. Louis Althusser, "Ideology and Ideological State Apparatuses," in *Lenin and Philosophy and Other Essays*, trans. Ben Brewster (New York: Monthly Review Press, 2001), 118.

61. Kaplan, *Scroll of Agony*, 360; translation modified according to the Hebrew version.

62. The manner in which the Other reads the subject, even as he harms her, is decisive. Thus, for example, the Auschwitz Sonderkommando Zalman Gradowski compares Auschwitz to the departure from Spain. In Auschwitz there is no national pride and, rather than leaving their countries, the Jews are forcibly expelled from them, "not . . . as a people, but as despicable creatures" (Zalman Gradowski, "Writings," in *The Scrolls of Auschwitz*, ed. Ber Mark, trans. Sharon Neemani [Tel Aviv: Am Oved, 1985], 182). The way in which the Jews are expelled determines their status.

63. The murder takes place during a death march at the end of the war. Robert Antelme, *The Human Race*, trans. Jeffrey Haight and Annie Mahler (Evanston, IL: Marlboro, 1992), 224.

64. See Rosenfeld, *In the Beginning Was the Ghetto*, 184 (18 April 1943), in which he describes a murder committed out of boredom. The account of the murder is identical to that of the murder of Jews by gas in the same entry: both accounts are anonymous, do not seek motives for the murder, and express a lack of recognition of the subjectivity of the victim.

65. See the description by Shlomo Frank from the Lodz ghetto, in Shlomo Frank, *Togbuch fun Lodzer Geto* [Diary from the Lodz ghetto] (Tel Aviv: Menorah, 1959), 19 (19 January 1941). Frank also describes a sadistic murderer by the name of Fuchs, who particularly liked killing women from behind (ibid., 348). See also Opoczynski, *Reshimot*, 253.

66. Accounts of such arbitrary murders are very frequent in diaries from the Holocaust period. See, for example, the story told by Peretz Opoczynski: "The new gendarmes shot today . . . at a Jew who passed by wearing a velvet hat, killing him on the spot. It's unclear whether they killed him because he had not taken his hat off to them or because . . . he was wearing a velvet hat" (Opoczynski, *Reshimot*, 244). See also Kahane, *Lvov Ghetto Diary*, 9–10.

67. A diary characterized by the passive voice is that of Rosina Sorani, "Mitokh Yoman Redifot (Kta'im Miyomanah shel Pkidah Bikehilat Roma Bitkufat Hakibush Hagermani)"

[From a diary of persecution (selections from the diary of a secretary in the Jewish community of Rome during the German occupation], *Yalkut Moreshet* 10 (1969): 72–78.

68. Kaplan uses similar terms to describe a similar incident that occurred opposite his window, in an entry dated 21 July 1942, the day before the beginning of the deportations to Treblinka (see an interesting analysis of this incident and its narration, in Leociak, *Text in the Face of Destruction*, 155–156).

69. It is, once again, the voice of the sadistic obscene father who enjoys without limit. See Reik, "The Shofar."

70. See Boaz Neumann, *Re'iyat Ha'olam Hanatzit: Merhav, Guf, Safah* [The Nazi weltanschauung: Space, body, language] (Haifa: Haifa University, 2002), 255–268, 291–297. For example, Stefan Zweig wrote in March 1936: "Our Germany has become a very silent land. Although it now thunders with singing and shouting." Bella Fromm, too, writes in her diary that the German mind has gone "berserk" and that Germans have become "a nation shouting too loudly and too insanely to hear the voice of reason" (both Zweig and Fromm are cited in Neumann, *Re'iyat Ha'olam Hanatzit,* 255; see Bella Fromm, *Blood and Banquets: A Berlin Social Diary* [New York: Harper, 1942], 285). See also Yaron Jean, *Re'ashei Hamoderniyut: Havayot shel Shmi'ah Begermanyah 1914–1945* [Noises of modernity: Hearing experiences in Germany 1914–1945] (Tel Aviv: Resling, 2011), 126, as well as the entire fourth chapter, 125–163.

71. Quoted in Neumann, *Re'iyat Ha'olam Hanatzit,* 329–330, 292; Bursztein, *Hapsikho'analizah shel Hanatzizm*, 64. The quote appears in Neumann, *Re'iyat Ha'olam Hanatzit*, 259. In this sense, the voice that Hitler's opponents heard was not so different from the one described by Goebbels. Ruth Andreas-Friedrich describes Hitler's voice as "the hated barbershop voice" (*die verhasste Knödelstimme*) (Ruth Andreas-Friedrich, *Berlin Underground 1938–1945* [New York: Holt, 1947], 56).

72. In the introduction to his English translation of Kaplan's diary, Abraham Katsh claims that Hirsch is an imaginary figure (see Katsh, introduction to Kaplan, *Scroll of Agony*, 10). Yechiel Szeintuch also asserts with complete certainty that Hirsch is not a real person (Yechiel Szeintuch, *Yitzhak Katzenelson: Ktavim Shenitzlu Migeto Varshah Umimahaneh Vittel* [Yitzhak Katzenelson's rescued manuscripts from the Warsaw ghetto and the Vittel concentration camp] [Jerusalem: Magnes and the Ghetto Fighters' House, 1990], 9n9), and David Roskies follows suit (David Roskies, *Against the Apocalypse: Responses to Catastrophe in Modern Jewish Culture* [Cambridge, MA: Harvard University Press, 1984], 221). It is worth noting that all three use the term "alter ego" to describe Reb Hirsch, as if relying on a single, uncited source. Similarly, Alexandra Garbarini refers to Hirsch as a "fictional friend" created by Kaplan (Garbarini, *Numbered Days*, 4). In a personal conversation, Yisrael Gutman told me that he doubted this theory, arguing that it is not in keeping with the documentary spirit of Kaplan's writing, which generally recounts only facts, and in as objective a manner as possible. Kaplan's "Hirsch" may be Josef Hertz, whom Stanislaw Adler describes as a man who suffered from some mental illness and constantly argued that hope in Hitler's defeat was merely an illusion and that all of the ghetto's inhabitants were condemned to death (see Adler, *In the Warsaw Ghetto*, 75).

73. See Christopher R. Browning and Israel Gutman, "The Reports of a Jewish 'Informer' in the Warsaw Ghetto: Selected Documents," *Yad Vashem Studies* 17 (1986): 247–293. The information about the Chelmno death camp had already reached the ghetto in February 1941.

74. Garbarini, *Numbered Days*, 84.

75. So too in entries dated 16 May 1942; 10 July 1942; 13 July 1942.

76. This is not to suggest, of course, that the "final solution" was inscribed in advance in Nazi policy. Like Confino, however, in his recent book *A World without Jews*, and following

Arendt in *The Origins of Totalitarianism*, 290, I think that from the very early stages of the Nazi period, the Jews had no place in the Nazi symbolic order. They had to disappear—whether by emigration, deportation, or annihilation. In this sense the Jews of Warsaw who were outside the law were symbolically dead from the very beginning of the Nazi occupation. This does not mean that this symbolic death had, deterministically, to be translated into actual total killing. It does suggest, however, that, in many ways, the "final solution" was a radicalized outcome of the Nazi logic, in which the Jews had no symbolic place from the very beginning.

9

BETWEEN PERPETRATORS AND VICTIMS

The Gray Zone of Consciousness in the Diary of Chaim Kaplan

On 18 May 1941, Chaim Kaplan wrote in his diary: "Nazism came to annihilate us. It is the enemy of Judaism in its spirit and in its practice. We fight it and await its defeat. However—the human spirit is inexplicable. *Unconsciously, we accept its ideology and follow in its ways. Nazism has conquered our entire world.* It severely damages our public life. And yet we do not cease to declare day and night that it is ugliness and that one ought to distance oneself from it."[1] This startling passage deserves close examination. As perhaps the keenest observer of ghetto life, Kaplan believes that Jewish life in Warsaw ghetto can tell us something new, profound, and perhaps unprecedented about "the human spirit." A radical schism has occurred within the downtrodden collective identity of the ghetto's Jews. On the one hand, on the conscious and articulated level Nazism is perceived as an enemy. Jewish identity is defined in relation to it by way of absolute negation—"it is ugliness and . . . one ought to distance oneself from it." Nazism is a bitter enemy "in its spirit and in its practice," with which cooperation cannot be contemplated. And so, Kaplan proceeds, "we fight it and await its defeat."

Yet on the other hand this does not provide a complete picture of the Warsaw Jews' mental makeup. Identity is split into a conscious stratum within which the Nazi is a stranger, an enemy and a criminal, and a hidden, unconscious stratum, in which he serves as a model. According to Kaplan, the victim imitates the Nazi perpetrator both ideologically and practically ("we accept its ideology and follow in its ways"). At this level the division between the two entities becomes blurred, and the overt "enemy" is implicitly internalized, becoming a part of the Jewish social "self." This stratum exerts a decisive influence, as Kaplan's radical declaration tells us: "Nazism has conquered our entire world." In other words, no corner of the Jewish world, either "within" or "without," is free of it.

The concrete event to which Kaplan refers here is the inequitable distribution of food in the Warsaw ghetto, which works to his disadvantage. The Writers and Journalists Association, which was allocated food coupons by the Joint Distribution Committee[2] (as part of its policy to assist the intelligentsia in particular), was controlled by the "journalists," who exploited their position to distribute the limited number of coupons among themselves, leaving none for the "writers."[3] Kaplan, a "writer," was naturally angered by this discrimination.[4] He considered the behavior of the "journalists" to be a manifestation of the manner in which adoption of Nazi "social-Darwinist" values and modes of behavior had corrupted and poisoned public life in the ghetto.

It is reasonable to presume that Kaplan's use of such extreme terms was motivated by his understandable anger and frustration. Yet, as will soon become apparent, this outburst also expresses Kaplan's profound recognition of a system of ways in which the victims identified with their oppressors, of which they are only partially aware but which is far more pervasive and complex than it may appear at first glance. A further passage from Kaplan's diary in which he reiterates this assertion reinforces this conclusion.

On 12 December 1941, Kaplan refers to the apparatus of substitution that had emerged in the ghetto. In place of the wagons harnessed to a horse "we invented the rickshaws" pulled by human beings. Likewise, since "you had no hope of finding clothing or footwear material," people therefore "devised wooden soles" with which to repair worn shoes. Kaplan proceeds to list the makeshift articles manufactured in the ghetto that replaced unavailable products. He summarizes the matter in the following terms: "We learned from the Germans to cherish and value every remain and every remnant and all waste material." This condition of extreme frugality, however, extracts a heavy moral price: "The coarse life that is no more than the fulfillment of material needs turned you into an animal . . . and everyone in the ghetto turned into predatory animals . . . both personal and public morality was shorn from one. *I would say: we all but substituted 'Jewish teaching'* [*torat 'yisra'el'*] *with the 'teaching of Nazism'* [*'torat ha-natsizem'*] *even though we are at war with it*" (emphasis added). Once again, Kaplan remarks on the inherent paradox of Jewish life in the ghetto. On the one hand Nazism is an implacable enemy, while on the other hand its values are somehow internalized in public life, perhaps as part of a process whereby life was being increasingly reduced to its biological dimension.[5]

This internalized identification highlighted by Kaplan should not be mistaken for an overt bonding with Nazi ideology or acts perpetrated by the Nazis. Kaplan by no means indicates a Jewish desire to join the ranks of Nazism or to mimic it. The various manifestations noted by him are flimsy, subtle, and nuanced threads, unconscious for the most part, which imitate and internalize certain aspects of the thought and behavior of the Nazis or their associates. This is primarily a form of psychological identification, involving self-erasure and identification with the aggressor, which in some instances also acquires a cultural aspect, but it does not suggest political or ideological identification. Similarly, while this is merely a partial identification, which by no means exhausts the human complexity of the Jewish individual or collective in the Warsaw ghetto, its effects are patently apparent. These aspects as manifested in Kaplan's diary and in other Jewish sources form the focus of this chapter.

Primo Levi's essay "The Gray Zone," which Giorgio Agamben has hailed as Levi's most important discovery, will serve as the starting point for our discussion.[6] This concept, which Levi introduced, refers to the fundamental blurring between murderers and victims that emerged in the Nazi concentration camp (and in fact also outside of it, in the ghettos, for example). Levi implies that the entire camp population, perpetrators and victims alike, may be located somewhere along a "gray" axis, on which the distinction between victim and perpetrator is ambiguous and the separate identities tend to merge with one another.[7]

It may at first appear that Levi's assertion is an insult to common sense and one's moral instinct. Ostensibly, if there were a place in which dichotomous distinctions between groups of people were absolutely clear-cut, it would be the concentration camp, where the disparity between perpetrator and victim was total. The group of victims had nothing in common with the perpetrators: the latter operated on behalf of the institutions of the party and the totalitarian state, and to whom, in the words of Hannah Arendt, "everything is permitted and everything is possible."[8] This group exercised the most absolute control imaginable over a second group of people, imprisoned under coercion within the framework of a political order that deprived them of their very humanity and their right to life, to the extent that their existence touched upon what Agamben terms "bare life" itself.[9] Furthermore, as Boaz Neumann has emphasized, the concentration camp as a sphere of death (*Todesraum*) was the exact inverse of the Aryan living sphere (*Lebensraum*), and the *Musselmann* was the opposite of the superman (*Übermensch*).[10] This is a radical example of social reality that accords perfectly with rigid structuralist thought, according to which A is defined first and foremost as the opposite of B, and vice versa.[11]

Levi is well aware of the problematic nature of his "gray zone," in particular its moral aspects. He is thus sure to clarify that "I was a guiltless victim and I was not a murderer . . . and . . . to confuse them [the Nazis] with their victims is a moral disease or an aesthetic affectation or a sinister sign of complicity; above all, it is precious service rendered (intentionally or not) to the negators of truth."[12] Yet nevertheless, Levi's description portrays a gray zone shared by both groups. Among the characteristic figures that populate this gray area, Levi includes members of the Sonderkommando—prisoners forced to work in the extermination facilities who, among other tasks, were responsible for handling the bodies of those murdered in the gas chambers—and the head of the Lodz ghetto Judenrat, Haim Rumkowski, who behaved like a tyrant in the ghetto and collaborated with the Germans in transporting Jews to the extermination camps, with the sincere intention, one must add, of prolonging the lives of as many inhabitants of the ghetto as possible.[13]

Levi adopts a patently ethical perspective. He seeks to examine whether, and in what manner, one can judge the figures that operated within the "gray zone" and can hold them legally or morally responsible. Yet his ethical insights rest upon a fundamental epistemological premise regarding the way in which one may come to know the concentration camp. The essay begins with this insight: "Have we—we who have returned—been able to understand and make others understand our experience? What we commonly mean by 'understand' coincides with 'simplify' . . . in short, we are compelled to reduce the knowable to a schema: with this purpose in view we have built for ourselves admirable tools in the course of evolution, tools which are specifically the property of the human species—language and conceptual thought."[14] Levi speaks here of a cognitive schema relying on linguistic and conceptual distinctions that enables human beings to comprehend the world. This ability to impose a conceptual grid on the chaotic and brutal material of reality renders it meaningful. Historical writing, Levi proceeds to argue, and certainly the writing of the history of the Holocaust and Nazism, is dominated by the binary opposition of "we" and "they," "ally" and "enemy." Yet the epistemological shock that the *Lager* induced in the prisoners derived precisely from the breakdown of this fundamental distinction: "The world into which one was precipitated was terrible, yes, but also undecipherable. It did not conform to any model."[15] Levi cites two destructive processes that led to this indecipherability. On the one hand, the familiar boundary between "inside" and "outside" collapsed: "The enemy was all around but also inside—the 'we' lost its limits." On the other hand, a process of endless fragmentation was under way: "one could not discern a single frontier but rather many confused perhaps innumerable frontiers that stretched between each of us."

Fragmentation of identity and the blurring of boundaries between murderer and victim are thus the epistemological characteristics of the "gray zone," and they analytically precede the ethical aspects that Levi addresses later in his essay. This phenomenon will henceforth be termed "the epistemological gray area," and I shall focus on its appearances in Chaim Kaplan's diary and other works. In the following discussion I will suggest an analytical typology of this "epistemological gray area of the consciousness," which relates to three processes that occurred during the interaction between the victim and the perpetrator in the gray area: (1) imitation, (2) internalization of the perpetrator's perspective, and (3) a form of cultural identification.[16]

Imitation

Jewish wartime writings exhibit frequent expressions of criticism leveled at community institutions, mainly the Judenrat and the Jewish police, who are accused of imitating the Nazis' modes of thought and conduct. For example, in his eulogy of Leon Bernson, an assimilationist lawyer who attempted to combat the corruption and degradation that had, in his opinion, become rife among members of the Judenrat in the Warsaw ghetto, Emanuel Ringelblum noted that he (Bernson) had wished to establish a civil guard that would replace the corrupt Jewish police, but "very soon this dreaming idealist came to the conclusion that the institutions which the occupier establishes ought to *be in his own image*."[17] Bernson's assertion, according to Ringelblum, is thus of a structural nature: an institution founded by the Nazis, albeit administered by Jews, cannot escape the structural replication of the Nazis' corrupt value system.

Hersh Wasser, a leftist Zionist (PZL) and secretary of the clandestine Oyneg Shabes archive, provides a more psychologically oriented explanation of the Jewish police in the Warsaw ghetto in his diary entry of 22 January 1941: "Nobody . . . pays the least thought to a civic approach toward the ravaged Jewish population . . . they [the Jewish ghetto police] are rotten to the core [take bribes] . . . the German-Prussian mentality has also penetrated the Jewish police: relentless beating and floggings, endless insults against entirely innocent people. With no cause whatsoever, people are dragged off to the district commissariat and on the whole, conduct is arrogant and impudent."[18] This criticism was voiced more insistently during the periods of roundups and deportations and regarding Jews who participated in gathering and assembling the population. For example, the teacher Avraham Lewin, on 21 August 1942 at the time of the mass deportation from the Warsaw ghetto to Treblinka, writes: "Yesterday evening after six o'clock the Jewish police raided the homes of residents who were forced to vacate them. They forced the occupants to leave, broke into the closed apartments, stole and robbed and destroyed whatever fell into their hands, and at the same time arrested women, particularly [those] who had no papers [*Meldenkarten*]. Such greediness toward Jews? The spirit of the German *passed onto them*. They also entered our shop at eight and created a commotion among the women. They received a bribe and left."[19] The head of the Lodz ghetto Judenrat, Chaim Rumkowski, who was mentioned earlier, was accused of such behavior more than anyone else: "Rumkowski adopted the mentality of his rulers. He not only carries out the orders of the regime, but has also adopted their spirit and he is therefore the only one to organize [things] in the ghetto and has no competitors whatsoever in all the land," writes Leon Horowitz in his diary.[20] Michal Unger maintains that this assessment is supported by others and that Rumkowski did indeed imitate several Nazi political practices. He initiated a grotesque personality cult in the Lodz ghetto, reminiscent of that of the Führer in Nazi Germany. He would, for example, travel around the ghetto in a regal carriage; his portrait adorned the notes of the ghetto currency, calendars, and numerous other official publications; he appropriated authority over most aspects of ghetto life, including the arrangement of weddings, and the judges of the ghetto swore allegiance directly to him, in a manner reminiscent of the judges' oath of allegiance sworn directly to the Führer, in complete contrast to the custom of liberal legal systems. Unger has no doubt that Rumkowski's behavior manifested internalization of Nazi modes of comportment and governance.[21]

Obviously not all Jewish Judenrat leaders and policemen were perceived as collaborators. Many elicited positive assessments from among their fellow Jews, both during and after the war.[22] However, on occasion, Jewish policemen or others holding positions of authority likewise displayed this type of imitation.[23] An amazing example of this were the Jewish policemen in the town of Konin, who ceased to converse in Yiddish and began to give their orders in broken German with a Nazi intonation.[24]

These and similar episodes recorded in the writing of the period indicate a certain type of interpretative framework adopted by contemporary observers, who speak of imitation or adoption of Nazi codes of behavior among Jewish officials in the ghettos.[25] Several extremely common psychological dimensions in the victims' writings may explain this phenomenon. Adulation of the strong and powerful perpetrator who resorts to unbridled violence is repeatedly observed among groups that have experienced political violence, and is indeed also manifested in the writings of this period. From the very first moment, in fact, of the Germans' entry into the decimated city of Warsaw, Kaplan and many other witnesses refer to the Germans as heroes: "Today at eight in the evening the divisions of Hit.(!) enter the gates of Warsaw as victorious heroes" (29 September 1939). Two days later, referring to the impressive appearance of the German soldiers, he writes: "You almost begin to believe that this is a people that deserves to rule over everything, and has the courage and the authority."

This troubling sentiment of admiration generated criticism that was leveled not only at the Jewish policemen and leaders who, as we have seen, were frequently compelled to maneuver along the thin line dividing the Jewish community from the Nazi regime. The underground newspaper of the leftist Zionist youth movement Ha-shomer ha-tsa'ir, *Płomienie*, published in Warsaw, addresses this issue in an article that appeared in September 1940, titled "The Situation of the Youth in the Wake of the Occupation":

> And in the meantime the soul of the slave is solidified and the back is bent. Our youth have learned to doff their hats in front of the Germans. They have learned to smile a smile of slavery and obedience. Deep in their hearts burns jealousy and a deep appreciation of the evil Fascist arrogance. And disguised in the depths of their heart is the dream of being one of them—handsome, elegant, firm and full of self confidence so we too can kick someone without being brought to justice; to hit, rob, despise others as I am now despised.[26]

In the field of psychoanalysis, Sigmund Freud was the first to discern these mechanisms of imitation and adoption, which involve identification with the wielders of power and might and their adulation. He asserted, for example, that cannibalism was the manner in which the victor appropriated the admired attributes of the hated enemy.[27] Within this context he likewise explained in his book *Totem and Taboo* the Oedipal foundations of culture.[28]

It was his daughter Anna Freud, however, who methodically observed these processes and proceeded to conceptualize them. She regarded what she termed "identification with the aggressor" as a defense mechanism against attack from the outside. When a person's "ego" is subjected to a significant and anxiety-provoking threat, the defense manifests itself in the internalization of the anxiety-provoking figure.[29]

Most of Anna Freud's examples refer to the experiences of young people and children. It would appear that she considered the tendency toward identification with the aggressor to be linked to the childish condition, when the personality is not yet fully formed and reacts with anxiety to every threat. In his book *Surviving*, which deals with the period of his imprisonment in the Dachau and Buchenwald camps between 1938 and 1939, the psychoanalyst Bruno Bettelheim continues this line of thought.[30] Bettelheim maintained that prisoners in the camp regressed to a childlike state and tended to admire, identify with, and respect the camp guard, of all people, who functioned as the adult figure in that situation. The words of Robert Antelme, a French resistance prisoner in the Bad-Gandersheim concentration camp, illustrate this phenomenon very forcefully: "Yes! You are the strongest. We are telling you so because you deserve to be told that you are the strongest. We have never seen anybody stronger than you. Once we too thought that we were strong, but now we know that you are stronger than we ever were. . . . No matter what you do, we will never try to measure our strength against yours, not even in our imagination."[31]

According to Bettelheim, this "regressive" state generated a particular personality structure that predisposed the prisoner to accept, albeit not always consciously, the value system and behavior of the SS men. Bettelheim viewed the violence of veteran prisoners in particular toward their fellow inmates as a regressive emulation of their tormentors, citing their violent body language: longtime prisoners would on occasion imitate the guards' dress, appearance and bodily gestures. They would, for example, slap one another as a game, to see who could endure the longest without falling down, a game that they adopted from the SS personnel.[32]

Sandor Ferenczi, a student and subsequently opponent of Sigmund Freud, articulated the identification mechanism in the most interesting and precise manner. In a lecture titled "The Confusion of Tongues," which he delivered in 1932, Ferenczi addressed the phenomenon of identification with the aggressor on the part of children subjected to sexual abuse. He argued that victims of trauma develop a split personality: "Detailed examination of the phenomena . . . teaches us that there is neither shock nor fright without some trace of splitting personality."[33] This split is in fact part of the "ego's" defense mechanism in the face of unpredictable individuals who are liable to do whatever they please to the subject: "In order to defend himself against dangers coming from people without self-control he must know how to identify himself completely with them."[34]

Unlike Sigmund Freud and Bettelheim, Ferenczi did not address the (naturally unfounded) sense of empowerment that the victim acquires by imitating and identifying with the omnipotent perpetrator. Ferenczi rather underscores the logic of survival encompassed in imitating the perpetrator and in "stepping into his shoes." The more profound the internalization, the better it appears to enable the victim to predict the abuse and to prepare for it, even though the perpetrator's actions are generally unpredictable and unreasonable. This is not a cognitive process and the victim is unable to control it. Rather, the victim must genuinely and utterly internalize the standpoint of the perpetrator, and weave it fully into his emotional makeup. For this reason, the consciousness of the victim of violence is a "split" or "dual" one. His language is likewise dualistic. It at once retains something of his authentic voice and tongue and also manifests the violent consciousness of the violent and aggressive perpetrator, which is inevitably expressed verbally. Jean Améry, a Jewish intellectual who survived Auschwitz, went as far as to assert that Auschwitz prisoners had to fully internalize the Nazi world of values, and not merely its rationale, in order to survive.[35]

The historian Raul Hilberg addressed this issue on a more worldly and historical level, rather than a psychological one. In all encounters with the Nazis, he maintained, the Jews were implicitly forced to accept the Nazi premises, since this was a necessary condition for any interaction with them. Thus, for example, a Jew from Bukovina could claim that he was being "unjustly" deported (southern Bukovina was not under Soviet rule and he could therefore not be accused of collaboration with the Soviets), implying that there was a measure of justice in the deportation of Jews who had lived under Soviet rule.[36] This dual structure of consciousness may explain the expressions of imitation, internalization, identification, and also the admiration to which writers of the period testify on occasion.

Internalization of the Perpetrator's Perspective: A Psychosis of Effacement

Processes of identification may occur in very different and varied ways. Following Lacan, Slavoj Žižek points to two principal structures of identification. The first, which we have discussed thus far, is linked to processes of imitation in the simple and overt sense of the word, in which the individual seeks, perhaps unconsciously, to resemble the object of his identification and admiration. The second type of identification, which was actually already assumed by Ferenczi, is far more subtle and complex, and refers to an individual who internalizes the perspective and the voice of his or her object of admiration, and apparently seeks to *view things from the location at which the object of identification views things*, as he ostensibly adjusts his voice and focuses it through the vocal chords of the object of identification.[37] Numerous tragic examples of this way of internalizing the Nazi perpetrator's view are to be found in Kaplan's diary.

As early as 18 November 1939, Kaplan writes: "We are like horses . . . we are embarrassed to look one another in the eye. And worse than this, . . . we ourselves have become in our own eyes 'inferior beings' devoid of the divine image." Shortly after the sealing of the ghetto, in a passage written on 17 November 1940, he concludes: "We thus began a new life and one cannot imagine the panic and the anxiety that arose in the Jewish quarter. Suddenly, *we see ourselves* fenced in from all sides, differentiated and excluded from the entire world, excluded from the society of mankind, an abominable people ordered to get out, impure and leprous, who must be removed and cast out from the surroundings of human beings lest they defile and infect the atmosphere" (emphasis added). Moreover, he continues thus: "In short, we were divested of the image of God. We became lowly and degraded *in our own eyes*, we were gripped by a psychosis of effacement. *We ourselves almost began to believe that our nature was corrupt and that we should not be compared to the rest of humanity*" (emphasis added). Two days later Kaplan returns to the matter of shame: "A closed ghetto is nothing but a prison for criminals . . . after all, this is really not a ghetto but a concentration camp for the wicked . . . we began to feel ashamed in the eyes of our fellows." Kaplan goes on to analyze the ways in which the Jews sustained themselves in the new circumstances, explaining that "At moments such as these you become affected by the slurs of Jew haters and the growing number of antisemitic Jews among us . . . a psychosis of racist effacement penetrates us too. And as you listen to such vile words you begin to realize the cause of the 'eternal hatred for the Jewish people.' . . . The conqueror too justifies all his deceit by claims of 'profiteering' and concealment of goods. There is some truth to these allegations." These expressions of identification with the Nazi's racist and degrading viewpoint recur frequently in the diary in various forms. At several points Kaplan employs an explicit generalization to describe the Jews' feelings of guilt, which lead them to justify the Nazis' behavior toward them. In the entry of 25 September 1940, he writes of the resignation with which the Jews accept the Nazis' acts of robbery and theft. "It is a thing of wonder! The Jew accepts the sentence with equanimity as if he believes in his heart—I am deserving of this." On another occasion he is astonished at the eagerness with which Jews read the Nazi papers suffused with enmity and venom toward them: "And the Jewish readers are prepared for all kinds of invective and cursing and 'lovingly' accept the tub of sewage that this murderous press pours on their head" (6 May 1940).

At times it appears as though the internal Jewish criticism, of which Kaplan was by no means the sole representative, itself tends to adopt the Nazi viewpoint. While Kaplan was indeed among the fiercest critics of Jewish society in general, and of the Jewish institutions such as the Judenrat and the Joint in particular, many others joined him in criticizing the manner in which the communal institutions operated, as well as the comportment of Jewish society under Nazi oppression and persecution from the beginning of the war in autumn 1939 up to the demolition of the Warsaw ghetto in the spring of 1943.[38] The lack of solidarity, tremendous social and economic disparities, exploitation and corruption, the flawed and scandalous behavior of institutions, favoritism, moral turpitude at both the individual and public levels, sexual promiscuity, and so forth were all subjected to severe criticism by the Jews of Warsaw themselves throughout the war. In Kaplan's writing, however, both implicit and explicit anti-Semitic rhetoric interwoven with his criticism is particularly evident.

On 21 February 1940, for example, Kaplan describes his impressions in the wake of his visits to the various offices of the Joint organization in Warsaw. He was well aware of the fact that, as a welfare organization funded primarily from abroad, the Joint was the sole life belt for Warsaw Jews, and that "without it we would really have expired of weakness." Yet in his diary entries he constantly decries the administrative chaos prevalent in this enterprise, and claims that its administrators lack the skill required to bear the burden of the period: "The ant is unable to carry on its shoulders a load that is meant for a donkey." The weight of their tasks is far greater than the means, the capabilities, the organizational power, and quality of manpower at their disposal. The outcome, as Kaplan sees it, is catastrophic. It is, however, not the substance of Kaplan's critique that is of most interest to us, but rather his rhetoric, which, in my opinion, echoes anti-Semitic rhetoric. The entry of 27 April 1940 illustrates this internalization.

Kaplan declares that his criticism is not directed at the practical successes or failures of the Joint's activity, but first and foremost at the organization's essential nature: "In order to assess an enterprise, one should not view its dry numbers, which merely provide material for official statistics, but rather look into its living soul. And here I was a witness." How, then, does he portray this living soul? The typical Joint official is an "upstart" according to Kaplan. He particularly objects to the lack of consideration that the managers show toward the clientele. He complains that the managers hold meetings precisely during reception hours and wonders: "Where have these Jew boys (*yehudonim*) seen such Asian customs?"[39] He goes on to refer to the manager as "some Jew boy."

Use of the words "Jew boy" (*yehudon*) as a derogatory term denoting lowliness and abjection requires no interpretation, but it is significant that the depiction of the Jews as an "Asian nation" constitutes one of the components of the anti-Semitic stereotype of the Jew, which in Nazi rhetoric was always associated with primitivism and Soviet Bolshevism. Kaplan internalizes this stereotype and projects it onto a particular group, namely, the Joint officials.[40]

At the same time, it is quite evident that the rhetoric Kaplan employs to criticize the Joint and its officials closely resembles the rhetoric he uses to complain about the Nazis' behavior. As was demonstrated in the previous chapter, in Kaplan's diary the Nazis, and in particular their campaign against the Jews, are characterized by "exemplary disorder." This is one of the Nazis' attributes that particularly perturbs Kaplan, since it expresses the arbitrary nature of Jewish existence under Nazi rule. Yet it transpires that the Joint officials are portrayed in precisely the same manner. They create "havoc" and the more they "sit and discuss in secret how to put things in order," "this always results in disorder." This disorder is compounded by "shaming, disgrace and humiliation" of those who seek their assistance by the duty official, who is frequently depicted as "a little sadist," "evil through and through," and a "misanthrope."

Moreover, in the same way that Kaplan sarcastically portrays the Nazis in his diary by paraphrasing religious Jewish texts traditionally employed to describe the Deity, so too he depicts the Joint.[41] The entry begins with this passage: "The Joint! 'His honor' fills the world of Polish Jewry at this time of distress."[42] In a very similar manner Hitler is described as "the leader whose heroism fills the world" (9 February 1940).[43] The same rhetoric similarly characterizes both phenomena with regard to the inadequacy of language to depict them. Kaplan writes as follows about the reality the Nazis, "Even a skilled writer would be unable to express the terrors in our lives" (26 February 1941), and turning to the Joint, he notes, "The havoc that reigned in the Joint's enterprises prior to the holiday cannot be put into words. For the lifeless word cannot adequately convey all that occurred there." Thus, just as only the victims of Nazism, according to Kaplan, are able to describe it—only he "who has offered his back to the lash of his whip" (3 February 1940)—so too it is "only he who has been in need of its assistance . . . and has had to argue with its 'directors' " who can sense and document the Joint's havoc.

Kaplan's description of the Joint thus merges two opposing clusters of linguistic images: on the one hand, the organization's personnel are portrayed according to anti-Semitic parameters ("Jew boys," "Asians"), and are ostensibly observed through the Nazi lens. On the other hand, they are described according to the parameters of the Jewish perspective on the Nazis (sadists, characterized by disorder, Deists). In each case one finds a subtle form of identification with the Nazis—either by adopting their point of view or by perceiving the object (Jewish institutions) in their image.

Cultural Identification: Biographical Contexts

Thus far the discussion has offered mainly psychoanalytical and linguistic explanations and contexts for the phenomena of "the epistemological gray zone." However, Kaplan's diary contains several expressions of conscious and positive identification with certain ideological and phenomenological components of Nazism. Such expressions require a further level of explanation, beyond the psychoanalytical and the linguistic.

Kaplan naturally refers to the Nazis and Nazism with blatant hostility and loathing. The major semantic field through which he relates to Nazism is that of mental disease: madness, sadism, and psychosis. This is the diary's primary characteristic and dominant theme, even prior to the outbreak of war. Upon hearing of the events of *Kristallnacht,* Kaplan writes (on 2 December 1938) that "The Germans have a pathological, sadistic and insane hatred toward the Jews." Likewise, having listed the flood of new edicts that rained down on German Jews, he concludes, "Is this not a psychotic government?"[44] From this point onward he expresses this attitude toward the Nazis dozens, and perhaps hundreds, of times throughout the diary.

These attempts to "diagnose" Nazism in fact reveal Kaplan's sense of helplessness in the face of a radical historical phenomenon that transcends his epistemological capacities and that he finds difficult to understand and describe. On more than one occasion he describes the Germans as a "conundrum,"[45] and in many respects they are the focus and object of his work of documentation, as Kaplan himself declares in the early stages of his writing:

> The time will come when my testimony will perhaps be made public. In any event it will constitute historiographical material for the account of our disaster. Polish Jewry is undergoing a national catastrophe unprecedented in our history. A cruel and tyrannical enemy that knows no shame has risen up to annihilate us and brazenly admits fully before the peoples and the states that this is its aspiration. And this obliges those who write things down to record every event and each small detail, *which can shed light on the darkness of its impure and abhorrent soul.* I am unable to record each event for the protocol. This will perhaps be done by others when the appropriate time comes. But events that are recorded in the form of reportage are also of important historical value. *It is not some dry, embalmed truth that is reflected in them, but rather a living and alert truth, a truth that struggles to emerge into daylight, which declares and cries out: see, there is no pain such as mine.* (20 February 1940; emphasis added)

Kaplan distinguishes between documenting the perpetrator and documenting the victim. As an attempt at deciphering, documentation is primarily directed toward the Nazis in order to clarify his motives and his inner makeup, and in Kaplan's words, "to shed light on the darkness of his impure and abhorrent soul." Documentation of the victim, on the contrary, is not "explanatory" by nature. Its mission is to expose Jewish suffering, not as an object of analysis but in its own right: "a living and alert truth, a truth that struggles to emerge into daylight, which declares and cries out: see, there is no pain such as mine."

This, then, is the dominant voice in the diary: one of rage and hatred toward the Nazis and of empathy and identification with Jewish suffering, of which he himself is of course a part. Moreover, as we have seen, Kaplan's voice rests on a broad foundation of cultural, religious, and communal Jewish identity. At this level Kaplan is far removed from any form of ideological identification with the Nazis. Yet a different awareness nevertheless infiltrates his diary almost against his will, expressing clear admiration for certain aspects or manifestations of Nazism.

On 29 November 1940, shortly after the establishment of the ghetto and once he had recovered somewhat from the shock he experienced upon its closing, Kaplan writes:

> The recognition of collective responsibility which was so lacking in our brethren has penetrated everyone. Everyone has come to realize *that he is an organic part of a whole body. . . . The concept of Volksgemeinschaft was introduced to us by the conqueror. That which is good must be accepted from whatever source it may come.* The concept that "all Jews are responsible for one another" [*kol yisrael arevim ze laze*] has ceased to be merely a slogan or metaphor. The ancient saying "I have learned from all my teachers and even from my enemies" has been realized for us. (emphasis added)

In this passage Kaplan approvingly reports on the inner solidarity that emerged within the Warsaw ghetto. He claims that this was a new phenomenon in the social life of Warsaw's Jews, which actually (and this is extremely surprising for him) originated in the Nazi ideology, in the concept of *Volksgemeinschaft*, the ethnic/racial community.[46]

Kaplan's use of such a charged concept demands particular attention. Although they did not coin the term, *Volksgemeinschaft* was a cornerstone of the Nazi worldview. The concept emerged and became dominant within *völkisch* nationalist thought since the end of the nineteenth century and particularly following World War I in Germany. The word *Gemeinschaft* denotes community and marks the organic ethnic and quasi-familial nature of relationships within the nation, by contrast *Gesellschaft* (society) refers to civil, functional and more technical aspects of social belonging.[47] In national and nationalist thought the latter term was generally employed in the context of castigating modern alienation, whereas the former was depicted as the lost paradise. Against this backdrop, the integration of the Jews into the "*Volksgemeinschaft*" was frequently described as a problematic and even futile attempt on the part of foreigners to penetrate a tribe in whose mythical past they play no part and in which they have no roots.

Nazi language greatly enhanced the importance of the concept of *Volksgemeinschaft*, transforming it into a fundamental component of its racist political doctrine.[48] According to the Nazi worldview, the German *Volksgemeinschaft* would be unable to realize its full identity and be redeemed as long as aliens—first and foremost the Jews, but also the chronically ill, the mentally ill, and other such groups—continued to infect, defile, and even to pollute it from within. These aliens disrupt the harmony and inner health of the national community, causing schisms, antagonisms, and divisions of interest, and eventually dismantle the *Volksgemeinschaft* from within. There can be no common denominator between this evil and the good embodied in the racial community; someone who supports the one is obliged to hate the other.[49] Nazism thus regarded it as its mission to restore the *Volksgemeinschaft* to its original and primordial unity, sacrificing the "other" that disrupted this covenant.[50]

Both practically and legally, the concept of *Volksgemeinschaft* became the principle of absolute and unconditional preference of the "Aryan race" and its direct interests over every other group or any other considerations. Every act of mass violence was justified by this principle, which became the primary touchstone of policy in Nazi Germany and thereby acquired constitutional validity. Hitler's figure and voice embodied this unity of the *Volksgemeinschaft*, and his pronouncements acquired mandatory legal validity. The concept of *Volksgemeinschaft* thus occupied a central position in the rhetoric and shaping of the policy of exclusion, persecution, and murder of the Jews in Germany and throughout Europe. "The starting point for all interpretation that addresses the centrality of 'the Jewish policy' [in the Nazi regime] must be the recognition that Nazism posted itself the goal of creating a completely new social order—the racially homogenous *Volksgemeinschaft*," maintains the historian Peter Longerich.[51]

Kaplan, as every educated person in Europe of the 1940s, was well aware of this. It is therefore amazing to find this open expression of admiration precisely in the context of this problematical concept (which unsurprisingly is omitted from the English edition of the diary). Moreover, on another level this passage creates a kind of hermeneutics of identification with the aggressor. Kaplan is clearly not content to use the Hebrew expression "all Jews are responsible for one another" in order to assess the ethical transformation that occurred among the ghetto's inhabitants. He derives the Hebrew expression's current validity and significance from the concept of *Volksgemeinschaft*, which is manifestly associated with the Nazi conqueror, while stripping it of its negative connotations and yet not concealing its source: "accept the good from he who has brought it."

In a previous entry, dated 23 December 1939 (again omitted from the English publication), Kaplan articulates another expression of identification and admiration:

> This week a reflection of mine caused me sadness and gloom! In the *Deutsche Allgemeine Zeitung* . . . I read a report titled Bücher Bücher Bücher! and my hopes to be delivered from the Nazi distress waned . . . this article made me realize that this villainous Nazi harbors some power that is based not merely on violence and physical *heroism*, but on an ideology that resides deep within the impure Nazi's emotional resources. *Heroism* may reside also in impure forces, in the Devil's children. We are confronting here a people with a high culture, *a people of the book*. The article . . . reports on the craze for books that has assailed Germany . . . say what you may: I fear such a people! In a place in which theft is based on ideology, on a worldview that is essentially spiritual, it enjoys unrivalled validity, robustness and endurance. Such a people will not go astray. *The Nazi has stolen from us not only material property but also our reputation as the "people of the book." The Nazi is both a writer and a warrior, and this is his strength and his heroism.* (emphases added)

Beyond overt admiration for the spiritual Nazi hero that the Nazi press sought to portray for its European readership, and even beyond the fact that the Nazis are perceived here as heirs to the Jews, what stands out particularly is that this admiration is directed at the very act of usurping the Jews' reputation. Just as the Nazis forcibly appropriated Jewish property, they now rob and appropriate the reputation of the Jews as "people of the book." And it is precisely this appropriation that becomes an object of admiration.

Admiration for the Nazis as the ones who had taken over the reputation of the Jewish people is not merely motivated by the Germans' fondness for books and culture but also by ideological components, and precisely the most abhorrent of these, certainly from the Jewish point of view. Kaplan writes as follows on 25 December 1939 (a passage that is once again omitted from the English publication): "The principles of the Nazis are not new after all. . . . In fact, they have stolen the principle of race from us Jews. Race as a fundamental principle of all histories of the nation—is the teaching of Judaism. We should not be ashamed of that."[52]

It is worth reiterating that remarks in this vein were made before the persecution of the Jews had turned into mass extermination. The Nazism to which Kaplan refers, however violent, imperialistic, and dictatorial, has not yet focused on extermination of the Jews. Yet, nevertheless, it appears that Kaplan's remarks transcend the universal psychological identification of the weak with the powerful and of the oppressed with the oppressor. Sympathy for some of the most problematical elements of the Nazi ideology and culture emerges between the lines.[53] The case of Kaplan thus displays a further aspect that should be taken into account when tracing the map of "the epistemological gray zone," and this pertains to the cultural and intellectual context of the writer. Comparing Kaplan's writings to those of Emanuel Ringelblum, we discover no trace of expressions such as these in the latter's works, whose spiritual world was totally different.[54] A comparison between the two might then be useful and illuminating to explain Kaplan's ambivalence toward some Nazi elements.

Between Ringelblum and Kaplan

There can be no doubt that Ringelblum and Kaplan were acquainted. As I have noted, Ringelblum asked Kaplan's permission to copy his diary to the Oyneg Shabes archive, but Kaplan agreed to this only toward the final days of the ghetto, and thus only a part of the diary is preserved in that archive.[55] As we have seen, Ringelblum did not hold Kaplan in particularly high esteem and referred to him as "mediocre."[56] Kaplan, for his part, does not mention Ringelblum at all in his diary, but we can assume that he was not one of his supporters. Kaplan's profound and prolonged enmity toward the "Yiddishists," of whom Ringelblum was a prominent spokesman, along with his loathing of anything to do with Marxism, a principal component of the credo of the Left Po'alei Tsiyon party of which Ringelblum was a member, obviously did not improve the strained relationship between them.[57] This may, indeed, have been the reason for Kaplan's initial refusal to hand his diary over to Ringelblum.

The conspicuous differences between their approaches and preferences notwithstanding, the writings of Kaplan and Ringelblum display several important similarities. They both seek to provide documentation "from the field" of Jewish society under Nazi occupation; both men regard the exposure of historical truth and its documentation as a mission and a calling and devote themselves to this task with fervor; both write from a position of total identification with their community; and they are both extremely critical of the ghetto's formal institutions. Their styles of writing are of course very different. While Ringelblum's diary tends toward a factual account couched in dry language, Kaplan's is subjective and filled with his experiences and feelings. The thematic foci of observation are likewise different, and this is particularly evident in the objects of observation beyond the Jewish world.

Ringelblum is obsessed by Jewish–Polish relations. This theme runs through all his writings and diaries, and he devoted an entire book to the topic, which he wrote from his hideout on the Aryan side following the ghetto's destruction and prior to his capture and murder.[58] Kaplan, on the other hand, displays little interest in the Poles and their relations with the Jews.[59] He has no sense of belonging to the Polish people and held them in very low esteem even prior to the war.[60] He did not even possess a good command of the Polish language.[61] For his part, he makes an obsessive effort to decipher the "conundrum" of Nazism. It would appear that the roots of this difference between Kaplan and Ringelblum are to be found in their divergent intellectual and ideological orientations. As will be demonstrated shortly, this in all probability influenced their writing.

Both Kaplan and Ringelblum were Zionists, although they harbored extremely different perceptions of Zionism. Ringelblum, as mentioned, was among the prominent activists and intellectuals of the Left Po'alei Tsiyon movement founded by Ber Borochov, which sought to link Zionism to Marxism. Faithful to this position, Ringelblum favored the existence of two autonomous cultural centers for the Jewish people—a sovereign political center in Palestine and a diaspora Jewish national center in Poland. Borochov's slogan "do dortn" (here–there) underscores this dual interest in the two centers. Ringelblum's prewar writing as well as his political, educational, and cultural activity during that period thus focused on the desired pattern of relations between Poles and Polish Jews. This outlook was naturally subjected to serious challenges during the war, which Ringelblum addressed extensively in his writing. In this respect, the conception of Jewish nationality in his writings was couched in economic, political, social, and existential terms. His worldview grew out of a social context and was aimed at "the Jewish masses." Romantic and essentialist concepts such as "race" and "*Volksgemeinschaft*" were utterly foreign to Ringelblum, and all the more so in their Nazi context. We find no trace of them in his diary, and certainly no hint of their appreciation as manifested in Nazism.[62]

This was not the case as far as Kaplan was concerned. His spiritual world and intellectual orientation were very different. Kaplan, for his part, was preoccupied before the war with the meeting between traditional Judaism on the one hand, and the enlightened, scientific, and modern world that he admired on the other. He strongly advocated a cultural merging of these poles. It was Nahum Sokolow rather than Borochov whom Kaplan viewed as the exemplary figure within Zionism. He particularly admired what he termed "the Sokolowian blending": "The blending of the original and deep-rooted Jewish culture, the culture of the seminary and the Talmud that is the true complexion of the nation, with the foreign gentile culture . . . apart from Maimonides' blending, the Sokolowian blending is almost unique in Jewish history . . . when Sokolow entered the European foyer, the ancient spirit of the Jewish traditional seminary (*Beit Midrash*) trailed behind him. But just as he introduced [components] from Shem (Jewish culture) to Japheth (gentile culture) so did he introduce [components] from Japheth to Shem."[63] From his prewar writings it emerges that, in contrast to Ringelblum, Kaplan took recourse to western scientific thought in attempting to comprehend Jewish nationalism, and adopted the romantic scientific discourse typical of Social Darwinism. He believed that the "nation" was a natural phenomenon whose heritage was passed on to its sons and daughters in an almost genetic manner. In his article "National Education from a Scientific Point," he writes: "A French child will grow up and become a Frenchman by attribute even were he to be educated among a foreign people, and this is true of a Jewish child and of the children of all peoples."[64] In the same vein, Kaplan asserts that when a Jew, however assimilated and remote from Judaism he may be, writes about general European topics, his writing will differ from that of "Aryans." Thus, for example, he characterizes the writing of Max Nordau, which dealt with altogether general topics: "The fact that these articles are written by a Semite could not be concealed from scholars of the people's psychology; since even were he to share Nordau's political views, an Aryan would have written them somewhat differently."[65] Kaplan can thus sympathize with "the scientists among the antisemites," who warn that "European culture is transforming its Aryan shape and core—and becoming Jewish."[66]

Throughout his adult life, Kaplan regarded himself as a pedagogue by calling and expertise, and many of his prewar writings address topics related to this discipline. His pedagogical views were explicitly influenced by the Social Darwinist Herbert Spencer, who coined the slogan "the survival of the fittest" also with regard to societies and races.[67] Although, like Darwin himself, Spencer was a liberal, his theory and studies are mentioned in almost every genealogical reconstruction of the ideas of Social Darwinism and political racism.[68] Kaplan eagerly and explicitly adopted its principles. In his aforementioned article he seeks to establish the necessity of national education by invoking the scientific foundations of Social Darwinism. Teachers who educate their pupils according to the spirit of nationalism are therefore "fulfilling here neither some obligation toward some sacred nationalism as they see it . . . nor toward political programs, but are simply not entitled to do otherwise. Because should they do otherwise they would be infringing the laws of pedagogical science."[69]

In a further pedagogical essay on educational punishment, Kaplan once again refers to Spencer's theory in order to weave it into the thread of his argument: "Do not demand excessive morality from the infant. Observe its tiny and puerile facial contours, its prominent and puerile nose, its fat lips, its sloping forehead—and you will find that they bear some similarity to the facial contours of the savage. And from this you will gather why young children naturally tend toward all the evil and shameful qualities, such as to be cruel, to steal and to lie."[70] According to the narrative of Social Darwinism, the development of the child is analogous to the teleological evolution of human civilization from primitive man to the refined and moral European man of culture. In this article Kaplan approvingly refers to a further figure whose role in the development of eugenics and political racism is undeniable, namely, the Italian Jew Cesare Lombroso who, according to Kaplan, succeeded in establishing the "congenital criminal" type.[71]

This Darwinian discourse, which likewise reveals the clearly orientalist themes in Kaplan's prewar writings, makes an appearance in his diary on more than one occasion. For example, in 1937, his son-in-law's Arab partner in their business exporting oranges from Palestine to Poland was invited to join them for the Passover Seder. The guest is an educated man who speaks fluent French and also reads Hebrew. Kaplan is greatly impressed by him, yet adds a reservation: "With all his formal education, there is a something Asian about him. He was invited as a guest at a festive feast in the house of strangers and did not bring with him a present for courtesy's sake." He likewise failed to shake hands with the women and did not leave a tip for the servant. "These are not cardinal matters but they indicate a lack of European manners. The son of a rather savage tribe, simple and primitive."[72] In a far more tragic context, on 5 November 1939, a month after Warsaw was overrun by the Germans, Kaplan reaches the conclusion that "Polish Jewry faces total extinction . . . one third will die of hunger; a third will be exiled to the Soviets; and a third will live a life of grinding poverty . . . [they] will be incapable of any cultural creation and through economic and cultural deterioration will reach the level of abjectness of the Jewish collective in Yemen or in Persia."[73]

The ideas of Social Darwinism infiltrated Kaplan's political positions with the help of Nietzschian ethics.[74] On 25 April 1936, following the outbreak of the great Arab revolt and the murder of Jews in Palestine, Kaplan devoted a lengthy diary entry to the nature of the struggle between the Jews and Palestine's Arab population.[75] He begins by complaining that "In the lands of the Diaspora we are persecuted for being 'strangers' and compromise the lives and living of the locals. And in 'our land'? We have brought it life, we revived it from its desolation and its wretchedness and in it too we are persecuted." Yet he immediately continues: "Let us admit to the truth that all the above is merely a platitude derived from propaganda articles in the Zionist press." The comparison is inappropriate, so he admits. The hatred of Jews in Europe is totally irrational. True, the anti-Semites, as well as some Zionists, try to find a justification for this hatred, as though this were a struggle over resources—as if the Jews had come to dispossess "the locals"—but in truth this is a racial hatred: "When we move out we will not benefit the country . . . we are not superfluous in any country because there are no superfluous citizens."

This is not the case as far as Palestine is concerned. There the Arabs' claim is justified. They would relinquish all the wealth and prosperity that the Jews bring as long as they did not take their land from them. Indeed, Kaplan maintains, the Jews did not formally declare war on the Arabs, but "we were the cause of this war and subjective justice is with those who declared it."[76]

How, then, can one justify this confrontation from a Jewish perspective? Kaplan is very forthright on this matter: "Every people goes to war for the sake of new conquests and sacrifices blood and money . . . the right of the sword remains valid. Happy is the people whose sword obeys it and does its national work and woe betide the people whose hands have slackened and dried up and instead of holding a sword approaches the war for its existence with utterances of morality." And he continues: "At a time of battle for one's existence . . . one does not seek justice. The fighters have only one justification: the will to live." Regarding the Arabs' claims, he declares, "These are all just moral claims but who will listen to them? And does Abyssinia have no claims? And do the Jews have no claims? And do the Ukrainians in Poland have no claims? And do the Irish in Britain have no claims?" Questions of morality and justice have no place in collective life; issues of power and will are the only valid ones: "Morality—is merely the invention of the defeated and the weak. Justice is born of weakness. Much of Jewish morality is insincere." What the Jews call morality is merely a tactical tool for survival. Kaplan holds up the Germans vis-à-vis the Jews (it is important to remember that this was written in April 1936, almost three and a half years after the Nazis' rise to power in Germany): "A different people—such as the Germans, for example—has tempered itself a moral sword. And a weak people such as the Jews has tempered itself a 'moral ideal.' Each fights with the tools it likes best so long as it achieves its final goal: making itself a place in the world."

The meaning of these passages is abundantly clear. Kaplan justifies the Jewish struggle against the Arabs of Palestine by employing the Nietzschean ethos, particularly as manifested in *On the Genealogy of Morality,* as well as Social Darwinism's discourse of survival.[77]

In conclusion, like many of his contemporaries, Kaplan's spiritual world drew upon sources very close to those from which the Nazis also drew. Nietzsche, as we know, was considered the political prophet of National Socialism in Nazi Germany. The cult of Nietzsche flourished in Germany during these years, both among the wider public and among the intellectual elite, and his writing was exploited, albeit minus several of its components, to justify the Nazi regime and ideology.[78] The contribution made by Social Darwinism to the development of Nazi racism is widely known.

Together with a large proportion of the European intelligentsia, many Jews of the late nineteenth and first half of the twentieth century were deeply influenced by nationalist, Nietzschean, Social Darwinist, and even blatantly racist concepts and took part in the discourse pertaining to them. During the Holocaust period, however, they encountered something akin to cognitive dissonance and even inner alienation when the discourse with which they identified was appropriated by a regime hostile to them in order to justify their radical and murderous persecution. Kaplan's text illustrates this. We have seen how, in a similar manner, Klemperer's identification with *Völkerpsychologie,* which contained chauvinist-nationalist and essentialist elements, led him to reflect on several occasions as to whether he too bore some responsibility for the growth of the discourse that facilitated the rise of the Nazis.[79] Although Kaplan does not always explicitly address this matter, it appears that this dissonance contributes to the creation of "the epistemological gray zone" in his diary.

When, at the outbreak of the war, Kaplan realizes that "Nazi ideology claims that power is justice, that power is honesty, that power is truth. That power is the sole ruler in the world" (22 October 1939),[80] his words echo his perception of Jewish justice vis-à-vis the Arab revolt several years earlier. Yet now this theory of morality as interpreted by the Nazis establishes the persecution of the Jews (as well as others), and Kaplan is aware of this: "And thus wherever the Nazis arrive there is only theft and robbery." Nevertheless, as we have observed, he does not recoil from concepts such as "*Volksgemeinschaft*" and "race," and even adopts them.

This dissonance occasionally surfaces in the diary. In an entry dated 14 November 1941, for example, Kaplan expresses the Social Darwinist position that many nationalist and fascist thinkers throughout Europe used, namely, that war encompasses considerable value for the evolution of human culture:

> Our prophets foresaw that one day people would beat their swords into ploughshares . . . and wars would cease in the land. But this is merely a poetic vision which real life does not obey . . . some are of the opinion that war in itself brings considerable benefit to the world. Human development . . . is revealed only through wars, which have never ceased . . . the collision between peoples sets in motion latent forces that through war become active whereas during times of peace they are in a state of slumber and passivity . . . and should you fail to be equipped, armed and prepared for war, you will end up by being atrophied and will be annihilated. *Its murderous aspect is the Nazi doctrine, and in itself—there is much that is good in it.* (emphasis added)

Kaplan is no racist, in the sense that concepts of race do not serve as a significant foundation for his worldview in general and his political positions in particular. He certainly does not express any open ideological identification with Nazism. Moreover, in his diary we find passages that express the absolute inverse of the one just quoted. On 31 April 1940, for example, he expresses a blatantly antinationalist sentiment:

> Thousands of people are dying every day on the killing fields and in Flanders . . . there is no purpose to their death . . . the platitude about the death of heroes will be voiced. But it is unable to bend what is straight. I insist. Even a homeland is not deserving or worth a man sacrificing his soul for it, for all the world is his homeland. When love and fraternity will pervade the world there will be no need for a homeland. Any homeland is merely a good thing for several millions or for several tens of thousands and the masses are merely as submissive slaves to the holders of office and government.

And he continues: "And I say: this attitude toward the war dead is merely a punishment for 'the homeland's heroes,' who refer to simple murder as heroism. I am the grandson of the prophet Isaiah. I and my grandfather likewise abhor bloodshed of any kind, you may say this is merely cowardice! So be it! I am not ashamed of this reprehensible quality." He thus not only loathes

Nazism, derides it, and primarily suffers from it, but from an ideological perspective too is at odds with it. Kaplan is a liberal Zionist, and the discourse of human rights that grew out of the French Revolution is no less dear to him than the Romantic, Social Darwinist, or Nietzschean discourse. Inspired by this discourse, prior to the war Kaplan attempted to pioneer a debate on children's rights within Eastern European Jewish education.[81] Politically speaking, Kaplan was a liberal nationalist Zionist. While he loathed Communism, he did not support any specific party on either the right or the left.[82] Yet like many other intellectuals among the European intelligentsia of the first half of the twentieth century, Jews and Gentiles alike, Kaplan adopted the concepts of a romantic and essentialist nationalism that drew on the contemporary scientific discourse of race and Social Darwinism, and on the Nietzschian ethos of "the will for power."[83] These served as extremely dominant discursive frameworks for the last third of the nineteenth century in Europe and deeply influenced mainstream fields of science such as anthropology, genetics, biology, and to a significant extent also disciplines in the humanities, such as linguistics, history, and geography.

Kaplan, who was deeply influenced by these discourses before the war, employed this conceptual world to confront the tragedy that beset Polish Jewry from 1939 onward. This may to some extent explain the dualist consciousness manifested in his diaries, and in particular his expressions of respect and admiration for, and identification with, certain aspects of the Nazi discourse and phenomenon found throughout the diary. Kaplan's "encounter" with the Nazis and Nazism is manifested in his diary by the entry of a different voice, apart from the dominant voice therein, which abhors Nazism and awaits its downfall. This additional voice, however weak, is clearly identifiable and tells a different story, one of jealousy, identification with, and at times even admiration for, certain aspects manifested by the Nazis, which had until then been highly respected. It was only after World War II and the Holocaust, once the catastrophic results of the views and approaches associated with racial and Social Darwinist thought and with Nazism had fully emerged, that these ideas fell into disrepute and became almost taboo, to the point that they were excluded from the overt and respected intellectual panorama of the western world.[84] Kaplan, who did not survive to see the postwar period and absorbed these frames of thought into his world, was unable to disengage from them fully during the war, and they occasionally surface in the diary and express an additional voice other than the dominant one. Embedded as it was in the prewar conceptual world, this voice could not but on occasion voice respect and even admiration for certain manifestations of Nazism, and partly because of this a dual language and split consciousness, is created in the diary.[85]

After tracing the psychological, linguistic, and cultural mechanisms of identification in Kaplan's diary, and in the works of other contemporary writers, we can return to the paragraph from Kaplan's diary with which this discussion began, and appreciate its full significance: "Nazism came to annihilate us. It is the enemy of Judaism in its spirit and in its practice. We fight it and await its defeat. However—the human spirit is inexplicable. Unconsciously, we accept its ideology and follow in its ways. Nazism has conquered our entire world. It severely damages our public life. And yet we do not cease to declare day and night that it is ugliness and that one ought to distance oneself from it."

Notes

1. Chaim Aron Kaplan, Diary, "Hayim Ahron Kaplan" file, Moreshet Archive, D.2.470; emphasis added.

2. The Joint Distribution Committee is an independent American relief and welfare organization that was founded in 1914 in order to assist Jews and Jewish communities around the world in times of crisis. During the war the Joint opened shelters and soup kitchens in Poland for the thousands of Jewish refugees who fled from the small towns to the large cities. Once the Warsaw ghetto was created, the Joint supported soup kitchens, Jewish hospitals, and educational and cultural programs within the ghetto. See also Yehuda Bauer, *American Jewry and the Holocaust: The American Jewish Joint Distribution 1939–1945* (Detroit: Wayne State University Press, 1982), 67–106.

3. See Yisrael Gutman, *The Jews of Warsaw 1939–1943: Ghetto, Underground, Revolt*, trans. Ina Friedman (Bloomington: Indiana University Press, 1982), 103. On such moral disputes over food in the Writers and Journalists Association, see Ber Mark, *Di Umgekumene Shrayber fun di Getos un Lagern un Zeyere Verk* (Warsaw: Yiddish Bukh Ferlag, 1954), 49–50; and Rokhl Oyerbakh's response in *Varshever Tsavoes* [Warsaw wills] (Tel Aviv: Farlag Yisroel Bukh, 1974), 63, and, more generally about the Writers and Journalists Association, 26–32.

4. This is just one instance of the blatant social injustice prevalent in the Warsaw ghetto and to which many of its writers referred. See, for example, Peretz Opoczynski, *Reshimot* [Sketches from the Warsaw ghetto] (Tel Aviv: The Ghetto Fighters' House and Hakibbutz Hameuchad, 1970). For a balanced description and analysis of this complex issue of solidarity in the Warsaw Jewish community during the war, see Samuel Kassow, *Who Will Write Our History? Emanuel Ringelblum, the Warsaw Ghetto, and Oyneg Shabes Archive* (Bloomington: Indiana University Press, 2007). See also Saul Friedländer's assessment of the "ongoing disintegration of overall Jewish solidarity" during the Holocaust in Saul Friedländer, *Nazi Germany and the Jews: The Years of Extermination 1939–1945* (London: Weidenfeld and Nicolson, 2007), 192.

5. This complaint is repeated on numerous occasions in many ghetto diaries. See, for example, in the Lodz ghetto: Oskar Rosenfeld, *In the Beginning Was the Ghetto: Notebooks from*

Łódź, ed. Hanno Loewy, trans. Brigitte M. Goldstein (Evanston, IL: Northwestern University Press, 2002), 229–331.

6. The essay appears in the last book published before his suicide: Primo Levi, *The Drowned and the Saved*, trans. Raymond Rosenthal (New York: Vintage, 1989), 36–69. Giorgio Agamben, *Remnants of Auschwitz: The Witness and the Archive*, trans. Daniel Heller-Roazen (New York: Zone Books, 1999), 26. For a critique of Agamben's conception of the "gray zone" and his interpretation of Levi, see Dominick LaCapra, *History in Transit: Experience, Identity, Critical Theory* (Ithaca, NY: Cornell University Press, 2004), 144–194.

7. Only recently have gray-zone issues gradually become the subject of more discussions. See, for example, Jonathan Petropoulus and John Roth, eds., *Gray Zones: Ambiguity and Compromise in the Holocaust and Its Aftermath* (New York: Berghahn, 2005). See also Omer Bartov, "Wartime Lies and Other Testimonies: Jewish–Christian Relations in Buczacz, 1939–1944," *East European Politics and Societies* 25 (2011): 486–511. See also Jacques Presser's classic work *The Night of the Girondists*, trans. Barrows Mussey (London: HarperCollins, 1992).

8. This is one of the principal themes of her book, articulated mainly in the introduction and the third section, which deals with totalitarianism. See Hannah Arendt, *The Origins of Totalitarianism* (Cleveland: World, 1958).

9. Giorgio Agamben, *Homo Sacer: Sovereign Power and Bare Life*, trans. Daniel Heller-Roazen (Stanford, CA: Stanford University Press, 1998).

10. Boaz Neumann, "The National Socialist Politics of Life," *New German Critique* 85 (2002): 107–132.

11. "To name is to know—to fit something in a taxonomic system of classification." Robert Darnton, *The Kiss of Lamourette: Reflections in Cultural History* (New York: Norton, 1989), 336.

12. Levi, *The Drowned and the Saved*, 48–49.

13. On the Sonderkomando, see Gideon Greif, *We Wept without Tears: Testimonies of the Jewish Sonderkommando from Auschwitz* (New Haven, CT: Yale University Press, 2005). On Rumkowski's dubious leadership, see Michal Unger, *Lodz: Ahron Hageta'ot BePolin* [Lodz: The last of the ghettos in Poland] (Jerusalem: Yad Vashem, 2005). See also Richard Rubenstein, "Gray into Black: The Case of Mordechai Chaim Rumkowski," in Petropoulous and Roth, *Gray Zones*, 299–310.

14. Levi, *The Drowned and the Saved*, 36.

15. Ibid., 37.

16. For a fourth lingual gray zone in which the Nazi language and metaphors penetrate and distort Kaplan's Hebrew, see Amos Goldberg, *Trauma Beguf Rishon: Ktivat Yomanim Bitkufat HaSho'ah* [Trauma in first person: Diary writing during the Holocaust] (Or Yehuda: Ben Gurion University and Kinneret Zmora–Bitan Dvir, 2012), 343–369.

17. Emanuel Ringelblum, *Ktavim Ahronim* [Last writings], vol. 2 (Jerusalem: Yad Vashem, 1994), 20; emphasis added.

18. Wasser, "Daily Entries of Hersh Wasser," *Yad Vashem Studies* 15 (1983): 247.

19. Avraham Lewin, *Mipinkaso shel Hamoreh MiYehudiyah: Geto Varshah April 1942–Mai 1943* [From the notebook of a teacher at the Yehudiah School: Warsaw ghetto April 1942–May 1943] (Tel Aviv: Hakibbutz Hameuchad and the Ghetto Fighters' House, 1969), 108; emphasis added.

20. Cited in Unger, *Lodz*, 230. In his diary, Leon Hurwicz frequently describes Rumkowski as a dictator (Leon Hurwicz, Diary, Archive of the Jewish Historical Institute in Warsaw [ZIH], 302/11–13). In March 1941, Hurwicz explains Rumkowski's mind-set: "You can't

slip away from my dictatorship alive, only death will set you free" (ZIH 302/11). Rumkowski admitted publicly that he was inspired by the Fascists and that he did not regard dictatorship as a bad word. See Kermish, *To Live with Honor, to Die with Honor: Selected Dolcuments from the Warsaw Ghetto Underground Archives* (Jerusalem: Yad Vashem, 1986), 298.

21. Michal Unger, *Reassessment of the Image of Mordechai Chaim Rumkowski* (Jerusalem: Yad Vashem, 2004). She reiterated this assessment in her presentation concerning the appointment of judges, at the conference "New Trends in the Study of the Jews during the Holocaust," held at Yad Vashem, 6 July 2008.

22. This issue has been hotly debated and the subject of overwhelming research. Trunk's seminal work is still the most comprehensive on this complex topic. Isaiah Trunk, *Judenrat: The Jewish Councils in Eastern Europe under Nazi Occupation* (New York: Macmillan, 1972). See also Yehuda Bauer, *The Death of the Shtetl* (New Haven, CT: Yale University Press, 2009).

23. Not all Jewish police units and not all Jewish policemen were corrupt: some (for example, those in the Minsk ghetto) cooperated with the underground. See Trunk, *Judenrat*, 416, 518–519. For cooperation of the Kovno ghetto Jewish police with the communist underground, see ibid., 521–522. Rokhl Oyerbakh dedicated a chapter called "The Jewish National Socialist" to the notorious Warsaw ghetto collaborator Abraham Gancwajch; see Rokhl Oyerbakh, *Baym Letsten Veg* (Tel Aviv: Farlag Yisroel Bukh, 1977), 184–201.

24. Moshe Maltz, *Years of Horror—Glimpse of Hope: The Diary of a Family in Hiding* (New York: Shengold, 1993), 52 (manuscript in Yad Vashem Archives O.33/2474). See also Emanuel Ringelblum's reflection on similar behavior in Warsaw (2–5 October 1940): Emanuel Ringelblum, *Yoman Ureshimot* [Diary and notes from the Warsaw ghetto] [Jerusalem: Yad Vashem and the Ghetto Fighters' House, 1992], 154.

25. For more on the Jewish police in the Lodz ghetto, see, for example, Shlomo Frank, *Togbuch fun Lodzer Geto* [Diary from the Lodz ghetto] (Tel Aviv: Menorah, 1959), 11–21 (16 January 1941). Many such indications can be found in the memoir of Stanislaw Adler, a Jewish police officer in the Warsaw ghetto: Stanislaw Adler, *In the Warsaw Ghetto, 1940–1943: An Account of a Witness*, trans. Sara Chmielewska Philip (Jerusalem: Yad Vashem, 1982),

26. Daniel Blatman, *Geto Varshah: Sipur Itona'i* [The Warsaw ghetto: A journalistic story] (Jerusalem: Yad Vashem, 2002), 263.

27. Sigmund Freud, "Totem and Taboo," in *The Standard Edition of the Complete Psychological Works of Sigmund Freud*, vol. 13, ed. and trans. James Strachey (London: Hogarth, 1953), 81–82. See also Freud, "The Ego and the Id," in *The Standard Edition of the Complete Psychological Works of Sigmund Freud*, vol. 19, ed. and trans. James Strachey (London: Hogarth, 1961), 29n2.

28. Freud, "Totem and Taboo," 127–129.

29. Anna Freud, *The Ego and the Mechanisms of Defense* (London: Hogarth, 1968), 109–120. On this issue, see also Sigmund Freud, "Moses and Monotheism," in *The Standard Edition of the Complete Psychological Works of Sigmund Freud*, vol. 23, ed. and trans. James Strachey (London: Hogarth, 1964), 107–110.

30. Bruno Bettelheim, *Surviving and Other Essays* (New York: Vintage, 1979).

31. Robert Antelme, *The Human Race*, trans. Jeffrey Haight and Annie Mahler (Evanston, IL: Marlboro, 1992), 31.

32. We should note that biographies published on Bettelheim reveal his cruelty, despotism, and sarcastic behavior, which bordered on sadism. He committed suicide in 1990 at the age of eighty-seven. It is therefore quite possible that in depicting the "regressive" identification on the part of camp prisoners with their tormentors he was also testifying about himself.

33. Sandor Ferenczi, "The Confusion of Tongues between Adults and Children," in *Final Contributions to the Problems and Methods of Psychoanalysis*, ed. Michael Balint, trans. Eric Mosbacher (London: Hogarth, 1955), 156–167.

34. Ibid., 164.

35. Jean Améry, *At the Mind's Limits: Contemplations by a Survivor on Auschwitz and Its Realities*, trans. Sidney Rosenfeld and Stella P. Rosenfeld (Bloomington: Indiana University Press, 1980), 10–11.

36. Raul Hilberg, *Sources of Holocaust Research: An Analysis* (Chicago: Ivan R. Dee, 2001), 134–136. Such expressions are prevalent in Victor Klemperer's linguistic analyses. See, for example, Victor Klemperer, *Ich will Zeugnis ablegen bis zum letzten*: vol. 2, *Tagebücher 1942–1945* (Berlin: Aufbau, 1995), 188–189 (29 July 1942). It is instructive to compare these processes to those found in other historical instances of oppression and genocide. See, for example, Mark Nichinian's observation with regard to the Armenian genocide: "The discourse concerning the genocide still resides within the claws of the murderer. We still utterly belong to the logic of the murderer." David Kazanjian and Marc Nichanian, "Between Genocide and Catastrophe," in *Loss: The Politics of Mourning*, ed. David Eng and David Kazanjian (Berkeley: University of California Press, 2003), 127. For the colonial context see Frantz Fanon, *Black Skin, White Masks*, trans. Richard Philcox (New York: Grove, 2008).

37. In narratological terms one can speak of "voices" and issues associated with focalizations. See Shlomith Rimmon-Kenan, *Narrative Fiction: Contemporary Poetics* (London: Routledge, 1983), 71–105. In psychoanalytical terms, this refers to the distinction between imagined identification, in which the subject seeks to resemble some "other," and symbolic identification, through which the subject seeks to discover how to become worthy of the gaze of the other. See Slavoj Žižek, *The Sublime Object of Ideology* (London: Verso, 1989), 105–107.

38. Kaplan was highly critical of the Jews of Warsaw and in general, even prior to the war. He himself was aware of this, as his comment of 7 July 1936 indicates: "Readers of my diary in future generations will consider me a misanthrope, who sees only [indistinct word] and shadows and who will find fault with everyone" (Archive of the Jewish Historical Institute in Warsaw, ZIH 302/218) (henceforth Kaplan Diary). See Blatman, *Geto Varshah*.

39. The image of the Jews as "Asians" is one of the most fundamental images originating from the time of emancipation. It seeks to underscore the Jews' essential foreignness to European culture. In Nazi language, the Asian association was frequently linked to Jewish Bolshevism. In this manner, for example, the commander of the sixth army Walter von Reichenau explained his notorious order at the time of the invasion of the Soviet Union: "The most essential objective in the war against the Bolshevik-Jewish system is the total destruction of their means of power and the removal of Asian influence on European culture." The text of the order can be found at the Nuremberg Trials website, http://web.archive.org/web/20091227042100/http://www.ess.uwe.ac.uk:80/genocide/ussr2.htm, accessed 2 September 2016.

40. See also the entry dated 19 August 1940, in which he complains that the many years spent in Europe have not uprooted the Jews' oriental nature and "an Aryan philanthropic office would certainly have had a different shape." In certain respects this manifests a mechanism that Sander Gilman has termed "Jewish self-hatred," although in this case the political situation and cultural conditions differ completely from those that Gilman had in mind. See Sander Gilman, *Jewish Self-Hatred: Anti-Semitism and the Hidden Language of the Jews* (Baltimore: Johns Hopkins University Press, 1986).

41. For an extensive analysis of this phenomenon, see Goldberg, *Trauma Beguf Rishon*, 313–326.

42. This expression originates from the Sabbath *Kedushah* prayer, "The whole earth is full of His glory; His servants ask one another: Where is the place of His glory that we may admire Him."

43. This turn of phrase is, of course, reminiscent of the traditional Jewish blessing that refers to thunder, winds, tempests, earthquakes, and so forth: "Blessed are You . . . whose power and might fills the world."

44. Kaplan Diary (ZIH 302/218).

45. See, for example, the entries dated 26 November 1940; 12 February 1941; 15 February 1941; 27 February 1941; and 14 May 1942.

46. The young Moshe Flinker listens in his hiding place in Holland to a speech by Goebbels and prays to the Lord that "He might instill in our hearts such spirit," though not as "an all-encompassing mania in the name of which millions of people are sacrificed." Moshe Flinker, *Young Moshe's Diary: The Spiritual Torment of a Jewish Boy in Nazi Europe*, trans. Geoffrey Wigoder (Jerusalem: Yad Vashem, 1965), 79 (12 February 1943).

47. This dichotomy is attributed to the sociologist Ferdinand Tönnies. On this conception and its link to murderous *volkist* anti-Semitism, see Enzo Traverso, *The Origins of Nazi Violence*, trans. Janet Lloyd (New York: New Press, 2003), 135–136.

48. Michael Wildt, *Hitler's Volksgemeinschaft and the Dynamics of Racial Exclusion: Violence against Jews in Provincial Germany, 1919–1939*, trans. Bernard Heise (New York: Berghahn, 2012). See also Avraham Barkai, "*Volksgemeinschaft*, 'Aryanization' and the Holocaust," in *The Final Solution: Origins and Implementations*, ed. David Cesarani (London: Routledge, 1994), 33–50; Shelly Baranowski, *Nazi Empire: German Colonialism and Imperialism from Bismarck to Hitler* (Cambridge: Cambridge University Press, 2011).

49. See Friedländer, *Nazi Germany and the Jews: 1939–1945*, 38, 48. See also Martina Steber and Bernhard Gotto, eds., *Visions of Community in Nazi Germany: Social Engineering and Private Lives* (Oxford: Oxford University Press, 2014), esp. the editors' introduction, 1–25, and chap. 15, Christopher Browning, "The Holocaust: Basis and Objective of the Volksgemeinschaft?," 217–225. Browning asserts that: "There was a strong ideological connection between the understanding of the Volksgemeinschaft as a racial community and the rationalization and justification of the Holocaust" (217).

50. See Dominick LaCapra, *Writing History, Writing Trauma* (Baltimore: Johns Hopkins University Press, 2014); Dan Stone, "Genocide as Transgression," *European Journal of Social Theory* 7, no. 1 (2004): 45–65.

51. Peter Longerich, "The Wannsee Conference in the Development of the 'Final Solution,'" in *The Holocaust: Critical Concepts in Historical Studies*, vol. 3, ed. David Cesarani (London: Routledge, 2004), 124.

52. Kaplan expresses a completely different attitude in the entry dated 21 May 1940: Chaim Aron Kaplan, *Megilat Yisurin: Yoman Geto Varshah* [Scroll of agony: Warsaw ghetto diary] (Tel Aviv: Am Oved and Yad Vashem, 1966), 246.

53. A further, albeit less clear-cut, example is Kaplan's reference to the concept of the "new world" that the Nazis claim to be founding. This optimistic, liberating, and revolutionary rhetoric enchants him, and apparently it is for this reason that he feels obliged to confront it. On 18 December 1940, for example, he writes: "Nazism wants to build a new world. A world ruled by new concepts. Yet it is really not worthy and not fair and not qualified to create something 'new,' not merely because of its title but also because of its essence and nature. It merely roused from its sleep the animal in humans, which under the influence of the nineteenth century's humanism slumbered in its lethargic sleep and dared not raise its head." He furthermore

realizes that there was no room for the Jews in Nazism's new world. See, for example, the entries dated 5 February 1940; 4 May 1940; 6 September 1940; and 3 November 1940.

54. For a similar reading, which regards cultural background as a decisive component in understanding diaries, see Rachel Feldhay Brenner, "Voices from Destruction: Two Eyewitness Testimonies from the Stanisławów Ghetto," *Holocaust and Genocide Studies* 22, no. 2 (2008): 320–339.

55. Ringelblum, *Ktavim Ahronim*, 19.

56. Ibid.

57. The Yiddishists were a cultural group that regarded Yiddish as the national and cultural tongue of East European Jews. On this basis, among others, some demanded cultural autonomy for the Jews within the Polish nation state. On Kaplan's attitude toward them, see, for example, the entry dated 7 June 1941.

58. Ringelblum, *Ktavim Ahronim*, 173–302.

59. Obviously, he was not completely indifferent to the Poles. See, for example, his appreciation of their empathy with the Jews, after the latter had been forced to wear the badge (Kaplan, *Megilat Yisurin*, 104 [5 December 1939]).

60. On his attitude toward Poles, see, for example, the entries of 28 June 1936 and 30 June 1939 (in which he calls the Polish state an "upstart"); and that of 18 March 1937, among many others. He maintains this attitude to Poles during the war as well (see, e.g., *Megilat Yisurin*, 412 [8 December 1940]).

61. He states this explicitly on 3 March 1937.

62. On Ringelblum's Zionist and Marxist ideology and conceptualization, see Kassow, *Who Will Write Our History?*, 27–89.

63. Chaim Kaplan's eulogy for Sokolow, "Rabi Nahum," in Chaim Aron Kaplan, *Pezurai: Mehkarim, Reshimot Ufelyetonim: Kol Kitvei Hamehaber Bitkufat Hashanim 1900–1936* [My scatterings: Studies, articles, and feuilletons: The author's complete writings during the years 1900–1936] (Warsaw: Va'ad Hayovel, 1937), 382–386. See also his diary entry of 22 May 1942, and *Pezurai*, 37, for his admiration of Bialik and especially his nostalgic and ambivalent attitude toward the traditional Beit Midrash.

64. Kaplan, *Pezurai*, 30.

65. For an extensive discussion of the *Völkerpsychologie* and its relations to *volkisch* and nationalist concepts and attitudes, see chapters 4 and 5 on Victor Klemperer.

66. Kaplan, *Pezurai*, 28.

67. Herbert Spencer, *The Evolution of Society: Selections from Herbert Spencer's Principles of Sociology*, ed. Robert L. Carneiro (Chicago: University of Chicago Press, 1974), 72–81, esp. 78.

68. On perceptions of Social Darwinism within the pacifist movement in Europe, see Richard Weikart, *From Darwin to Hitler: Evolutionary Ethics, Eugenics, and Racism in Germany* (New York: Palgrave Macmillan, 2004), 163–183. On Spencer's importance in the evolution of Social Darwinist thought, see Mike Hawkins, *Social Darwinism in European and American Thought, 1860–1945: Nature as Model and Nature as Threat* (Cambridge: Cambridge University Press, 1997), esp. 82–103 (chap. 4).

69. Chaim Kaplan, "Hahinukh Hale'umi" [National education], in *Pezurai*, 32.

70. Chaim Kaplan, "Sakhar Ve'onesh Behinukh" [Reward and punishment in education], in *Pezurai*, 17–18.

71. A founding father of modern criminology, Lombroso asserted that the tendency toward crime is hereditary and that a "born criminal" can be identified by outward attributes. Even in the writings of a humanist such as Janusz Korczak one finds echoes of a worldview that

at times reflects the ideas of Social Darwinism. He proposes, for example, to kill violent children who are beyond redemption and who will harm society in their adulthood, namely, for "fifty years." Janusz Korczak, *Ghetto Diary*, trans. Jerzy Bachrach and Barbara Krzywicka (New Haven, CT: Yale University Press, 2003), 92; in this regard, see also 112. On Lombroso's contribution to the evolution of modern racism, see Mosse, *Toward the Final Solution: A History of European Racisim* (New York: Harper and Row, 1980), 83–87.

72. Kaplan Diary, 30 March 1937 (ZIH 302/218). Very similar accusations reeking of social anti-Semitism were leveled by Gentile businessmen at their Jewish competitors from the nineteenth century onward. See Arendt, *The Origins of Totalitarianism*, 169.

73. Kaplan's prewar diaries likewise display his orientalist attitude on numerous occasions. In the entry dated 6 August 1936, for example, reflecting on the future of the Arab revolt, he recognizes that the Arabs' campaign is directed at those "who are stealing his land," but consoles himself by remarking that "we have a powerful rule on our side: culture vanquishes savagery." And with regard to Darwinism, he makes an optimistic pronouncement of 26 October 1939, a few weeks after the occupation of Warsaw, that "individuals will be lost; the Jewish collective will live," echoing to some extent the Darwinist discourse.

74. Nietzsche's antirationalist conception that (in Kaplan's words) "the will is father to the idea," in other words that will dictates reason rather than vice versa, serves as one of the most fundamental principles in Kaplan's perception of reality. See, for example, the entries dated 20 February 1940; 11 April 1940; 5 September 1940; and many others.

75. Kaplan Diary (ZIH 302/218).

76. Although Kaplan was by no means a follow of Ze'ev Jabotinsku, his argument is reminiscent of and, consciously or unconsciously, quite probably rests upon Jabotinsky's 1923 essay, "The Iron Wall," https://www.jewishvirtuallibrary.org/jsource/Zionism/ironwall.html, accessed 21 August 2016.

77. Friedrich Nietzsche, *On the Genealogy of Morality*, ed. Keith Ansell-Pearson, trans. Carol Diethe (Cambridge: Cambridge University Press, 1994).

78. In fact, very similar assertions about the superiority of might over the law were already brutally uttered by German liberal nationalists in 1848, at the Frankfurt German Assembly as they fantasized about a great Germany: "Our right is that of the stronger, the right of the conquest. . . . Legal rules appear nowhere more miserable than where they presume to determine the fate of nations." Hitler admired them for this attitude (in contradistinction to the despised "November traitors"—the liberals of the Weimar Republic), which he completely endorsed. See Lewis Namier, *1848: The Revolution of the Intellectuals* (Garden City, NY: Anchor Books, 1964), 108, 150 (see also 85, 86, 128, 129, 146–150). See also Mark Mazower, *Hitler's Empire: How the Nazis Ruled Europe* (New York: Penguin, 2008), 16 (see also 64).

79. On these connections, see Heide Gerstenberger, "Meine Prinzipien über das Deutschtum und die Verschiedenen Nationalitäten sind ins Wackeln gekommen wie di Zähne eines alten Mannes," in *Im Herzen der Finsternis: Victor Klemperer als Chronist der NS-Zeit*, ed. Hannes Heer (Berlin: Aufbau, 1997), 10–20. This should be compared to the position adopted by Matti Bunzl and Egbert Klautke, who fail to see any link between *Völkerpsychologie* and Racism or Nazi ideology: see Matti Bunzl, "*Völkerpsychologie* and German-Jewish Emancipation," in *Worldly Provincialism: German Anthropology in the Age of Empire*, ed. H. Glenn Penny and Matti Bunzl (Ann Arbor: University of Michigan Press, 2003), 47–85; Egbert Klautke, *The Mind of the Nation: Völkerpsychologie in Germany 1851–1955* (Oxford: Berghahn, 2013).

80. See also the entry dated 25 December 1939.

81. Kaplan, *Pezurai*, 39, and the entire article.

82. On the basis of diary entries of 1936, he did not support a particular political party. He abhorred the left, but he was not enamored with right wing Beitar either.

83. On Jewish scientists and intellectuals who adopted the concept of race in their work, see John Efron, *Defenders of the Race* (New Haven, CT: Yale University Press, 1994); Nancy Leys Stepan and Sander L. Gilman, "Appropriating the Idioms of Science: The Rejection of Scientific Racism," in *The "Racial" Economy of Science: Toward a Democratic Future*, ed. Sandra Harding (Bloomington: Indiana University Press, 1993), 170–194. A prominent and controversial figure in the debate on this issue is Arthur Ruppin. See Amos Morris-Reich, "Arthur Ruppin's Concept of Race," *Israel Studies* 11, no. 3 (2006): 1–30; and Etan Bloom, "What 'The Father' Had in Mind: Arthur Ruppin (1876–1943), Cultural Identity, Weltanschauung and Action," *Journal for History of European Ideas* 33, no. 3 (2007): 330–349. See also Raphael Falk, *Tziyont Vehabiologyah shel HaYehudim* [Zionism and the biology of the Jews] (Tel Aviv: Resling, 2006). On Nietzsche's tremendous influence on Hebrew and Jewish culture, see Steven Aschheim, "Nietzsche and the Nietzschean Moment in Jewish Life (1890–1939)," *Leo Baeck Institute Year Book* 37 (1992): 189–212. See also Jacob Golomb, ed., *Nitshe Batarbut HaIvrit* [Nietzsche, Zionism and Hebrew culture] (Jerusalem: Magnes, 2002).

84. These approaches remained alive in various disguised discursive configurations. On this matter, see Etienne Balibar, "Is There a 'Neo-Racism'?," in *Race, Nation, Class: Ambiguous Identities*, by Etienne Balibar (trans. Chris Turner) and Immanuel Wallerstein (London: Verso, 1991), 17–28 (and the entire volume). The best summary of this issue, to my knowledge, is provided by Yehouda Shenhav and Yossi Yonah, eds., *Gizanut BeYisra'el* [Racism in Israel] (Tel Aviv: Van Leer Jerusalem Institue and Hakibbutz Hameuchad, 2008), 13–46.

85. Ferenczi, "The Confusion of Tongues."

CONCLUSION

Believing she had succeeded in recovering from the traumas of her life, Anaïs Nin wrote the following in her diary: "Stories are the only enchantment possible, for when we begin to see our suffering as a story, we are saved."[1] These words reflect the optimistic approach to the power of stories to deliver the victim from the suffering of trauma. Nin refers both to fictional writing and to autobiographical, diary writing. There are situations, however, in which narrative appears to lack sufficient power—situations in which the force of shock is so great that it disintegrates even the story and greatly limits its therapeutic, redemptive power. Suzette Henke addressed this issue, circumscribing Nin's conclusions regarding the power of stories: "Only the historical trauma of Nazi aggression proved too powerful an enemy."[2]

At the close of this book, I can only agree with Henke's conclusion regarding the victims of Nazi aggression, although the exclusivity she affords this particular phenomenon is certainly debatable. From the examination of many Holocaust diaries, some of which have been discussed here at length, it seems that in the context of radical trauma such as that experienced by Holocaust victims, narrative written as the events themselves unfold lacks the ability to deliver the authors from their distress. Life stories were unable during this period to restore the self and its identity or to serve as a therapeutic alternative in the face of the immense and catastrophic power of the trauma. In this concluding chapter, I will try to tie together all the threads spun (or rather unraveled) over the course of the book.

Trauma is an experience at the heart of which lies a void; an experience in which the shock is so immense that it cannot be completely woven into the cognitive and psychic systems and thus, to a certain extent, remains external to them. Traumatic experience is an encounter with a tangible lack that refuses to be integrated into systems of meaning—including those of narrative. The immediate effect of the encounter with this absence is numbness on the one hand, and terror and rage on the other, bearing immense destructive potential. Not only does void escape all human meaning (hence the terror it evokes) and not only does it threaten to disintegrate the way in which we afford meaning to the events of our lives (i.e., our narrative identities), but it jeopardizes the mechanism by which meaning is afforded: the conceptual network that enables meaning in the first place. It thus threatens the very possibility of narrative. Following Lacan, I have called such situations symbolic or second death. Once the frameworks of knowledge and law that organize the human world into meaningful reality have disintegrated, the victim continues to exist only on the biological plane. Symbolic death is the catastrophic potential embodied in trauma—that which lies beyond it.

Diaries written during the Holocaust are a kind of battlefield on which the writers seek to reconstitute their words, if only at first, around the lack, in order to enclose it and try to limit its harm and exposure. Due to the preliminary nature of the writing and its proximity to the shocking, traumatic events, it ultimately fails in its effort to reorganize the writer's narrative identity—to the point that, at times, the text itself disintegrates. The text thus walks a fine line that delimits extreme trauma, while striving not to fall into the catastrophic abyss of symbolic death.

In Victor Klemperer's diaries, we saw how the narrative organization of identity through diary writing subverts itself and, especially, how the organization of narrative time fails. We saw how the conception of (Augustinian and Ricoeurian) autobiographical time as a three-dimensional present—the past in the present as memory, the future in the present as expectation and hope, and the present itself as a form of "attention" to the world in which the future consciously becomes the past—collapses almost entirely. As a result of this collapse in Klemperer's narrative, his German identity is undermined, as is his conceptual world—rooted in the principles of *Völkerpsychologie* ("peoples' psychology"). We also saw how the traumatic present tarnishes and distorts his childhood past.

As a reminder of the extent of the temporal disintegration in Klemperer's diary, the passage with which the discussion began bears repeating. On 14 September 1944, Klemperer writes:

> But something else made a greater impression on us—it was the same for both Neumark and myself—the impotence of memory to fix all that we had so painfully experienced in time. When—insofar as we remembered it at all—had this or that happened, when had it been? Only a few facts stick in the mind, dates not at all. One is overwhelmed by the present, time is not divided up, everything is infinitely long ago, everything is infinitely long in coming; there is no yesterday, no tomorrow, only an eternity. And that is yet another reason one knows nothing of the history one has experienced: The sense of time has been abolished; one is at once too blunted and too overexcited, one is crammed full of the present. The chain of disappointments also unfolded in front of me again.[3]

In the previous chapters, we have seen how these processes sometimes reach the extreme at which there is no longer a point of reference within the symbolic order, and the text collapses toward symbolic death. We encountered these processes, inter alia, in the diaries of Victor Klemperer, particularly from his time in prison; in the diary of Janusz Korczak, who would have celebrated a mass but found that his words had disappeared; in the diary of Fela Szeps from the Grünberg camp, who wonders whether there is any point in writing; and, in a slightly different fashion, in Kaplan's relation to the law, which excludes the Jews from its framework—thereby, in a certain sense, excluding them from their humanity. In effect, we have observed these processes in most of the texts examined here. Symbolic death is thus the abyss into which the texts we have seen throughout the book seek not to fall. As harsh and extreme as trauma may be, it does not preclude writing. Beyond it, however, lies annihilating, paralyzing, and silencing symbolic death.

If symbolic death is the collapse of meaning-producing systems in the victim's world, that is to say that it creates an infinite distance between the victim and the structures of meaning, placing the victim outside these structures, then "death by the master's signifier" is the very opposite. Here the Nazi mark is affixed to the body of the Jewish victim, leaving no gap into which words might be directed in the constant search for new words to express changing, living self-perception and desire, thereby constituting identity (narrative identity, in our case). The victims thus become, consciously or unconsciously, the murderer's mouthpieces or automatic executioners of the murderer's will, necessarily assuming the place assigned to them by the murder. The ultimate expression of this phenomenon is the Nazi decree of marking (the "badge of shame") and imprinting numbers on the bodies of the prisoners at Auschwitz. Another expression of this can be found in Kaplan's diary, in what I have called the "epistemological gray zone"—when the Nazi voice penetrates and "adheres" to the voice of the victim, even threatening to overwhelm it in the context of diary writing. In such cases, the victim internalizes the gaze or voice of the murder, to one extent or another, making it the text's central focalizer. One of the gravest expressions of this phenomenon can be observed when figurative language collapses—as Chaim Kaplan writes on 19 November 1940, following the sealing of the Warsaw ghetto: "If it were said that the sun has darkened for us at noon it would not be merely a metaphor."[4]

In the face of such threats of destruction, the writer strives to reconstitute himself through autobiographical assertion: saying "I." This statement seeks to establish a possible distance from reality—neither to be cast out of it nor to be swallowed up by it; to reopen the gap between "words and things," remaining within the boundaries of trauma. It seeks to avoid falling into that which lies beyond it—the abyss of symbolic death—while escaping the suffocating death of Nazi marking. This endeavor encounters serious obstacles, however, in the Holocaust diaries.

On the most basic level, we have seen that the diary genre itself changes character, undergoing a veritable metamorphosis—from a genre that focuses on the writer's personal life and "I," to one that draws attention to tremendous forces that change the world as well as the writer. The diary does not declare "I!" but, on the contrary, its radical reduction in the face of the raging traumatic exterior. The "I" as the focus of the autobiographical story practically ceases to exist. The change in the nature of the genre highlights a fundamental cultural and cognitive metamorphosis. But there is more to it.

Analysis of the diaries in this book is largely based on the distinction between narrator and protagonist in autobiographical writing. In the introductory chapters, I argued that autobiographical writing largely depends on maintaining the appropriate distance and connection between these two domains of the self. The two domains cannot be identical in autobiographical writing, nor can they be entirely detached from one another. In the diaries I have discussed, the authors find it difficult to maintain an appropriate distance between the two domains. The numbness so evident in these texts often expresses the fact that the protagonist is not present as an active consciousness at the events described, but only as a body; while all that remains for the narrator is to accurately (and at times even analytically) document the protagonist's absence and disappearance. The narrator thus tells a "non-story," in which, at times, the protagonist no longer exists.

In the diaries of Klemperer and Kaplan, as in most of the other diaries mentioned throughout the book, an unbridgeable gap is often variously created between the two domains. Klemperer calls this experience of detachment "cinema"—moments of severe dissociation, in which Klemperer manages to detach himself from the course of events and watch them as if they were a film, examining them from the documenter's perspective. This dissociative phenomenon is well-known as one of the symptoms of traumatic exposure. Charlotte Delbo, an Auschwitz survivor, wrote about these two types of consciousness from the perspective of "after" and about the protective role of the split: "I live within a twofold being. The Auschwitz double doesn't bother me, doesn't interfere with my life. As though it weren't I at all. Without this split I would not have been able to revive."[5] As we have seen however, it also comes at a high psychological price.

In relation to Kaplan's diary, extensive discussion was devoted to the gap between the narrative's Jewish protagonists and the voice of the narrator, heavily tarnished by the annihilating voice of the Nazis. This huge gap, given many and varied but always catastrophic expression, appears in most of the Holocaust diaries. The words of Pal Kovacs, from the Neuengamme camp, cited in chapter 1, offer a clear illustration of the gap: "We arrived at Neuengamme at dawn. From that moment, we ceased to exist as human beings. No sooner had we left the railway car than I received the first kick, after which they also set a dog on me. To this day the reason is not clear. At that moment, reality penetrated my consciousness, I understood where I was and sunk into a feeling of unconsciousness, from which I have not yet awoken."[6] In this passage, the author describes in great detail the disappearance of the protagonist. Similarly, he writes a few days later: "It is hard to believe I too was once a human being and it wasn't long ago. Here I am merely a prisoner, and no one can imagine that I too might have a home and a family, that I too am a human being."[7] One domain of the self—the narrating "I"—recounts the disappearance of the other domain: the protagonist who has ceased being a human being and has even forgotten that he ever was one. It is a consciousness that observes the process of its own disintegration. In this sense, the life story as a form of organizing the human temporal experience loses its validity. The life story becomes the death story of the protagonist who is, biologically, still alive. This can be explained in terms of the constant movement of subjectification and desubjectification, to borrow the words of Agamben cited in chapter 9, with regard to shame.

However, not only the autobiographical protagonist is harmed. As we have seen, the narrator is also not immune to the detrimental effects of the traumatic situation. In the discussion of the language of the victim, as expressed in the diary of Chaim Kaplan, we saw how Nazi language infiltrates his own. We saw how the diary explicitly or implicitly exhibits various levels of internalization, identification, and even admiration for certain aspects of Nazism. We also saw how this occurs not only in his manner of reporting and documenting but also on a performative level, as an act of language. The text sometimes adopts the Nazi perspective, and the rhetoric is sometimes permeated with the effects of catastrophic "dialogical" interaction with Nazi discourse. And we saw how Kaplan's imagery is heavily influenced by Nazi imagery and perhaps even by elements of social Darwinism, which, in its Nazi version, denies the human status of the Jews.

The penetration of the powerful, annihilating voice and gaze of the Nazis, into the heart of Jewish narrative is indicative of what I would term, paraphrasing Primo Levi, the "epistemological gray zone."[8] This is the space in which human identities are fundamentally undermined, to the point that it becomes impossible to distinguish between oneself and the other, or between inside and outside. As noted by Primo Levi, the concentration camp experience highlights the extent to which the existence of an "I" and an "inside" depends upon an "other" and an "outside," and the extent to which the destructive behavior of the latter fundamentally harms the former.[9] Over the course of the book we have seen that these processes occur, albeit with lesser intensity, in places other than the concentration camp. There too, on certain planes, the boundaries and even the sharp distinctions between murderers and victims become blurred (on other planes they are acutely maintained and must be maintained). Trauma thus blurs the most basic distinction (murderers/victims) that brought it about in the first place. Over the course of the book, I have tried to locate the specific places in the autobiographical writing of the victims where this blurring of identities occurs—harming, first and foremost, the narrator who, at certain times, wholly or partially adopts the murderer's voice and gaze that denies his or her own existence. Or, to use Ferenczi's terminology, victims of trauma always speak in two tongues: their own and that of the aggressor who brought catastrophe upon them.[10]

The question thus arises, what is left of the individuals and their "life stories" written during the Holocaust, in which the protagonist and the narrator—generally understood as distinct domains—received a blow so deadly that it brought about their near-total collapse? This volume has dealt with mapping the disintegration of the language, narrative, and identity of the subject. Now, at its conclusion, I would like to suggest a number of reflections, to which I have already alluded, in order to facilitate discussion of the existence of the "I" even in the extreme situations experienced by diarists during the Holocaust period.

The basic premise of this book is that something nevertheless remained of the framework of human identity, as the diaries before us attest to the fact that their authors—despite the difficult limitations imposed on them—did succeed in reflecting both inwardly, on themselves, and outwardly, on the events around them. I believe that ethical responsibility and a commitment to historical accuracy demand that we view the consciousness that reveals itself in these diaries as a representation of real human subjects who appeals to us, at times even directly, to serve as their readers.[11] This phenomenon cannot be dismissed as an illusion that conceals the truth of the complete disappearance of the writer's "I," for ultimately there is someone (the narrator) who is telling us something. What is the nature, however, of this narrating "I"?

I would like to suggest three possibilities of subject-presence, each constituting a different type—and even a different genre—in the context of the Holocaust diaries:

1. The first "I" is the "I" of the ongoing scream of the suffering of the body. Ludwig Wittgenstein distinguished between expressive and reflexive speech, and language—certainly documentary language—is generally reflexive, reporting events while reflecting on them from a point outside of them—the point in which the "writing 'I'" exists.[12] In certain conditions, however, the words do not report the event but are a part of it: its expressive part. In such conditions, the sentences employed not only serve to describe feelings but also embody them. For example, a child who falls might report his injury and say "It hurts," and the sentence would be declarative. The same child, however, might cry out the very same words, in pain, at the time of the injury. The effect would then be expressive rather than a mere reporting of fact. The words would thus be part of the pain and a continuation of it, and not just linguistic signifiers. Expressive sentences are part of the "thing

itself" and they incorporate both the subject and the object—both the narrator and the protagonist, in the case of autobiographical writing.

An example of expressive speech can be found in the following passage from Avraham Lewin's diary (quoted in chapter 1):

> The blood of our children will never be erased from the Cain's forehead of the German people! It is only now that I understand Bialik's sorrow and rage in the poem "On the Slaughter." . . . If Kishinev alone could arouse such reverberations of suffering in a Jewish heart, what is happening in our hearts after the greatest tragedy we have ever known? And perhaps because the tragedy is without measure, we are entirely unable to express all of our feelings. Only if we were to be given the possibility of uprooting the greatest of all mountains, Everest, by the strength of our choked suffering, to cast it with rage and force on the head of all the Germans . . . this would be the only response worthy of our time. We have lost the ability to use words.[13]

In this passage, Lewin points to the fact that language, with all the cultural resources it entails, ceased functioning as an instrument of mediation and communication between writer and potential reader. Declarative language collapsed ("We have lost the ability to use words") and it is no longer possible to convey the catastrophic experience through language. The only option that remains is to use words in order to be heard but not necessarily with the goal of being understood. Ultimately, what Lewin does here, is to shout his pain. Diary writing is thus a continuation of psychological and physical suffering.

2. The second "I" is the questioning or doubting "I." In order to explain its nature, I would like to return to a passage from the Bergen-Belsen diary of Hannah Lévy-Hass: "Everything we see here, everything that happens under our eyes makes us begin to question our own human qualities. A dark and heavy doubt awakens. Doubt in mankind."[14] The doubt raised by Lévy-Hass is the most terrible doubt of all—concerning the victim's subjective, human existence. Nevertheless, it is hard to escape the feeling that this penetrating question in fact brings the author's critical and keen subjective consciousness to the fore, evoking a very present and significant "I." As Descartes discovered, the very act of doubting one's own existence constitutes the self as a subject. Here, however, the discovery emerges not from philosophical speculation but from the very heart of terrible, concrete experience. In this context, it is the question rather than the answer that holds meaning because it sustains the "I" of doubt, and in it, the "I" can survive.[15] We must remember, however, that this is a very minimal "I,"

lacking positive content and existing only as a formal entity to which the doubt is attributed.

3. The third "I" is the documenting "I," which has been addressed here at length, particularly in relation to the diary of Victor Klemperer.

Trauma, as noted, embodies consciousness's nonpresence to itself in the midst of a catastrophic event, thereby rendering it present-less or, to be more precise, the present that is uprooted from it is the present that develops within the framework of the past-present-future temporal order. This was discussed primarily in the chapters dealing with Victor Klemperer's diary, where I also pointed out the option of documentation, which offers another temporal order. Documentary time is born on the ruins of Augustinian-Ricoeurian life-story time, which is based on a threefold present. In documentary time, the future as future perfect ("will have been") logically precedes the present and will constitute it retrospectively. The documentary subject "pays" with her nonpresence in the present, in order to be "resurrected" in the future, where she is assured a place as the representative of a past that never fully came into being as present.

All these forms of "I" that survive in the diaries are very "minimal," and it is hard to "celebrate" the fact of their survival. Primo Levi would perhaps note that they did indeed survive but were not redeemed. They are not the forms of "I" or "self" that we experience in our everyday lives. In the extreme moments, they bear no positive meaning. "Self" in the sense of identity, continuity, coherence, and unity (even in a limited and relative fashion), and in relation to the writers' ability to afford meaning to their reality and experiences, is very limited in these stories, and the narrative performs none of the constructive or therapeutic functions generally ascribed to "normal" life stories. The narrators cannot heal the collapse of the protagonist or prevent the Nazis from infiltrating their own act of narration. What did not cease to exist for these writers was the impulse of narrators to tell their stories and of writers to write their diaries.

Emanuel Ringelblum attests to this impulse in his diary, in an entry of February 1941: "The drive to write down one's memoirs is powerful: Even young people in labor camps do it. The manuscripts are discovered, torn up, and their authors beaten."[16] The most significant part of this passage, in my opinion, is the word "drive" (*drang* in the original Yiddish). It is the drive to cry out the pain, to document for the future while doubting, at times, the existence of reality and even the very existence of the writer himself. The narrating "I," although its voice and gaze are irremediably entangled with the Nazi gaze and voice, is the one who desires to write and the one who takes up the pen or the pencil to do so.

I believe that Victor Klemperer best encapsulated the status of writing, and the relationship between writing and the question of survival of the person writing, in the passage in which he discusses the pencil he received on the fourth day of his imprisonment. I would like to return to the passage now, adding another layer to the previous reading. Klemperer described the change that came over him after having received the pencil, as follows: "The pencil really had made a profound difference to me. . . . I had certainly clambered up out of hell on my pencil—but not as far as earth itself, only as far as limbo."[17] This "limbo" is, in my opinion, the space between the minimal form of "I" that writing enables and the full self that people experience in "normal" life. It is a space in which the "I" and the "world," although they exist, bear virtually no meaning. This lack of meaning, which arouses the impulse to shout it, question it, and document it, attests—in retrospect—to the existence of an "I," first and foremost as the "I" that desires to write.

Thus, something does remain of the self in the Holocaust diaries, but it is a self who is profoundly and extremely helpless. This fundamental helplessness—in the face of external forces, the collapse of time, the voice of the Nazi other, the reduction of the protagonist's space to the point of its destruction, the threat of fundamental disintegration, and all of the other destructive forces that impinge on the story—raises the question of whether anything remains in these diaries of the "life story" that constitutes narrative identity, as described in chapter 1.

I would therefore argue that life story and narrative identity, in the ordinary sense, do not exist in these diaries, which are characterized, above all, by the helplessness and deep ruptures they reveal in the continuity of identity. Nevertheless, as we have noted, something did survive in them: vestiges that I call *life-story fragments*.[18] Despite the shattering of the life story in most of these diaries, the resulting fragments did not entirely lose the fundamental qualities of the master concept. First of all, something is maintained of temporal continuity and of the relevancy of language and culture, without which writing itself would not have been possible. Although this narrative organization is minimal and what remains outside it—the traumatic reality—has the potential to destroy and paralyze the writer, something of the order and organization of the temporal experience, at least in writing itself, nevertheless manages to survive. Ultimately, it is the act of narration that enables and even constitutes the emergence of the screaming/documenting/questioning "I." These appear even when the narrative itself, as an organization of the human temporal experience, disintegrates, at times collapses, and even disappears.

The "I" of the life-story fragments as reflected in the diaries we have examined is a particular kind of "I," characterized primarily by the great gaps and contrasts that the story and the act of narrative are unable to bridge. The fragments scatter in various and opposing directions, expressing acute disintegration.

As early as 1948, Emil Utiz, a psychologist and philosopher, survivor of the Theresienstadt ghetto, wrote about the "schizophrenic nature" of the ghetto prisoners, oscillating between extremes of numbness and rage.[19] Dominick LaCapra described the aporia of trauma in a similar fashion: "The radically disorienting experience of trauma often involves a dissociation between cognition and affect. In brief, in traumatic experience one typically can represent numbly or with aloofness what one cannot feel, and one feels overwhelmingly what one is unable to represent. . . . Here one has an aporetic relation between representation and affect with the possibility of uncontrolled oscillation between poles of a double bind."[20] On another plane, Lawrence Langer describes the texts written during the Holocaust as reflecting "a constant wavering" between expectation of deliverance and futility, draining the self of its inner strength.[21]

The "fragments" metaphor that I have used to characterize what remained of the life stories seeks to capture the way in which the story disintegrates into unbridgeable poles—numbness and lively analytical consciousness; apathy and terror and rage; narrator and protagonist; autobiographical time and documentary time; moments of inspiration and moments of disintegration; hope and deep, fundamental despair; disintegration and preservation of identity; radical rupture and forms of continuity. There are hardly any continuous threads between these contrasting poles. This, in itself, is the central traumatic characteristic of autobiographical writing during the Holocaust, destroying it from within. Different parts of the personality, consciousness, experience, and identity are in constant radical discord, in a kind of atomization of the psyche. The coherence and continuity that "normal" life stories create, if only in a partial and limited fashion, are conspicuously absent in the Holocaust diaries. In their place, as if after a big explosion, we find fragments scattered in all directions, separated by the abysses of traumatic and terrifying experience.

What are the possible ramifications of these conclusions? I will suggest a number of initial considerations.

Introducing trauma as a central concept for the understanding of the lives of Jews during the Holocaust may be presented as a completion and rectification of previous historiography or, alternatively, as a call for a radical shift. On one plane, relating to the story of the Holocaust in terms of trauma rather than crisis (see chapter 2) constitutes a complementary rectification of existing historiography, directing attention to dimensions and aspects of the topic that have largely been ignored: radical disintegration, severe narrative gaps and ruptures, the penetration of the Nazi "other" into the Jewish story and, above all, the extreme helplessness of Jews during the Holocaust.[22]

On another plane, adopting trauma as a key concept for the reading of the Holocaust diaries represents a radical shift in historiographical thought and writing about the Jews during the Holocaust. It is in the nature of historical writing to focus on "what is." In the case of the Holocaust, such writing generally deals with various aspects of the actions taken by Jews during this period—resistance, leadership, social frameworks, family, gender, and so forth. If we consider the meanings and ramifications of trauma, however, it is clear that the reconstruction of all aspects of life, objective and complete as it may be, will fail to address the essence of the period. This is precisely what Jorge Semprún claimed with regard to his own testimony:

> Even if one had given evidence with absolute precision, with perfect objectivity (something by definition beyond the powers of the individual witness), even in this case one could miss the essential thing. Because it wasn't the accumulation of horror, which could be spelled out, endlessly, in detail. One could have spent hours testifying to the daily horror of the camp without touching upon the essence of this experience. . . . One could recount the story of any day at all—from reveille at 4:30 in the morning to curfew—the fatiguing labor, the constant hunger, the chronic lack of sleep, the persecution by the *Kapos*, the latrine duty . . . the exhaustion, the death of friends—yet never manage to deal with the essential thing.[23]

The essential thing cannot be fully represented in the reconstruction of facts and, therefore, cannot be described solely in positive terms. What is essential during this period is precisely that which cannot be accurately described and is therefore termed traumatic. It is the terrifying aspects that so severely undermine subjective status and narrative identity. The concepts of trauma thus allow us to approach the "essential thing." They do more than that, however. The "man" whom they place at the center of the story is not the same as the one we find at the center of the standard historiographical narrative. The traumatic "I" is the liminal self, constantly oscillating within the "gray zone" of identity; within the areas that lie between "myself" and the murderous "other," between developing time and standing time, existence and absence, the metaphorical and literal, the brutish and the human, life and death, biological death and symbolic death—and between these two and the death inflicted by the Nazi marking procedures (see chapter 4). The writer thus oscillates between writing and silence. It is the self whose identity is constantly subverted and no longer belongs to its natural and obvious owner. On the contrary, it must arduously and constantly struggle to prevent its complete disintegration. Historical writing with such a figure of "man" at its center will be different by its very nature, and as such will also change history itself.

I began with Saul Friedländer's question: "What is the nature of human nature?" Hannah Arendt, in her seminal work *The Origins of Totalitarianism*, asserts that the fundamental belief of totalitarian regimes is not merely that "everything is permitted" but that "everything is possible" and that a new kind of "man" and a new kind of humanity are a worthy and feasible project. At the heart of this belief, however, for which the concentration camps served as a kind of test laboratory, lies "not the transformation of the outside world or the revolutionizing transmutation of society, but the transformation of human nature itself."[24]

Did human nature then change in the concentration camps, under the Nazi regime? Did the Nazi "outside" succeed in penetrating the "inner" human nature of its victims and in constituting a new kind of "man"?

The answer suggested in this book is a complex one. On the one hand, the texts discussed over the course of the book point to radical disintegration, to the crushing of human identity, and, at times, even to the reduction of "man" to a purely biological state. These phenomena would seem to indicate a different kind of (anti-)narrative "man"—inherently different from the familiar narrative "man" of "normal" human experience. Such disintegration cannot be examined or described, however, without resorting to familiar conceptual frameworks. Here, I have used psychoanalytical and narratological concepts such as "trauma," "life story," "symbolic death," and so forth. In using these concepts I have been able to create a conceptual link between such extreme phenomena and everyday life and to connect them to conceptual and historical continua—not by means of comparison but by establishing continuity along a common human, conceptual, and historical axis.[25] And if we have seen that the fragments of a life story retain something of the narrative identity constituted by the life story, the same path can be followed in reverse: the fragments of a life story can teach us something about the life story itself.

Dominick LaCapra distinguished between historical and structural trauma.[26] Historical trauma is the effect on the human psyche produced by the experience of concrete historical events. Structural trauma, on the other hand, is a kind of framework or structure that offers a conceptual explanation of fundamental components of the human psyche and human epistemological abilities.. It assumes that trauma is the basic structure of the human psyche. Although the two traumas are not identical, they are not entirely unrelated. Trauma as a structure (structural trauma) allows us to identify processes within traumatic experience (historical trauma). It is limited, however, inasmuch as it is unable to fully explain it, as concrete reality always exceeds theoretical frameworks.

In this sense, the unmediated exposure of historical trauma may also have something to teach us about everyday experience, on the basis of conceptual trauma. The traumatic life story may thus afford insight into the ordinary life story that is, by nature, also rooted in the attempt to contend with the traumatic "real" that escapes the story, albeit in situations in which one may be far less exposed and threatened. Therefore, in retrospect, some of the characteristics formulated here with regard to the Holocaust diaries may also be identified—in a far milder fashion—in "normal" life stories as well (and all the more so in first-person writing by victims of other extreme situations). They allow us to see such narratives as less stable, concrete, and coherent structures than they may initially appear to be. "How could I have wished for that unifying utopia?" remarks Philippe Lejeune, as he explains his preference, as a scholar and an autobiographer, for the diary genre rather than the complete and harmonious autobiography.[27] The narrative fragments of trauma, as reflected in the Holocaust diaries, thus tell us something about the deep ruptures harbored in all human life.

Notes

1. Anaïs Nin, *The Diary of Anaïs Nin,* vol. 3, *1939–1944,* ed. Gunther Stuhlmann (New York: Harvest/Harcourt Brace Jovanovich, 1969), 296. Similarly, but in relation to the power of memory (rather than the story), Shlomo Breznitz concludes his memoirs with the following

observation: "The fields of memory are unbounded. Locations are their servants, and time their playground. As we travel through life, it is hard to find a truer friend" (Shlomo Breznitz, *Memory Fields* [New York: Knopf, 1993], 179).

2. Suzette A. Henke, *Shattered Subjects: Trauma and Testimony in Women's Life-Writing* (New York: St. Martin's, 1998), 142.

3. Victor, Klemperer, *I Will Bear Witness: A Diary of the Nazi Years, 1942–1945*, trans. Martin Chalmers (New York: Modern Library, 2001), 357.

4. The realization of metaphor is an expression of its death. Susanna Egan associates this phrase of Kaplan's with the feeling of witnesses to these events that they lack the linguistic and narrative tools to describe them (Susanna Egan, *Mirror Talk: Genres of Crisis in Contemporary Autobiography* [Chapel Hill: University of North Carolina Press, 1999], 173).

5. Charlotte Delbo, *Days and Memory*, trans. Rosette Lamont (Marlboro, VT: Marlboro, 1990), 3.

6. Pal Kovacs, "Yomano shel Pal Kovacs" [The diary of Pal Kovacs], *Dapim Leheker Tkufat HaSho'ah* 1 (1979): 232 (3 December 1944).

7. Ibid., 234 (14 December 1944).

8. Primo Levi, *The Drowned and the Saved*, trans. Raymond Rosenthal (New York: Vintage, 1989), 36–69. As noted in the previous chapters, I relate to Levi's "gray zone" not in the context of areas of collaboration between the victims and murderers but with regard to areas in which the distinct identity of each side is obfuscated.

9. Primo Levi, *If This Is a Man/The Truce*, trans. Stuart Woolf (London: Abacus, 2004), 178.

10. Sandor Ferenczi, "The Confusion of Tongues between Adults and Children," in *Final Contributions to the Problems and Methods of Psychoanalysis*, ed. Michael Balint, trans. Eric Mosbacher (London: Hogarth, 1955), 156–167.

11. In this I differ from Boaz Neumann, who defines the prisoners in the death camps as ontologically dead. Ontological death is absolute, as long as the relevant ontology remains valid. The concept I have employed is that of "symbolic death," which is a structural state that enables passage to other states. See Boaz Neumann, *Re'iyat Ha'olam Hanatzit: Merhav, Guf, Safah* [The Nazi weltanschauung: Space, body, language] (Haifa: Haifa University, 2002). Many of the diaries appeal directly to the reader as, for example, in the introduction to a diary written by one of the Sonderkommandos at Auschwitz: "Take interest in this document which contains very important material for the historian" (see Ber Mark, ed., *The Scrolls of Auschwitz*, trans. Sharon Neemani [Tel Aviv: Am Oved, 1985], 173).

12. Ludwig Wittgenstein, *Philosophical Investigations*, trans. G. E. M. Anscombe (Oxford: Basil Blackwell, 1953), 89. This distinction forms the basis of Lorna Martens's discussion of the question at the heart of her own research: "What does it mean to say 'I'?" (Lorna Martens, *The Diary Novel* [Cambridge: Cambridge University Press, 2009]).

13. Avraham Lewin, *Mipinkaso shel Hamoreh MiYehudiyah: Geto Varshah April 1942–Mai 1943* [From the notebook of a teacher at the Yehudiah School: Warsaw ghetto April 1942–May 1943] [Tel Aviv: Hakibbutz Hameuchad and the Ghetto Fighters' House, 1969], 51–52.

14. Hanna Lévy-Hass, *Diary of Bergen-Belsen: 1944–1945*, trans. Sophie Hand (Chicago: Haymarket, 2009), 113.

15. See Paul Ricoeur, "Narrative Identity," in *On Paul Ricoeur: Narrative and Interpretation*, ed. David Wood (London: Routledge, 1991), 188–199.

16. Emanual Ringelblum, *Notes from the Warsaw Ghetto: The Journal of Emanuel Ringelblum*, trans. Jacob Sloan (New York: Schocken, 1974), 133.

17. Victor Klemperer, *I Will Bear Witness: A Diary of the Nazi Years, 1933–1941* (New York: Modern Library, 1999), 415.

18. "Fragments" is the term used by Fiona Kaufman in her study on the diaries. See Fiona Kaufman, "De Emplotment," in "By Chance I Found a Pencil: The Holocaust Diary Narratives of Testimony, Defiance, Solace and Struggle" (PhD diss., University of Melbourne, 2010), 12–34, and the entire dissertation. I would like to thank the author, who sent me a copy of her work before its publication.

19. Emil Utiz, *Psychologie des Lebens im Konzentrazionslager Theresienstadt* (1947; reprint, Vienna: Continental Edition Verlag A. Sezl, 1948), 9–16.

20. Dominick LaCapra, *History in Transit: Experience, Identity, Critical Theory* (Ithaca, NY: Cornell University Press, 2004), 117.

21. Lawrence L. Langer, *Admitting the Holocaust: Collected Essays* (Oxford: Oxford University Press, 1995), 41.

22. One historian who has sought to address the traumatic dimension of the events in the context of historical writing is Saul Friedländer, Introduction to *Probing the Limits of Representation: Nazism and the Final Solution* (Cambridge, MA: Harvard University Press, 1992), 19–20; Saul Friedländer, "The Final Solution: On the Unease in Historical Interpretation," in *Lessons and Legacies: The Meaning of the Holocaust in a Changing World*, ed. Peter Hayes (Evanston, IL: Northwestern University Press, 1991), 23–35. The practical expression of this approach can be observed in Friedländer's inclusion of passages from contemporary diaries in the historical narrative he presents in his monumental works, *Nazi Germany and the Jews: The Years of Persecution 1933–39* (Frome, UK: Phoenix, 1997) and *Nazi Germany and the Jews: The Years of Extermination 1939–1945* (London: Weidenfeld and Nicolson, 2007). For a sharp critique of this approach, see Inga Clendinnen, *Reading the Holocaust* (Cambridge: Cambridge University Press, 1999), 83–88. Regarding the degree to which Friedländer was successful in writing a different kind of history, see Dan Stone, *Constructing the Holocaust* (London: Vallentine Mitchell, 2003), 161–165; and Amos Goldberg, "The Victim's Voice in History and Melodramatic Esthetics," *History and Theory* 48, no. 3 (2009): 220–237.

23. Jorge Semprún, *Literature or Life*, trans. Linda Coverdale (New York: Viking, 1997), 87–88.

24. Hannah Arendt, *The Origins of Totalitarianism* (Cleveland: World, 1958), 458.

25. Similarly, Eliezer Schweid writes, with regard to ethical dilemmas that arose during the Holocaust: "These dilemmas, as anomalous or distant as they may seem to us, today, from conditions of 'normal' human existence, reveal profound dimensions hidden within the human soul, and deepen our understanding of ourselves. . . . Despite their extreme nature, they should not be considered irrelevant to the reality of our time. On the contrary, they lie very close to the surface and are reveal themselves more often than we would like to believe" (Eliezer Schweid, "Hadilema Hakiyumit Vehamusarit shel Hahitnagdut Hamezuyenet Bageto" [The existential and moral dilemma of armed resistance in the ghetto], in *Kedushat Hahayim Veheruf Hanefesh: Kovetz Ma'amarim Lezikhro shel AmirYekutiel* [Sanctity of life and martyrdom: Studies in memory of Amir Yekutiel], ed. Isaiah M. Gafni and Aviezer Ravitzky [Jerusalem: The Zalman Shazar Center, 1992], 277).

26. Dominick LaCapra, *Writing History, Writing Trauma* (Baltimore: Johns Hopkins University Press, 2014), 43–85.

27. Philippe Lejeune, *On Diary*, ed. Jeremy D. Popkin and Julie Rak, trans. Katherine Durnin (Manoa: University of Hawai'i Press, 2009), 168.

BIBLIOGRAPHY

Adelson, Alan, and Robert Lapides, eds. *Lodz Ghetto: Inside a Community under Siege*. New York: Viking, 1989.

Adler, Stanislaw. *In the Warsaw Ghetto, 1940–1943: An Account of a Witness*. Translated by Sara Chmielewska Philip. Jerusalem: Yad Vashem, 1982.

Adorno, Theodor W. "The Liquidation of the Self." In *Can One Live after Auschwitz? A Philosophical Reader*, 427–436. Edited by Rolf Tiedemann. Stanford, CA: Stanford University Press, 2003.

———. "Meditations on Metaphysics." In *A Holocaust Reader: Responses to the Nazi Extermination*, 42–47. Edited by Michael L. Morgan. New York: Oxford University Press, 2001.

Agamben, Giorgio. *Homo Sacer: Sovereign Power and Bare Life*. Translated by Daniel Heller-Roazen. Stanford, CA: Stanford University Press, 1998.

———. *Remnants of Auschwitz: The Witness and the Archive*. Translated by Daniel Heller-Roazen. New York: Zone Books, 1999.

———. *State of Exception*. Translated by Kevin Attell. Chicago: University of Chicago Press, 2005.

Aharony, Michal. *Hannah Arendt and the Limits of Total Domination: The Holocaust, Plurality, and Resistance*. New York: Routledge, 2015.

Alexander, Sally, and Barbara Taylor, eds. *History and Psyche: Culture, Psychoanalysis, and the Past*. Basingstoke: Palgrave Macmillan, 2013.

Alter, Robert. *The Book of Psalms: A Translation and Commentary*. New York: Norton, 2007.

Althusser, Louis. "Ideology and Ideological State Apparatuses." In *Lenin and Philosophy and Other Essays*, 127–186. Translated by Ben Brewster. New York: Monthly Review Press, 2001.

Améry, Jean. *At the Mind's Limits: Contemplations by a Survivor on Auschwitz and Its Realities*. Translated by Sidney Rosenfeld and Stella P. Rosenfeld. Bloomington: Indiana University Press, 1980.

Anderson, Linda. *Autobiography*. London: Routledge, 2001.

Andreas-Friedrich, Ruth. *Berlin Underground 1938–1945*. New York: Holt, 1947.

Antelme, Robert. *The Human Race*. Translated by Jeffrey Haight and Annie Mahler. Evanston, IL: Marlboro, 1992.

Appelfeld, Aharon. *The Story of a Life: A Memoir*. Translated by Aloma Hallter. New York: Schocken, 2004.

Arad, Yitzhak, Israel Gutman, and Abraham Margaliot, eds. *Documents on the Holocaust: Selected Sources on the Destruction of the Jews of Germany and Austria, Poland, and the Soviet Union.* Jerusalem: Yad Vashem, 1981.

Arendt, Hannah. "The Concentration Camps." In *A Holocaust Reader: Responses to the Nazi Extermination*, 47–63. Edited by Michael L. Morgan. New York: Oxford University Press, 2001.

———. *The Origins of Totalitarianism.* Cleveland: World, 1958.

———. "What Remains? Language Remains." In *The Portable Hannah Arendt*, 3–22. Edited by Peter Baehr. New York: Penguin, 2000.

Aron, Yitzhak. *Mayn Klayne Tsavoe* [My little Will]. Yad Vashem Archives (uncataloged, in the author's possession).

Aronson, Yehoshua Moshe. *Alei Merorot* [Leaves of bitterness]. Bnei Brak: private publication, 1996.

Aronstein, Raphael F. "Hineh Hayehudi Klemperer" [Here is the Jew Klemperer]. *Orlogin* 1 (1950): 226–234.

Aschheim, Steven E. "Comrade Klemperer: Communism, Liberalism and Jewishness in the DDR. The Later Diaries 1945–59." *Journal of Contemporary History* 36, no. 2 (2001): 325–343.

———. "Nietzsche and the Nietzschean Moment in Jewish Life (1890–1939)." *Leo Baeck Institute Year Book* 37 (1992): 189–212.

———. *Scholem, Arendt, Klemperer: Intimate Chronicles in Turbulent Times.* Bloomington and Cincinnati: Indiana University Press and Hebrew Union College, 2001.

Ataria, Yochai, David Gurevitz, Haviva Pedaya, and Yuval Neria, eds. *Interdisciplinary Handbook of Trauma and Culture.* Switzerland: Springer, 2016.

Augustine. *Confessions.* Translated by Henry Chadwick. Oxford: Oxford University Press, 2008.

Bacharach, Walter Zwi. "Jews in Confrontation with Racist Antisemitism 1879–1933." *Leo Baeck Institute Year Book* 25 (1980): 197–219.

Bakhtin, Mikhail M. "Forms of Time and of the Chronotope in the Novel: Notes toward a Historical Poetics." In *The Dialogic Imagination: Four Essays*, 84–258. Edited by Michael Holquist. Translated by Caryl Emerson. Austin: University of Texas Press, 1981.

Balibar, Etienne. "Is There a 'Neo Racism'?" In *Race, Nation, Class: Ambiguous Identities*, by Etienne Balibar (translated by Chris Turner) and Immanuel Wallerstein, 17–28. London: Verso, 1991.

Baranowski, Shelly. *Nazi Empire: German Colonialism and Imperialism from Bismarck to Hitler.* Cambridge: Cambridge University Press, 2011.

Barkai, Avraham. "*Volksgemeinschaft*, 'Aryanization' and the Holocaust." In *The Final Solution: Origins and Implementations*, 33–50. Edited by David Cesarani. London: Routledge, 1994.

Bartov, Omer. *Germany's War and the Holocaust.* Ithaca, NY: Cornell University Press, 2003.

———. "Wartime Lies and Other Testimonies: Jewish–Christian Relations in Buczacz, 1939–1944." *East European Politics and Societies* 25 (2011): 486–511.

Bataille, Georges. *Death and Sensuality: A Study of Eroticism and Taboo.* New York: Walker, 1962.

Bauer, Yehuda. *American Jewry and the Holocaust: The American Jewish Joint Distribution 1939–1945.* Detroit: Wayne State University Press, 1982.

———. *The Death of the Shtetl.* New Haven, CT: Yale University Press, 2009.

———. *Hashlahot Mehkar Hasho'ah al Toda'atenu Hahistorit* [The Holocaust today: An attempt at a new evaluation]. Jerusalem: The Institute of Contemporary Jewry, 1972.
———. *Rethinking the Holocaust.* New Haven, CT: Yale University Press, 2001.
———. *Tguvot Be'et Hasho'ah: Nisyonot Amidah, Hitnagdut, Hatzalah* [Reactions during the Holocaust: Attempts to withstand, resist, rescue]. Tel Aviv: Ministry of Defense, 1983.
Bauman, Zygmunt. *Modernity and the Holocaust.* Cambridge: Polity, 1989.
Belke, Ingrid. Introduction to *Moritz Lazarus und Heymann Steinthal: Die Begründer der Völkerpsychologie in ihren Briefen.* Edited by Ingrid Belke. Tübingen: Mohr, 1971.
Ben-Amos Batsheva. "A Multilingual Diary from the Lodz Ghetto." *Gal-Ed* 19 (2004): 51–74.
Benjamin, Walter. "Thesis on the Philosophy of History." In *Illuminations*, 253–264. Edited by Hannah Arendt. Translated by Harry Zohn. New York: Schocken, 1969.
Ben-Sasson, Havi. "Polin Upolanim Be'einei Yehudei Polin Bitkufat Milhemet Ha'olam Hashniyah" [Poland and Poles in the eyes of Polish Jews during the Second World War, 1939–1944]. PhD diss., Hebrew University, 2005.
Ben-Sasson, Havi, and Lea Prais. "Twilight Days: Missing Pages from Avraham Lewin's Warsaw Ghetto Diary, May–July 1942." *Yad Vashem Studies* 33 (2005): 7–60.
Ben-Shem, Reuven. "Mitokh Yoman Geto Varshah 1941" [From a diary of the Warsaw ghetto 1941]. *Yalkut Moreshet* 25 (1978): 25–44.
Benveniste, Emile. *Problems in General Linguistics.* Coral Gables, FL: University of Miami Press, 1971.
Berg, Mary. *The Diary of Mary Berg: Growing up in the Warsaw Ghetto.* Edited by Susan Lee Pentlin. Oxford: Oneworld, 2009.
Berr, Hélène. *The Journal of Hélène Berr.* Translated by David Bellos. New York: Weinstein Books, 2008.
———. *Yoman* [Diary]. Translated by Nir Rachkovsky. Ben Shemen: Modan, 2010.
Bersani, Leo. *The Culture of Redemption.* Cambridge, MA: Harvard University Press, 1990.
Bethke, Svenja. "Crime and Punishment in Emergency Situations: The Jewish Ghetto Courts in Lodz, Warsaw and Vilna in World War II—A Comparative Study." *Dapim: Studies on the Holocaust* 28, no. 3 (2014): 173–189.
Bettelheim, Bruno. *The Informed Heart.* New York: Thames and Hudson, 1961.
———. *Surviving and Other Essays.* New York: Vintage, 1979.
Blatman, Daniel. *Geto Varshah: Sipur Itona'i* [The Warsaw ghetto: A journalistic story]. Jerusalem: Yad Vashem, 2002.
Bloom, Etan. "What 'The Father' Had in Mind: Arthur Ruppin (1876–1943), Cultural Identity, Weltanschauung and Action." *Journal for History of European Ideas* 33, no. 3 (2007): 330–349.
Bonfil, Robert. "The Devil and the Jews in the Christian Consciousness of the Middle Ages." In *Antisemitism through the Ages*, 91–105. Edited by Shmuel Almog. Translated by Nathan H. Reisner. New York: Pergamon, 1988.
Börner, Peter. *Tagebuch.* Stuttgart: Metzlerische, 1969.
Bowie, Malcolm. *Lacan.* Cambridge, MA: Harvard University Press, 1991.
Brett, Edward A., and Robert Ostroff. "Imagery and Posttraumatic Stress Disorder." *American Journal of Psychiatry* 142 (1985): 417–424.
Breznitz, Shlomo. *Memory Fields.* New York: Knopf, 1993.
Browning, Christopher. "The Holocaust: Basis and Objective of the Volksgemeinschaft?" In *Visions of Community in Nazi Germany: Social Engineering and Private Lives*, 217–225. Edited by Martina Steber and Bernard Gotto. Oxford: Oxford University Press, 2014.

———. *The Origins of the Final Solution*. London: Arrow, 2005.
———. *Remembering Survival: Inside a Nazi Slave-Labor Camp*. New York: Norton, 2010.
Browning, Christopher, and Israel Gutman. "The Reports of a Jewish 'Informer' in the Warsaw Ghetto: Selected Documents." *Yad Vashem Studies* 17 (1986): 247–293.
Brunner, José. "Political Fetishism on the Left and Right in Israel." Paper presented at the "Thera-P-olitics" Psychoactive Conference, Tel Aviv University, 28 January 2008.
Bruss, Elizabeth W. *Autobiographical Acts: The Changing Situation of Literary Genre*. Baltimore: Johns Hopkins University Press, 1976.
Bryman, Jerakhmil. "The Nature of Ghetto Prayer Services." In *Lodz Ghetto: Inside a Community under Siege*, 399–405. Edited by Alan Adelson and Robert Lapides. New York: Viking, 1989.
Bunkers, Suzanne I., and Cynthia A. Huff. *Inscribing the Daily: Critical Essays on Women's Diaries*. Amherst: University of Massachusetts Press, 1996.
Bunzl, Matti. "*Völkerpsychologie* and German-Jewish Emancipation." In *Worldly Provincialism: German Anthropology in the Age of Empire*, 47–85. Edited by H. Glenn Penny and Matti Bunzl. Ann Arbor: University of Michigan Press, 2003.
Burleigh, Michael. *The Third Reich: A New History*. London: Pan Macmillan, 2001.
Bursztein, Jean-Gérard. *Hapsikho'analizah shel Hanatzizm: Masah al Heres Hatzivilizatzyah* [The psychoanlysis of Nazism: An essay on the destruction of civilization]. Translated by Miriam Meir. Tel Aviv: Resling, 2004.
Busak, Meir. "Yamim Aharonim Bamahaneh Hagermani Brnenetz (Pirkei Yoman Milifnei 40 Shanah)" [Final days at the German camp of Brnenec (Diary excerpts from 40 years ago)]. *Yalkut Moreshet* 41 (June 1986): 181–188.
Caruth, Cathy. *Unclaimed Experience: Trauma Narrative and History*. Baltimore: Johns Hopkins University Press, 1996.
Clendinnen, Inga. *Reading the Holocaust*. Cambridge: Cambridge University Press, 1999.
Coe, Richard N. *When the Grass Was Taller: Autobiography and the Experience of Childhood*. New Haven, CT: Yale University Press, 1984.
Cohn, Willy. *Kein Recht, Nirgends: Tagebuch vom Untergang des Breslauer Judentums, 1933–1941*. Cologne: Böhlau, 2006.
Confino, Alon. *Foundational Past*. Cambridge: Cambridge University Press, 2012.
———. "Narrative Form and Historical Sensation: On Saul Friedländer's *The Years of Extermination*." *History and Theory* 48 (2009): 199–219.
———. *A World without Jews: The Nazi Imagination from Persecution to Genocide*. New Haven, CT: Yale University Press, 2014.
Consonni, Manuela. *Rezistentzyah o Sho'ah: Zikaron, Gerush Vehashmadah Be'italyah 1945–1985* [Resistance or Holocaust: The memory of the deportation and the extermination in Italy 1945–1985]. Jerusalem: Magnes, 2009.
Culler, Jonathan. *Ferdinand de Saussure*. Sussex: Harvester, 1976.
Culley, Margo. Introduction to *A Day at a Time: The Diary Literature of American Women from 1764 to the Present*. Edited by Margo Culley. New York: Feminist Press at the City University of New York, 1985.
Czerniakow, Adam. *The Warsaw Diary of Adam Czerniakow: Prelude to Doom*. Edited by Raul Hilberg, Stanislaw Staron, and Josef Kermisz. New York: Stein and Day, 1979.
———. *Yomanei Geto Varshah* [The diaries of the Warsaw ghetto]. Jerusalem: Yad Vashem, 1970.
Dadrian, Vahram. *To the Desert: Pages from My Diary*. Princeton, NJ: Gomidas Institute, 2003.

Darnton, Robert. *The Kiss of Lamourette: Reflections in Cultural History.* New York: Norton, 1989.

Daub, Lori, and Nanette C. Auerhahn. "Knowing and Not Knowing Massive Psychic Trauma: Forms of Traumatic Memory." *International Journal of Psychoanalysis* 74 (1993): 287–302.

De Costa, Denise. *Anne Frank and Etty Hillesum: Inscribing Spirituality and Sexuality.* New Brunswick, NJ: Rutgers University Press, 1998.

DeKoven Ezrahi, Sidra. *By Words Alone: The Holocaust in Literature.* Chicago: University of Chicago Press, 1980.

———. "Racism and Ethics: Constructing Alternative History." In *Humanity at the Limit: The Impact of the Holocaust on Jews and Christians,* 27–35. Edited by Michael A. Singer. Bloomington: Indiana University Press, 2000.

———. "Representing Auschwitz." *History and Memory* 7, no. 2 (1996): 121–154.

———. "See under: Memory: Reflections on When Memory Comes." *History and Memory* 9, nos. 1–2 (1997): 364–375.

Delbo, Charlotte. *Days and Memory.* Translated by Rosette Lamont. Marlboro, VT: Marlboro, 1990.

De Man, Paul. *Allegories of Reading: Figural Language in Rousseau, Nietzsche, Rilke and Proust.* New Haven, CT: Yale University Press, 1979.

———. "Autobiography as De-facement." *MLN* 94 (1979): 919–930.

Derrida, Jacques. *The Ear of the Other: Otobiography, Transference, Translation.* Edited by Christie McDonald. Translated by Peggy Kamuf and Avital Ronell. Lincoln: University of Nebraska Press, 1988.

———. "Shibboleth." In *Midrash and Literature,* 307–347. Edited by Geoffrey H. Hartman and Sanford Budick. New Haven, CT: Yale University Press, 1986.

———. "To Speculate on Freud." In *A Derrida Reader,* 516–568. Edited by Peggy Kamuf. New York: Columbia University Press, 1991.

Diner, Dan. *Beyond the Conceivable: Studies on Germany, Nazism, and the Holocaust.* Berkeley: University of California Press, 2000.

Dolar, Mladen. "The Object Voice." In *Gaze and Voice as Love Objects,* 7–31. Edited by Renata Saleci and Slavoj Žižek. Durham, NC: Duke University Press, 1996.

Dworzecki, Mark. "Ha'adam Vehahevrah Nokhah Hasho'ah" [Man and society in view of the Holocaust]. *Yedi'ot Yad Vashem* 2 (June 1954): 10, 12.

Eakin, Paul John. *How Our Lives Become Stories: Making Selves.* Princeton, NJ: Princeton University Press, 1999.

Eco, Umberto. *Semiotics and the Philosophy of Language.* Southampton, UK: Macmillan, 1984.

Efron, John. *Defenders of the Race.* New Haven, CT: Yale University Press, 1994.

Egan, Susanna. *Mirror Talk: Genres of Crisis in Contemporary Autobiography.* Chapel Hill: University of North Carolina Press, 1999.

Eisenstein, Miriam. *Jewish Schools in Poland 1919–1939.* New York: King's Crown, 1950.

Ellman, Maud, ed. *Psychoanalytic Literary Criticism.* London: Longman, 1994.

Engel, David. "On the Bowdlerization of a Holocaust Testimony: The Wartime Journal of Calek Perechodnik." *Polin* 12 (1999): 316–329.

———. "'Will They Dare?' Perceptions of Threat in Diaries from the Warsaw Ghetto." In *Holocaust Chronicles: Individualizing the Holocaust through Diaries and Other Contemporaneous Personal Accounts,* 71–82. Edited by Robert Moses Shapiro. Hoboken, NJ: Yeshiva University Press and KTAV, 1999.

Engelking, Barbara, and Jacek Leociak. *The Warsaw Ghetto: A Guide to a Perished City*. Translated by Emma Harris. New Haven, CT: Yale University Press, 2009.

Erikson, Kai T. *A New Species of Trouble: The Human Experience of Modern Disasters*. New York: Norton, 1994.

Evans, Dylan. *An Introductory Dictionary of Lacanian Psychoanalysis*. London: Routledge, 1996.

Even-Shoshan, Avraham. *Hamilon Haivri Hamerukaz* [The concise Hebrew dictionary]. Jerusalem: Kiryat Sefer, 1984.

Ewen, Joseph. *Milon Munahei Hasiporet* [A dictionary of narrative fiction]. Jerusalem: Akademon, 1978.

Falk, Raphael. *Tziyont Vehabiologyah shel HaYehudim* [Zionism and the biology of the Jews]. Tel Aviv: Resling, 2006.

Fanon, Frantz. *Black Skin, White Masks*. Translated by Richard Philcox. New York: Grove, 2008.

Farbstein, Esther. "Diaries and Memoirs as a Historical Source: The Diary and Memoir of a Rabbi at the 'Konin House of Bondage.'" *Yad Vashem Studies* 26 (1998): 87–128.

Feldhay Brenner, Rachel. "Voices from Destruction: Two Eyewitness Testimonies from the Stanisławów Ghetto." *Holocaust and Genocide Studies* 22, no. 2 (2008): 320–339.

———. *Writing as Resistance: Four Women Confronting the Holocaust: Edith Stein, Simone Weil, Anne Frank, Etty Hillesum*. University Park: Pennsylvania State University Press, 1994.

Felman, Shoshana, and Lori Daub. *Testimony: Crises of Witnessing in Literature, Psychoanalysis, and History*. New York: Routledge, 1992.

Ferenczi, Sandor. "The Confusion of Tongues between Adults and Children." In *Final Contributions to the Problems and Methods of Psychoanalysis*, 156–167. Edited by Michael Balint. Translated by Eric Mosbacher. London: Hogarth, 1955.

Fink, Bruce. *The Lacanian Subject: Between Language and Jouissance*. Princeton, NJ: Princeton University Press, 1995.

Fiszkin, Sara. "Yomanah shel Sarah Fishkin" [The diary of Sara Fiszkin]. *Yalkut Moreshet* 2, no. 4 (1965): 21–35.

Flinker, Moshe. *Young Moshe's Diary: The Spiritual Torment of a Jewish Boy in Nazi Europe*. Translated by Geoffrey Wigoder. Jerusalem: Yad Vashem, 1965.

Föllmer, Moritz. *Individuality and Modernity in Berlin: Self and Society from Weimar to the Wall*. Cambridge: Cambridge University Press, 2013.

Fothergill, Robert. *Private Chronicles: A Study of English Diaries*. London: Oxford University Press, 1974.

Foucault, Michel. "What Is Enlightenment?" In *The Foucault Reader: An Introduction to Foucault's Thought*, 32–50. Edited by Paul Rabinow. New York: Pantheon Books, 1984.

Frank, Anne. *The Diary of a Young Girl: Definitive Edition*. Edited by Otto H. Frank and Mirjam Pressler. Translated by Susan Massotty. London: Puffin, 2007.

Frank, Shlomo. *Togbuch fun Lodzer Geto* [Diary from the Lodz ghetto]. Tel Aviv: Menorah, 1959.

Frankl, Viktor. *Man's Search for Meaning*. Part 1. Translated by Ilse Lasch. Boston: Beacon, 2014.

Frenk, Hanan. "God Is Not Accountable to Us." *Haaretz*, 13 December 2002. http://www.haaretz.com/jewish/books/god-is-not-accountable-to-us-1.25464. Accessed 13 April 2017.

Freud, Anna. *The Ego and the Mechanisms of Defense*. London: Hogarth, 1968.

Freud, Sigmund. "Beyond the Pleasure Principle." In *The Standard Edition of the Complete Psychological Works of Sigmund Freud,* vol. 18, 7–66. Edited and translated by James Strachey. London: Hogarth, 1955.

———. "The Ego and the Id." In *The Standard Edition of the Complete Psychological Works of Sigmund Freud,* vol. 19, 3–66. Edited and translated by James Strachey. London: Hogarth, 1961.

———. "From the History of Infantile Neurosis." In *The Standard Edition of the Complete Psychological Works of Sigmund Freud,* vol. 12, 7–122. Edited and translated by James Strachey. London: Hogarth, 1958.

———. "Moses and Monotheism." In *The Standard Edition of the Complete Psychological Works of Sigmund Freud,* vol. 23, 3–143. Edited and translated by James Strachey. London: Hogarth, 1964.

———. "Mourning and Melancholia." In *The Standard Edition of the Complete Psychological Works of Sigmund Freud,* vol. 14, 237–260. Edited and translated by James Strachey. London: Hogarth, 1957.

———. "Remembering, Repeating and Working Through." In *The Standard Edition of the Complete Psychological Works of Sigmund Freud,* vol. 12, 145–156. Edited and translated by James Strachey. London: Hogarth, 1958.

———. "Totem and Taboo," in *The Standard Edition of the Complete Psychological Works of Sigmund Freud,* vol. 13, 1–164. Edited and translated by James Strachey. London: Hogarth, 1953.

Friedländer, Saul. "The Final Solution: On the Unease in Historical Interpretation." In *Lessons and Legacies: The Meaning of the Holocaust in a Changing World,* 23–35. Edited by Peter Hayes. Evanston, IL: Northwestern University Press, 1991.

———. *History and Psychoanalysis: An Inquiry into the Possibilities and Limits of Psychohistory.* New York: Holmes and Meier, 1978.

———. Introduction to *Probing the Limits of Representation: Nazism and the Final Solution,* 1–21. Edited by Saul Friedländer. Cambridge, MA: Harvard University Press, 1992.

———. *Nazi Germany and the Jews: The Years of Extermination 1939–1945.* London: Weidenfeld and Nicolson, 2007.

———. *Nazi Germany and the Jews: The Years of Persecution 1933–39.* Frome, UK: Phoenix, 1997.

———. "Trauma, Transference and 'Working Through.'" *History and Memory* 4 (1992): 39–55.

———. *When Memory Comes.* Translated by Helen R. Lane. New York: Farrar, Straus and Giroux, 1979.

Friedländer, Saul, and Martin Broszat. "Martin Broszat/Saul Friedlander: A Controversy about the Historicization of National Socialism." *Yad Vashem Studies* 19 (1988): 1–47.

Friedman, Philip. "The Jewish Badge and the Yellow Star in the Nazi Era." *Historia Judaica* 17 (1955): 41–70

———. "Problems of Research on the Holocaust." In *Roads to Extinction: Essays on the Holocaust,* 554–567. Philadelphia: Jewish Publication Society, 1980.

Fritzsche Peter, *Life and Death in the Third Reich.* Cambridge MA: Harvard University Press, 2008.

Fromm, Bella. *Blood and Banquets: A Berlin Social Diary.* New York: Harper, 1942.

Garbarini, Alexandra. *Numbered Days: Diaries and the Holocaust.* New Haven, CT: Yale University Press, 2006.

Gerstenberger, Heide. "Meine Prinzipien über das Deutschtum und die Verschiedenen Nationalitäten sind ins Wackeln gekommen wie di Zähne eines alten Mannes." In *Im Herzen der Finsternis: Victor Klemperer als Chronist der NS-Zeit*, 10–20. Edited by Hannes Heer. Berlin: Aufbau, 1997.

Gilman, Sander L. *Jewish Self-Hatred: Anti-Semitism and the Hidden Language of the Jews*. Baltimore: Johns Hopkins University Press, 1986.

Ginsburg, Ruth. "'Whose Trauma Is It Anyway?' Some Reflections on Freud's Traumatic History." In *New Perspectives on Freud's "Moses and Monotheism,"* 77–92. Edited by Ruth Ginsburg and Ilana Pardes. Tübingen: Max Niemeyer, 2006.

Glückel of Hameln. *Memoirs of Glückel of Hameln*. Translated by Marvin Lowenthal. New York: Schocken, 1977.

Goebbels, Josef. "Die Juden sind schuld." *Das Reich*, 16 November 1941.

———. *The Goebbels Diaries 1942–1943*. Edited and translated by Louis P. Lochner. New York: Doubleday, 1948.

Goffman, Erving. "On the Characteristics of Total Institutions." In *Asylums: Essays on the Social Situation of Mental Patients and Other Inmates*, 1–124. New Brunswick, NJ: Aldine Transaction, 2009.

Golan, Ruth. "The Secret Bearers: From Silence to Testimony, from the Real to the *Phantasme*." In *Loving Psychoanalysis: Looking at Culture with Freud and Lacan*, 101–126. Translated by Jonathan Martin. London: Karnac, 2006.

Goldberg, Amos. "Haktivah Bitkufat Hasho'ah: Ti'ud Hahistoriyah o 'Ti'ud' Hatraumah? Kri'ah Beyomanah shel Fela Szeps" [Writing during the Holocaust: Documenting history or "documenting" the trauma? A reading of Fela Szeps's diary]. *Dapim: Studies on the Shoah* 19 (2005): 95–113.

———. "Jews' Diaries and Chronicles." In *The Oxford Handbook of Holocaust Studies*, 397–414. Edited by Peter Hayes and John K. Roth. Oxford: Oxford University Press, 2011.

———. *Trauma Beguf Rishon: Ktivat Yomanim Bitkufat HaShoah* [Trauma in first person: Diary writing during the Holocaust]. Or Yehuda: Ben Gurion University and Kinneret Zmora-Bitan Dvir, 2012.

———. "Trauma, Narrative, and Two Forms of Death." *Literature and Medicine* 25, no. 1 (2006): 122–141.

———. "The Victim's Voice in History and Melodramatic Esthetics." *History and Theory* 48, no. 3 (2009): 220–237.

———. "Yomanei HaSho'ah: Samkhut She'einah Medaberet Kahalakhah" [Holocaust diaries: An authority that doesn't speak appropriately]. In *Kanoni Upopulari: Mifgashim Sifrutiyim* [Popular and canonical: Literary dialogues], 131–140. Edited by Tamar Hess, Omri Herzog, and Yael Shapira. Tel Aviv: Resling, 2007.

Golomb, Jacob, ed. *Nitshe Batarbut HaIvrit* [Nietzsche, Zionism and Hebrew culture]. Jerusalem: Magnes, 2002.

Gorodenchik, Rinat. "Brihat Tnu'ot Hano'ar MiZaglembie, 1943–1945" [The flight of the youth movements from Zaglembie, 1943–1945]. MA thesis, Hebrew University, 1986.

Gradowski, Zalman. "Writings." In *The Scrolls of Auschwitz*, 173–205. Edited by Ber Mark. Translated by Sharon Neemani. Tel Aviv: Am Oved, 1985.

Greif, Gideon. *We Wept without Tears: Testimonies of the Jewish Sonderkommando from Auschwitz*. New Haven, CT: Yale University Press, 2005.

Guterman, Simcha. *Leaves from Fire*. Translated by Mindle Crystel Gross. Charleston, SC: Self-published by Yaakov Guterman, printed by CreateSpace, 2015.

Gutman, Yisrael (Israel). Afterword to *Ktavim Ahronim* [Last writings], vol. 2, by Emanuel Ringelblum. Jerusalem: Yad Vashem, 1994.

———. *The Jews of Warsaw 1939–1943: Ghetto, Underground, Revolt.* Translated by Ina Friedman. Bloomington: Indiana University Press, 1982.

———. "'Kidush Hashem' Ve 'Kidush Hahayim'" [The "sanctification of (God's) name" and the "sanctification of life"]. In *Ba'alatah Uvema'avak: Pirkey Iyun Basho'ah Uvehitnagdut Yehudit* [In darkness and struggle: Studies on the Holocaust and Jewish resistance], 72–90. Tel Aviv and Jerusalem: Moreshet, Hebrew University and Sifriyat Poalim, 1985.

———. *Sugiyot Beheker Hasho'ah: Bikoret Utrumah* [Issues in the study of the Holocaust: Criticism and contribution]. Jerusalem: Yad Vashem and the Zalman Shazar Center, 2009.

———. "Trumato shel Hati'ud Hayehudi Hamekori Leheker Hasho'ah" [The contribution of original Jewish documentation to Holocaust research]. In *Mignizah Letziyunei Derekh Historiyim: Arkhiyonim Yehudi'im Mitkufat Hamilhamah VehaSho'ah* [From hidden treasures to historical landmarks: Jewish archives from the period of the war and the Holocaust], 181–195. Jerusalem: Yad Vashem, 1997.

———. *Yehudai Varshah 1939–1943: Geto, Mahteret, Mered* [The Jews of Warsaw 1939–1943: Ghetto, underground, uprising]. Tel Aviv: Yad Vashem, the Institute of Contemporary Jewry, and Sifriyat Poalim, 1977.

Gutterman, Bella, ed. *Bevo Ha'emah: Yehudei Lvov Tahat Hakibush Hagermani: Dapei Edut Yuni 1941–April 1942* [Days of horror: Jewish testimonies from German-occupied Lemberg 1941–1943: Testimonies from June 1941 to April 1942]. Tel Aviv: The Institute for the History of Polish Jewry and the Diaspora Research Center, 1991.

Habermas, Jürgen. "Modernity: An Unfinished Project." In *Habermas and the Unfinished Project of Modernity: Critical Essays on the Philosophical Discourse of Modernity*, 38–58. Edited by Maurizio Passerin d'Entrèves and Seyla Benhabib. Cambridge, MA: MIT Press, 1997.

———. *The Theory of Communicative Action.* Translated by Thomas McCarthy. Boston: Beacon, 1984–1987.

Hartman, Geoffrey. *The Longest Shadow: In the Aftermath of the Holocaust.* Bloomington: Indiana University Press, 1996.

Hawkins, Mike. *Social Darwinism in European and American Thought, 1860–1945: Nature as Model and Nature as Threat.* Cambridge: Cambridge University Press, 1997.

Heer, Hannes, ed. *Im Herzen der Finsternis: Victor Klemperer als Chronist der NS-Zeit.* Berlin: Aufbau, 1997.

Heilbrunn, Stefania. *Children of Dust and Heaven.* Pacific Palisades, CA: Remember Point, 2012.

Heim, Susanne. "The German–Jewish Relationship in the Diaries of Victor Klemperer." In *Probing the Depths of German Antisemitism*, 312–325. Edited by David Bankier. New York: Berghahn, 1999.

Heise, Ursula K. "Chronoschisms." In *Chronoschisms: Time Narrative, and Postmodernism*, 11–76. Cambridge: Cambridge University Press, 1997.

Henke, Suzette A. *Shattered Subjects: Trauma and Testimony in Women's Life-Writing.* New York: St. Martin's, 1998.

Herman, Tamar. "Gam Kan Mutar Lahlom Vele'ehov (Yoman Migeto Terezin)" [Here too one may dream and love (A diary from the Theresien ghetto)]. *Yalkut Moreshet* 47 (1989): 195–208.

Hever, Hannan. "Avru Toldot He'amim Keshod Batzaharayim: Natan Alterman Bitkufat Hasho'ah" [The history of the nations passed like a robbery at noon: Nathan Alterman during the Holocaust]. In *Sho'ah Mimerhak Tavo* [When disaster comes from afar], 48–84. Edited by Dina Porat. Jerusalem: Ben-Zvi Institute, 2009.

Hilberg, Raul. *Sources of Holocaust Research: An Analysis.* Chicago: Ivan R. Dee, 2001.

Hillesum, Etty. *An Interrupted Life: The Diaries of Etty Hillesum, 1941–1943.* Translated by Arnold Pomerans. New York: Henry Holt, 1996.

Hocke, Gustav Rene. *Europäische Tagebücher aus vier Jahrhunderten.* Frankfurt am Main: Fischer Taschenbuch, 1991.

Hurwicz, Leon. Diary. Archive of the Jewish Historical Institute in Warsaw (ZIH), 302/11–13.

Jabotinsky, Ze'ev. "The Iron Wall." 4 November 1923. https://www.jewishvirtuallibrary.org/jsource/Zionism/ironwall.html. Accessed 21 August 2016.

Jacobs, Peter. *Victor Klemperer: Im Kern ein deutsches Gewächs.* Berlin: AtV, 2000.

Jakobs, Rose. *Yomanah shel Na'arah Bemahbo Bishnot Hasho'ah* [Diary of a girl in hiding during the Holocaust]. Bnei Brak: privately printed, 2002.

Jean, Yaron. *Re'ashei Hamoderniyut: Havayot shel Shmi'ah Begermanyah 1914–1945* [Noises of modernity: Hearing experiences in Germany 1914–1945]. Tel Aviv: Resling, 2011.

Kahane, David. *Lvov Ghetto Diary.* Translated by Jerzy Michalowicz. Amherst: University of Massachusetts Press, 1990.

Kalmanovitch, Zelig. "A Diary of the Nazi Ghetto in Vilna." In *YIVO Annual of Jewish Social Science*, vol. 8, 9–81. New York: YIVO, 1953.

Kambanellis, Iakovos. *Mauthausen.* Translated by Gail Holst-Warhaft. Athens: Kedros, 1996.

Kaplan, Chaim Aron. *Amei HaTanakh: Tziurim Histori'im Mihayei Amei Hamizrah* [The peoples of the Bible: Historical portraits from the lives of the peoples of the East]. Warsaw: Limud, 1926.

———. Diary. Archive of the Jewish Historical Institute in Warsaw (ZIH), 302/218.

———. Diary. "Hayim Ahron Kaplan" file. Moreshet Archive D.2.470.

———. Diary entries. *Bitzaron* 53, no. 1 (254) (October–November 1965): 7–18.

———. Diary entries. *Bitzaron* 69, no. 5 (28) (April–May 1969): 15–17, 39.

———. Diary entries. *Yalkut Moreshet* 3 (December 1964): 7–22.

———. *Dikduk Halashon Veshimushah* [The grammar of the language and its usage]. New York: Hebrew Publishing, 1926.

———. *Haggadah shel Pesah: Hotza'ah Omanutit Umada'it, im Be'ur Ivri Hadash* [Passover Haggadah: An artistic and scientific edition with new Hebrew explanations]. Warsaw: Limud, 1924.

———. *Megilat Yisurin: Yoman Geto Varshah* [Scroll of agony: Warsaw ghetto diary]. Tel Aviv: Am Oved and Yad Vashem, 1966.

———. *Pezurai: Mehkarim, Reshimot Ufelyetonim: Kol Kitvei Hamehaber Bitkufat Hashanim 1900–1936* [My scatterings: Studies, articles, and feuilletons: The author's complete writings during the years 1900–1936]. Warsaw: Va'ad Hayovel, 1937.

———. *Scroll of Agony: The Warsaw Diary of Chaim A. Kaplan.* Translated and editted by Abraham I. Katsh. Bloomington: Indiana University Press, 1999.

———. *Sefer Hamis'hakim Hasha'ashuim Vehahit'amlut: Sefer Ezer Lehorim, Lemorim Uletalmidim* [The book of games, quizzes, and exercises: A reference book for parents, teachers, and students]. Warsaw: Limud, 1922.

Kaplan, Marion. *Between Dignity and Despair: Jewish Life in Nazi Germany.* New York: Oxford University Press, 1998.

Kassow, Samuel. *Who Will Write Our History? Emanuel Ringelblum, the Warsaw Ghetto, and the Oyneg Shabes Archive*. Bloomington: Indiana University Press, 2007.

Katsh (Katz), Abraham I. Introduction to *Megilat Yisurin: Yoman Geto Varshah* [Scroll of agony: Warsaw ghetto diary], by Chaim Aron Kaplan. Tel Aviv: Am Oved and Yad Vashem, 1966.

———. Introduction to *Scroll of Agony: The Warsaw Diary of Chaim A. Kaplan*. Edited and translated by Abraham I. Katsh. Bloomington: Indiana University Press, 1999.

———. "Kaplan, Chaim Aron." In *Encyclopaedia Judaica*, vol. 11, 774–775. 2nd ed. Edited by Michael Berenbaum and Fred Skolnik. Detroit: Macmillan Reference, 2007.

Katzenelson, Yitzhak. "Pinkas Vittel" [Vittel notebook]. In *Ktavim Ahronim 5700–5704* [Last writings 1940–1944], 177–239. Tel Aviv: Hakibbutz Hameuchad, 1956.

Kaufman, Fiona. "By Chance I Found a Pencil: The Holocaust Diary Narratives of Testimony, Defiance, Solace and Struggle." PhD diss., University of Melbourne, 2010.

Kazanjian, David, and Marc Nichanian. "Between Genocide and Catastrophe." In *Loss: The Politics of Mourning*, 125–147. Edited by David Eng and David Kazanjian. Berkeley: University of California Press, 2003.

Kermish, Josef, ed. *To Live with Honor, to Die with Honor: Selected Documents from the Warsaw Ghetto Underground Archives*. Jerusalem: Yad Vashem, 1986.

Kermisz (Kermish), Josef (Joseph). Introduction to *The Warsaw Diary of Adam Czerniakow*. Edited by Raul Hilberg, Stanislaw Staron, and Josef Kermisz. New York: Stein and Day, 1979.

Kermisz, Josef, ed. *Itonut Hamahteret* [The underground press]. Vol. 2. Jerusalem: Yad Vashem, 1980.

Kershaw, Ian. *Hitler: A Biography*. New York: Norton, 2008.

Kertész, Imre. *Fatelessness*. Translated by Tim Wilkinson. London: Vintage, 2004.

Khan, Masud R. "The Concept of Cumulative Trauma." *Psychoanalitic Study of the Child* 18 (1963): 286–306.

Kidron, Carol. "Surviving a Distant Past: A Case Study of the Cultural Construction of Trauma Descendant Identity." *Ethos* 31, no. 4 (2003): 513–544.

Kijek, Kamil. "Was It Possible to Avoid 'Hebrew Assimilation'? Hebraism, Polonization and Tarbut Schools in the Last Decade of Interwar Poland." *Jewish Social Studies* 21, no. 2 (2016): 105–141.

Klautke, Egbert. *The Mind of the Nation: Völkerpsychologie in Germany 1851–1955*. Oxford: Berghahn, 2013.

Kleinberg, Aviad. "Shalosh Otobiografiyot Miyemei Habeinayim" [Three autobiographies from the Middle Ages]. *Alpayim* 13 (1996): 44–64.

Klemperer, Victor. Correspondence with Teubner. Nachlass Klemperer, Victor (1881–1960)/5. Briefe. Sächsische Landsbibliothek—Staats und Universitätsbibliothek Dresden (SLUB). Mscr.Dresd.App.2003, 465–469.

———. *Curriculum Vitae*. 2 vols. Berlin: AtV, 1996.

———. Diaries. Nachlass Klemperer, Victor (1881–1960)/4. Tagebücher und Notizkalender. Sächsische Landsbibliothek—Staats und Universitätsbibliothek Dresden (SLUB), Mscr.Dresd.App.2003, 134–139.

———. *Ich will Zeugnis ablegen bis zum letzten*. Vol. 1: *Tagebücher 1933–1941*. Berlin: Aufbau, 1995.

———. *Ich will Zeugnis ablegen bis zum letzten*. Vol. 2: *Tagebücher 1942–1945*. Berlin: Aufbau, 1995.

———. *I Will Bear Witness: A Diary of the Nazi Years, 1933–1941*. Translated by Martin Chalmers. New York: Modern Library, 1999.
———. *I Will Bear Witness: A Diary of the Nazi Years, 1942–1945*. Translated by Martin Chalmers. New York: Modern Library, 2001.
———. *The Language of the Third Reich: LTI, Lingua Tertii Imperii: A Philologist's Notebook*. Translated by Martin Brady. London: Continuum, 2006.
———. *Leben sammeln, nicht fragen wozu und warum: Tagebücher 1918–1932*. 2 vols. Berlin: Aufbau, 1996.
———. Letter to Victor Klemperer from the Continental News Agency. Berlin, 1932. Nachlass Klemperer, Victor (1881–1960)/5. Briefe. Sächsische Landsbibliothek—Staats und Universitätsbibliothek Dresden (SLUB). Mscr.Dresd.App.2003, 426.
———. *Und so ist alles schwankend: Tagebücher Juni bis Dezember 1945*. Berlin: AtV, 1996.
———. *Yomanim 1933–1945 (Mivhar)* [Diaries 1933–1945 (A selection)]. Edited by Ilana Hammerman. Translated by Tali Kunes. Tel Aviv: Am Oved, 2004.
Klinger, Chajka. *Miyoman Bageto* [From a diary in the ghetto]. Merhavia: Sifriyat Poalim and Kibbutz Haogen, 1959.
Klonicki, Aryeh. *The Diary of Adam's Father*. Translated by Avner Tomaschoff. Jerusalem: The Ghetto Fighters' House and Hakibbutz Hameuchad, 1973.
———. *Yoman Avi Adam* [Adam's father's diary]. Jerusalem: The Ghetto Fighters' House and Hakibbutz Hameuchad, 1969.
Korczak, Janusz. *Ghetto Diary*. Translated by Jerzy Bachrach and Barbara Krzywicka. New Haven, CT: Yale University Press, 2003.
Kovacs, Pal. "Yomano shel Pal Kovacs" [The diary of Pal Kovacs]. *Dapim Leheker Tkufat HaSho'ah* 1 (1979): 229–252.
Kristeva, Julia. *Desire in Language: A Semiotic Approach to Literature and Art*. New York: Columbia University Press, 1980.
Kruk, Herman. *The Last Days of the Jerusalem of Lithuania: Chronicles from the Vilna Ghetto and the Camps 1939–1944*. Edited by Benjamin Harshav. Translated by Barbara Harshav. New Haven, CT: Yale University Press, 2002.
———. *Togbuch fun Vilner Geto* [Diary from the Vilna ghetto]. New York: YIVO, 1961.
Lacan, Jacques. *The Ethics of Psychoanalysis*. Translated by Dennis Porter. New York: Norton, 1992.
———. "Kant with Sade." *October* 51 (1989): 55–75.
———. "The Mirror Stage as Formative of the Function of the I." In *Ecrits: The First Complete Edition in English*, 1–6. Translated by Bruce Fink. New York: Norton, 2002.
———. *The Seminar of Jacques Lacan, Book I: Freud's Papers on Technique, 1953–1954*. Edited by Jacques-Alain Miller. Translated by John Forrester. New York: Norton, 1988.
———. *The Seminar of Jacques Lacan, Book XI: The Four Fundamental Concepts of Psychoanalysis*. Edited by Jacques-Alain Miller. Translated by Alan Sheridan. New York: Norton, 1998.
LaCapra, Dominick. *History and Memory after Auschwitz*. Ithaca, NY: Cornell University Press, 1998.
———. *History in Transit: Experience, Identity, Critical Theory*. Ithaca, NY: Cornell University Press, 2004.
———. *Representing the Holocaust: History, Theory, Trauma*. Ithaca, NY: Cornell University Press, 1994.
———. *Writing History, Writing Trauma*. Baltimore: Johns Hopkins University Press, 2014.

Lang, Berel. *Act and Idea in the Nazi Genocide*. Chicago: University of Chicago Press, 1990.
Langer, Lawrence L. *Admitting the Holocaust: Collected Essays*. Oxford: Oxford University Press, 1995.
———. Foreword to *The Diary of Dawid Sierakowiak*. Edited by Alan Adelson. Oxford: Oxford University Press, 1996.
———. *Holocaust Testimonies: The Ruins of Memory*. New Haven, CT: Yale University Press, 1991.
Laplanche, Jean, and Jean-Baptiste Pontalis. *The Language of Psychoanalysis*. New York: Norton, 1973.
Laqueur, Walter Ze'ev. "Three Witnesses: The Legacy of Viktor Klemperer, Willy Cohn and Richard Koch." *Holocaust and Genocide Studies* 10, no. 3 (1996): 252–266.
Laqueur Weiss, Renata. "Writing in Defiance: Concentration Camp Diaries in Dutch, French and German, 1940–1945." PhD diss., New York University, 1971.
Laurent, Éric. "Alienation and Separation (I)." In *Reading Seminar XI*, 19–28. Edited by Richard Feldstein, Bruce Fink, and Maire Jaanus. Albany: State University of New York Press, 1995.
Lazerson-Rostovsky, Tamar. *Yomanah shel Tamara: Kovno 1942–1946* [Tamara's diary: Kovno 1942–1946]. Lohamei Hageta'ot: The Ghetto Fighters' House and Hakibbutz Hameuchad, 1976.
Lejeune, Philippe. *On Diary*. Edited by Jeremy D. Popkin and Julie Rak. Translated by Katherine Durnin. Manoa: University of Hawai'i Press, 2009.
Lemkin, Raphaël. *Axis Rule in Occupied Europe*. Washington, DC: Carnegie Endowment for International Peace, 1944.
Leociak, Jacek. *Text in the Face of Destruction: Accounts from the Warsaw Ghetto Reconsidered*. Translated by Emma Harris. Warsaw: Żydowski Instytut Historyczny, 2004.
Levi, Primo. *The Drowned and the Saved*. Translated by Raymond Rosenthal. New York: Vintage, 1989.
———. *If This Is a Man/The Truce*. Translated by Stuart Woolf. London: Abacus, 2004.
Lévy-Hass, Hanna. *Diary of Bergen-Belsen: 1944–1945*. Translated by Sophie Hand. Chicago: Haymarket, 2009.
Lewin, Avraham. *Mipinkaso shel Hamoreh MiYehudiyah: Geto Varshah April 1942–Mai 1943* [From a notebook of a teacher at the Yehuduiah School April 1942–May 1943]. Tel Aviv: Hakibbutz Hameuchad and the Ghetto Fighters' House, 1969.
Lewis Herman, Judith. *Trauma and Recovery*. New York: Basic Books, 1997.
Leys, Ruth. *Trauma: A Genealogy*. Chicago: University of Chicago Press, 2000.
Lifton, Robert Jay, and Eric Olson. *Explorations in Psychohistory*. New York: Simon and Schuster, 1975.
Linde, Charlotte. *Life Stories*. New York: Oxford University Press, 1993.
Littel, Jonathan. *The Kindly Ones*. Translated by Charlotte Mandell. New York: Harper, 2009.
Loewenthal, Zalman. "Writings." In *The Scrolls of Auschwitz*. Edited by Ber Mark. Translated by Sharon Neemani. Tel Aviv: Am Oved, 1985.
Longerich, Peter. "The Wannsee Conference in the Development of the 'Final Solution.'" In *Holocaust: Critical Concepts in Historical Studies*, vol. 3, 121–153. Edited by David Cesarani. London: Routledge, 2004.
Lyotard, Jean François. *The Differend: Phases in Dispute*. Translated by Georges Van Den Abbeele. Minneapolis: University of Minnesota Press, 1989.
Majer, Diemut. *"Non-Germans" under the Third Reich*. Baltimore: Johns Hopkins University Press, 2003.

Maltz, Moshe. Diary. Yad Vashem Archives O.33/2474.
———. *Years of Horror—Glimpse of Hope: The Diary of a Family in Hiding.* New York: Shengold, 1993.
Marcus, Laura. *Auto/biographical Discourses: Theory, Criticism, Practice.* Manchester: Manchester University Press, 1994.
Mark, Ber. *Di Umgekumene Shrayber fun di Getos un Lagern un Zeyere Verk.* Warsaw: Yiddish Bukh Ferlag, 1954.
———, ed. *The Scrolls of Auschwitz.* Translated by Sharon Neemani. Tel Aviv: Am Oved, 1985.
Markowska, Marta, ed. *The Ringelblum Archive: Annihilation—Day by Day.* Warsaw: Karta Centre, 2008.
Marrus, Michael. "Killing Time: Jewish Perceptions during the Holocaust." In *The Holocaust: History and Memory: Essays Presented in Honour of Israel Gutman*, 10–38. Edited by David Bankier, Daniel Blatman, Dalia Ofer, and Shmuel Almog. Jerusalem: Yad Vashem, 2001.
Martens, Lorna. *The Diary Novel.* Cambridge: Cambridge University Press, 2009.
Mazower, Mark. *Hitler's Empire: How the Nazis Ruled Europe.* New York: Penguin, 2008.
Michman, Dan. "Is There an 'Israeli School' of Holocaust Research?" In *Holocaust Historiography in Context: Emergence, Challenges, Polemics and Achievements*, 37–65. Edited by David Bankier and Dan Michman. Jerusalem and New York: Yad Vashem and Berghahn, 2008.
Milch, Baruch. *Can Heaven Be Void?* Edited by Shosh Milch-Avigal. Translated by Helen Kaye. Jerusalem: Yad Vashem, 2003.
Mintz, Alan. *Ḥurban: Responses to Catastrophe in Hebrew Literature.* New York: Columbia University Press, 1984.
———. *Popular Culture and the Shaping of Holocaust Memory in America.* Seattle: University of Washington Press, 2001.
Miron, Guy. "'Lately, Almost Constantly, Everything Seems Small to Me': The Lived Space of German Jews under the Nazi Regime." *Jewish Social Studies* 20, no. 1 (2013): 121–149.
———. "The 'Lived Time' of German Jews under the Nazi Regime." *Journal of Modern History* (forthcoming).
———. "'The Politics of Catastrophe Races On. I Wait': Waiting Time in the World of German Jewry under Nazi Rule." *Yad Vashem Studies* 43, no. 1 (2015): 45–76.
Misch, Georg. *A History of Autobiography in Antiquity.* London: Routledge and Kegan Paul, 1950.
Moi, Toril. "From Femininity to Finitude: Freud, Lacan, and Feminism, Again." *Signs: Journal of Women in Culture and Society* 29, no. 3 (2004): 841–878.
Morris-Reich, Amos. "Arthur Ruppin's Concept of Race." *Israel Studies* 11, no. 3 (2006): 1–30.
Morson, Gary Saul. *The Boundaries of Genre.* Austin: University of Texas Press, 1981.
Moseley, Marcus. *Being for Myself Alone: Origins of Jewish Autobiography.* Stanford, CA: Stanford University Press, 2006.
Mosse, George L. *Toward the Final Solution: A History of European Racism.* New York: Harper and Row, 1980.
Namier, Lewis. *1848: The Revolution of the Intellectuals.* Garden City, NY: Anchor Books, 1964.
Neumann, Boaz. "The National Socialist Politics of Life." *New German Critique* 85 (2002): 107–132.
———. *Re'iyat Ha'olam Hanatzit: Merhav, Guf, Safah* [The Nazi weltanschauung: Space, body, language]. Haifa: Haifa University, 2002.

Nieden, Suzanne zur. "Aus dem vergessenen Alltag der Tyrannei." In *Im Herzen der Finsternis: Victor Klemperer als Chronist der NS-Zeit*, 110–121. Edited by Hannes Heer. Berlin: Aufbau, 1997.

Nietzsche, Friedrich. *On the Genealogy of Morality*. Edited by Keith Ansell-Pearson. Translated by Carol Diethe. Cambridge: Cambridge University Press, 1994.

Nin, Anaïs. *The Diary of Anaïs Nin*. Vol. 3: *1939–1944*. Edited by Gunther Stuhlmann. New York: Harvest/Harcourt Brace Jovanovich, 1969.

Nowojski, Walter. Afterword to *Leben sammeln, nicht fragen wozu und warum: Tagebücher 1918–1932*, by Victor Klemperer. Berlin: Aufbau, 1996.

Nussbaum, Felicity A. *The Autobiographical Subject: Gender and Ideology in Eighteenth-Century England*. Baltimore: Johns Hopkins University Press, 1989.

Ofer, Dalia. "Everyday Life of Jews under Nazi Occupation: Methodological Issues." *Holocaust and Genocide Studies* 9, no. 1 (1995): 42–69.

Opoczynski, Peretz. *Reshimot* [Sketches from the Warsaw ghetto]. Tel Aviv: The Ghetto Fighters' House and Hakibbutz Hameuchad, 1970.

Oppenheim, Menachem. "Yomano shel Menahem Oppenheim Migeto Lodz" [The diary of Menachem Oppenheim of the Lodz ghetto]. *Sinai* 28 (1951): 241–278.

Oyerbakh, Rokhl. *Baym Letsten Veg* [In the last path]. Tel Aviv: Farlag Yisroel Bukh, 1977.

———. *Varshever Tsavoes* [Warsaw wills]. Tel Aviv: Farlag Yisroel Bukh, 1974.

Patterson, David. *Along the Edge of Annihilation: The Collapse and Recovery of Life in the Holocaust Diary*. Seattle: University of Washington Press, 1999.

———. "The Collapse and Recovery of Time in the Holocaust Diary." *Modern Jewish Studies Annual* 9 (1994): 131–137.

Perechodnik, Calel (Calek). *Am I A Murderer? Testament of a Jewish Ghetto Policeman*. Translated by Frank Fox. Boulder, CO: Westview, 1996.

———. *Hatafkid He'atzuv shel Hati'ud* [The sad role of documentation]. Jerusalem: Keter, 1993.

Petropoulus, Jonathan, and John Roth, eds. *Gray Zones: Ambiguity and Compromise in the Holocaust and Its Aftermath*. New York: Berghahn, 2005.

Petsche, Hans-Joachim. "Victor Klemperer: Ein Missverständnis?" In *Victor Klemperers Werk: Texte und Materialien für Lehrer*, 150–168. Edited by Karl-Heinz Siehr. Berlin: AtV, 2001.

Piekarz, Mendel. *Sifrut Ha'edut al Hasho'ah Kemakor Histori: Veshalosh Teguvot Hasidiyot Be'artzot Hasho'ah* [The literature of testimony as a historical source of the Holocaust and three Hasidic reflections on the Holocaust]. Jerusalem: Bialik Institute, 2003.

Polen, Nehemia. *The Holy Fire: The Teachings of Rabbi Kalonymus Kalman Shapira, the Rebbe of the Warsaw Ghetto*. Northvale, NJ: Jason Aronson, 1994.

Polkinghorne, Donald. *Narrative Knowing and the Human Sciences*. Albany: State University of New York Press, 1988.

Porat, Dina. *The Fall of a Sparrow: The Life and Times of Abba Kovner*. Translated by Elizabeth Yuval. Stanford, CA: Stanford University Press, 2010.

———. Introduction to *Geto Yom Yom: Yoman Umismakhim Migeto Kovno* [Ghetto everyday: diary and documents from the Kovno ghetto], by Avraham Tory. Edited by Dina Porat. Jerusalem: Bialik Institute and Tel Aviv University, 1988.

———. "The Vilna Ghetto Diaries." In *Holocaust Chronicles: Individualizing the Holocaust through Diaries and Other Contemporaneous Personal Accounts*, 157–169. Edited by Robert Moses Shapiro. Hoboken, NJ: Yeshiva University Press and KTAV, 1999.

———. "Yomanah shel Anna Frank Umakhishei HaSho'ah" [Anne Frank's diary and Holocaust deniers]. In *Hasho'ah—Hayihudi Veha'universali: Sefer Yovel LeYehuda Bauer* [The Holocaust—The unique and the universal: Essays presented in honor of Yehuda Bauer], 160–183. Edited by Shmuel Almog, Daniel Blatman, David Bankier, and Dalia Ofer. Jerusalem: Yad Vashem and the Institute of Contemporary Jewry, 2001.

Poznanski, Renée. Afterword to *Yoman* [Diary], by Hélène Berr. Ben Shemen: Modan, 2010.

Prais, Lea. *Displaced Persons at Home: Refugees in the Fabric of Jewish Life in Warsaw, September 1939–July 1942*. Jerusalem: Yad Vashem, 2015.

Presser, Jacques. *The Night of the Girondists*. Translated by Barrows Mussey. London: HarperCollins, 1992.

Radlitzky, Zvi. "Reshimot Miyemei Hakibush HaGermani BeLvov (Lemberg) 1941–1943" [Notes from the days of the German occupation in Lvov (Lemberg) 1941–1943]. *Yalkut Moreshet* 21 (1976): 7–34.

Rak, Julie. "Dialogue with the Future: Philippe Lejeune's Method and Theory of Diary." Introduction to *On Diary*, 16–26. Edited by Jeremy D. Popkin and Julie Rak. Translated by Katherine Durnin. Manoa: University of Hawai'i Press, 2009.

Redlich, Egon (Gonda). *Hayim Ke'ilu: Yoman Egon Redlich Migeto Terezienstat (1943–1944)* [Life as if: The diary of Egon Redlich from the Theresienstadt ghetto (1943–1944)]. Lohamei Hageta'ot: Hakibbutz Hameuchad and the Ghetto Fighters' House, 1984.

———. *The Terezin Diary of Gonda Redlich*. Edited by Saul Friedländer. Translated by Laurence Kutler. Lexington: University Press of Kentucky, 1992.

Reik, Theodor. "The Shofar." In *Ritual: Psychoanalytic Studies*, 221–361. Translated by Douglas Bryan. New York: Farrar, Strauss, 1946.

Richardson, Margaret Ravenel. "Trauma and Representation in Women's Diaries of the Second World War." PhD diss., University of St Andrews, 2012.

Ricoeur, Paul. "Life in Quest of Narrative." In *On Paul Ricoeur: Narrative and Interpretation*, 20–33. Edited by David Wood. London: Routledge, 1991.

———. "Narrative Identity." In *On Paul Ricoeur: Narrative and Interpretation*, 188–199. Edited by David Wood. London: Routledge, 1991.

———. *Time and Narrative*. 3 vols. Translated by Kathleen McLaughlin and David Pellauer. Chicago: University of Chicago Press, 1984–1988.

Rimmon-Kenan, Shlomith. "Narration as Repetition: The Case of Günther Grass's *Cat and Mouse*." In *Discourse in Psychoanalysis and Literature*, 176–187. Edited by Shlomith Rimmon-Kenan. New York: Methuen, 1987.

———. *Narrative Fiction: Contemporary Poetics*. London: Routledge, 1983.

———. "The Story of 'I': Illness and Narrative Identity." *Narrative* 10, no. 1 (January 2000): 9–26.

Ringelblum, Emanuel. *Ksovim fun Geto: Togbuch fun Varshover Geto 1939–1942* [Writings from the ghetto: A diary from the Warsaw ghetto 1939–1942]. Warsaw: Yiddish Bukh, 1961.

———. *Ktavim Ahronim: Yahasei Yehudim–Polanim* [Last writings: Jewish–Polish relations]. Vol. 2. Jerusalem: Yad Vashem, 1994.

———. *Notes from the Warsaw Ghetto: The Journal of Emanuel Ringelblum*. Translated by Jacob Sloan. New York: Schocken, 1974.

———. *Yoman Ureshimot Mitkufat Hamilhamah* [Diary and notes from the Warsaw ghetto]. Jerusalem: Yad Vashem and the Ghetto Fighters' House, 1992.

Roethler, Shulamit. "Miyomanah shel Metta Lande" [From the diary of Metta Lande]. *Edut* 6 (1991): 85–96.

Rogers, Kim Lacy, Selma Leydesdorff, and Graham Dawson, eds. *Trauma and Life Stories: International Perspectives*. London: Routledge, 1999.

Rosenberg, Kurt F. *"Einer, der nicht mehr dazugehört": Tagebücher 1933–1937*. Edited by Beate Meyer and Björn Siegel. Göttingen: Wallstein, 2012.

Rosenfeld, Alvin. *A Double Dying: Reflections on Holocaust Literature*. Bloomington: Indiana University Press, 1980.

Rosenfeld, Oskar. *In the Beginning Was the Ghetto: Notebooks from Łódź*. Edited by Hanno Loewy. Translated by Brigitte M. Goldstein. Evanston, IL: Northwestern University Press, 2002.

Roskies, David G. *Against the Apocalypse: Responses to Catastrophe in Modern Jewish Culture*. Cambridge, MA: Harvard University Press, 1984.

———. *Holocaust Literature: A History and a Guide*. Waltham, MA: Brandeis University Press, 2012.

Rothkirchen, Livia. *Hurban Yahadut Slovakia: Te'ur Histori Bete'udot* [The destruction of Slovak Jewry: A documentary history]. Jerusalem: Yad Vashem, 1961.

Rubenstein, Richard. "Gray into Black: The Case of Mordechai Chaim Rumkowski." In *Gray Zones: Ambiguity and Compromise in the Holocaust and Its Aftermath*, 299–310. Edited by Jonathan Petropoulus and John Roth. New York: Berghahn, 2005.

Rubinowicz, Dawid. *The Diary of Dawid Rubinowicz*. Translated by Derek Bowman. Edmonds, WA: Creative Options, 1982.

Rudashevski, Yitskhok. *The Diary of the Vilna Ghetto, June 1941–April 1943*. Translated by Percy Matenko. Jerusalem: The Ghetto Fighters' House, 1973.

Salecl, Renata. "I Can't Love You Unless I Give You Up." In *Gaze and Voice as Love Objects*, 179–207. Edited by Renata Saleci and Slavoj Žižek. Durham, NC: Duke University Press, 1996.

Santner, Eric L. "History beyond the Pleasure Principle: Some Thoughts on the Representation of Trauma." In *Probing the Limits of Representation: Nazism and the Final Solution*, 143–154. Edited by Saul Friedländer. Cambridge, MA: Harvard University Press, 1992.

Schlissel, Lillian. *Women's Diaries of the Westward Journey*. New York: Schocken, 1982.

Schmitt, Carl. *The Concept of the Political*. Translated by George Schwab. New Brunswick, NJ: Rutgers University Press, 1976.

———. *Political Theology: Four Chapters on the Concept of Sovereignty*. Translated by George Schwab. Cambridge, MA: MIT Press, 1985.

Schweid, Eliezer. "Hadilema Hakiyumit Vehamusarit shel Hahitnagdut Hamezuyenet Bageto" [The existential and moral dilemma of armed resistance in the ghetto]. In *Kedushat Hahayim Veheruf Hanefesh: Kovetz Ma'amarim Lezikhro shel AmirYekutiel* [Sanctity of life and martyrdom: Studies in memory of Amir Yekutiel], 277–312. Edited by Isaiah M. Gafni and Aviezer Ravitzky. Jerusalem: The Zalman Shazar Center, 1992.

Sechehaye, Marguerite, ed. *Autobiography of a Schizophrenic Girl*. New York: Grune and Stratton, 1951.

Seidman, Hillel. *The Warsaw Ghetto Diaries*. Translated by Yosef Israel. Southfield, MI: Targum, 1997.

———. *Yoman Geto Varshah*. New York: Di Yiddishe Vokh, 1947.

Semprún, Jorge. *Literature or Life*. Translated by Linda Coverdale. New York: Viking, 1997.

Sepp, Arvi. "The Reception of Victor Klemperer's Diaries 1933–1945 in Contemporary American Holocaust Scholarship." In *Tales of the Great American Victory: World War II*

in *Politics and Poetics*, 131–142. Edited by Diederik Oostdijk and Markha G. Valenta. Amsterdam: VU University Press, 2006.
———. *Topographie des Alltags: Eine Kulturwissenschaftliche Lektüre von Victor Klemperers Tagebüchern 1933–1945*. Antwerp: University of Antwerp, 2008.
Seshadri-Crooks, Kalpana. *Desiring Whiteness: A Lacanian Analysis of Race*. London: Routledge, 2000.
Shahar, Yigal. *Ho Madre: Sipur Ahavah Be'auschwitz* [Ho Madre: A love story in Auschwitz]. Jerusalem: Yad Vashem, 2002.
Shandler, Jeffrey, ed. *Awaking Lives: Autobiographies of Jewish Youth in Poland before the Holocaust*. New Haven, CT: Yale University Press, 2002.
Shapira, Kalonymus Kalman. *Esh Kodesh* [Sacred fire]. 1960. Reprint, Jerusalem: Yad Vashem, 1979.
Shapiro, Robert Moses. "Diaries and Memoirs from the Lodz Ghetto in Yiddish and Hebrew." In *Holocaust Chronicles: Individualizing the Holocaust through Diaries and Other Contemporaneous Personal Accounts*, 95–116. Edited by Robert Moses Shapiro. Hoboken, NJ: Yeshiva University Press and KTAV, 1999.
Shenhav, Yehouda, and Yossi Yonah, eds. *Gizanut BeYisra'el* [Racism in Israel]. Tel Aviv: Van Leer Jerusalem Institute and Hakibbutz Hameuchad, 2008.
Shulman, Yani. "Der Elteste der Yuden" [The eldest of the Jews]. *Yediot Beit Lohamei Haghetaot* 29 (1960): 61–89.
Silverman, Kaja. *The Subject of Semiotics*. New York: Oxford University Press, 1983.
Singer, Oskar. "Hamatzod Hagadol Begeto Lodz" [The great manhunt in the Lodz ghetto]. *Yediot Beit Lohamei Haghetaot* 21 (1959): 69–83.
Soler, Colette. "The Subject and the Other (II)." In *Reading Seminar XI*, 45–54. Edited by Richard Feldstein, Bruce Fink, and Maire Jaanus. Albany: State University of New York Press, 1995.
Sorani, Rosina. "Mitokh Yoman Redifot (Kta'im Miyomanah shel Pkidah Bikehilat Roma Bitkufat Hakibush Hagermani)" [From a diary of persecution (Selections from the diary of a secretary in the Jewish community of Rome during the German occupation)]. *Yalkut Moreshet* 10 (1969): 72–78.
Spencer, Herbert. *The Evolution of Society: Selections from Herbert Spencer's "Principles of Sociology."* Edited by Robert L. Carneiro. Chicago: University of Chicago Press, 1974.
Steber, Martina, and Bernhard Gotto, eds. *Visions of Community in Nazi Germany: Social Engineering and Private Lives*. Oxford: Oxford University Press, 2014.
Stepan, Nancy Leys, and Sander L. Gilman. "Appropriating the Idioms of Science: The Rejection of Scientific Racism." In *The "Racial" Economy of Science: Toward a Democratic Future*, 170–194. Edited by Sandra Harding. Bloomington: Indiana University Press, 1993.
Steuwer, Janosch. *"Ein Drittes Reich wie ich es auffasse": Politik, Gesellschaft und Privates Leben in Tagebüchern 1933–1939*. Göttingen: Wallstein, 2017.
Stolleis, Michael. *The Law under the Swastika: Studies on Legal History in Nazi Germany*. Translated by Thomas Dunlap. Chicago: University of Chicago Press, 1998.
Stolzfus, Nathan. *Resistance of the Heart: Intermarriage and the Rossenstrasse Protest in Nazi Germany*. New York: Norton, 1996.
Stone, Dan. *Constructing the Holocaust*. London: Vallentine Mitchell, 2003.
———. "Genocide as Transgression." *European Journal of Social Theory* 7, no. 1 (2004): 45–65.
Swindells, Julia. *The Uses of Autobiography*. London: Taylor and Francis, 1995.

Szac-Wajnkranc, Noemi. *Halaf im Ha'esh: Reshimot al Geto Varshah Shenikhtevu Bemahbo* [Gone with the fire: Notes on the Warsaw ghetto written in hiding]. Jerusalem: Yad Vashem, 2003.

Szeintuch, Yechiel. *Yishayahu Spiegel: Prozah Sipurit Migeto Lodz* [Isaiah Spiegel: Yiddish narrative prose from the Lodz ghetto]. Jerusalem: Magnes, 1995.

———. *Yitzhak Katzenelson: Ktavim Shenitzlu Migeto Varshah Umimahaneh Vittel* [Yitzhak Katzenelson's rescued manuscripts from the Warsaw ghetto and the Vittel concentration camp]. Jerusalem: Magnes and the Ghetto Fighters' House, 1990.

Szeps, Fela. *Balev Ba'arah Hashalhevet: Yomanah shel Fela Szeps* [A blaze from within: The diary of Fela Szeps]. Jerusalem: Yad Vashem, 2002.

Tal, Uriel. *Christians and Jews in Germany: Religion, Politics and Ideology in the Second Reich, 1870–1914*. Translated by Noah Jonathan Jacobs. Ithaca, NY: Cornell University Press, 1975.

Temkin-Berman, Batya. *Yoman Bamahteret: Parshiyot Udmuyot Mivarshah Hakvushah* [Underground diary: Episodes from occupied Warsaw]. Tel Aviv: Hakibbutz Hameuchad and the Ghetto Fighters' House, 1956.

Timm, Uwe. *In My Brother's Shadow: A Life and Death in the SS*. Translated by Anthea Bell. New York: Farrar, Straus and Giroux, 2005.

Toker, Leona. "Towards a Poetic of Documentary Prose: From the Perspective of Gulag Testimonies." *Poetics Today* 18, no. 2 (Summer 1997): 187–222.

Tory, Avraham. *Surviving the Holocaust: The Kovno Ghetto Diary*. Edited by Martin Gilbert. Notes by Dina Porat. Translated by Jerzy Michalowicz. Cambridge, MA: Harvard University Press, 1990.

Traverso, Enzo. *The Origins of Nazi Violence*. Translated by Janet Lloyd. New York: New Press, 2003.

Traverso, Paola. "Victor Klemperers Deutschlandbild: Ein jüdisches Tagebuch." *Tel Aviver Jahrbuch für deutsche Geschichte* 36 (1997): 307–344.

Trunk, Isaiah. *Judenrat: The Jewish Councils in Eastern Europe under Nazi Occupation*. New York: Macmillan, 1972.

Unger, Michal. *Lodz: Ahron Hageta'ot BePolin* [Lodz: The last of the ghettos in Poland]. Jerusalem: Yad Vashem, 2005.

———. *Reassessment of the Image of Mordechai Chaim Rumkowski*. Jerusalem: Yad Vashem, 2004.

United States Holocaust Memorial Museum. "Tattoos and Numbers: The System of Identifying Prisoners at Auschwitz." *Holocaust Encyclopedia*, http://www.ushmm.org/wlc/article.php?lang=en&ModuleId=10007056. Last modified 2 July 2016.

Utiz, Emil. *Psychologie des Lebens im Konzentrazionslager Theresienstadt*. 1947. Reprint, Vienna: Continental Edition Verlag A. Sezl, 1948.

Vice, Sue. *Introducing Bakhtin*. Manchester: Manchester University Press, 1997.

Wasser, Hersh. "Daily Entries of Hersh Wasser." *Yad Vashem Studies* 15 (1983): 201–282.

Weikart, Richard. *From Darwin to Hitler: Evolutionary Ethics, Eugenics, and Racism in Germany*. New York: Palgrave Macmillan, 2004.

Weinreich, Max. *Hitler's Professors*. New York: YIVO, 1946.

Weintraub, Karl Joachim. *The Value of the Individual: Self and Circumstance in Autobiography*. Chicago: University of Chicago Press, 1978.

Wiener, Wendy J., and George C. Rosenwald. "A Moment's Monument: The Psychology of Keeping a Diary." In *The Narrative Study of Lives*, vol. 1, 30–58. Edited by Ruthellen Josselson and Amia Lieblich. Newbury Park, CA: Sage, 1993.

Wigren, Jodie. "Narrative Completion in the Treatment of Trauma." *Psychotherapy* 31, no. 3 (1994): 415–423.

Wildt, Michael. *Hitler's Volksgemeinschaft and the Dynamics of Racial Exclusion: Violence against Jews in Provincial Germany, 1919–1939*. Translated by Bernard Heise. New York: Berghahn, 2012.

Wisse, Ruth R. *The Modern Jewish Canon: A Journey through Language and Culture*. New York: Free Press, 2000.

Wittgenstein, Ludwig. *Philosophical Investigations*. Translated by G. E. M. Anscombe. Oxford: Basil Blackwell, 1953.

Wünschmann, Kim. *Before Auschwitz: Jewish Prisoners in the Prewar Concentration Camps*. Cambridge, MA: Harvard University Press, 2015.

Yahil, Leni. "Mekomah shel Hasho'ah Bahistoryografyah Hayehudit" [The place of the Holocaust in Jewish historiography]. In *Al Natzim, Yehudim Umetzilim* [On Nazis, Jews, and rescuers], 153–168. Jerusalem: Yad Vashem, 2002.

———. "Mekorot Hasho'ah Uve'ayot Mehkaran" [Holocaust: Original sources and the problems of their investigation]. *Yalkut Moreshet* 2, no. 3 (December 1964): 155–161.

"The Yellow Badge: A Shibboleth in Nazi Europe." *Wiener Library Bulletin* 8, nos. 5–6 (September–December 1954): 40, 42.

Yomano shel Na'ar Almoni MiLodz [Diary of an anonymous boy from Lodz]. Yad Vashem Archives, O.33/1032.

Young, Allan. *The Harmony of Illusions: Inventing Post-Traumatic Stress Disorder*. Princeton, NJ: Princeton University Press, 1995.

Young, James E. *Writing and Rewriting the Holocaust*. Bloomington: Indiana University Press, 1988.

Zapruder, Alexandra. *Salvaged Pages: Young Writers' Diaries of the Holocaust*. New Haven, CT: Yale University Press, 2004.

Żbikowski, Andrzej. "Yahasei Yehudim VePolanim Tahat Hakibush HaGermani" [Jewish–Polish relations under German occupation during World War II]. *Dapim: Studies on the Shoah* 22 (2008): 169–238.

Zelkowicz, Josef. *In Those Terrible Days: Notes from the Lodz Ghetto*. Edited by Michal Unger. Translated by Naftali Greenwood. Jerusalem: Yad Vashem, 2002.

Zimmermann, Moshe. Foreword to *The Law under the Swastika: Studies on Legal History in Nazi Germany*, by Michael Stolleis. Chicago: University of Chicago Press, 1998.

Zimmermann, Moshe, and Oded Heilbronner, eds. *Prakim Mitokh "Ma'avaki" shel Adolf Hitler* [Selections from Adolf Hitler's *Mein Kampf*]. Jerusalem: Akademon, 1994.

Ziv, Effi. "Traumah Ikeshet" [Persistent trauma]. *Mafteakh* 5 (2012): 55–74.

Žižek, Slavoj. "I Hear You with My Eyes." In *Gaze and Voice as Love Objects*, 90–127. Edited by Renata Saleci and Slavoj Žižek. Durham, NC: Duke University Press, 1996.

———. *Looking Awry: An Introduction to Jacques Lacan through Popular Culture*. Cambridge, MA: MIT Press, 1992.

———. *The Metastases of Enjoyment: Six Essays on Woman and Causality*. London: Verso, 1995.

———. *On Belief*. London: Routledge, 2001.

———. *The Sublime Object of Ideology*. London: Verso, 1989.

Zur, Avichai. "'The Lord Hides in Inner Chambers': The Doctrine of Suffering in the Theosophy of Rabbi Kalonymus Kalman Shapira of Piaseczno." *Dapim: Studies on the Shoah* 25 (2011): 183–237.

Zylberberg, Michael. *A Warsaw Diary*. London: Vallentine Mitchell, 1969.

INDEX

AMOS GOLDBERG is a Holocaust historian and chair of the Department of Jewish History and Contemporary Jewry at the Hebrew University of Jerusalem. His major fields of research are the cultural history of the Jews in the Holocaust, Holocaust historiography, and Holocaust memory in a global world. The Hebrew edition of *Trauma in First Person* won the Eggit Prize for Holocaust literature and research in Israel.

www.ingramcontent.com/pod-product-compliance
Lightning Source LLC
LaVergne TN
LVHW050148080826
844660LV00002B/123

* 9 7 8 0 2 5 3 0 2 9 7 4 4 *